Metrics 2.0

Metrics 2.0

Creating Scorecards for
High-Performance Teams
and Organizations

Ruth A. Huwe

 PRAEGER

AN IMPRINT OF ABC-CLIO, LLC
Santa Barbara, California • Denver, Colorado • Oxford, England

Copyright 2010 by Ruth A. Huwe

All rights reserved. No part of this publication may be reproduced, stored in a retrieval system, or transmitted, in any form or by any means, electronic, mechanical, photocopying, recording, or otherwise, except for the inclusion of brief quotations in a review, without prior permission in writing from the publisher.

Library of Congress Cataloging-in-Publication Data
Huwe, Ruth A.
   Metrics 2.0 : creating scorecards for high-performance work teams and organizations / Ruth A. Huwe.
      p. cm.
   Includes bibliographical references and index.
   ISBN 978-0-313-38456-1 (hbk. : alk. paper) — ISBN 978-0-313-38457-8 (ebook)
   1. Organizational effectiveness—Measurement. 2. Performance—Measurement. 3. Total quality management. 4. Benchmarking (Management) I. Title.
   HD58.9.H89 2010
   658.4′013—dc22   2010000810

ISBN: 978-0-313-38456-1
EISBN: 978-0-313-38457-8

14 13 12 11 10   1 2 3 4 5

This book is also available on the World Wide Web as an eBook.
Visit www.abc-clio.com for details.

Praeger
An Imprint of ABC-CLIO, LLC

ABC-CLIO, LLC
130 Cremona Drive, P.O. Box 1911
Santa Barbara, California 93116-1911

This book is printed on acid-free paper ∞

Manufactured in the United States of America

To Brian Spitzberg:
Measure for Measure,
a truly great professor

We will waste little time arguing that it is better to express standards and performance in terms of numbers rather than adjectives. Our century is fully aware that measurement has been a basic contributor to the march of science. Our managers have all gone through the frustration of debating how "high" are costs, how poor is "poor" quality. They know that once we set up units of measure, the debate shifts from the meaning of adjectives to doing the job, which is as it should be.

—Joseph M. Juran, *Quality Control Handbook*

Contents

Preface		*ix*
Acknowledgments		*xi*

Part One: Intellectual Foundation   1

1	Introduction to Metrics	3
2	Introduction to Scorecards	17
3	Systems Theory: The Foundation for Contemporary Metric Systems	33
4	The Measurement of Productivity, Quality, and Other Scorecard Variables	47

Part Two: Creating Metrics   61

5	Metrics for Individuals: Performance Appraisals	63
6	First-Level Team Scorecards	81
7	Departmental Scorecards	103
8	Organization Scorecards	117

Part Three: Surveys and Scale Construction   133

| 9 | Scale Construction | 135 |
| 10 | Customer Surveys | 155 |

Part Four: Scrutiny of Metrics   169

11   Measurement Issues   171
12   Statistics Primer   185

Part Five: Using Metrics   207

13   Engagement: Getting from Metrics to Action   209
14   Metrics as Feedback   223
15   Metrics and Motivation   241
16   Putting It All Together   267

Part Six: Reference   291

17   Special Topics   293
18   Collection of Indicators and Metrics   311
     Index   335

Preface

When I ask MBA students their reason for taking an entire class on metrics, I get some standard responses.

"Because my company is really into metrics."

"Because I keep hearing about metrics and wish I knew more."

"Because I was intrigued by the balanced scorecard in accounting class."

But several in my last group of students said something that truly surprised me: "I think this class will be fun."

Granted, I teach at the Foster School of Business at the University of Washington, where many students are techies who work at Microsoft and Boeing. But metrics as *fun*? Was I being punked?

These students finally explained that they had seen me do a guest-lecture in Dr. Mitchell's motivation class and figured that metrics were about motivation. I was just about to say, "But metrics aren't about motivation . . ."

And I caught myself.

Thanks to that class, this book is different from other metrics books in many ways. First, this book goes beyond *creating* scorecards (what I call "Metrics 1.0") to both *creating and using* scorecards ("Metrics 2.0"). Metrics are treated here as just one of many types of feedback messages, and feedback messages are just one of many motivation techniques. Entire chapters cover feedback, motivation, and engagement. Second, that class was filled with informal "lead" project leaders and first-level managers. No one has written a book on metrics for this audience. While most books focus on high-level organizational scorecards, this book walks readers through the process of creating scorecards for all levels: individuals, teams, departments, and organizations. Third, this book is written for both creators and consumers of metrics. Some of you are managers or informal project leaders who need to design your own scorecards. Others will hire outside firms but would still like to understand what on earth they are doing. The statistics and measurement chapters will get you up to speed. Entire chapters cover survey construction. Fourth, this book has a reference function. Definitions for terms are provided throughout. An entire reference section addresses special topics and provides an inventory of possible metrics. Fifth, and also influenced by the MBA crowd, I address the cynics who question the power of metrics and motivation theory by giving a quantitative report of effects at every turn.

Will this book be fun? I have to admit that I have seen actual rocket scientists develop headaches from this task. It would be so simple if this book were about dashboard technology or giving a fancy data report, but it's not. This book is about coming up with the metric content that fuels the dashboard. It's not a fun task. But if you're like many leaders, it's one that you are desperate to learn how to do.

How do I measure that desperation? Remember, measures begin with indicators. Maybe it's the retired consultant in a Wichita bar who tugged at my arm to tell me (at least five times while waiting on take-out), "But if you can't measure it, you can't control it!" Or maybe it's finding myself in an extended metric conversation at a Rotary ball in the middle of Kyrgystan. Or perhaps it's the time in a Berlin airport when an airline had to hold up a plane because a frequent-flying company president was pummeling me with metric questions. Or maybe it's having an Australian CEO pull me aside to say that he could set me up with a private supply of wine from his vineyards if I'd help his company with their metrics. (Hint to future CEOs: shiraz would be the right choice.)

People have many reasons for studying metrics and here is mine: Many things motivate me, but nothing does so quite like hitting a new level on the elliptical machine, receiving a better evaluation, seeing a lower number on the scale, or when I was younger, getting the grades. There is nothing like numbers because they represent a duality of life: metrics are both a method and marker of human motivation.

Acknowledgments

First and foremost, I thank Walt Gillette, formerly of the Boeing Company. Functioning as my friend and mentor, he told me that I had to write a book. It took someone with his extraordinary integrity and credibility to motivate me to take on a project of this scale. I also credit the labor leader Charles Bofferding and then Vice President of Engineering Mike Denton. Their conversations led me to flesh out the "step-by-step" format used throughout this book. Also from my Boeing experience, I have to thank Alan Mulally for sending me books. He led me to read material that made a solid contribution to the special topics chapter. As well, my long-time "Boeing boss" Jim Hoch deserves credit for sponsoring the original feedback workshops that evolved into an entire metrics curriculum and the basic outline of this book.

I wish my parents were alive to see this book get published because they certainly deserve credit for steering me toward math. Beyond that, it is hard to name all the people who provided support but several deserve mention: Michaela Sweatt, Darlene Sweatt, Dorothy Graham, Bill Knight, Ted Gates, Lisa Anderson, April Stempniak, Dave Carson, Dave Wingsness, Gary Rood, Jill Pizzuto, Diane Stollenwerk, Carola Hibbard, Tina Fahy, Majia Holmer, Meghan Szczebak, Sherri Green, Hiro Tamura, Saundra Cope, Don and Charlotte Stuart, and Carolyn and Vince Cheverine. My sister Joan gets special credit as my writing-break phone-call-of-choice. I also can't forget the nephews and nieces who served as additional reasons to take writing breaks.

One person stands out for the final project: Veronica Howell, the most amazing assistant in the world. She was the true difference between failure and success. I also thank my signing editor, Jeff Olson. He suffered through the endless "first-time author" questions. And last but not least, I have to thank Maureen O'Driscoll for her truly heroic "catches" as my copyeditor.

Part One
Intellectual Foundation

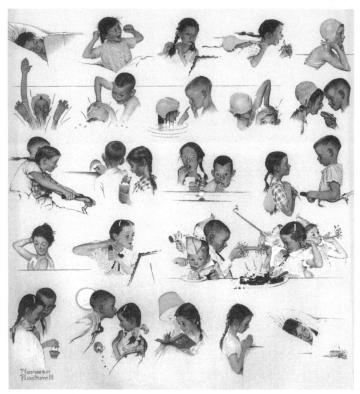

Photo 1.1 A Day in the Life of a Girl
Source: Reprinted by permission from the Norman Rockwell Family Agency.

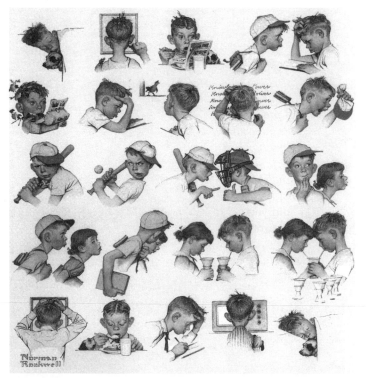

Photo 1.2 A Day in the Life of a Boy
Source: Reprinted by permission from the Norman Rockwell Family Agency.

1 INTRODUCTION TO METRICS

A DAY IN THE LIFE OF A MANAGER

Bed. Awake. Already time to get up? Digital alarm clock. 5:46. (Metric!) Need bathroom. The scale! Depressing weight. (Metric!) Must have coffee. Two scoops coffee (Metric!), two cups water (Metric!). Make breakfast. Two eggs (Metric!) will have 240 calories (Metric!), 5 grams of fat, 6 grams protein, and 1 gram of carbohydrate (Metric! Metric! Metric!). What else is in the fridge. Hmmm, a beef steak. "Never eat a beef steak. Its eyes will follow you forever they say." Think. Dread bathroom scale. Eggs and toast will do. And maybe a glass, a 12-ounce glass (Metric!) of juice.

Eat breakfast. Newspaper. Some ugly story about lawsuit settlements. (Metric!) Baseball salaries. (Metric!)

Commute. Just what I need, an accident. Estimated commute time: 50 minutes. (Metric!) Minutes late: 20 minutes. (Metric!) Time it takes Pat to make some crack laced with innuendo: 2 minutes. (Metric!)

Office. Better put my lunch in the fridge. What's this? That sicko stealing food is at it again. Last week, someone left a burrito with one bite (Metric!) taken out. He actually cut it in half (Metric!) and left the half (Metric!) with the bite.

Cubicle. Boss! Boss! Boss! Boss!

"Well, Wilhelm, did you get the memo on the metric initiative? We've got a team together. Latisha from engineering. Mung-wa from human resources. Ron from marketing."

What is this, one of those "incredible journey" sort of deals?

"And you're going to head this up. You get to be the leader of a cross-functional team!"

"Ron agreed to that?"

"He's just tolerating you. But relax. Sam knows no one person can do a metric system alone. Marketing doesn't know operations, human resources doesn't

LEARNING OBJECTIVES

After studying this chapter, you should be able to achieve the following:

1. Differentiate the terms *metric* and *measure.*
2. Quantify the effects of metrics.
3. Identify several ways that metrics are used.
4. Describe how several intellectual advances influence the way we think about metrics: TQM, ISO, goal-setting theory, the Balanced Scorecard, stakeholder model, and Baldrige criteria.

know finance, etc., etc. You'll sail your ships together. A bureaucratic fight from task to task, mapping your system as you go. It's your chance to show yourself as a warrior, a leader! You'll be like Odysseus, rallying your troops to survive battle upon battle."

"Battle upon battle?"

"Wilhelm, think of the cold bitterness and paranoia that come from people who know they're about to be judged. The skeptical 'Flavor of the Month' cracks about anything that represents change. Bickering half-wits who resist anything they didn't invent, but can't possibly be bothered to invent something themselves. That's right. They'll try to make a mockery of you. Battles!"

"Not to nitpick, but aren't you supposed to be selling me on this?"

"You can brazen it out. It might seem perilous, but think of what would happen if we don't get a metric system?"

"But we *do* have a metric system!"

"Wilhelm, we have inscrutable databases. Paralysis from analysis. Baffling reports. It's time to create a coherent system once and for all."

"I don't even know where to start."

"Well, if you want my advice . . ."

"Hit the sauce?"

"Har, har, Wilhelm. Actually, the best thing you could do is hit . . . a good metrics book."

CHAPTER OVERVIEW

This chapter begins with basic definitions. A historical overview is then provided to illuminate the significance of metrics in society and in modern business practice.

What Are Metrics?

When comparing definitions, it is easy to see why the terms "metrics" and "measures" often are used interchangeably. A *metric* is a "quantitative measure of the degree to which a system, component, or process possesses a given attribute" (IEEE, 2006, p. 651). A *measure* is a set of rules for assigning numbers to reflect attributes of an object (Kerlinger, 1979; Nunnally, 1978). However, "metric" has been treated as a broader term, reflecting "a comparison of two or more measures, for example, body temperature over time" (Kankanhalli & Tan, 2005. p. 21).[1] To be more specific about the comparison measure, this book nominally defines a **metric** as a measure typically attached to a measurement unit.

A **measurement unit** is the scope of observations that will be summarized when reporting a score on a measure. For example, suppose we want to measure the amount of training received by a given work team. The *object* is a "work team." The *attribute* of interest is "training." We decide that we will make observations of the team's training for an entire quarter before reporting a summary of observations as a score on a measure. Hence, a *measure* might be "number of training hours," a *measurement unit* might be "per quarter," and the training *metric* would be "number of training hours per quarter" for this given work team.

It is worth stressing that creating metrics is a subjective endeavor. In the previous example, we could have decided the *object* was a "person," the *attribute* was "morale," the *measure* was "number of hours of free overtime worked," and the *measurement unit* was "daily." The morale *metric* would have been "number of hours of free overtime worked per day" for each person. These all are subjective decisions.

The approach used here, disciplining ourselves to include *both* measure and measurement unit when creating metrics, is extremely practical in the business context because it the removes ambiguity that arises when people "forget" to consider the measurement unit. It is tempting to argue, "Well, why not insist that metrics include all three: the measure, measurement unit, and the object?" For example, why not say that the training metric is "number of training hours per quarter, per team?" This would be helpful in that it removes even more ambiguity, but it just does not happen to be the way metrics typically are worded in actual usage.

It is tempting to think that a measurement unit will always be some time increment such as "per week" or "per day," but this is an ill-advised assumption. Sometimes a measurement unit is in reference to a scope of observations, such as the number of errors "per project" or number of errors "per batch."

A measurement unit should not be confused with a unit of observation. A **unit of observation** is the number of objects that are observed when an individual score is recorded on a measure. For example, consider the metric "Number of defective pistons per 1,000 batch." The measure is "number of defective pistons," and we might create a system for assigning attributes to numbers such as a "defective" piston counting as "1" and a "not defective" piston counting as "0." What is the unit of observation when we make the judgment of "defective" or "not defective?" One. We observe one piston at a time. What is the measurement unit for our chosen metric? A batch of 1,000. Now here is the trick question: What, then, is a unit of analysis? The terms "unit of observation" and "unit of analysis" are one of the rare cases in this book where the terms actually are interchangeable (cf. Babbie, 2007). And finally, where did we get the 1,000? It was the unit that we arbitrarily decided on when creating the metric.

A final definition point concerns the idea that a metric is "typically" attached to a measurement unit. A standard exception is the case in which people create metrics to mark progress on a one-shot initiative or project. As an example, take the case of a cross-functional team formed to update a process to include a new technology. The goal is to achieve the update by a certain date. The measure might be something like "Percentage of Milestones Met." Per what? Per week? There is no clear need for a measurement unit. The measure and the metric are "Percentage of Milestones Met."

The term *metric* is often greeted with vexation as our minds trail to ridiculous "bum" metrics that organizations often force upon us. If you are a manager, you probably have some favorite stories. How about the efficiency experts that convinced managers to measure productivity by measuring the number of people who were on the phone when managers walked into the room. What happened? Every time the employees heard the manager coming, they picked up their phone and pretended to be talking. How about the police officers who were told that their performance would be measured by numbers of miles on their odometers? What did they do? They drove. Soon police cars were racing up and down country roads in the middle of the night. Metrics are never quite perfect or fully objective.

Why Metrics?

The quickest answer is "that which gets measured gets done." For over a century, psychology researchers have studied the idea that the sheer potential for being evaluated will influence task performance (Triplett, 1898). A growing body of evidence demonstrates that numbers can both help and hurt performance. Some argue that numbers help performance because the reality of others knowing how you are doing triggers a concern for failure. Others argue that concern for evaluation gets in the way of being able to concentrate. However, the most compelling evidence comes from a recent string of studies that show that whether the task is simple or complex, a "mere effort" effect takes place. When people know they are measured, they try harder (McFall, Jamieson, & Harkins, 2009).

Since the 1990s, metrics have meant financial gain for companies that have adopted a balanced metric system in the form of a Balanced Scorecard (Kaplan & Norton, 1996). Underscoring the need for balance, the Saratoga Institute analyzed more than 1,000 companies and identified those that had the highest scores in employee and financial performance. The top 110 companies had eight common traits. The "prime hallmark" was the balance of human and financial values (Fitz-enz, 2000). The *Harvard Business Review* highlighted the Balanced Scorecard as one of the 75 most influential ideas of the 20th century.

A recent review of five major management journals found that performance was the dependent variable in 29% of the published articles. The disturbing statistics emerge from how people *use* metrics. They found that 49% of the performance studies used single measures rather than a scorecard that would provide balanced metrics. Worse yet, "few, if any, empirical papers using firm performance as a dependent variable account for the internal incentive systems operating in the firms they are studying" (Richard, Devinney, Yip, & Johnson, 2009, p. 725). In the popular press, we see anecdotes that companies are trying to link their internal metrics to their scorecards (Kaplan & Norton, 2007), but linking is still so rare that it has not hit academic journals.

But you do not need a study of high-brow journals to understand the significance of metrics. How far could you get in a given day without being confronted by a metric? As demonstrated by the hapless manager in the chapter opening, you probably could not make it out of the house. Have you glanced at the monitor on a piece of gym equipment? Checked the temperature? Stepped on a scale? Looked at your child's grades? Although managers have countless motives for measures specific to business contexts, they generally cite the following typical reasons for metrics:

- Monitor employees
- Solve problems
- Present required reports
- Prevent problems
- Motivate employees
- Improve performance
- Develop an incentive system
- Report results to shareholders
- Compare to others
- Develop forecasts that help decisions
- Align teams with corporate indicators
- Create forecasts
- Facilitate communication
- Distribute compensation
- Provide recognition
- Monitor a value chain
- Change behaviors
- Organization alignment and execution
- Reports to stakeholders

As a book for people who wish to create "high-performance teams and organizations," the focus of this book is on *performance improvement*. Metrics are considered here as both method and marker of human motivation.

Historical Overview

The earliest examples of "measures" can be traced back to archaeological findings. As early as 30,000 B.C.E., people of the Old Stone Age devised a measure by grouping tally marks on wolf bones (Burton, 1985). Skipping forward several millennia, we arrive at the 20th century when several intellectual advances formed the current paradigm for how we think about metrics: total quality management (Deming, 1986; Feigenbaum, 1951; Juran, 1951), the standards movement (ISO, 2009), goal-setting theory (Locke & Latham, 1984), the Balanced Scorecard (Kaplan & Norton, 1996), the stakeholder model (Richard et al., 2009), and the culmination of metrics systems as articulated in the current criteria for the Baldrige Award (NIST, 2009). Each advance will now be discussed in turn.

Total Quality Management. Total quality management (TQM) "is an integrative management philosophy aimed at continuously improving the quality of products and processes to achieve customer satisfaction" (Ahire, Landeros, & Golhar, 1995, p. 278). Where "Six Sigma" or "Lean Manufacturing" are examples of programs, TQM is a philosophy that provides a paradigm for programs. **Paradigms** are "the fundamental models or frames of reference we use to organize our observations and reasoning" (Babbie, 2007, p. 31).

Many names are associated with TQM. In the 1950s, Joseph M. Juran lectured in Japan and developed ideas of quality control. Armand V. Feigenbaum coined the phrase "Total Quality Control" and wrote a seminal work while still a doctoral student at MIT: *Quality Control: Principles, Practices, and Administration.* However, the name most popularly associated with TQM is W. Edwards Deming.

Deming was an advisor on sampling methods to the U.S. Bureau of Census and taught at New York University. He was one of 200 scientists and specialists brought to Japan by General MacArthur to help the Japanese rebuild the country after World War II. The rest is well known: Japan rose from the ashes to become an economic giant within 30 years. Though Deming had been relatively ignored in the United States before that time, U.S. companies discovered him in the 1980s. His popularity surged throughout the 1990s, and his ideas became a standard element of business school curricula. In fact, in the early 1990s, if I were to ask students to name important sources of performance feedback, they would say something like "bosses, peers, and, subordinates." From the late 1990s on, they were quick to include "customers" and "suppliers" in their answer.

Deming's approach to problem solving was one of the biggest drivers of the current push for metrics in corporate America. He presented the "Plan, Do, Check, Act" cycle that requires metrics (the "Check") for virtually every organizational initiative (Walton, 1990). TQM is explicitly credited as the paradigm that grounds the philosophy of the International Organization for Standards (ISO), to which we now turn.

The Standards Movement. Were you reluctant to shift from VCRs to DVDs? Or if you're a bit older, from forty-fives and eight-tracks to CDs? If you are a homeowner, think of what happens if you need to replace the hood on your stove. You go to Home Depot and find out that the range just happens to fit exactly with your stove, even though it was made in China by someone who did not possibly know your building contractor. How is it possible that all of the manufacturers got together and decided to do the same thing in the same sizes? You do not have to be a paranoid conspiracy theorist to conclude that somehow, someone somewhere is in collusion to make consistent standards across the globe. That someone is ISO.[2]

ISO's roots go back to 1906 with the creation of the International Electrotechnical Commission (IEC), but the current organization was created on February 23, 1947, following a meeting in London of delegates from 25 different countries. The original goal was to provide standards for industry, but the current mission has evolved to a focus on three domains: economic, environmental, and societal. More than 50,000 experts contribute to the standards set by ISO, but it is then up to individual nations to adopt them (ISO, 2005). ISO has evolved into a nongovernmental organization with delegates from 161 countries (ISO, 2009).

The term **standard** is a broader term than metric, basically meaning a "specification." ISO may specify that a certain metric be used to measure an object, but a specification can also mean specifying that a certain material or object be classified as belonging to a certain group or taxonomy.

Not only does ISO provide standards, it also specifies an entire management system based on the premise that metrics are central to organizational functioning. The two most famous management systems refer to ISO 9000 and ISO 14000. ISO 9000 provides definitions for conformance to quality standards and ISO 14000 provides standards for conformance to environmental standards (ISO, 2009).

Goal-Setting Theory. In the late 1960s, Edwin A. Locke began a series of studies that sparked the beginning of contemporary goal-setting theory (Locke, 1968). In the 1970s, Locke teamed with Gary P. Latham and their collaboration led to an explosion of goal-setting research. In 1984, they published *Goal Setting: A Motivational Technique that Works.* By the 1990s, more than 500 studies had tested various hypotheses and questions advanced by the theory. By 2003, goal-setting theory was rated as number one in importance when 95 experts rated 73 management theories (Miner, 2003). In the early 21st century, it would be nearly impossible to open a contemporary motivation textbook that does not include a reference to goal-setting theory.

Although people have set goals through the ages, Locke and Latham specified the conditions in which goals would work. They articulated a succinct basic theoretical statement: hard, specific goals—if accepted—will lead to increased performance. This implies three hallmarks of "scientific" goals: goal difficulty, goal specificity, and goal acceptance. That is, hard goals are more effective than easy goals. Specific goals are more effective than ambiguous goals. Goals are effective only if they are accepted.

However, significant corollaries have been added to goal-setting theory. Setting a goal to *learn*, a "mastery orientation," is very different than setting a goal to *perform*, a performance orientation (Kanfer & Ackerman, 1989; Payne, Satoris, & Beaubien, 2007). A growing body of evidence demonstrates that giving hard goals may be useful when people perform tasks they already understand, but actually may hurt performance on complex tasks (Yeo, Loft, Xiao, & Kiewitz, 2009). As well, distal goals in the future may not produce effects if they are not aligned with proximal (shorter-term) goals. For practitioners, this means that it is important to break down larger "outcome" goals to consider simpler and more immediate "behavioral" goals.

Another corollary to goal-setting theory was that feedback is a "necessary but not sufficient" condition for goal-setting effects (Erez, 1977). In goal-setting theory, feedback is defined as "knowledge of results" (KR). In other words, the terms "feedback" and "metric" are basically synonymous and the statement that goals don't work without *feedback* is the same as saying that goals don't work without *metrics*.

Goal-setting theory basically cements the case for metrics because it builds a huge body of evidence that establishes the power of feedback. How important is feedback? Chapter 14 is devoted to this subject, but for now consider the extent to which metric feedback is rendered more powerful when coupled with goals. To understand this effect size, this text often turns to meta-analyses to reflect bodies of research.

A **meta-analysis** is an analysis of analyses, a study that pools the data from all similar studies together and combines the data to find one grand result. As an example, suppose there were 10 similar studies with 100 subjects each. A meta-analysis would combine all studies and do the investigation as if it was a huge study with 1,000 subjects. Although a recent "meta-analysis of meta-analyses" demonstrated that results of these studies can vary simply because of research decisions (Geyskens, Krishnan, Steenkamp, & Cunha, 2009), meta-analyses still provide an excellent method for combining large bodies of often-conflicting data to express general conclusions.

Getting back to feedback and goal effects, one meta-analysis (Stajkovic & Luthans, 1998) gave a comparison of scores found in other meta-analyses, showing there was a 10.39% increase in performance from goal setting (an examination of Wood, Mento, & Locke, 1987), 13.6% increase in performance from feedback interventions (an examination of Kluger & DeNisi, 1996), and a 17% increase performance from organizational behavior modification (an examination of Stajkovic & Luthans, 1997). Coincidentally, behavior modification is a motivational method that stresses the use of feedback specifically in the form of metrics.

The Balanced Scorecard. During the Industrial Revolution, roughly 1850–1950, "scorecards" were basically accounting practices that reflected the tangible value of a company. What changed? The rise of the service economy turned statistics reflecting tangible assets upside down. A 2005 study by the World Bank reported that natural capital accounts for 5% of the world's wealth, produced capital for 18%, and intangible capital for 77% ("Our Intangible Riches," 2007).

In 1992, the challenge to reflect intangible assets in metric systems was greeted when Robert S. Kaplan and David P. Norton introduced their concept of a "Balanced Scorecard" in a *Harvard Business Review* article (Kaplan & Norton, 1992). Their seminal work, *The Balanced Scorecard,* was published in 1996 and, according to one editor, "revolutionized conventional thinking about performance metrics" (Kaplan & Norton, 2007). These authors focused on measurement systems for entire organizations that balance a concern for the intangible and tangible. They emphasize a number of balances, including a concern for the external (e.g., shareholders) and the internal (e.g., operations) as well as a measure of lagging indicators and leading indicators. In this book, lagging indicators typically are referred to as outcome metrics and leading indicators are covered by behavioral metrics.

The hallmark of the Balanced Scorecard is four key scorecard categories: customer, learning and growth, internal business process, and financial. In 1999, a survey by the consulting firm Bain and Company reported that more than 50% of Global 1,000 companies had some version of the Balanced Scorecard (Burton Organisation Development, 2003).

By 2001, the Financial Accounting Standards Board (FASB) advanced a formal proposal to grapple with the problem of reflecting nonfinancial indicators in accounting practices. They called for measuring intangible factors such as market size and share, research and development, and employee retention (FASB, 2001).

Originally, the Balanced Scorecard led to an emphasis on performance measurement at the organization level of analysis. Although it is now recognized that scorecards need to be pushed down to lower levels (Kaplan & Norton, 2007), no new set of attributes goes with the various levels of analysis. Moreover, the Balanced Scorecard's original four categories are not the only model to depict high performance at an organizational level. Different scorecards, reflecting different attributes to reflect performance, are found in two other important models: the stakeholder model and the Baldrige criteria.

Stakeholder Model. Recently, Richard et al. (2009) reviewed 213 papers that used organizational performance as a dependent variable and found 207 different measures of performance. To aid the quest to be able to compare organizations, they advanced the following definition: **Organizational performance** encompasses three specific areas of firm outcomes: (a) financial performance (profits, return on assets, etc.); (b) product market performance (sales, market share, etc.), and (c) shareholder return (total shareholder return, economic value added, etc.) (Richard et al., 2009, p. 722). They went on to argue that organizational scorecards need to measure performance from the perspective of all primary stakeholders. Primary stakeholders reflect categories on the scorecard.

Baldrige National Quality Award. The Baldrige Award was created in 1987 to honor Malcolm T. Baldrige, who served as secretary of commerce from 1981 until his tragic death in 1987, and is administered by the National Institute for Standards and Technology (NIST, 2009). The award is referred to as a "quality" award, but the categories of scoring criteria demonstrate that it is another variation of a Balanced Scorecard. Over time, it has come to be considered the most prestigious award in American business.

The Baldrige Award committee explicitly advances systems theory as *the* paradigm for describing a contemporary system of measures. The Baldrige Award reflects yet another intellectual push for the importance of metrics in that it literally includes "measurement" as a key organizational function.

The assertion that metric systems are best understood from a systems theory lens is carried forth throughout this book. Hence, we come full circle from marks on a wolf bone, TQM, goal-setting, and balanced scorecards, to the Baldrige Award and system theory as prescribing the way that metrics will be considered in the future.

Future Sociological Trends. At least four trends will make metrics even more important to managers of the future: virtual work teams, telecommuting, hotelling, and flextime. The forces of globalization push for *virtual work teams*, workers who span time zones and are geographically dispersed. For example, British Petroleum implemented a pilot program to link five drilling platforms via satellite. They estimated that they saved $40 million in the first 18 months after a $13 million initial investment. Not surprisingly, the program is being expanded across the company (Virtualworkteams.com, n.d.). If managers are not physically present with teams, how can they monitor performance? Metrics will be needed not just to improve performance but also to ensure basic monitoring and accountability.

Telecommuting also takes managers away from actual presence of employees. The Bureau of Labor Statistics reports that the number of people over 25 with bachelor degrees working at home rose from 33% to 35% from 2007 to 2008 alone. Of those with less than a high school diploma, the number dropped from 12% to 9% (Bureau of Labor Statistics, 2007; 2009). Others predict that telecommuting will become the predominant workplace trend in the next 20 years (Campbell, 2007). When the work being done at home appears to have intangible white-collar outputs rather than intangible blue-collar outputs, how can managers tell the work is getting done without metrics?

Hotelling is a relatively newer trend where companies acknowledge employees may not need a permanent office at all, providing hotelling centers where employees can come in and do their work on company workstations. For example, the Boeing Company has employees who routinely need to work in Renton (20 miles south of Seattle) as well as Everett (20 miles north of Seattle). If you live in Everett and your office is in Renton, it's easier to work out of the hotelling center in Everett than to commute to Renton. Yet, how do your bosses in Renton know you're getting your work done? Perhaps informal checks. Perhaps formal metrics.

Flextime allows workers to vary the time when they begin and end their work. Government figures show that the trend is leveling out, but flextime is still practiced by a large portion of the workforce. In May 2004, more than 27 million full-time and salary workers had flexible schedules, accounting for 27.5% of all full-time wage and salary workers, down only slightly from 28.6% in May 2001 when data were previously collected. Men were more likely to have flextime than women, 28.1% and 26.7% percent, respectively. Flextime was most common among management, professional, and related occupations (36.8%) as well as sales and office workers (29.5%). Only 17.6% of natural resources, construction, and maintenance workers and 14.3% of production, transportation, and material moving workers were given these freedoms (Bureau of Labor Statistics, 2007). Flextime reflects empowerment as well as the idea that most managers aren't even interested in "how many" hours people work just so long as the work gets done. But then, metrics are still needed to tell that the work *does* get done and done well.

So, why metrics? On a practical level, metrics are as old as the Old Stone Age and are an inescapable part of contemporary life. Metrics are practical in that scorecards are primary mechanisms used to describe, explain, and predict what goes on in organizations. Metrics are part of a future that brings globalization, flextime, hotelling, and the rise of the virtual organization.

On an academic level, metrics are a key element of goal-setting theory. Moreover, as motivation is known through performance and performance is known through metrics, then metrics are a part of any motivation theory or practice. Metrics are a dualism of concept and action: metrics not only *are* results, metrics *get* results.

CHAPTER SUMMARY

This chapter presented a vocabulary of basic terms for managers who are charged with implementing a metric system. A historical overview revealed many reasons why metrics are important. On a personal level, metrics are an inescapable part of our human existence that date back to the time of cavemen. On a professional level, this chapter included several intellectual milestones and practices that demonstrate the significance of metrics in organizations: total quality management, the standards movement, goal-setting theory, the balanced scorecard, stakeholder approaches, and the Baldrige National Quality Award.

NOTES

1. An even broader approach yet conceives "The term 'metric' refers to definition of the measure, how it will be calculated, who will be carrying out the calculation, and from where the data will be obtained" (Gunasekaran & Kobu, 2007, p. 2821).

2. To account for translations in different languages, the International Organization for Standards goes by the acronym ISO because "isos" means "equal" in Greek.

REFERENCES

Ahire, S., Landeros, R., & Golhar, D. (1995). Total quality management: A literature review and an agenda for future research. *Production and Operations Management, 4,* 277–307.

Babbie, E. (2007). *The practice of social research* (11th ed.). Belmont, CA: Wadsworth.

Bureau of Labor Statistics. (2007, May 29). *American time use survey.* Retrieved July 28, 2007, from http://www.bls.gov/tus/charts/work.htm.

Bureau of Labor Statistics. (2009, June 26). *American time use survey.* Retrieved July 10, 2009, from http://www.bls.gov/news.release/pdf/atus.pdf.

Burton, D. M. (1985). *The history of mathematics: An introduction.* Boston, MA: Allyn & Bacon.

Burton Organisation Development. (2003). *The balanced scorecard.* Retrieved June 23, 2006, from http://www.burtonod.co.uk/a_balanced.html.

Campbell, A. (2007). *Virtual workplace trend changes business.* Small Business Trends.com. Retrieved December 10, 2007 from http://www.smallbiztrends.com/2004/10/virtual-workplace-trend-changes.html.

Deming, W. E. (1986). *Drastic changes for western management.* Madison, WI: Center for Productivity and Quality Improvement, University of Wisconsin–Madison.

Erez, M. (1977). Feedback: A necessary condition for goal setting-performance relationship. *Journal of Applied Psychology, 62,* 624–627.

FASB (Financial Accounting Standards Board). (2001, August 17). *Proposal for a new agenda project: Disclosure of information about intangible assets not recognized in financial statements.* Retrieved June 21, 2006, from http://www.fasb.org/proposals/intangibles.pdf.

Feigenbaum, A. V. (1951). *Quality control: Principles, practice, and administration; an industrial management tool for improving product quality and design and for reducing operating costs and losses.* New York: McGraw-Hill.

Fitz-enz, J. (2000). *The ROI of human capital.* New York: Amacom.

Geyskens, I., Krishnan, R., Steenkamp, J-B. E. M., & Cunha, P. V. (2009). A review and evaluation of meta-analysis practices in management research. *Journal of Management, 35,* 393–419.

Gunasekaran, A., & Kobu, B. (2007). Performance measures and metrics in logistics and supply chain management: A review of recent literature (1995–2004) for research and applications. *International Journal of Production Research, 45,* 2819–2840.

IEEE (Institute of Electrical and Electronics Engineers). (2006). *The IEEE standard dictionary of electrical and electronics terms. IEEE Std. 100–1996.* New York: IEEE.

ISO (International Organization for Standards). (2005, July 4). *Overview of the ISO system.* Retrieved June 21, 2006, from http://www.iso.org/iso/en/aboutiso/introduction/index.html.

ISO (International Organization for Standards). (2009). *About ISO*. Retrieved July 10, 2009, from http://www.iso.org/iso/about.htm.

Juran, J. M. (1951). *Quality control handbook*. New York: McGraw-Hill.

Kanfer, R., & Ackerman, P. L. (1989). Motivation and cognitive abilities: An integrative/aptitude treatment interaction approach to skill acquisition. *Journal of Applied Psychology, 74*, 951–956.

Kankanhalli, A., & Tan, B. C. Y. (2005). Knowledge management metrics: A review and directions for future research. *International Journal of Knowledge Management, 1*, 20–32.

Kaplan, R. S., & Norton, D. P. (1992, January/February). The balanced scorecard—measures that drive results. *Harvard Business Review, 70.1*, 71–79.

Kaplan, R. S., & Norton, D. P. (1996). *The balanced scorecard: Translating strategy into action*. Boston, MA: Harvard Business School Press.

Kaplan, R. S., & Norton, D. P. (2007, July-August). Using the balanced scorecard as a strategic management system. *Harvard Business Review, 85.4*, 150–161.

Kerlinger, F. N. (1979). *Behavioral research: A conceptual approach*. New York: Holt, Rinehart, & Winston.

Kluger, A. N., & DeNisi, A. (1996). The effects of feedback interventions on performance: A historical review, a meta-analysis, and a preliminary feedback intervention theory. *Psychological Bulletin, 119*, 254–284.

Locke, E. A. (1968). Toward a theory of task motivation and incentives. *Organizational Behavior and Human Performance, 3*, 157–189.

Locke, E. A., & Latham, G. P. (1984). *Goal setting: A motivational technique that works*. Englewood Cliffs, NJ: Prentice Hall.

McFall, S. R., Jamieson, J. P., & Harkins, S. G. (2009). Testing the mere effort account of the evaluation-performance relationship. *Journal of Personality and Social Psychology, 96*, 135–154.

Miner, J. B. (2003, September). The rated importance, scientific validity, and practical usefulness of organizational behavior theories: A quantitative review. *Academy of Management Learning and Education, 2.3*, 250–268.

NIST (National Institute of Standards and Technology). (2009). *Baldrige national quality program: Criteria for performance excellence*. Baldrige National Quality Program. Retrieved July 8, 2009, from http://www.baldrige.nist.gov/PDF_files/2009_2010_Business_Nonprofit_Criteria.pdf.

Nunnally, J. C. (1978). *Psychometric theory*. (2nd ed.). New York: McGraw-Hill.

"Our Intangible Riches." (2007, August). *Growth strategies*. Retrieved September 19, 2007, from http://findarticles.com/p/articles/mi_qa3908/is_200708/ai_n19511507.

Payne, S. C., Satoris, S. Y., & Beaubien, J. M. (2007). A meta-analytic examination of the goal orientation nomological set. *Journal of Applied Psychology, 92*, 128–150.

Richard, P. J., Devinney, T. M., Yip, G. S., & Johnson, G. (2009). Measuring organizational performance: Towards methodological best practice. *Journal of Management, 35*, 718–804.

Stajkovic, A. D., & Luthans, F. (1997). A meta-analysis of the effects of organizational behavior modification on task performance, 1975–1995. *Academy of Management Journal, 40,* 1122–1149.

Stajkovic, A. D., & Luthans, F. (1998). Self-efficacy and work-related performance: A meta-analysis. *Psychological Bulletin, 124,* 240–261.

Triplett, N. (1898). The dynamogenic factors in pacemaking and competition. *American Journal of Psychology, 9,* 507–533.

Virtualteamworks.com. (n.d.). Retrieved July 9, 2008, from http://www.virtual teamworks.com/08.htm.

Walton, M. (1990). *Deming management at work.* New York: Perigee Books.

Wood, R. E., Mento, A. J., & Locke, E. A. (1987). Task complexity as a moderator of goal effects: A meta-analysis. *Journal of Applied Psychology, 72,* 416–425.

Yeo, G., Loft, S., Xiao, T., & Kiewitz, C. (2009). Goal orientations and performance: Differential relationships across levels of analysis and as a function of task demands. *Journal of Applied Psychology, 94,* 710–726.

2 INTRODUCTION TO SCORECARDS

You're a first-level manager and you have just been told to come up with metrics for the new metric system. Top management keeps talking about balanced-scorecard this and Tobin's Q that.

They may as well be speaking in riddles.

The teams creating the high-level scorecards have high-powered consulting help, but you're just a small fry with a small work group and suddenly you're supposed to come up with numbers that are apparently objective and obvious to all. The bewildering stacks of (really thick!) performance measurement books all speak to leaders of organizations or strategic business units. If only something was written to describe scorecards at all levels, particularly for the folks who supervise first-line workers . . .

CHAPTER OVERVIEW

The chapter begins with conceptualization, laying out a basic vocabulary of terms used throughout this book and in any discussion of metrics. A *basic metric model* is introduced with the example of weight loss to demonstrate how principles of metrics apply to anything people wish to measure. The basic model is then applied to a business example to present a *basic metric model of work performance*.

Conceptualization

Recall that a metric refers both to a measure and measurement unit. In this section, we will explore other key terms associated with metrics in general. To make learning the dry basic scientific vocabulary participative, both readers and teachers are invited to consider associations between terms in Figure 2.1. Before reading further, look at the concepts in Figure 2.1 and guess for yourself how these terms are related.

LEARNING OBJECTIVES

After studying this chapter, you should be able to achieve the following:

1. Define and use a basic vocabulary of terms related to metrics.
2. Use a basic metric model to remember essential elements of a metric scorecard: motive, object, attributes, dimensions, measurement units, behavioral metrics, outcome metrics, and goals.
3. Understand five key criteria for choosing a measurement unit.
4. Know practical and theoretical reasons why it is so important to couple behavioral metrics and outcome metrics.
5. Design a "Basic Metric Model" and a "Basic Metric Model of Work Performance."

To unpack the associations among the terms presented in Figure 2.1, eight comparisons will be discussed. Warning: plan for some confusion. If you have guessed by now that many terms are used interchangeably, you would be right.

First, consider the terms *indicator* and *measure*, terms that are often (and erroneously) used interchangeably. An **indicator** is something that signifies the presence or absence of an attribute. A **measure** is a quantification that provides a set of rules for assigning numbers to reflect that attribute. To drive home the distinction between the terms indicator and measure, refer to the following example:

Nerd Index for a Group of Software Engineers
A. Gender.
B. Intensity of employee anger when deprived of time surfing game sites where 12-year-olds around the world think they are heroes: low, medium, high = 1, 2, 3.
C. Rating of 1 to 10 measuring bad dancing at Christmas parties (sober), low being 1 and high being 10.
D. Total number of employees whose entire wardrobes consist of company t-shirts.
E. Yes or No: Cubicle decorations include pictures of little girls holding hands, skipping through fields.

Metric	Measure	Index	Unit of Analysis	Unit of Observation
Feedback	Indicator	Attribute	Object	Phenomenon Dimension
Level of Measurement	Level of Analysis	Survey	Scale	Statistic
	Parameter		Variable	Census

Figure 2.1. Key Metric Concepts
Source: ©Ruth A. Huwe.

All of the items include indicators, but only items B, C, and D are measures. Item A can be translated into a measure if we make the rule that Male = 1 and Female = 0. Similarly, Item F can be easily translated into a measure if we claim that Yes = 1 and No = 0 and take our observations from there.

Second, consider the terms *attribute* and *object*. In the classic textbook *Psychometric Theory*, Nunnally (1978) stressed a point that is worth repeating: *measures are not about objects, measures are about attributes*. In the examples above, the items do not measure the "groupiness" of the software group, the items measure the attribute of nerdiness. An **attribute** is a facet, aspect, or characteristic of an object. The **object** is the phenomenon we wish to observe. A phenomenon could be anything we are able to define: an individual, a team, a department, an entire organization, or a batch of parts. The phenomenon is what we observe, but the attributes are what we measure.

Third, consider the terms *indicator* and *dimension*. What indicates whether or not an employee is a top performer? In the case of the software employee, is it that he writes a lot of code? Rarely has work that needs to be rewritten? Does not forget key details in crucial PowerPoint presentations? Smiles when he greets internal customers? Helps fellow employees? Displays a positive attitude? Notice that these indicators might fall into a couple of categories: data behaviors or people behaviors. A grouping of indicators is known as a *dimension*. In this example, indicators of attributes would be divided into dimensions of "data" (lines of code, rewrites, details) and "people" (smiling, helpful, positive) indicators of performance. A **dimension** refers to "a specifiable aspect of our concept" (Babbie, 2007, p. 126), but the aspects are then described with indicators.

Fourth, consider together the concept of *attribute* and *dimension*. An attribute is a broader concept; a dimension is basically an attribute of an attribute. For example, consider a human as an object. Attributes of the human might be "home behavior and work behavior." We could look at "dimensions" of work behavior, such as "dealing with data" and "dealing with people." Alternatively, some people will refer to a dimension as if it is an attribute and then use the term subdimension as an attribute of the dimension. In all cases, dimensions, subdimensions, and attributes are all variables. A **variable** is something that takes on different values.

Fifth, consider the distinction between the terms *unit of analysis, level of analysis*, and *level of measurement*. As with a unit of observation, a **unit of analysis** is the number of objects observed when an individual score is recorded on a measure. For example, it could be an individual respondent's score on a satisfaction survey. Similar to a measurement unit, the **level of analysis** is a specification of what counts as the object we are observing when summarizing scores. In business, we might measure our "level of analysis" according to how we conceptualize systems and subsystems: the individual, group/team, organization, industry, or society (Gupta, Tesluk, & Taylor, 2007). For example, a team's average satisfaction score could be taken at the team or department "level of analysis."

A unit or level of analysis refers to the *objects* we observe or measure at a given time, but a **level of measurement** is a reference to the *precision* with which we take measures. The nerdiness factors described earlier provide examples of the four levels of measurement: nominal (Item A), ordinal (Item B), interval (Item C), and ratio (Item D). Level of measurement is discussed at length in Chapter 11.

Sixth, consider the terms *index, scale,* and *survey*. The terms scale and survey often are used interchangeably. A **survey** is a set of subjective-response items that are added to together to reflect quantified attributes of an object. Put in simpler terms, a survey is a set of items that reflect a score on a measure. A **scale** is referred to as a set of survey items added together, but the term "scale" also can refer to the units of measure that go with individual survey items (e.g., a scale of 1 to 7). An **index** is also a composite set of scores on a measure, but the measures might be subjective or objective. For example, a quality "index" might be a mix of subjective survey items and objective error counts. Alternatively, an index might be purely based on objective measures such as "number of housing starts" and "dollars earned" as an index to reflect health of the construction industry.

Seventh, consider the difference between the terms *statistic, parameter,* and *census.* All three terms refer to a number that is a summary. For example, my salary last month is just a score on a salary metric. The average salary of all lecturers is a *summary* of other scores. Although all three (statistic, parameter, and census) are summaries, the concepts vary in terms of (a) whether the numbers are used to make descriptions (inferences) about samples or populations, and (b) the data on which the numbers are based. A **statistic** is a summary number used to describe a sample and is based on data gathered from a sample. A **parameter** is a summary number used to describe a population but is based on data gathered from a sample that is a subset of the population. A **census statistic** is a summary number used to describe a population and is based on data from every member of the population.[1]

For an example of the difference between a statistic and a parameter, consider a number that *Time* magazine published: "655,000[.] The number of civilians estimated to have died as a result of the current war" ("Numbers," 2006, p. 26). It is unlikely that someone counted every one of the projected 655,000 casualties of the Iraq war. It is more likely that this statistic was based on some sample of data and an inference was made about the overall population of casualties; the estimate is a parameter. To the contrary, the same story lists as "0" the number of the 12,000 Federal Bureau of Investigation (FBI) agents who speak Arabic with the fluency of a native. The number "0" reflects the outcome of a census as the FBI likely would be able to count every one of their employees.

Eighth, consider the terms *attribute* and *variable*. For decades, people have fallen into the trap of using the terms "attribute" and "variable" interchangeably (Gould & Kolb, 1964), but this is a mistake. Defined earlier, an attribute is a *characteristic* and a **variable** is a concept that takes on *different values*.

At this point, you are probably clinically depressed about the realization that endless conceptual distinctions go along with the art of creating metrics. So far, we have hit the key terms that give us a basic scientific language for going forward. To link metric concepts to actual practice, let's now turn to a basic metric model.

Technique: Basic Metric Model

The basic metric model shown in Table 2.1 was initially developed as a diagram for teaching concepts in masters of business administration elective course on metrics and in a feedback class at the Boeing Company. Over the years, it evolved into a tool that has been used by dozens of managers at both for-profit and nonprofit companies.

When creating metrics, the $64,000 question is, "How do you come up with the measures in the first place?" One way would be to "brainstorm" different metrics. Another approach is to choose from some collection of indicators or measures such as those presented in Chapter 18. The basic metric model presents yet another alternative, a "fill-in-the-blank" approach.

A "fill-in-the-blank" approach serves as a memory device, triggering us to remember all of the elements that should be specified: the object to measure, measurement units, attributes, dimensions, behavioral metrics, outcome metrics, and goals. The model will be described in reference to a weight-loss example. The letters on the model indicate the order in which blanks are typically completed.

This example may seem incredibly hokey (even "nerdy") at first. But as students have learned in countless classes, when we get to the actual work applications of metric models, the ability to reflect on this simple example will be invaluable.

(A) The process for creating any kind of metrics begins with a basic motive question, "What is my **reason** for developing these metrics?" This initial question intuitively leads us to the next step, asking, "What is my ultimate goal?" In the case of weight loss, you would ask, "What is the reason for developing

Table 2.1 Basic Metric Model

(B) Name of Object Being Measured: _____

(C) Level of Analysis: _____

(A) Reason for Metrics	(F) Attributes of Object Being Measured	(G) Dimensions of Attributes	(H) Behavior Metric (Measure/ Unit)	(I) Behavior Goal	(E) Outcome Metric (Measure/ Unit)	(D) Outcome Goal

Source: © Ruth A. Huwe.

weight loss metrics?" One motivation might be "I live in fear of bathing-suit season."

(B) Before continuing, it is helpful to name the object being measured and (C) observe your level of analysis. In the example shown in Table 2.2, the name of the object measured in this case is "Pat," and the level of analysis is an individual.

The level of analysis is basically the same across a scorecard. Part Two of this book describes scorecards that vary in unit of analysis for individual performance appraisals (Chapter 5), teams (Chapter 6), departments (Chapter 7), and organizations (Chapter 8).

(D) Your ultimate goal is reflected in your **outcome goal**, the tangible result you hope to achieve. As shown in Table 2.2, if you live in fear of the upcoming bathing suit season, a logical outcome goal might be something like "lose 20 pounds."

Outcome goals do not always include a time goal, but it is helpful if they do. An outcome goal without a time goal is saying, "I want to lose 20 pounds!" An outcome goal with a time goal is the more powerful statement, "I want to lose 20 pounds *in 12 weeks*" (and spare myself the humiliation at vacation resort X, public pool Y, or class reunion Z).

You might also notice that we could have completed steps A, B, C, or D in any order, but we could not have continued until we completed these four steps. This reminds us that the steps for creating metric scorecards follow a somewhat logical process, but it is not perfectly linear.

(E) Once stating an outcome goal, the **outcome metric** typically follows logically. For example, if our outcome goal is to "lose 20 pounds," then a sensible outcome metric is "number of pounds lost per week." As with all metrics, we are making two decisions: choice of measure (pounds lost) and choice of measurement unit (per week).

(F) The reason for a metric and the outcome goal will lead us to **attributes** of the object that should be measured. These attributes are known as the "drivers" of the outcome we seek. For example, if the outcome we care about is losing weight, we know that we must focus on two key attributes of the object's behavior: eating and exercise. If we were measuring "eating," but our outcome goal was "drop 100 cholesterol points," the relevant attribute of eating would be the amount of saturated fat in our diet. But if our goal is weight loss (and it is), we would consider the most relevant dimension to be the "overall amount" that we eat.

(G) To continue with the example in Table 2.2, we need to consider the possibility that an attribute has *dimensions*. For example, if you want to lose weight, the exercise attribute has two key dimensions: aerobic exercise and weight-training exercise. If the outcome goal was "tone," you might have considered a different attribute of exercise. In some diet plans, eating would be broken down into dimensions. For example, Weight Watchers would break eating attributes into three dimensions: calories, fat, and fiber. Alternatively, the Zone diet would look at dimensions such as fat, carbohydrates, and protein. Once we

Table 2.2 Dimensions of Metrics (Weight Example)

Name of Object Being Measured: Pat

Level of Analysis: Individual

Scorecard Owner: Manager X

Example: Reason for Metrics	Attributes	Dimensions	Behavior Metric (Measure/Unit)	Behavior Goal	Outcome Metric (Measure/Unit)	Goal
I live in fear of bathing suit season	Eating	Amount	Calories per day	Under 1,800 calories, 7 days in a row	No. of pounds per week	Lose 20 pounds in 12 weeks
	Exercise	Aerobic	No. of minutes per day	30 per day, 7 days in a row		
		Weight	No. of 30-min. workouts per week	3 per week		

Source: ©Ruth A. Huwe.

have identified both attributes and dimensions, we are in a position to come up with behavioral metrics.

(H) The process of creating a *behavior metric*[2] involves two steps. First, we ask, "How would we measure the attributes?" In this case, "What is a measure of the amount we eat?" For example, "calories," Weight Watchers "points," or Zone units are measures of the amount we eat. Second, we translate the measure into a metric by adding a measurement unit: calories *per day*.

To develop behavior metrics for exercise, we would ask, "How do you measure aerobic exercise? How do you measure weight training?" Given that our goal is weight loss, it would be tempting to answer "number of calories burned from aerobic exercise" and "number of calories burned from weight training." However, consider the feasibility of that choice. Would we really want our exercise measure to be calories burned? Is that an easy metric to track? Does that tell us exactly what behavior to do? A more practical approach might be to measure the "number of 30-minute workouts per week" to aerobic exercise and "number of workouts per week" to weights.

(I) A well-established principle in feedback research is that feedback (particularly metric feedback) is more powerful if attached to goals (Pritchard, Jones, Roth, Stuebing, & Ekeberg, 1988). To finish our example in Table 2.2, we decide on **behavior metric goals**: "Eat less than 1800 calories for 7 days in a row" and "Do seven 30-minute aerobic workouts and three weight workouts per week" as our exercise goal.

Preconscious Decisions behind our Metric Choices

We make dozens of measurement decisions at what has been called a "preconscious" level. A *conscious* level means we are aware of what we are doing. An *unconscious* level means we are not aware of what we are doing. A **preconscious** level of awareness is one in which a decision is made out of awareness, but the decision maker could explain the rationale behind the decision if asked (Giddens, 1984). A lengthy list of potential preconscious metric decisions is presented in Chapters 11 and 12, but several issues warrant conscious attention at the outset.

Key Issues Related to the Choice of Measures

An important set of issues about measures can be remembered with the mnemonic RVFLAPS: reliability, validity, feasibility, logic, actionable, parsimony, and statistical soundness.[3] First, we consider **reliability**, the consistency of a measure. For example, you can hurt the reliability of your weight scores from one weigh-in to the next by craning your head back and tipping away from the scale when you see numbers you don't like. For a business example, the ratings of "product delivered" can be gamed ("manipulated") if one team measures it by shipping date and another measures it by the date the product is received; the gaming makes the measure less consistent and, hence, less reliable.

Second, we consider **validity**, the extent to which the metric measures what we think it measures. If you weighed yourself on a daily basis, would the variation reflect what you think it measures (weight loss) or something else (retained water)? For a business example, sometimes people claim they are measuring productivity when in fact they are only measuring efficiency.

Third, we consider **feasibility**, a reference to how difficult or easy it is to gather data for a measure. In the weight example, it can be more feasible to count the "number of workouts" rather than "calories burned per workout." In business, we might be interested in open-ended opinions of every customer, but it would not be feasible to gather and crunch such an amount of data.

Fourth, we consider **logic**, just plain horse sense. Logic is a catchall category that makes us consider other questions beyond the other areas of scrutiny. For example, we might ask, "Does it really make sense create metrics that lead us to eat all the fat we want on a low-carb diet—even when we are shooting calories and cholesterol through the roof?" For a business example, would it make sense to measure productivity by the amount of time one spends on the phone?

Fifth, the measures should be **actionable** in that the people actually can influence scores on the metric. It is a stretch, but some people would argue that weight is not necessarily actionable because of genetics. A fairly standard business example is to count "turnaround time" of work flow, even though another department holds up the work of your team and your team cannot do anything about it. These examples are not actionable because people seemingly cannot take action to influence the metric.

Sixth, measures need to be **parsimonious**, that is, they should contain the fewest variables that explain the most variation. This is the scientist's way of saying that things should be as simple as possible while maintaining relevance. For example, the main variables that influence weight loss are eating and exercise. We could add a host of others such as stress, restaurant invites, alcohol, family matters, tobacco intake, and on and on, but we go with the simplest list of things to track that have the biggest impact on the outcomes we wish to produce. In business, it is possible to measure every single process down to the seconds it takes to turn on a computer, but the list of metrics would not be parsimonious.

Seventh, measures need to be **statistically sound.** In cases in which we use our measures to represent characteristics of a larger population, we need to consider an entire set of statistical criteria. In simpler cases such as the weight loss example, we use questions of statistical soundness to check whether our math is right. For example, Weight Watchers assigns a point value that is associated with the fat, fiber, and calories associated with a given portion of food. A question of statistical soundness would simply be one of whether their equation is correct. In fact, over the years, they have changed their slide-rule measurement mechanism to count a different effect from fiber. In business, an example of statistical soundness would be one of comparing average performance appraisal scores across teams. Would we use the average as a metric—or the median?

Key Issues Related to the Choice of Measurement Units

We make at least four important considerations when choosing our measurement unit. First, what is the purpose of the measure? For example, is this metric being used to control variation in some process down the line? If so, this would pose an argument for making the unit of measure more frequent. In the weight loss example, some would argue that you should weigh yourself daily and not weekly so things don't have a chance to get out of control.

Second, if a measurement unit is time (per day, per week, etc.), the period of time needs to be long enough to detect variability. This is the argument to make the measurement unit less frequent. For example, what would happen if you weighed yourself every hour? Is that long enough to detect valid weight loss? In business, you might not measure "training hours per day," but you might measure some manufacturing processes by the hour.

Third, another issue related to periods of time is that measures need to be timely enough so the metric can be used as feedback. If someone is only weighed once a month, the impact of watching numbers will be minimal. In business, who cares about metrics that are outdated before you even get them?

Fourth, consider feasibility of the measurement unit. We cannot have people running to weight scales all day. In business, we can't have people recording metrics all day.

In Table 2.2, Pat went with a "weekly" unit of measure because that is common to most weight loss programs. Hence, the outcome metric is number of pounds lost per week. Table 2.2 also demonstrates how the choice of measurement unit may be different for different measures. In the weight loss example, the number of calories is measured per day but the number of workouts is measured per week.

Linking Behavioral and Outcome Metrics

It is worth stressing the importance of developing both behavioral metrics and outcome metrics. An accepted principle of psychology is that human behavior is influenced by outcomes we expect from our environment. Consider the reverse: What if we felt that our actions *were not* linked to outcomes in the environment? A classic experiment tested this proposition on dogs. The creatures were put in an apparatus in which they had no control over whether or not they would receive an electric shock. What did the dogs do? What would you do if every time you moved you got an electric shock no matter what you did? Dogs, as with humans, learned to feel "helpless." In the face of helplessness, a condition in which behaviors are unconnected to outcomes, creatures give up (Seligman & Maier, 1967). That sounds pretty dramatic, but it is precisely what managers are doing when they hold employees accountable for metrics over which they have no control. The helplessness condition is aroused when managers set outcome metrics and goals and then give employees absolutely no guidance on the behaviors needed to achieve those goals.

Beyond thinking of the dogs in the electric box, the idea of linking behaviors and outcomes is considered essential in several theories of motivation, including reinforcement theory (Stajkovic & Luthans, 2003), behavior modification (Stajkovic & Luthans, 1997), cognitive evaluation theory (Deci, Koestner, & Ryan, 1999), expectancy theory (Vroom, 1964), self-determination theory (Gagne & Deci, 2005), and social cognitive theory (Bandura & Locke, 2003). If people cannot see how their behaviors are linked to outcomes, they feel helpless, demoralized, and lack the self-efficacy necessary for goal achievement.

Most dieters seek a specific outcome: lose pounds, lose inches, fit into diet pants, and so forth. Most successful diet plans insist that you begin by recording behavior: how much you eat and exercise. As an example, if you go to a Weight Watchers meeting and listen to people report "how they did it," you are guaranteed to hear a variation on the phrase "I was writing it down!" Tracking both outcomes and behaviors is akin to the basketball coach who doesn't just look at overall points (the outcome), but also tracks behaviors such as blocks, rebounds, and assists. Keeping an eye on both behavioral and outcome metrics is a fundamental step in any logical set of metrics, including those created for the work place.

Finally, another reason to spell out behavior metrics is because of potential regulations. There are many paths to the same outcome, but in the case of heavily regulated business environments, some methods may be explicitly illegal.

Technique: A Basic Metric Model of Work Performance

Nunnally (1978) emphasized a point that cannot be repeated enough: measurement is about attributes, not objects. We don't measure a "team," we measure attributes about a team such as their work performance.

At the most basic level, **performance** is the behaviors that people enact to complete a task. A useful synonym for "behaviors" is to think of the "actions" people take to get something done. Although the emphasis here is on job performance, there are obviously as many forms of performance as there are roles that we can conjure (parental performance, student performance, civic performance, etc.).

Specific attributes and dimensions we choose to measure will depend on our reasons for developing measures, consequent goals, and the object we wish to judge. The attributes we choose to measure also vary by perspective, in that we would focus on different things if we were an accountant, economist, or organization development specialist. Just as the attributes focused on by a dieter will be different than those of a triathlete, specific attributes will be relevant in the judgment of work performance.

This book translates the "Basic Metric Model" into a specific "Basic Metric Model of Work Performance" by taking the perspective of a manager and focusing on the goal of performance improvement. As shown in the generic model in Table 2.3 and the engineering example in Table 2.4, this model assumes that three attributes of work performance will be relevant: quantity, quality, and efficiency. Where do these come from? From the insistence (1) that every model considers both productivity and quality and (2) that productivity is defined as having both a quantity dimension and an efficiency dimension. An expanded conceptualization of productivity and quality is provided in Chapter 4.

Applying the basic metric model to work performance is facilitated by adding one opening step: begin by considering the team's mission. This logical step has three helpful consequences. First, it provides focus. Second, it clarifies the motive in that it specifies what performance you wish to improve. Third, it helps identify key deliverables.

The following is a mission format that is particularly useful for creating metrics:

Mission: to provide _____ products/services to _____ customers.

Four features of the "Basic Metric Model of Work Performance" warrant discussion. First, notice that main attribute that concerns work is the performance on a deliverable. A **deliverable** is a product and/or service delivered by the team. Although we focus on one deliverable in this example, it is likely that teams will produce more than one major deliverable. The exact number will vary from team to team.

Rather than use the term "deliverable," some organizational cultures like to think of their work in terms of "processes" that they execute. One can easily see how attributes of deliverable performance (quantity, quality, efficiency) compare to standard attributes of process performance (cycle time, quality, cost). This book goes with the broader deliverable perspective because it leads us to consider a wider variety of metrics. For example, there are many other efficiency metrics to consider beyond costs. Moreover, this book's focus on deliverables does not eliminate the relevance of processes, as any process can be thought of in terms of the deliverable (product or service) it is meant to create.

Second, this book follows a contemporary definition of productivity (Pritchard et al., 1988) where the concept is taken to have two dimensions: quantity and efficiency. Why is this necessary? It is nice if you are so efficient that you can do 100 widgets per hour, but who cares if you are only able to keep that up for one hour and we need 800 widgets? Alternatively, it is nice if you can get out 800 widgets in a day, but not if your goofing off makes you so inefficient that it took you 12 hours and we have to pay you overtime.

Third, this model and every model in this book will always couple productivity with quality. Quality can refer to either a product or service. An expanded delineation of product quality is discussed in Chapter 4. Service quality generally requires scale construction and is the topic of Chapter 10. Whether considering product or service quality, this book follows a Total Quality Management (TQM) philosophy in which "quality" is judged from the perspective of a customer (Sousa & Voss, 2002).

Why is it so important to couple productivity measures with quality measures? Consider what would happen if you *only* measured work quantity. Remember those earlier examples of bum metrics? People could "game" or "manipulate" the metric to increase quantity but do it in a way that sacrifices quality—unless you also measure quality.

Table 2.3 Basic Metric Model of Work Performance

Name of Unit Being Measured: Generic Engineering Team.

Team Mission: Provide Drawings X for Customers Y.

Level of Analysis (Who is Being Measured): Team Z.

Example: Reason for Metrics	Attribute	Dimensions	Behavior Metric (Measure/ Unit)	Behavior Goal	Outcome Metric (Measure/ Unit)	Outcome Goal
Improve Performance	Performance on X	Quantity Quality Efficiency				

Date of Scorecard Update: _____ *Metric Owner: Manager X*

Source: ©Ruth A. Huwe.

Table 2.4 Basic Metric Model of Work Performance: Engineering Example

Name of Unit Being Measured: Generic Engineering Team.

Team Mission: Provide Generic Drawings to Generic Customers.

Level of Analysis (Who is Being Measured): First-Level Team with Eight
Employees.

Example: Reason for Metrics	Attribute	Dimensions	Behavior Metric (Measure/Index)	Behavior Goal	Outcome Metric (Measure/Unit)	Outcome Goal
Improve Engineering Work Performance	Drawing performance	Productivity (Quantity)	Milestones met	100%	No. of drawings per month	30
		Productivity (Efficiency)	Amount of overtime (checked monthly)	0%	Average costs per project (checked monthly)	$2k for small projects, $10k for large projects
		Quality	No. of checklists completed (checked monthly)	100%	Customer Satisfaction Score (1–10 scale, checked monthly)	9

Date of Scorecard Update: _____   *Metric Owner:* _____

Source: ©Ruth A. Huwe.

Fourth, this model begins with consideration of the object (or "team") that is the focus of measurement and the level of analysis at which this occurs (individual, first-level team, departmental, or organizational). The intellectual argument for this focus of analysis is grounded in systems theory and is described in detail in Chapter 3.

From Metric Model to Scorecard

The basic metric model of work performance is meant as a visual checklist of sorts. It is a tool to remind managers to consider all key concepts when creating metrics: productivity and quality, behavioral and outcome, metrics and goals, and all key deliverables or processes. Once the entire model is completed, managers typically select a subset of four or five key metrics for actual use.

How is the metric model different from a scorecard? A scorecard includes additional attributes of teams that should be considered. As discussed in Chapter 3, it is not sufficient just to consider productivity and quality of a team; it is also important to consider how the team renews itself and the extent to which it supports the overall organization's strategy. It is also the case that scorecards will vary by level of analysis. For this reason, Part Two of this book discusses the basic process for creating a performance appraisal at the individual level of analysis (Chapter 5) and includes step-by-step processes for using and creating scorecards at three levels of analysis: team (Chapter 6), department (Chapter 7), and organization (Chapter 8).

CHAPTER SUMMARY

The example of weight loss was used to introduce a Basic Metric Model, a fill-in-the-blank tool that helps people consider all key concepts when creating a metric. The example of engineering work was then used to demonstrate a Basic Metric Model of Work Performance. The work performance version includes consideration of a team's mission as well as the attributes that would be considered in any measure of work performance: quality, quantity, and efficiency.

NOTES

1. One more way to distinguish a statistic and a parameter is to consider the difference between what is known as descriptive statistics and inferential statistics. **Descriptive statistics** are summary numbers used to describe a sample; descriptive statistics *are not* parameters. **Inferential statistics** are summary numbers used to describe a larger population; inferential statistics *are* parameters. The term "inferential" derives from the idea that a statistic is a prediction about a population and the prediction is "inferred" from a sample.

2. Behavior metrics are typically leading metrics and always should be linked as drivers of performance.

3. Why RVFLAPS? Because metric mistakes are as bad as following RV Flaps. (Heh.) It's just a difficult set of letters to put into a mnemonic. Ambitious Scrabble players are encouraged to write in an improvement for future editions.

REFERENCES

Babbie, E. (2007). *The practice of social research* (11th ed.). Belmont, CA: Wadsworth.

Bandura, A., & Locke, E. A. (2003). Negative self-efficacy and goals revisited. *Journal of Applied Psychology, 88*, 87–99.

Deci, E. L., Koestner, R., & Ryan, R. M. (1999). A meta-analytic review of experiments examining the effects of extrinsic rewards on motivation. *Psychological Bulletin, 125*, 627–668.

Gagne, M., & Deci, E. L. (2005). Self-determination theory and work motivation. *Journal of Organizational Behavior, 26*, 331–362.

Giddens, A. (1984). *The constitution of society: Outline of the theory of structuration.* Berkeley: University of California Press.

Gould, J., & Kolb, W. L. (1964). *A dictionary of the social sciences.* New York: Macmillan.

Gupta, A. K., Tesluk, P. E., & Taylor, M. S. (2007). Innovation at and across multiple levels of analysis. *Organization Science, 18*, 885–897.

"Numbers." (2006, October 23). *Time, 168*(17), p. 26.

Nunnally, J. C. (1978). *Psychometric Theory* (2nd ed.). New York: McGraw-Hill.

Pritchard, R. D., Jones, S. D., Roth, P. L., Stuebing, K. K., & Ekeberg, S. E. (1988). Effects of group feedback, goal setting, and incentives on organizational productivity. *Journal of Applied Psychology, 73*, 337–358.

Seligman, M. E., & Maier, S. F. (1967). Failure to escape traumatic shock. *Journal of Experimental Psychology, 74*, 1–9.

Sousa, R., & Voss, C. A. (2002). Quality management re-visited: A reflective review and agenda for future research. *Journal of Operations Management, 20*, 91–109.

Stajkovic, A. D., & Luthans, F. (1997). A meta-analysis of the effects of organizational behavior modification on task performance, 1975–1995. *Academy of Management Journal, 40*, 1122–1149.

Stajkovic, A. D., & Luthans, F. (2003). Behavioral management and task performance in organizations: Conceptual background, meta-analysis, and test of alternative models. *Personnel Psychology, 56*, 155–194.

Vroom, V. H. (1964). *Work and motivation.* New York: Wiley.

3 SYSTEMS THEORY: THE FOUNDATION FOR CONTEMPORARY METRIC SYSTEMS

Emotional intelligence. Knowledge capturing. Out-of-the-box thinking. Leader by example. Open to conflict. Theory Y. Level Five. Sensitive to diversity. Systems thinker.

Managers are expected to be many things. In most cases, the application of new concepts is pretty clear. If someone tells you "be emotionally intelligent," it is fairly obvious that they mean in your dealings with people. If someone tells you to be "knowledge capturing," it is not a big leap to see that they mean you should have a knowledge-management system.

Everyone these days is also supposed to be a "systems thinker," but exactly what is that supposed to mean? Systems theory provides a way to conceptualize things, but where is the application to actual practice?

One direct application of systems theory is to the manner in which metrics systems are created. Systems theory provides an answer to an essential question of this text: What is a metric scorecard supposed to measure?

CHAPTER OVERVIEW

If you were to measure "an organization," how on earth would you know where to place your focus? On the wall colors? On the organization chart? On buildings located north of the 45th parallel?

Systems theory tells us how to go about deciding the focus of our measures. We do not create a random "list" of metrics, but create a system of metrics that are oriented toward the general purpose of improving performance.

This chapter describes three variations on systems theory: the open-system properties, General Systems Theory, and a socio-technical systems perspective. The goal is to demonstrate how system theory provides the basic ideas behind

---

LEARNING OBJECTIVES

After studying this chapter, you should be able to achieve the following:

1. Distinguish open and closed systems.
2. Define a system, subsystem, and suprasystem.
3. Describe the 10 properties of open systems.
4. Understand associations between system elements.
5. Know key subsystems prescribed by Baldrige criteria.
6. Describe principles of metric systems that are based on open-systems properties.
7. Describe principles of metric systems that are based on General Systems Theory.
8. Describe principles of metric systems that are based the socio-technical systems approach.
9. Understand how systems theory provides the foundation for all scorecards presented in this book.

---

contemporary metric systems. These metric principles are the intellectual foundation for all metric models and scorecard models presented in this book (Chapters 6, 7, and 8).

The 10 Properties of Open Systems

What would happen if we slammed shut the doors on the room we are sitting in right now and hermetically sealed the cracks in the walls. How long would we survive? We might have some air. We might have some food sitting around. But without input from our environment, we would slowly dehydrate and die—if we didn't go crazy first. Shutting the room creates a *closed system*, a type of system that does not receive inputs from the external environment. A closed system is in contrast to an *open system*, a type of system that does receive inputs from the external environment. A **system** is a group of interacting elements that function together as a whole.

In 1966, Daniel Katz and Robert L. Kahn published their seminal text *Social Psychology of Organizing* (Katz & Kahn, 1966; 1978). Their central thesis was that organizations are **open systems**, "an energic input-output system in which the energic return from the output reactivates the system" (Katz & Kahn, 1978, p. 20). Their basic example is that, in many organizations, outcomes are converted into money and the money then represents the input that refurbishes the system. They note, however, that not all outputs convert into money. They give the example of a society of birdwatchers whose output and energizing input are the edification and enjoyment gained from watching birds.

An open system is distinguished from a **closed system**, self-contained structures that do not depend on the environment for their existence. Katz and Kahn grant that closed systems exist and are the typical domain of physical sciences. However, they argue that all living systems—either biological or social—depend on inputs and are, therefore, open systems. Organizations are social, open systems.

Another open-system feature is the idea that every open system is dependent on **subsystems, systems, and suprasystems**, which vary by how we define units of analysis. To illustrate, we may consider a company a system, with departments as its subsystems and its industry as a suprasystem. Whether a department is a subsystem or a system entirely depends on how we define it. For example, we could define the accounting department as a system unto itself, or define it as a subsystem of the larger organizational system. Alternatively, we could consider that company's computer lines as a system, its intranet lines as one subsystem, and its public lines as another subsystem; the Internet represents a suprasystem.

Katz and Kahn also stressed that each system is defined by a **boundary**, the lines of definition between the system and its environment. They argued that one cannot define a system by the purpose of its members because the system would then have as many definitions as motives. Instead, they argue that the system should be defined by its output.

The idea of the boundary has two important implications for metric systems. First, any practitioner must define **scope**, the range of objects to which measures will be applied. For example, managers must define who does and does not count as part of a "team." Second, output is an excellent place to focus our metrics. As an example, an essential step to creating a team scorecard is to begin by defining the mission of the team in terms of the products or services it provides to its customers.

A detailed description of Katz and Kahn's open-system properties is shown in Box 3.1 along with a running example of a hospital. These 10 properties give a vocabulary for understanding key open-system contributions to metric systems, to which we now turn.

Properties 1, 2, and 3 are aligned with General Systems Theory in depicting that systems are composed of inputs, throughputs, and outputs. For metric systems, this provides attributes that need to be considered for measurement. This extends the emphasis of metrics from mere financial metrics that reflect outputs to a concomitant concern for (a) the renewal of employees and others sources of inputs and (b) processes reflected in throughputs. Measuring attributes to mark employee performance and internal processes are standard categories on Balanced Scorecards (Kaplan & Norton, 2007), scorecards based on Baldrige criteria (NIST, 2009), and stakeholder categories (Richard, Devinney, Yip, & Johnson, 2009).

Property 4 conceives of systems as cycles of events. For metrics, this emphasizes the idea that different metrics are needed at different points in time. For example, Kaplan and Norton (1996) note that metrics will vary over time

Box 3.1. Katz and Kahn's 10 Properties of an Open System

"1. *Importation of energy.* Open systems import some form of energy from the external environment" (p. 23).

Hospital Example: Organizations requires two kinds of input: maintenance and production (Katz & Kahn, 1978). The maintenance inputs support the system, the production inputs are processed to yield the final product. In a hospital, human resources and electricity are examples of support inputs. The patients, wraps, and medicines are elements of the final product that goes out the door.

"2. *The throughput.* Open systems transform the energy available to them" (p. 23).

Hospital Example: Patients are treated, transformed from sick to healing, and are relieved of some of their financial resources.

"3. *The output.* Open systems export some product into the environment, whether it be the invention of an inquiring mind or a bridge constructed by an engineering firm" (p. 24).

Hospital Example: The restored patient is sent into the environment and the hospital has earned profit. The profit, in turn, also goes out into the environment as the hospital purchases more of the human resources, materials, and electricity needed to run the hospital.

"4. *Systems as cycles of events.* The pattern of activities of the energy exchange has a cyclic nature" (p. 24).

Hospital Example: The process of patient and resource inputs, treatment throughput, hospital release, and payment output is repeated.

"5. *Negative entropy.* To survive, open systems must reverse the entropic process; they must acquire negative entropy. The entropic process is a universal law of nature in which all forms of organization move toward disorganization or death" (p. 25).

Hospital Example: The hospital could stop having patients or input resources, have a breakdown in the throughput processes to treat them, or have its doors blockaded so that the patients cannot be released. Unless efforts are taken to stop these entropic forces, the hospital system will shut down. However, Katz and Kahn also note that it is characteristic for systems to have some storage capacity and the hospital does have the ability to carry on in the face of problems. As an example, if electricity is halted, there are generators. If staff is not available, existing staff can work overtime. Storage rooms could be used to keep patients.

"6. *Information input, negative feedback, and the coding process.* The inputs into living systems do not consist only of energic materials. . . . The simplest type of informational input found in all subsystems is negative feedback" (p. 26).

Hospital Example: Suppose a hospital's throughput processes are broken; patients have to wait too long, wounds fester, and people die. If the released hospital patients complain bitterly to the health board, this "feedback" in turn would be fed into the hospital systems and changes in processes would be demanded.

The concept of coding is also important. Do personnel of the hospital sit in front of screens that show them shifts in stock prices through the day? Do they monitor changes in troop movements by the Taliban? The buzzing confusion of information from the world is "coded" into information that is relevant to the system. For example, the hospital personnel pay attention to feedback such as that provided on customer service surveys or health board inspections.

"7. *The steady state and dynamic homeostasis.* The importation of energy to arrest entropy operates to maintain some constancy in energy exchange, so that open systems that survive are characterized by a steady state" (p. 27).

A qualification to the homeostatic principle is that living systems tend toward growth and expansion to counteract entropy.

Hospital Example: The hospital has a relatively fixed number of beds and staff and, on average, a typical patient flow. But suppose there is an apartment fire and the hospital is overwhelmed with patients. The hospital system may speed up to some frenetic pace to deal with the patients, but then it spirals back toward its normal pace of operation. The normal pace is the steady state, though we expect the hospital to grow over time.

Meanwhile, the organization has ploughed its profits back into improvements that require additional staff, means to acquire raw materials, and so forth. A new bureaucracy is created to handle the additions and the overall system proceeds toward expansion.

"8. *Differentiation.* Open systems move in the direction of differentiation and elaboration" (p. 29).

Hospital Example: Does everyone in a hospital participate in the insurance billing? Treating of patients? Fixing of electrical appliances? Individual throughput functions become specialized and differentiated. Doctors treat patients. Maintenance personnel fix appliances. Administrators deal with insurance.

Another system principle is that of system survival, including that of subsystems. Once a department is established, it is difficult to dismantle it.

"9. *Integration and Coordination.* As differentiation proceeds, it is countered by processes that bring the system together for unified functioning" (p. 29).

According to Katz and Kahn (1978), three interrelated bases provide the integration of social systems: roles, norms, and values. In their example, roles will tell people what job functions they perform. Norms will provide the extent to which workers will do a satisfactory job. Values provide a rationale for their activities.

Hospital Example: Can the doctors, maintenance personnel, or insurance processors conduct themselves in isolation? At some point, they are integrated. As an example, the insurance processor signals the doctor to proceed with a patient. The doctor complains to maintenance about appliances. Overall, someone is coordinating the flow of the communication that integrates the actions of the various parties.

"10. *Equifinality.* . . . a system can reach the same final state from differing initial conditions and by a variety of paths" (p. 30).

Hospital Example: At the hospital, a patient comes in with a torn ligament. Many paths, or solutions, can be taken to taken the same outcome. The surgeon may wish to do surgery, the physical therapist may wish to do physical therapy. Even the choice of physical therapy exercises is an example of different ways to do the same thing. It could also be that two doctors see the patient, only one doctor, or just a nurse. Again, many paths can be taken to achieve the same ending.

Source: © Ruth A. Huwe.

according to whether an organization is in a growth, sustain, or harvest stage of evolution. For work teams and departments, metrics need to evolve as deliverables and strategies evolve.

Property 5, the idea of negative entropy, along with Properties 8 and 9 concerning differentiation and integration, leads to an important point: "roll-up" or "cascade" metrics are insufficient. **Roll-up** metrics attempt to depict an organization by "adding up" the scores of individual teams. Unfortunately, this misses the idea that entropic and synergic forces influence the value of the whole. It also misses the idea that the output of one team is not the same as the output of another team. As an example, it is senseless to add the "number of drawings" by an engineering department with the "number of interviews" conducted by a human resources department. What is the manager to do? Metric systems must include both measures of subsystems (e.g., departments) as well as measures of the suprasystem (e.g., entire organization).

Property 5 leads one to consider the idea of capacity. Whether this means backup stock of the technical system or backup, cross-trained personnel for the human system, this system concept alerts managers to consider capacity as another attribute that needs to be included in contemporary metric systems.

Property 6 makes an important point about informational input and the coding process associated with negative feedback. An organization does not just take in "feedback," it "codes" the feedback and considers only that which is relevant. This underscores the importance of the need for parsimony in metric systems. In fact, most managers do not complain that they have "too few" metrics. The typical lament is that they have "too many," and they need to choose "*which* few" do the best job. The quest for parsimony is aligned with the quest for developing a metric system that is feasible.

Taking Properties 1 and 6 together leads scorecard categories based on strategic renewal. Formally defined, "**strategic renewal** includes the process, content, and outcome of refreshment or replacement of attributes of an organization that have the potential to substantially affect its long-term prospects" (Agarwal & Helfat, 2009, p. 282). From a systems theory perspective, this can be broken into two scorecard categories: inputs that need to be renewed (Property 1) and a strategy that meets the demands of negative feedback to ensure long-term survival (Property 6). In this book, these will be labeled *renewal* and *strategic contribution*.

Agarwal and Helfat (2009) also distinguish two types of strategic renewal that correspond to two types of negative feedback: "(i) discontinuous strategic transformations and (ii) incremental renewal" (p. 283). Discontinuous strategic transformations refer to major changes in the environment such as technology, customer demand, or political events. For example, consider challenges faced by the manufacturers of cameras, mainframe computers, personal computers, or the telephone. Agarwal and Helfat point out that an organization's response to these major demands involves change along multiple dimensions such as the business model, technological base, resources and capabilities, and organizational mind-set.

Incremental strategic renewal is more likely to be undertaken proactively and allows organizations to cope with negative feedback as it emerges. This change comes from sources such as research and development (R&D), enlightening results from metric systems, globalization, and the type of employee entrepreneurship that leads to spinout companies.

What kinds of metrics address major discontinuous strategic transformations and incremental renewal? Reactions to major changes are likely beyond business as usual and are reflected in organizational initiatives, a major subject of Chapter 13. Hopefully, incremental adjustments are taken proactively and the need to change is signaled ahead of time by metrics. Taken together, both forms of change should be reflected in the company's overall strategy, and metrics are then a tool for strategy execution.

Property 7 describes the homeostasis principle that systems tend toward a steady state, characterized by running smoothly rather than in erratic leaps of high and low activity. Similar to Property 4, Property 7 alerts the metrics observer to consider time. Rather than consider the "cycle" or "stage" of the organization, however, this property underscores the need for metrics to consider *trends* reflecting growth or deterioration over time.

Properties 8 and 9 also make an important distinction for how units of analysis are conceived in the era of globalization. Writing in 1978, Katz and Kahn considered units such as job, work group, and organization. These units, however, do not reflect the work that is done in collaborations. Consider engineers who interface across time zones with engineers at a subcontracting firm. Those engineers together represent a work group that does not appear on any organization chart. Another example is cross-functional teams who work together to execute important projects. Not only do metrics need to reflect units of analysis, but also metrics need to depict the efforts of the workers who actually do the work. The organizational chart may not be relevant, but systems theory gives a solution for defining collaborative or cross-functional teams: define the unit of analysis around the outputs.

Property 10 advances equifinality as a characteristic of open systems. **Equifinality** is the idea that many paths can be taken to the same outcome. A subtle but important point is that this lays the foundation for the idea of continuous improvement. If there was just one optimal way of doing things, the idea of continuous improvement would be meaningless. Contemporary metric systems also reflect the idea that improvement should be considered continuous and that an update of processes should be continuous.

General Systems Theory

This section describes several important ideas that are implied by General Systems Theory (GST). As with open-systems properties, these metric principles provide the foundation for all metric models and scorecards within this text.

Metric Principle: The need for input and output metrics cuts across any kind of organization because the concepts are relevant to any kind of open system.

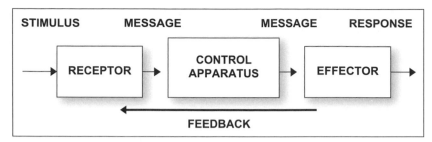

Figure 3.1 Simple Feedback Scheme
Source: von Bertalanffy, L. (1968). *General systems theory* (Rev. ed.). New York: George Braziller, p. 43. Reprinted by Permission from George Braziller, Inc.

Ludwig von Bertalanffy is generally considered to be the grandfather of GST. As a theoretical biologist, von Bertalanffy gave the human body as an example of an open system, a suprasystem that is composed of a variety of subsystems: skeletal system, respiratory system, nervous system, and so forth.

However, von Bertalanffy was not content to describe just the human body as an open system. GST was meant to be "general" in the sense that the concepts of open systems could cut across all scientific disciplines. For example, we might consider the earth as a system: inputs come from the atmosphere, inputs enter a throughput process, and outputs from the earth are returned to the atmosphere. An electrical impulse is pumped into a stereo system, the stereo translates the impulses, and the output produced is sound. A customer inputs an order to a company's Web site, the organization processes the order, and the product is shipped as output to the customer. Meteorologists. Engineers. Organizational psychologists. Any scientist could use the concepts of input-through-put-output and environment to depict the phenomena they seek to describe.

Figure 3.1 presents Bertalanffy's depiction of an open system. The main idea is that this model is generic and can be used to describe any given system.

Metric Principle: It is not sufficient only to look at the performance of individual subsystems, but we must also look at how the performance of one subsystem causally affects the performance of other subsystems.

One of the major contributions of the Balanced Scorecard model (Kaplan & Norton, 1996) is that it begins with a strategy map. Rather than find metrics for financial, growth and learning, operations, and customer categories, they urge practitioners to consider the causal associations between those variables. Why is this important? One reason is that goals expressed on a scorecard could be conflicting and actually hurt performance. For example, a given organizational scorecard could call for reducing costs and improving quality. Where does the company place its focus? At the team level, a given sales person could be given goals to increase her customer base and to increase satisfaction scores among current customers. Where does the salesperson spend her time? One

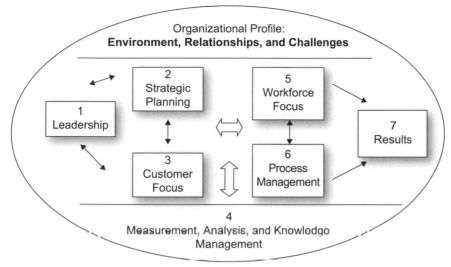

Figure 3.2 Baldrige Representation of Organizational Systems
Source: NIST (National Institute of Standards and Technology). (2009). *Baldrige national quality program. Criteria for performance excellence.* Baldrige National Quality Program, p. iv. Retrieved on July 8, 2009, from http://www.baldrige.nist. gov/PDF_files/2009_2010_Business_Nonprofit_Criteria.pdf. Reprinted by permission from the Baldrige National Quality Program.

study conducted a series of simulations to question the effects of multiple goals and found that performance is higher when the goals are positively associated (Ethiraj & Levinthal, 2009). Customer base? Satisfaction? The answer is not clear.

Richard et al. (2009) report that a study of more than 3,000 global firms in 38 countries concluded that a minimum of three dimensions is necessary to characterize basic aspects of performance. They conclude, however, "it is not clear that simply having more and varied measures increases the clarity of measured performance unless they are also modeled appropriately" (Richard et al., 2009, p. 738).

The call for causal associations is grounded in systems theory. In the Baldrige criteria (NIST, 2009), the NIST states on the first page that they take a systems orientation. As shown in Figure 3.2, they advance a model not just of scorecard categories, but a consideration of how those categories are related.

What do those arrows in Figure 3.2 mean? That is, how are subsystems related to one another? In his seminal work *The Social Psychology of Organizing,* Karl E. Weick (1979) made the concept of associations come alive by depicting what goes on in a given meeting. He asked readers to connect the following variables:

- Variety of ideas suggested
- My irritation at speaker

- Amount of group concentration on problem
- My feelings of boredom
- Amount of horsing around in group
- Number of ideas I think of
- My understanding of material that is presented
- My willingness to volunteer a comment
- Quality of ideas suggested

Draw a line to connect each dot and note a plus ("+") when one variable has a positive association with another variable and a minus ("–") when one variable has a negative association with another variable. Write in as many lines as you can. A **positive association** occurs when two variables "vary together," as one goes up the other goes up; as one goes down, the other goes down. A **negative association** occurs when two variables "vary opposite," as one goes up, the other goes down and vice versa. For example, if an increase in the "number of ideas I think of" leads to a decrease in "my feelings of boredom," then the two variables have a negative association (one increases as the other decreases).

Now apply this systems thinking to the Baldrige criteria diagramed in Figure 3.2. See the arrow between workforce focus and process management? From a systems perspective, we would ask questions about how one affects the other in cause-effect terms. Do human resources have a positive effect on processes? Or negative?

It is likely that systems thinking seems so intuitive to you that you might be wondering, "Well, how else might they be connected?" Consider any given organization chart, also a depiction of a system. If those lines do not represent cause and effect, what do they mean? The manager's team is a subsystem of a director's organization, the director's organization is a subsystem of a vice president's larger organization, and so forth. But what do those lines represent? Authority. *Not* cause/effect associations. Thinking in causal terms is a hallmark of system thinking.

Metric Principle: Learning is an organizational attribute that should be measured.

Double-loop learning is another seminal idea that underscores contemporary metric systems, an idea explicated in the seminal text *Organizational Learning II: Theory, Method, and Practice* (Argyris & Schon, 1978). A good way to understand double-loop learning is to consider the idea of meta-learning. Recall that with few exceptions (e.g., "metaphor," "metaphysics"), the prefix meta turns a word on itself. Just as metacommunication is communication about communication, meta-learning is learning about learning. A single-loop is learning, the **double-loop learning** is meta-learning. For example, single-loop learning is learning a foreign language. Double-loop learning is noting that the most successful ways for studying the language is to use a computer program rather than immersion course and to study twelve 10-minute increments each day rather than 2 hours on 1 day.

In this book, double-loop learning is advanced two ways. First, each model is marked by the "Date of Update." Second, whenever there is a set of steps for creating scorecards, the section begins with a stern reminder to document the processes used to create metrics. This knowledge capture is so important that the Baldrige committee goes so far as to include an entire section on "Measurement, Analysis, and Knowledge Management" as a major area of scoring (NIST, 2009).

Socio-Technical Systems and Metrics

The socio-technical systems (STS) perspective is a variation on GST that provides several additional metric principles. The names most commonly associated with this perspective are Eric Trist and Frederick E. Emery who collaborated on a series of STS studies. Trist was also a cofounder of the Tavistock Institute in London, which still conducts STS interventions. Although Trist's original research goes back to the 1930s, the perspective did not get a boost until the 1960s when STS researchers were asked to help with labor problems.

The STS perspective emphasizes that two types of systems operate in any given organization: a technical system and a social system. **Technical systems** represent the objective world of raw materials and information that flows through machines, tools, and conveyances. **Social systems** are composed of humans who work with the objective world. The study of the technical system is typically the domain of industrial and technical engineers, the study of the social systems is the domain of psychology. The organization development practitioner makes an effort to understand both systems and, where the industrial engineer's goal is optimal productivity in terms of throughput time, the OD practitioner is concerned with both productivity (technical orientation) and satisfaction (human orientation) (Wall, Corbett, Martin, Clegg, & Jackson, 1990).

A basic STS approach to organizational change is exemplified in a study by Rice (1958), a member of the Tavistock Institute. This study was conducted in Ahmedabad, India. There were 8,000 employees in two textile mills. The "technical" problem was that new automatic looms were introduced, but workers assigned to them had no change in roles. That is, there was a change in the technical system but not a change in the human system. The workers were basically just using the looms the same as "nonautomatics" and did not change their processes. The new looms improved neither quality nor quantity of cloth produced.

A socio-technical analysis revealed that the "socio" problem was that there were 12 different occupational roles that, with the exception of a couple of categories ("jobbers" and "assisted jobbers" that tuned the looms), were spread across 29 employees who worked as an aggregate across 224 automatic looms. A classic example of a socio-technical interface problem was that changes in yarn completely threw how many looms a given person could attend.

As a standard socio-technical intervention, workers were formed into teams. The team made a decision on role change, designating three levels of status: a leader, experienced workers, and less-skilled workers who were nonetheless considered "members" of the team over newcomers. Jobs were expanded to include some of the previously fractionated roles. Production rose to 95% of potential (compared to 80% before the intervention) and, in the long run, quality (measured by damaged cloth) improved from 32% before the experiment to 15% in the final 6 months of the experiment. Morale was relatively high before the experiment and remained so if not improved. This story demonstrates the hallmarks of a socio-technical approach:

- A technical change requires a regrouping of roles and teams.
- The focus of analysis is a group.
- Employees are considered in decisions about how to organize themselves.
- Productivity, quality, and morale are all measured as outcome variables.

The STS approach holds several key tenets that can be seen in contemporary metric systems. First, technical changes should be accompanied by social changes. Processes need to specify how humans will interface with new technologies.

Second, STS models consider the group to be the level of analysis where all interventions should be focused. Interventions at the organizational level would be too far removed. For metrics, this means that it is insufficient to stop with organization-level scorecards. Companies need to drill down to create lower-level scorecards for individual departments and work teams.

Third, the STS model emphasizes that individuals closest to the work have the greatest amount of knowledge about the work at hand. For this reason, workers should be involved in all decisions regarding work design. Later, the STS framework evolved to be known as "socioecology," basically an open-systems conceptualization of organizations that is linked to "action research" practices (Emery, 2000). This idea not only emphasizes that metrics be used to improve processes, but also stresses that the way to bring about improvement ideas is through what companies variously call "engagement," "employee involvement," and "participative decision making." Chapter 13 addresses how to involve employees in interventions such as metric scorecards.

Fourth, the STS model involves measuring productivity, quality, and morale. Conceiving morale as a form of renewal, the STS model gives attributes that can be applied at any level of analysis.

Basic Team Scorecard

A "fill-in" model allows managers a simple way to follow the system properties described in this chapter. The basic team scorecard presented in Table 3.1 is the basic "fill-in" model for all scorecards included in this text. This builds

Table 3.1 Basic Team Scorecard

Name of Unit Being Measured:

Team Mission:

Level of Analysis:

Attribute	Dimensions	Behavior Metric (Measure/ Unit)	Behavior Goal	Outcome Metric (Measure/ Unit)	Outcome Goal
Work Performance	Productivity (Quantity)				
	Productivity (Efficiency)				
	Quality				
Strategic Contribution					
Renewal					

Date of Scorecard Update: _____ Scorecard Owner: _____

Source: © Ruth A. Huwe.

on the "Basic Metric Model of Work Performance" presented in Chapter 2, to include attributes from system theory: *strategic contribution and renewal.*

The introduction to systems theory presented in this chapter gives the reader an orientation to where major pieces of this model came from. Notice that the model begins with a clear definition of the "subsystem" (unit being measured, unit of analysis) and its output (team mission) as prescribed by Katz and Kahn. The idea of measuring attributes is drawn from psychometric principles (Nunnally, 1978) and specific dimensions of performance behavior are based on STS theory (productivity, quality). The idea of double-loop learning is the reason for the "update" line. The open-system property of cycles also calls for the "update" line in the model. The need for behavior and outcome goals is described more under the topic of motivation (Chapter 15). The need for the "renewal" dimension reflects the need for an open-system property that open systems require "inputs." The *strategic contribution* dimension reflects the organization's vision; it is a mechanism to halt entropic processes from the larger suprasystem. The renewal and strategy contribution categories also reflect efforts to monitor strategic renewal (Agarwal & Helfat, 2009).

CHAPTER SUMMARY

This chapter demonstrated how principles of open systems, General Systems Theory, and socio-technical approaches provide several prescriptions for metric scorecards. Systems theory tells us significant organizational attributes that should be considered in any given scorecard, particularly making the case that any given scorecard should include measures of renewal and strategic contribution.

REFERENCES

Agarwal, R., & Helfat, C. E. (2009). Strategic renewal of organizations. *Organization Science, 20*, 281–293.

Argyris, C., & Schon, D. A. (1996/1978). *Organizational learning.* Reading, MA: Addison-Wesley.

Emery, F. E. (2000). Emery's open system theory. *System Practice and Action Research, 13*, 623–643.

Ethiraj, S. K., & Levinthal, D. (2009). Hoping for A to Z while rewarding only A: Complex organizations with multiple goals. Organization Science, 20, 4–21.

Kaplan, R. S., & Norton, D. P. (1996). *The balanced scorecard: Translating strategy into action.* Boston, MA: Harvard Business School Press.

Kaplan, R. S., & Norton, D. P. (2007, July–August). Using the balanced scorecard as a strategic management system. *Harvard Business Review, 85.4*, 150–161.

Katz, D, & Kahn, R. L. (1966). *The social psychology of organizations.* New York: Wiley.

Katz, D, & Kahn, R. L. (1978). *The social psychology of organizations* (2nd ed.) New York: Wiley.

NIST (National Institute of Standards and Technology). (2009). *Baldrige national quality program: Criteria for performance excellence.* Baldrige National Quality Program. Retrieved on July 8, 2009, from http://www. baldrige.nist.gov/PDF_files/2009_2010_Business_Nonprofit_Criteria.pdf.

Nunnally, J. C. (1978). *Psychometric theory* (2nd ed.). New York: McGraw-Hill.

Rice, A. K. (1958). *Productivity and social organization: The Ahmedabad experiment.* London, England: Tavistock Publications Ltd.

Richard, P. J., Devinney, T. M., Yip, G. S., & Johnson, G. (2009). Measuring organizational performance: Towards methodological best practice. *Journal of Management, 35*, 718–804.

von Bertalanffy, L. (1968). *General systems theory* (Rev. ed.). New York: George Braziller.

Wall, T. D., Corbett, J. M., Martin, R., Clegg, C. W., & Jackson, P. R. (1990). Advanced manufacturing technology, work design, and performance: A change study. *Journal of Applied Psychology, 75*, 691–697.

Weick, K. E. (1979). *The social psychology of organizing* (2nd ed.). Reading, MA: Addison-Wesley.

4 THE MEASUREMENT OF PRODUCTIVITY, QUALITY, AND OTHER SCORECARD VARIABLES

It seems some crusty manager always has to resist change. The one who treats change leaders as though their stuff is just a bunch of baloney. The one who mocks OD people for producing endless flavor-of-the-month initiatives. The one who gripes about anything that pulls his people from their "real" work. The one who thinks human resources does nothing more than make him jump through endless hoops of performance evaluation paperwork. The crusty manager cringes at words like "mission" and likes to brag that no one knows the words to the vision statement.

The crusty manager feels like the OD people are always trying to drag him off to get some sort of training when he already knows what he needs to know. For him, it is impossible that industry advances or process improvements could improve his bottom line. No, he already knows everything.

But our crusty manager makes quotas! And his team produces high-quality work!

What gives? Is his way the right way? Or is he missing something?

CHAPTER OVERVIEW

We can create team scorecards at various levels of analysis: first-level team, department, or organization. Whatever the level, certain attributes of work performance always need to be measured: productivity and quality. However, there is more to a team than sheer performance. Any scorecard must also consider attributes that contribute to an organization's vision, strategy, and renewal.

This chapter describes five basic attributes that should at least be considered when creating any given metric scorecard: quantity and efficiency (reflecting productivity), quality, employee renewal, and strategic variables. The rationale

---

LEARNING OBJECTIVES

After studying this chapter, you should be able to achieve the following:

1. Identify the two key dimensions of *productivity.*
2. Know the difference between hard and soft measures.
3. Describe five dimensions of team productivity as measured through a survey approach.
4. Understand how the concept of *renewal* is derived from system theory and from the Balanced Scorecard model.
5. Identify variables that reflect renewal.
6. Explain why *renewal* variables should be included on any team scorecard.
7. Identify variables that reflect *strategic contribution.*
8. Explain why *strategic contribution* should be included on any team scorecard.
9. Describe a wide variety of approaches to measuring *productivity.*
10. Describe a wide variety of approaches to measuring *quality.*

---

for this choice of attributes is based on systems theory and was presented in Chapter 3.

Team Attributes: Quantity, Efficiency, and Quality

A model of productivity that dominates current management literature emphasizes that productivity has two dimensions. First, **efficiency** is an input-to-output ratio, comparing the resources needed to create a product or service to the number of products or services that are produced. Second, **effectiveness** is the overall amount of work done as compared with a given goal (Pritchard, Roth, & Jones, 1991). The term effectiveness just begs for ambiguity: Do we mean effectiveness on the productivity dimension? Or overall team effectiveness? Rather than use the word "effectiveness," this book uses the term "quantity" to mean the amount of work that has been completed.

A four-year program of research uncovered other key attributes of team performance. In this study, Christina B. Gibson and her colleagues sought to develop a team effectiveness measure that cut across departments, organizations, and cultures. To gather their collection of possible attributes, they interviewed workers from countries that they felt reflected key differences in power distance and collectivism: France, the Philippines, Puerto Rico, and the United States (Gibson, Zellmer-Bruhn, & Schwab, 2003).

Gibson, Zellmer-Bruhn, and Schwab's (2003) work uncovered five key dimensions of team performance: goals, customers, timeliness, quality, and productivity. The *goals* category reflects whether the team meets objectives. The *customer* category reflects whether the team addresses customer needs. The *timeliness* category reflects efficiency and adherence to goals. The *quality* category reflects whether the work is error free. The *productivity* category reflects the ratio of inputs to outputs, efficiency.

The final instrument to measure these terms is shown in Table 4.1. Notice that potential confusion between the Pritchard and Gibson models rests on definitions of terms. The Gibson model defines overall *goal achievement* in the way that the Pritchard model defines *effectiveness*. The Gibson model defines *productivity* in a way that the Pritchard model defines *efficiency*.

To clear any confusion, this book defines **work performance** as the quantity of output, quality of output, and efficiency with which output is produced; it reflects execution of the ongoing mission of the team. **Quantity** is the amount of work that gets completed. The quantity variable is reflected in Pritchard, Roth, and Jones's (1991) "effectiveness" dimension of productivity and Gibson's "timeliness" dimension of team effectiveness. **Quality** is a reflection of how well work is done and, if relevant, how well it meets a customer's needs. The quality variable is reflected both in Gibson's "quality" measure and "customer" variable. **Efficiency** is how well a system uses inputs to achieve its outputs. The efficiency variable is reflected in both Pritchard's and Gibson's definition of productivity.

Work performance is all well and good, but who cares if the "efficient" team does nothing to contribute to the organization's overall goals? What if a team is effective today, but burns itself out and can't continue into the future? Alternatively, what if a team can get products out the door but then slowly watches as its methods become obsolete and it is defeated by other teams who took the time to learn superior technologies and processes? To judge a team, is it sufficient to look at execution of work? Beyond work performance, a sensible team scorecard also will include some measure of attributes that allow the team to refuel and carry on performance on a long-term basis: renewal of inputs and execution of strategy.

Fourth Team Attribute: Renewal

As argued in Chapter 3, the need for the renewal category on scorecards is based on systems theory (Katz & Kahn, 1978) and on an organization's dynamic need for strategic renewal (Agarwal & Helfat, 2009). As well, the Balanced Scorecard model also includes growth and learning as an essential performance dimension (Kaplan & Norton, 1996; Kaplan & Norton, 2007). Learning basically reflects the capacity for the organization to renew itself. To draw this out, consider the company that has high profits, efficient processes, and happy customers, but that does not bother to document processes or train employees. In this case, lack of "learning" makes it impossible for the company to maintain its ongoing performance.

Stephen Covey (1997) used the children's story of the goose with the golden egg to describe the renewal concept. He reminded readers that the goose had the ability to lay only one egg per day. The goose's owner, the farmer, suspected that the goose had a whole bunch of golden eggs inside its belly. The farmer

Table 4.1 Pilot Survey Items to Measure Team Outcome Effectiveness

SCORING: 1 = very inaccurate; 2 = mostly inaccurate; 3 = slightly inaccurate; 4 = uncertain; 5 = slightly accurate; 6 = mostly accurate; 7 = very accurate

GOALS

This team fulfills its mission.

This team accomplishes its objectives.

This team meets the requirements set for it.

This team achieves its goals.

This team serves the purpose it was intended to serve.

CUSTOMERS

This team's customers are satisfied.

This team's customers are happy with the team's performance.

This team is responsive to its customers.

This team fulfills the needs of its customers.

This team responds to external demands.

TIMELINESS

This team meets its deadlines.

This team wastes time.

The team provides deliverables (e.g., products or services) on time.

This team is slow.

This team adheres to its schedule.

This team finishes its work in a reasonable amount of time.

QUALITY

This team has a low error rate.

This team does high quality work.

This team consistently provides high quality output.

This team is consistently error free.

This team needs to improve the quality of its work.

PRODUCTIVITY

This team uses too many resources.

This team is productive.

This team is wasteful.

Inputs used by this team are appropriate for the outputs achieved.

This team is efficient.

Note: To compare scores on this measure, the researchers reported the following statistics: Goals (Mean — 5.95, Std. Dev. = 0.34), Customer (Mean = 5.90, Std. Dev. = 0.35), Timeliness (Mean = 5.30, Std. Dev. = 0.51), Quality (Mean = 5.14, Std. Dev. = 0.51), and Productivity (Mean = 5.67, Std. Dev. = 0.43).

Source: Gibson, C. B., Zellmer-Bruhn, M. E., & Schwab, D. P. (2003). Team effectiveness in multinational organizations: Evaluation across contexts. *Group & Organization Management, 28*, p. 469. Recopied with Permission from Sage Publications.

got greedy, killed the goose, and found no trove of eggs inside. The story makes the point that burning out production resources (e.g., employees) is akin to the killing the goose that laid the golden egg.

Covey also likens "renewal" to the sharpening of a saw. You can saw away at a tree, but it will much more effective if you pause to sharpen the saw. The metaphor of "sharpening" represents training, team building, technological advances, or any other improvement activity.

Although many inputs are needed for a team's ongoing survival and performance, one resource is both a primary concern of any given manager and is needed on any given team: employees. **Employee renewal** refers to all variables that mark the capacity of employees to maintain an ongoing system on both a short- and long-term basis. This book uses the term "renewal" rather than "learning" because it considers all variables that mark employee capacity.

One way to think of employee metrics is in terms of **demographics**, facts about people. In this sense, we think of variables that are used to classify people into categories: age, race, gender, and other personnel classifications. In the context of developing performance metrics, employees are conceptualized as an energy resource that is input to a system. From a resource perspective, a different set of employee attributes are relevant to managers:

- Organization commitment
- Job satisfaction
- Employee training/skill proficiency
- Cross-training
- Knowledge capture activities
- Retention levels
- Skill utilization
- Overtime
- Attendance

There are still more variables to consider. Employee surveys center on variables that drive "job satisfaction" (Buckingham & Coffman, 1999). The science of organizational behavior focuses on absenteeism, turnover, job satisfaction, employee commitment, organization citizenship behavior, and employee deviance (Robbins & Judge, 2009). Motivation theories generally are focused on both attitudinal outcomes such as job satisfaction and organizational commitment, and on behavioral outcomes such as performance. In the behavioral realm, motivation theories then try to explain what causes performance improvement. This would lead us to consider antecedent variables such as job-person fit (Holland, 1973), the extent to which needs are met (Maslow, 1954; McClelland, 1961), justice perceptions (Adams, 1965), or even self-efficacy (Bandura, 1982). Managers need to consider leading measures such as "projected" turnover.

Which variables do managers use to track employee renewal? There is no one right answer. Managers can consult the list presented here, but in the end they need to choose the one or two variables that have the greatest impact on short- and long-term performance of the team. It is likely that the choice of variable will be influenced by corporate culture. For example, the employee survey is likely to include variables that are important in a given culture. Alternatively, the culture of a high-tech organization might place a special emphasis on knowledge-capture activities. A manufacturing organization might place a special emphasis on safety.

Fifth Team Attribute: Strategy Performance

Work performance reflects execution of an ongoing mission and is oriented to the present. **Strategic contribution** is the team's contribution toward the achievement of an organization's vision that will perpetuate the organization's survival into the future. For example, suppose a cornerstone of an automobile company's strategy is innovation. Even if a company (let's say Chrysler) had high productivity and high quality, we can see what happens when a company churns out cars that nobody wants to buy.

Yet innovation or other strategic variables such as safety or being "green" would not come up if the organization focused only on its current mission. Therein lies the problem with the crusty manager described at the outset of this chapter. Sure, he might make his quotas now, but will his methods take him into the future?

In that systems must both renew and prepare for the long term, they must be ambidextrous. **Ambidexterity** refers to a company's ability to exploit what is in the present and explore what is in the future simultaneously (O'Reilly & Tushman, 2004). For the present, team-level performance scorecards include metrics to mark productivity and quality. For the future, scorecards at all levels also need metrics that mark strategic contribution and renewal.

There are as many strategic variables as there are marketing approaches or leadership initiatives, which is to say a countless number. However, the following are some standard strategic variables:

- "Green" methods
- Customization
- Cost-cutting
- Innovation
- Quality improvement
- Lean production
- E-commerce
- Globalization

Attributes Summarized

This section has presented basic attributes that should be included in scorecards at any level: quantity, efficiency, quality, employee renewal, and strategic contribution. There are dozens of renewal and strategy variables, but two variables are staples on virtually every first-level scorecard: productivity and quality. An expanded discussion of each variable is presented in the following sections.

Technique: Measurement of Productivity

As discussed earlier, productivity has two dimensions: quantity of work accomplished and the efficiency with which it is accomplished. This book stresses that people designing performance metric systems should at least consider both types of measures, but it does not demand that both dimensions are relevant in every case. For example, an engineering team might only receive orders for 200 designs one month and then 130 designs the next month. A goal of 300 or 150 would be meaningless. The efficiency with which they did their work, however, would remain relevant. Alternatively, we might consider the example of the engineers answering technical support lines. We might measure their efficiency by counting the "number of calls handled per person, per day." As in the case of many human service metrics (doctor face time, bankers, technicians, and so forth), an efficiency metric might push them for "shorter duration" and then have the undesirable consequence of forcing them to end interactions too quickly. A quantity metric such as downtime (time spent on breaks per day) might be the better metric.

Taken together, **output** productivity metrics reflect quantity of work. The following are some typical examples of indicators that can be translated into metrics:

- Cycle time
- Output (count of number of items produced and/or services rendered)
- Output increases (or decreases)
- How much work completed versus how much work should have been completed
- On-time delivery
- Deadlines met
- Actual versus estimated time to complete a task
- Downtime
- Backlog
- Work that was missed (needed to be completed but was not)

To design efficiency metrics, we consider the inputs that are needed to achieve outputs. The following are some examples of **inputs** used in the denominators of efficiency metrics:

- Costs
- Amount of rework
- Amount of duplicated work
- Number of employees
- Number of labor hours

Putting it together as efficiency is an output-input ratio, the following are some examples of efficiency indicators that can be translated into metrics:

- Number of widgets per hour
- Number of designs per employee
- Cost per service call

Aside from input-output combinations, several approaches to productivity measurement warrant special attention. These approaches include the idea of an optimal scale, asset utilization, process measurement, classified count metrics, and milestones completed.

First, many things we wish to measure are best reflected in an **optimal scale**, a scale in which increments increase as one approaches an "optimal" number rather than scaling from lowest to highest. For example, consider a doctor's visit. One metrics fad for "managed care" pushed doctors to see more patients, driving down the number of minutes spent per patient. Another metric fad for "quality" pushed doctors to spend *more* time with patients. In this example, a perfectly healthy mountain climber could find herself in a doctor appointment in which the doctor was obviously dragging out the visit. Meanwhile, an elderly person with a complex mix of medicines could find himself short-changed by a doctor that rushed through his case. The need for optimality stretches across many situations, including any situation in which customer attention or employee utilization (idle versus working time) is being considered. In the doctor example, the metric would look something like this:

Optimal Minutes with Patient

Too few minutes   1   2   3   4   5   4   3   2   1   Too many minutes

Another productivity measure to consider is asset utilization. **Asset utilization** is the extent to which all resources are being utilized including extra resources gained from efficiencies.

Asset utilization presents an additional challenge for managers. Suppose you found some way to be efficient and the costs of creating a product went down because it took less time per worker to create the product. In fact, now you could say that it only takes 5 people to do the work of 10. Are those extra five workers still employed? Now that they are freed up from one task, are they being deployed to get more work done? Or are they sitting idle?

Process measurement is another approach to productivity measurement. **Process measurement** involves breaking down all key behaviors (or steps) in a process and statistically controlling the behaviors through measurement. For example, consider job hunting. If you only counted the outcome metric "job offers," the power of your metric system would go downhill very quickly. Relevant behavioral steps might include research activities, cold calls, networking calls, resumes mailed, and interviews attended.

Process approaches to productivity metrics have been popularized by the notion of "activity-based accounting" and "lean manufacturing." The basic scorecard model presented in Chapter 2 considers three key dimensions of deliverable performance (quantity, quality, and efficiency). Process measurement involves finding measures of quality, quantity, and efficiency for each step in a process. Chapter 18 provides a set of productivity metrics that are used to tap "processes" from an organizational level of analysis; many of these metrics can also be applied to individual work teams.

Another major approach to productivity metrics is to begin with the software that is used in the company's overall management information system (MIS). Manufacturing environments have a relatively easy time of it because they can make a "count" of completed products—unless the products are highly customized. If one product is a large, complex item and another is a simple product, then the matter of productivity is not a simple count. One solution is to use **classified count metrics**, classifying what are being counted as small-, medium-, and large-scale products and then taking separate counts for each category. Of course, to avoid gaming, you have to be careful to define what counts as "small," "medium," or "large."

The principle of a classified count metric can be applied to another standard productivity metric, milestones completed. Variously called "on-time performance," **milestones completed** is a metric that reflects the proportion of milestones that are completed on time. It is ridiculous to take a simple count of milestones completed because some are large and some are small. If, however, the milestones are classified as small, medium, or large, the metric comes closer to reflecting the true state of productivity.

At this point, the astute observer will say, "But the director or manager who signs off on the forecasts that set the milestones could game them to make it that the team finishes them every time." True (too true, in fact). But at some point, the director has a time limit at the end of all the milestones.

Technique: Measurement of Quality

This section will outline several techniques for measuring quality. These techniques are based on mixing (a) approaches to defining quality and (b) types of customers who make quality judgments.

Garvin (1984) advanced five approaches to *defining* product quality:

- A product's innate excellence (transcendent)
- Quantity of desired attributes (product-based)
- Satisfaction of individual consumer preferences (user-based)
- Conformance to requirements (manufacturing-based)
- Affordability (value-based)

According to TQM philosophy, quality is measured from the perspective of customers. However, questions arise over what is considered to be a customer (Ahire, Landeros, & Golhar, 1995; Sousa & Voss, 2002). The following is a basic summary of *types of customers*:

- Internal customers—other teams or divisions within your company using your product or service to build another product or service
- Internal customers of your product
- External customers
- Other stakeholders

Value quality metrics are generally comparisons, either judging your team's performance against its own performance in the past or contrasting the performance between your team and a competitor's team. The indicators can be either subjective (perceived value) or objective (price comparisons). The following are a few examples:

- Overall value: service was worth the price
- Relative perceived quality: our service quality versus competitor service quality
- Relative price: satisfaction with our price versus competitor price
- Inspections passed

External hard quality metrics consist of counts of phenomena that can be observed. The following are a few examples of indicators used in these metrics:

- Repeat or lost customers
- Number of defects
- Warranty costs
- Market share
- Complaints or returns
- Mean time to respond
- Mean time to complete request

Postsales service measures track customers after a purchase is complete. Tracking these indicators helps you keep an honest reflection of how well your processes are working.

- Warranty costs
- Repair costs

Product feature metrics are generally questions that ask the customer to rank the attributes of a product that are the most important to them. Consider a car, for example. What is most important to you? Cost? Color? Fuel efficiency? Safety? Another example is the choice of a university. What features are important? Geographic location? Cost? Programs offered? Prestige?

How does a company identify the list of attributes to ask customers about? The best way is to begin with open-ended questions through which you (or a research firm) directly ask customers what features are important. Later, the wording of this qualitative data is translated into formal survey questions.

Generic quality attributes are descriptors that describe the value of many types of products. Basic marketing principles and Garvin's (1987) list of product quality dimensions provides the following starting list:

- Price
- Variety
- Green
- Timeliness and ease of use
- Innovation and creativity
- Adaptability and multiple uses
- Consistency
- Completeness
- Reliability
- Conformance to law

Future-oriented marketing metrics reflect customer satisfaction but focus on future performance. For example, customer lifetime value (CLV) predicts future customer behavior and customer value as based on behavioral information about past customer interactions with the firm (Petersen et al., 2009). The following are examples:

- CLV
- Customer referral value
- Net promoter score
- Intention to be a repeat customer

Customer service surveys use pen and paper or electronic means to give formal surveys that reflect customer preferences and feelings. Chapter 10 is devoted to this topic, but here are some standard attributes to consider when developing measures:

- Flexibility
- Confidentiality
- Courtesy
- Attention to detail
- Understanding needs
- Follow-through
- Credibility
- Accuracy
- Responsiveness
- Clear communication
- Ease of contact
- Reliability
- Competency
- Tangibles and appearances

Open-ended quality measures ask customers to answer open-ended questions about their opinions about a product. These measures are not metrics unless they begin with a question that indicates overall favorability. **Global items** ask about an overall rating of a subject under consideration. For example, a survey can ask about many features of a customer's experience, but the global question would be some summary question asking, "Overall, your experience was A, B, or C?" In practice, global items can be coupled with qualitative questions to give an overall portrait of the customer's appraisal.

Standard Quantitative Questions

- Did you experience problems with our product?
  YES NO
- On a scale of 1 to 5, how would you rate our product?
  Poor 1 2 3 4 5 Excellent

Standard Qualitative Questions

- What could we do to improve?
- What were examples of problems that you had with our product?
- What did you like about our product?

There are several reasons why you should mix quantitative questions with qualitative questions. For one, counting up the quantitative answers is a quick computation. The process of analyzing the qualitative answers takes much longer as it (generally) cannot be computerized. Another reason to provide the "metric" or "quantitative" portion is because respondent answers may ramble in such a way that you cannot quite tell whether they meant for it to be favorable or unfavorable. The quantitative portion indicates direction of appraisal, positive or negative.

Here is a basic example of how you would couple quantitative and qualitative questions:

Did you experience problems with our product? YES NO
What were examples of problems that you had with our product? _____

An Implied Mix of Productivity and Quality Metrics

Before leaving the discussion of productivity and quality measurement, it is worth stressing (one more time) that the two concepts should not be measured in isolation. In fact, one effort to simplify metrics is to develop measures that are combinations of productivity and quality measures. The following are examples:

- Number of products that were both completed within 10% of milestones and at customer service rating X or higher
- Quantity $\times$ Quality (higher the rating, the higher the quality)
- Costs

A Note on Soft versus Hard Measures

A **hard measure** is objective—that is, the possibility of agreement exists between judges on what has been observed (Kerlinger, 1979). For example, the number of defects in a batch of parts can be counted by two different people and the same number of defects will be calculated. A **soft measure** is subjective—that is, it is based on the judgment of one individual and does not have some referent in reality that can be observed by others. A survey is an example of a soft measure.

Why can't we just use the survey of team effectiveness and forget the whole scorecard process? Most consider hard measures more believable but concede that some variables (e.g., customer attitudes) can be attained only through soft measures. In reality, most scorecards are a combination of soft and hard measures. A common mix is to measure quality through customer survey, productivity through a count of product, and efficiency through a count of money saved.

CHAPTER SUMMARY

This chapter provided an in-depth discussion about the conceptualization of productivity, quality, employee renewal, and strategic variables. This chapter also presented specific techniques and indicators that managers can use to measure productivity and quality. Productivity was conceived in terms of two dimensions: effectiveness (output, quantity of work) and efficiency (an output to input ratio). Quality was conceived in five dimensions: a product's innate excellence (transcendent), quantity of desired attributes (product-based), satisfaction of individual consumer preferences (user-based), conformance to requirements (manufacturing-based), and affordability (value-based).

REFERENCES

Adams, J. S. (1965). Inequity in social exchange. In L. Berkowitz (Ed.), *Advances in experimental social psychology* (Vol. 2, pp. 267–299). New York: Academic Press.

Agarwal, R., & Helfat, C. E. (2009). Strategic renewal of organizations. *Organization Science, 20,* 281–293.

Ahire, S., Landeros, R., & Golhar, D. (1995). Total quality management: A literature review and an agenda for future research. *Production and Operations Management, 4,* 277–307.

Bandura, A. (1982). Self-efficacy mechanism in human agency. *American Psychologist, 37,* 122–147.

Buckingham, M., & Coffman, C., (1999). *First break all the rules.* New York: Simon & Schuster.

Covey, S. R. (1997). *Seven habits of highly effective people.* Provo, UT: Covey Leadership Center.

Garvin, D. (1984). What does product quality really mean? *Sloan Management Review, 26*(1), 25–42.

Garvin, D. (1987). Competing on the eight dimensions of quality. *Harvard Business Review, 65,* 202–209.

Gibson, C. B., Zellmer-Bruhn, M. E., & Schwab, D. P. (2003). Team effectiveness in multinational organizations: Evaluation across contexts. *Group & Organization Management, 28,* 444–474.

Holland, J. L. (1973). *Making vocational choices.* Englewood Cliffs, NJ: Prentice-Hall.

Kaplan, R. S., & Norton, D. P. (1996). *The balanced scorecard: Translating strategy into action.* Boston, MA: Harvard Business School Press.

Kaplan, R. S., & Norton, D. P. (2007, July–August). Using the balanced scorecard as a strategic management system. *Harvard Business Review, 85.4,* 150–161.

Katz, D, & Kahn, R. L. (1978). *The social psychology of organizations.* (2nd ed.). New York: Wiley.

Kerlinger, F. N. (1979). *Behavioral research: A conceptual approach.* New York: Holt, Rinehart, & Winston.

Maslow, A. (1954). *Motivation and personality.* New York: Harper & Row.

McClelland, D. C. (1961). *The achieving society.* New York: Van Nostrand Reinhold.

O'Reilly, C. A., & Tushman, M. L. (2004, April). The ambidextrous organization. *Harvard Business Review, 82.4,* 72–81.

Petersen, J. A., McAlister, L., Reibstein, D. J., Winer, R. S., Kumar, V., & Atkinson, G. (2009). Choosing the right metrics to maximize profitability and shareholder value. *Journal of Retailing, 85,* 95–111.

Pritchard, R. D., Roth, P. L., & Jones, S. D. (1991). Implementing feedback systems to enhance productivity: A practical guide. *National Productivity Review, 10,* 57–67.

Robbins, S. P., & Judge, T. A. (2009). *Organizational behavior* (13th ed.). Upper Saddle River, NJ: Pearson/Prentice Hall.

Sousa, R., & Voss, C. A. (2002). Quality management re-visited: A reflective review and agenda for future research. *Journal of Operations Management, 20,* 91–109.

Part Two
Creating Metrics

5 METRICS FOR INDIVIDUALS: PERFORMANCE APPRAISALS

Performance appraisals can be one of the most negative experiences in corporate life. Consider the manager who is forced by company policy to rank his employees when he knows that they are all equally talented. Consider the employee in the hot seat, waiting to be judged. Consider the smirking Mr. Teflon who messes up even the simplest tasks but manages to snow his boss year after year, somehow getting good reviews when all of his coworkers know him to be an idiot.

Why do we endure this?

Done right, performance appraisals are an invaluable process. Appraisals give a record of the most valuable asset of any organization, its people. A long list of gripes can be made about performance appraisals, but an even longer list of benefits can be cited as well—if the appraisal is done correctly.

CHAPTER OVERVIEW

Although all metrics have a subjective bent, performance appraisals seem particularly difficult. A recent meta-analysis of 115 studies demonstrated that the correlation between self-ratings and supervisor ratings of performance is still extremely low ($r = 0.22$, $p < 0.05$), and that employees continue to be more lenient on themselves (Heidemeier & Moser, 2009). The goal is not to pretend the measure will be perfect, but to use what is known in the current research literature to make appraisals as accurate as possible.

This chapter describes the basic components of a performance appraisal and then turns to four relevant topics. First, a conceptualization section will orient the reader to key terms associated with performance appraisal. Second, a historical overview of job description taxonomies will demonstrate how competency categories evolved over time. Third, various scaling methods will be discussed

LEARNING OBJECTIVES

After studying this chapter, you should be able to achieve the following:

1. Explain how performance appraisals fit into overall performance management systems.
2. Recognize the various elements of a given performance appraisal form: Introduction, Employee Data, Job Descriptions/Responsibilities, Company Value Statements, Competencies and Ratings, Performance Planning, Comments, Signatures, and Thank You.
3. Define and differentiate key terms used to describe worker attributes on performance appraisals: *knowledge, skill, ability, personality,* and *competency.*
4. Understand why a competency approach evolved to be the dominant method used in contemporary performance appraisals.
5. Identify various taxonomies used to describe the performance of individuals: Functional Job Analysis, O*NET, and the "Eight Great" competencies.
6. Apply different types of rating scales to different types of survey items.
7. Describe several types of rating scales used on performance appraisals: Behaviorally Anchored Rating Scales, Behavior Observation Scales, Forced Distribution, Adjectival Anchors, and Adjectival Anchors Combined with Numbers.
8. Apply general steps for scale construction to the measurement of performance competencies.

in reference to performance appraisals. Fourth, a step-by-step process for creating a competency scale will be provided.

Components of a Performance Appraisal

A performance appraisal is basically a scorecard for which the unit of analysis is one person. **Performance appraisals** are measurement instruments used to judge the job performance of individuals and are part of an overall performance management system. A **performance management** system is a system to monitor and improve employee performance, typically composed of three elements: informal feedback (coaching), performance metrics related to goals, and performance appraisal. Performance appraisals are variously called "performance summaries," "annuals," or "evaluations." They are formal in that they are written and they are terminal in that they generally come at the end of a specified time period such as six months or a year.

In a touchy feely world in which political correctness is often a joke, we may quibble with words like "appraisal" or "evaluation" but make no mistake:

performance appraisals *are* judgments. They are judgments of individuals. This book uses the word "appraisal" because it is the most common term.

Performance appraisals are used by managers and human resources departments for several functions: promotion, training, hiring, termination, and evaluation. Verbiage for possible contents is provided in Chapter 18. The following are common appraisal sections: introduction, employee data, job description and responsibilities, company value statements, competencies, performance planning, competencies, signatures, and statement of thanks.

Introduction

Just as in a term paper or report of any sort, the introduction is going to state the purpose of the instrument and preview its contents. An electronic form also may include a listing of resources to go to in case of questions.

Employee Data

This section includes the basic information that the human resources department may need to process a file: Employee identification, Social Security number, department, organization, and so forth.

Job Description and Responsibilities

This section is helpful because it orients the manager (who is likely working through a pile of appraisal forms in a short period of time) to expectations of a given job. It is a basic description of duties and tasks associated with a given position.

Company Value Statements

Often, companies will use the occasion of the performance appraisal to reinforce communication about the company's strategic initiatives and values.

Rating Section (Competencies)

This section is the actual metric. Performance attributes are typically described in terms of competencies and are measured with generic scale items that apply across jobs. An entire company may have one or two versions of the performance appraisal, one for managers and one for nonmanagers.

Performance Planning

This section describes an individual's goals for the coming time period (6 or 12 months) and includes a plan for how the employee intends to achieve the goal. The plan may or may not describe support from the supervisor. This section can be used in the following year as a metric to assess goal achievement.

Comments

This is an open-ended section that allows the employee and supervisor to write in any additional information that they feel should go on record. People could write in achievements not noted elsewhere, make a notation about particular hardships, or make any kind of comment they feel appropriate.

Signatures

In some cases, companies require that employees or supervisors sign the appraisal to signify that an actual review session took place.

Thank You

This section may be a simple "thank you" or point to next steps in the performance management process.

Conceptualization

Managers who routinely deal with the analysis of individual performance likely have found themselves asking frustrating definition questions such as, "What on earth do you mean by KSA? What's the difference between a skill and ability anyway?" "What do you mean by competency? Isn't it some sort of category?" In this section, we describe the major issues in the conceptualization of performance and hopefully facilitate some of the annoying semantic disputes. To this end, begin by considering the relationship between the terms presented in Figure 5.1.

If you want to rate someone's performance in, say, typing, would you give that person a test that asks how much they like to type? Or, if they know concepts related to a keyboard? Or, would you just have them *perform the behavior*?

When it comes down to it, performance involves the actual typing itself. As observed by Campbell (1990), "**Performance** is behavior. It is something that people do and is reflected in the actions that people take. . . . Performance is not

Performance	Management	System	Performance Appraisal	
Knowledge	Skill	Ability	Capability	Competency
Traits	Motives	Personality		

Figure 5.1 Performance Appraisal Concepts
Source: © Ruth A. Huwe.

the consequence(s) or result(s) of action; it is the action itself" (p. 704). In turn, **behavior** on the job can be defined as "An observable activity exhibited by an employee in the performance of a job assignment" (Henderson, 1984, p. 91).

Measurable worker attributes include *knowledge, skills, ability*, and *other personality characteristics*. With a focus on the worker, we also consider what changes these variables: education, training, and experience.

Ability and Capability

As demonstrated in the discussion of definitions below, the words "capability" and "ability" provide an excellent example of circular definitions. This circularity also provides the grounds for the first conceptual move when creating the model of job performance: eliminate the word "capability." Using capability just adds a level of confusion because "ability" will suffice.

According to Dictionary.com (2009), capability is

The quality of being capable; capacity; capability; ability. *His capability was unquestionable.*

According to Dictionary.com (2009), ability is

The quality of being able to do something, especially the physical, mental, financial, or legal power to accomplish something.

Knowledge, Skill, and Ability

The terms *knowledge, skill*, and *ability* can be used as nouns to reflect performance attributes or be used as adjectives to reflect levels on a measure. We might describe one as "skilled or unskilled," "able or unable," and so forth.

Knowledge is the information, concepts, and abstract ideas that are known to an individual. Where *knowledge* is something in our head that marks a certain level of learning, *skill* and *ability* are reflected in action.

What is the difference between *ability* and *skill*? These terms are also circular concepts in that the word "ability" pops up in the word definition of "skill" (Boyzatis, 1982; Spencer & Spencer, 1993). **Skill** is the ability to perform behaviors at a certain level of proficiency. **Ability** is an overall capacity to perform a sequence of behaviors.

However, *ability* is a broader concept than *skill* or *knowledge*. You might say, "This person does not have the ability to program this statistical function. He just does not have the knowledge of statistics." The person may well have had typing skill, but not the knowledge. Alternatively, you might say "This person has knowledge of every note of Scott Joplin's ragtime *The Bethena*, but she will never have the skill to play that song without a mistake." Skill is the action side, knowledge is the thought side, but both are elements of ability.

Cognitive Ability and Knowledge

Taxonomies to describe attributes of worker performance often divide cognitive abilities and motor abilities (Buffardi, Fleishman, Morath, & McCarthy, 2000; Fleishman, 1967; Fleishman & Quaintance, 1984). It is clear that one is psychological and one is physical, but it is also tempting to equate cognitive ability with knowledge. **Cognitive ability** is the capacity to perform mental tasks such as adding, analyzing, and so forth. Knowledge reflects specific contents: information, ideas, or concepts.

Personality and Ability

An individual may have ability (knowledge and skill) but still cannot perform a task because of sheer personality. **Personality** is taken to be the sum total of ways that a person acts and reacts to his environment (Robbins & Judge, 2009). We might describe personality in terms of such traits as the "Big Five" (conscientiousness, agreeableness, openness to experience, neuroticism, and extraversion); internal versus external locus of control; Meyers Briggs Type Indicators; Machiavellianism; or basic descriptions such as gloomy, friendly, and so forth.

Different traits are needed for different jobs. Take the example of a nurse's job. This job calls forth people who can change the diaper of adult patients who are dying of cancer. The person who performs this job needs to have the ability: she has *knowledge* of how the patient should be lifted and the *skill* to perform the lifting.

But can *you* do this?

Some readers are likely thinking "I don't have it in me." To perform the task of changing the diaper on a patient dying of cancer, the nurse also needs *compassion*. That is, she needs to have a certain personality trait that is open to measure.

Competency

The term *competency* can be used to describe both worker and job domains: (a) **competency** is an *underlying attribute* (knowledge, skill, ability, or other personality characteristic) that enables an individual to perform at a certain level and (b) **competency** is a *set of behaviors* that results in a desired outcome. Jobs can also be described in terms of competencies required for execution.

Schippman (1999) distinguished what he called "can-do" and "will-do" competencies. Can-do competencies reflect skill and knowledge. Will-do competencies reflect personality and motivation.

Generic competencies are activities that apply across a range of jobs and occupations. For example, using the Microsoft suite of products may be considered a competency in a wide variety of jobs. **Job-specific competencies** are microlevel behaviors needed to carry out a specific job (e.g., creating an Excel spreadsheet to display a given hospital's inventory).

Kelner (2001) claimed that 57% of competencies are related to people and organizational influence, 29% are cognitive and involve knowledge competencies to make strategic sense of the world, and the remaining 14% are business-results competencies related to entrepreneurial thinking. Granted, knowledge, skills, and abilities have a bigger impact on an individual's job performance (Hunter & Hunter, 1984; Reilly & Chao, 1982; Schmitt, Gooding, Noe, & Kirsch, 1984), but meta-analyses have shown that personality explains a small but significant portion of the job performance variation (Barrick & Mount, 1991; Tett, Jackson, & Rothstein, 1991). Bartram's (2005) meta-analyses specifically linked both ability and personality to job performance. Hence, this book considers all concepts together (knowledge, skills, ability, and other personality characteristics) when it describes individual performance in terms of *competencies*.

Taxonomies of Competencies and Individual Performance Attributes

Huge research efforts have been made to identify lists of generic competencies that cut across all jobs (Bartram, 2005; Boyzatis, 1982; Fleishman & Quaintance, 1984; McCormick, Jeanneret, & Mecham, 1972; Spencer & Spencer, 1993). Based on research to create their taxonomy, Spencer and Spencer (1993) observed that generic competencies make up 80% to 98% of any given job and unique competencies make up 2% to 20%. If the generic competencies can be discovered, then a generic measure of competencies (i.e., generic performance appraisal) can be created.

The quest to describe all jobs can be traced to the 1930s when researchers in the "Manpower Administration" (renamed United States Employment Service [USES]) used job descriptions to generate taxonomies of job requirements. In the 1950s, Sidney Fine led a research effort by the U.S. government that culminated in Functional Job Analysis (FJA) (Fine & Cronshaw, 1999). In a FJA, each job is described in terms of the level of skill needed to deal with data, things, and people. These functional descriptions would be the content of the Department of Labor's *Dictionary of Occupational Titles* (DOT) from the 1930s through its final printing in 1991 (LaPolice, Carter, & Johnson, 2008).

Edwin A. Fleishman and his colleagues (Fleishman & Mumford, 1991; Fleishman & Quaintance, 1984) later developed the Fleishman Job Analysis Survey (FJAS) (formerly known as the Manual for Ability Requirements Scales [MARS]). Shifting from the job domain and functional focus, the MARS described the worker domain in the list of abilities such as "Oral Comprehension," "Inductive Reasoning," "Reaction Time," and "Trunk Strength." This became an important taxonomy because it later was reformulated into the replacement for the DOT, the Web-based O*NET (Jeanneret & Strong, 2003; Peterson, Mumford, Borman, Jeanneret, & Fleishman, 1999).

The O*NET is simply amazing. The classification system follows a standard listing of 1,000 occupations and describes each in terms of the abilities described in Fleishman's earlier research (Converse, Oswald, Gillespie, Field, & Bizot, 2004). Like the DOT, the O*NET was created by the U.S. Department of Labor. The O*NET includes 33 knowledge areas (e.g., administration and management, clerical, mechanical, computers and electronics and so forth), 46 skills (categorized as basic and cross-functional), and 52 abilities (categorized as cognitive, perceptual, psychomotor, physical, endurance, and sensory). This powerful tool goes well beyond description in terms of KSA, however, and presents information on the following categories of information for every occupation (Occupational Information Network, n.d.):

- Tasks
- Tools and technology
- Knowledge
- Skills
- Abilities
- Work activities
- Work context
- Job zone (title, requirements such as education)
- Interests
- Work styles
- Work values (relationships, working conditions, achievement)
- Related occupations
- Wages and employment trends (including demand)
- Associations that are sources of additional information

As you can tell from the "Wage and Employment Trends" category, the O*NET has powerful cross-research features that allows one to see where individual jobs stand in the entire economy. The O*NET also can adapt to other occupational classification systems. For example, an individual with a particular military classification can plug in the numbers (e.g., 96U for a radio operator) and the O*NET will spit back various current jobs in the industry and give information in all the categories noted above. Let's say you are a long-time human resources professional who is really devoted to your DOT categories. The O*NET can translate between categories.

Perhaps the most powerful feature of the O*NET is its ability to go backward *from* description *to* occupations. An individual can go into the "Skills" or "Tools and Technology" categories, check off proficiencies, and voilà, the O*NET spits back an entire list of occupations. This is definitely good to know if you're having a midlife crisis or have recently developed a grudge toward your boss.

Although the O*NET provides categories that are useful for job description, the next mental leap is to translate descriptions into "competencies" that can be measured. Although intellectual roots of the competency movement stem from David C. McClelland (1973), the publication of *The Competent Manager* (Boyzatis, 1982) is cited as a major turning point *toward* a competency-based approach and *away* from functions or abilities. Focusing on managerial jobs, Boyzatis did an analysis of behavioral event interviews from a number of competency studies of managers, focusing on those competencies that distinguished superior managers from average managers across organizations. That is, he was not trying to account for variation in managerial performance, but to identify those qualities that distinguished the good from the bad. To this end, his research included 12 organizations and more than 2,000 people in 41 management jobs within those organizations. The final 21 competencies identified by Boyzatis included categories such as "Conceptualization" and "Developing Others."

Spencer and Spencer (1993) turned the competency focus to nonmanagerial jobs. Their research team focused on 200 jobs for which competencies were available. They reduced 760 types of behaviors to 360 indicators and reduced the indicators to the 21 competency scales such as "Interpersonal Understanding Scale" and "Customer Service Orientation Scale."

Finally, managerial and nonmanagerial competencies were combined more recently in a meta-analysis of 29 studies that resulted in the "Eight Great" competencies (Bartram, 2005). Bartram also identified 20 competency dimensions and 112 competency component titles. The following "Eight Great" categories give a sense of basic categories found on contemporary performance appraisals:

- Leading and Deciding
- Supporting and Cooperating
- Interacting and Presenting
- Analyzing and Interpreting
- Creating and Conceptualizing
- Organizing and Executing
- Adapting and Coping
- Enterprising and Performing

Summary of Lists

This section described how the attributes of performance evolved over time from functions to abilities to competencies. An expanded list of performance descriptions from 55 actual performance appraisals is presented in Chapter 18. Once items are written, the next question centers on what scales to use, to which we now turn.

Types of Rating Scales

Once managers identify the competencies they wish to measure, they still have the task of selecting the appropriate rating scale. This section describes various choices, including the following:

- Behaviorally Anchored Ratings Scales (BARS)
- Behavior Observation Scales (BOS)
- Forced Distribution
- Adjectival Anchors
- Relative Percentile

Behaviorally Anchored Rating Scales

BARS describe performance in terms of behaviors that match varying degrees of value, most positive to most negative. A variation on the BARS is the Behavioral Expectation Scale (BES), where expected behaviors at the high end are what you would expect of a "competent" person who is "effective" and those at the low end describe someone who is "incompetent" and "ineffective." The product of the BES, however, is basically the same as the BARS (see Figure 5.2).

Job Dimension: Program Promotion and Public Relations Behaviors

This section includes standards for appraising the agent's behaviors in promoting programs and the Extension Service, raising funds, and using the mass media.

This agent can be expected to

7   *Conduct one of the best public information programs in the state.
      *Always get extensive media coverage for his/her programs.

6   *Be willing to work with all groups and organizations for promotion of
       Extension regardless of personal feelings.
      *Communicate effectively with publicity media.
      *Have developed a countywide mailing list of interested individuals.

5   *Localize some of the promotional material supplied by the Extension office.
      *Make reports to advisory groups and public officials on request or as
       opportunities arise.

4   *Maintain communication with some local leaders, organizations, and groups.
      *Assist with planning and implementing public relations programs even though
       efforts may lack consistency.

3   *Insufficiently use one or more of the mass media.
      *Make no effort to speak to community clubs or organizations.

2   *Continually mention mass media that should be contacted to increase potential
      audiences, but do nothing about it.
      *See some parts of the program as being unimportant and thus not be
       concerned with them.

1   *Show disrespect for local values and customs.
      *Fail to communicate events and activities to those interest.

Figure 5.2 Example of a Behaviorally Anchored Rating Scale
Source: Patterson, T. F. (1987) Refining performance appraisal. *Journal of Extension*, 25(4), p. 4. Reprinted by permission from Purdue University.

Behavior Observation Scales (BOS)

BOS have higher order competencies as categories and then describe the skills and abilities associated with the competency in terms of behaviors. The hallmark of this method is that items are written in a way that highlights the *frequency* of behavior. The example below shows the higher order competency of "communication," then reflects negotiation skill, listening ability, and audience adaptation skill. The items are written in a way that asks the rater to judge how frequently these skills are displayed.

Communication (Oral and Written)

- Utilizes interest-based negotiation principles to settle conflict.
  ALMOST NEVER   1   2   3   4   5   ALMOST ALWAYS
- Demonstrates active listening skills such as summarizing, eye contact, and clarification questions
  ALMOST NEVER   1   2   3   4   5   ALMOST ALWAYS
- Adapts communication to audience experience, background, and expectations.
  ALMOST NEVER   1   2   3   4   5   ALMOST ALWAYS

When using the BOS, the answers can be summarized and then translated into verbal descriptors such as "very poor" or "superior." For example, imagine that we had 10 items to measure communication. We might rate a person as follows:

Very Poor	Unsatisfactory	Satisfactory	Good	Superior
10–15	15–19	20–40	41–45	46–50

Notice that these were not necessarily equal intervals. You can have intervals reflect the actual distribution or you can have them reflect standard school categories (e.g., 90% is an "A" so make the top 10% superior). For calculation purposes, however, it is likely that you will want to make the intervals equal.

Forced Distribution. This method is where managers allocate members of the team to certain categories such as excellent, above average, average, below average, poor. These scales typically approximate a bell-shaped curve, for example 60% in the middle category, 15% in the next higher or lower, and then 5% in the highest and lowest categories.

Poor	Below Average	Average	Above Average	Excellent
(5%)	(15%)	(60%)	(15%)	(5%)

Adjectival Anchors. Another approach is to avoid numbers and use adjectives to describe performance level. The following is an example:

Unacceptable	**Marginally Acceptable**	**Good**	**Excellent**

Some organizations include paragraph-long sections that go into detailed instructions about what it means to be "excellent" or "good." The following example is taken from the performance appraisal form used by Drexel University (Drexel University, 2007):

Exceeds Expectations—contributions were clearly outstanding and identifiable as exceeding expectations, which strongly contributed to goals. Exhibited strong personal initiative and insight.

Meets Expectations—carried full workload and meets expectations in all/most areas, has competence derived from experience and training. Contributes to goals and outcomes.

Needs Improvement—carried adequate workload and met minimal expectations. Needs performance improvement in some areas.

Unacceptable	**Marginally**	**Acceptable**	**Good**	**Excellent**
1	2	3	4	5

Unacceptable—failed to carry adequate workload or failed to meet minimal expectations of the position.

Adjectival Anchors Combined with Numbers. The most common rating method used on performance appraisals is to combine numbers with anchors that provide verbal descriptions.

Relative Percentile Method. An example of the relative percentile method is shown below. Goffin, Jelley, Powell, and Johnston (2009) assessed the validity of this scaling method against the BOS and the Graphic Rating Scales. In their study ($N = 170$), rating scale outcomes were compared with Assessment Center scores. Confirming results from three prior meta-analyses, they found the social comparison method (composite score correlation to assessment center scores was $r = 0.29$, $p < 0.01$, one-tailed) to be superior to the noncomparative methods (composite score correlation to assessment center scores was $r = 0.18$, $p < 0.05$, one-tailed).

```
                  Mary              Pat          Sam
0 ----------------------- 50 --------------------------100
  Below average     Average for (Company)      Above Average
```

Global Items. In academic studies, researchers are cautioned to include a "global" item in any given scale so they can later compare the "composite" scores of individual items to the overall "global" item as a marker of scale validity. This is particularly important for people creating performance appraisals because it allows them to greatly reduce the number of scale items. For example, can you have just one item to measure administrative skill? Or do you need a subscale? In their study of scales using a social-comparative, relative percentile method, Goffin et al. (2009) found a strong correlation between composite scores and score on the global item ($r = 0.85$, $p < 0.01$). The same pattern held when assessing the BOS and Graphic Rating Scales as noncomparative methods ($r = 0.69$, $p < 0.01$).

Steps to Performance Appraisal Measurement

The actual "metric" in a performance appraisal is the competency scale that is used to calculate performance level. This next section describes the specific process for creating the competency scale. The following is an overview:

- **Step One: Define your reason for taking measures (motive).**
- **Step Two: Establish your scope.**
- **Step Three: Decide your unit of analysis.**
- **Step Four: Decide the variable(s) you want to measure.**
- **Step Five: Define your terms.**
- **Step Six: Make sure all relevant attributes are reflected in your conceptual definition.**
- **Step Seven: Identify all possible indicators of your attributes.**
- **Step Eight: Derive a subset of indicators that reflect the population of all possible attributes of your variable.**
- **Steps Nine (Iterative Step): Write items that reflect each competency and attach scales.**
- **Step Ten: Prepare the final instrument.**
- **Step Eleven: Proofread.**
- **Step Twelve: Pilot.**
- **Step Thirteen: Scrutinize.**
- **Step Fourteen: Use your measures.**

In the spirit of creating a learning organization that documents its processes, be sure to document your reasoning as you proceed through each step. This can be written into a "statement of method" that is not necessarily a part of future Power Point presentations, but rather is on hand to answer any kind of procedural questions that arise.

Step One: Define your reason for taking measures (motive).

At a minimum, performance appraisals can be used for promotion selection, recordkeeping, recognition, training, job design, compensation decisions, and though it may be politically incorrect to use this term, *appraise* people.

Step Two: Establish your scope.

At this step, you are asking "Who will use your appraisal instrument?" Is it for an entire company? One division? Will the same instrument be used for all employees? Which jobs will this instrument be used to judge?

Step Three: Decide your unit of analysis.

Performance appraisals generally are designed to measure the performance of an individual.

Step Four: Decide the variable(s) you want to measure.

In the business context, performance appraisals are about *job performance*.

Step Five: Define your terms.

Job performance is defined as the execution of a set of job competencies (behaviors) that results in a desired outcome.

Step Six: Make sure all relevant attributes are reflected in your conceptual definitions.

In this step, ensure that your definition covers everything that needs to be covered. Are you interested in the performance of competencies? Do you wish to include some sort of outcomes in your measure?

6a: Is there a previous measure that will suffice?

Step Seven: Identify all possible indicators of your attributes.

In this step, identify all possible competencies that describe the jobs your appraisal will be used to judge. Sometimes, surveys include an "other" category in which managers write in a specific KSA needed in a given position. They might also write specific employee goals into that line. Ultimately, these indicators will be translated into scale items. As an example, the manager might end up with something like "Other: Completed the new Web site for his team" and judge whether the employee "Exceed Expectations," "Met Expectations," or was "Below Expectations."

Step Eight: Derive a subset of indicators that reflect the population of all possible attributes of your variable.

Identify a parsimonious set of competencies that will cut across all the jobs you seek to measure. This can be done through expert judgment, committee, or formal study.

Steps Nine (Iterative Step): Write items that reflect each competency and attach scales.

At this point, you are doing two steps in one: translating the indicators into scale items and choosing your rating scale.

9a: Write the items.

If you are writing scale items, try to use the raw language of people who will answer the scale. Alternatively, you may choose competencies from this chapter's taxonomies or the list in Chapter 18, and then generate your own descriptions.

9b: Select the rating scale for your items.

Try to use the same rating scale for all items. Various types of scales were presented earlier in this chapter.

9c: Rewrite the items.

It is important that items match the scale being used to measure them. For example, consider the following item:

Job/Technical Knowledge
Possesses skills and technical competence to execute job duties; ability to learn and apply new skills; keeps up with current developments; understanding of how job relates to others; use resources effectively.
ALMOST NEVER   1   2   3   4   5   ALMOST ALWAYS

Instead, we would have to rewrite the item to something like this:

Demonstrates skills and technical competence when executing duties.
ALMOST NEVER   1   2   3   4   5   ALMOST ALWAYS

9d: Inspection.

This is a basic reminder step to proofread your appraisal form, making sure that the wording of your items matches your scales. You would be surprised how many official forms have incorrect scales.

9e: Rewrite the items.

Correct any flaws you have found.

Step Ten: Prepare the final instrument.

Beyond a competency scale, performance appraisals represent a special case where additional contents are required:

- Introduction
- Employee Data
- Job Descriptions/Responsibilities
- Company Value Statements
- Competencies and Ratings
- Performance Planning
- Comments
- Signatures
- Thank You

Examples of all of these contents are found in Chapter 18.

Step Eleven: Proofread.

Have several people proofread your instrument before proceeding to the next step.

Step Twelve: Pilot.

Still do not make mass copies. Have at least a dozen people complete the instrument and ask them to make critical marks about what they found to be confusing.

Step Thirteen: Scrutinize.

If you decided to create your own competency scale, then you will need to read Chapter 9, and review the procedures for carrying out the following steps:

Step 13a: Factor analysis.

Step 13b: Reliability analysis.

Step 13c: Validity check.

Step Fourteen: Use your measures.

We now return to the original motives for making the performance appraisal specified in step one: promotion selection, recordkeeping, recognition, training, job design, and compensation decisions. The goal is to describe a single individual or set of employees rather than infer behavior to a larger population.

CHAPTER SUMMARY

This chapter described basic performance appraisal contents: introduction, employee data, job descriptions/responsibilities, company value statements, rating section (competencies), performance planning, comments, signatures, and thank you.

REFERENCES

Barrick, M. R., & Mount, M. K. (1991). The big five personality dimensions and job performance: A meta-analysis. *Personnel Psychology, 44*, 1–26.

Bartram, D. (2005). The eight great competencies: A criterion-centric approach to validation. *Journal of Applied Psychology, 90*, 1185–1203.

Boyzatis, R. E. (1982). *The competent manager.* New York: Wiley.

Buffardi, L. C., Fleishman, E. A., Morath, R. A., & McCarthy, P. M. (2000). Relationships between ability requirements and human errors in job tasks. *Journal of Applied Psychology, 85*, 551–564.

Campbell, J. P. (1990). Modeling the performance prediction problem in industrial and organizational psychology. In M. D. Dunnette & L. M. Hough (Eds.), *Handbook of industrial and organizational psychology* (2nd ed., *Vol. 1*, pp. 687–732). Palo Alto, CA: Consulting Psychologists Press.

Converse, P. D., Oswald, F. L., Gillespie, M. A., Field, K. A., & Bizot, E. B. (2004). Matching individuals to occupations using abilities and the O*NET and an application in career guidance. *Personnel Psychology, 57*, 451–488.

Dictionary.com. (2009). Retrieved July 14, 2009, from http://dictionary.reference.com.

Drexel University. (2007). Performance appraisal form FY2007. Retrieved August 23, 2007, from http://www.drexel.edu/hr/forms/DU-PerfAppraisal.xls.

Fine, S. A., & Cronshaw, S. F. (1999). *Functional job analysis: A foundation for human resources management.* Mahwah, NJ: Lawrence Erlbaum.

Fleishman, E. A. (1967). Performance assessment based on an empirically derived task taxonomy. *Human Factors, 9,* 349–366.

Fleishman, E. A., & Mumford, M. D. (1991). Evaluating classifications of job behavior: A construct validation of the ability requirement scales. *Personnel Psychology, 44,* 523–575.

Fleishman, E. A., & Quaintance, M. K. (1984). *Taxonomies of human performance.* Orlando, FL: Academic.

Goffin, R. D., Jelley, R. B., Powell, D. M., & Johnston, N. G. (2009). Taking advantage of social comparisons in performance appraisal: The relative percentile method. *Human Resource Management, 48,* 251–268.

Heidemeier, H., & Moser, K. (2009). Self-other agreement in job performance rating: A meta-analytic test of a performance model. *Journal of Applied Psychology, 94,* 353–370.

Henderson, R. I. (1984). *Performance appraisal.* (2nd ed.). Reston, VA: Reston.

Hunter, J. E., & Hunter, R. F. (1984). Validity and utility of alternate predictors of job performance. *Psychological Bulletin, 96,* 72–98.

Jeanneret, P. R., & Strong, M. H. (2003). Linking O*NET job analysis information to job requirement predictors: An O*NET application. *Personnel Psychology, 56,* 465–492.

Kelner, S. (2001). A few thoughts on executive competency convergence. *Center for Quality of Management Journal, 10*(1), 67–72.

LaPolice, C., Carter, G. W., & Johnson, J. W. (2008). Linking O*NET descriptors to occupational literacy requirements using job component validation. *Personnel Psychology, 61,* 405–441.

McClelland, D. C. (1973). Testing for competence rather than for "intelligence." *American Psychologist, 28,* 1–14.

McCormick, E. J., Jeanneret, P. R., & Mecham, R. C. (1972). A study of job characteristics and job dimensions as based on the position analysis questionnaire (PAQ). *Journal of Applied Psychology, 56,* 347–368.

Occupation Information Network. (n.d.). O*NET online. Retrieved July 14, 2009, from http://online.onetcenter.org.

Peterson, N. G., Mumford, M. D., Borman, W. C., Jeanneret, P. R., & Fleishman, E. A. (1999). *An occupational information system for the 21st century: The development of O*NET.* Washington, DC: American Psychological Association.

Reilly, R. R., & Chao, G. T. (1982). Validity and fairness of some alternative employee selection procedures. *Personnel Psychology, 35,* 1–62.

Robbins, S. P., & Judge, T. A. (2009). *Organizational behavior.* (13th ed.). Upper Saddle River, NJ: Pearson/Prentice Hall.

Schippman, J. S. (1999). *Strategic job modeling.* Mahwah, NJ: Lawrence-Erlbaum.

Schmitt, N., Gooding, R. Z., Noe, R. A., & Kirsch, M. (1984). Meta-analyses of validity studies published between 1964 and 1982 and the investigation of study characteristics. *Personnel Psychology, 37*, 407–422.

Spencer, L. M., & Spencer, S. M. (1993). *Competence at work: Models for superior performance*. New York: Wiley.

Tett, R. P., Jackson, D. N., & Rothstein, M. (1991). Personality measures as predictors of job performance: A meta-analytic review. *Personnel Psychology, 44*, 702–742.

6 FIRST-LEVEL TEAM SCORECARDS

Welcome to the virtual world! You have just been assigned to work with an engineering team based in Noida, India. Your company knows that it is better if your counterparts meet you face to face, so off you go. Nice flight. Nice hotel. Now dinner with three of your new virtual coworkers.

Conversation is lively enough to begin with. They ask about your flight, your children, how you feel about soccer. At some point, and you aren't really sure which point, it becomes weird. Basically, you are on orders to "get to know" these people so you will be able to "work as a team."

You get back to the States and now your managers want results. They want evidence that you and your Indian counterparts are functioning "effectively." How do you know that you do? Because your counterparts are pleasant when they call? Come to think of it, how do you know that "any" team is functioning effectively?

CHAPTER OVERVIEW

A key challenge for implementers of any given metric system is to "push down" the metrics to the level at which they have meaning for workers on a day-to-day basis. Executives summarize high-level metrics in an organizational scorecard (Chapter 8), directors draw attributes from the corporate scorecards to create departmental scorecards (Chapter 7), but first-level managers have a different process. They may or may not draw from the departmental scorecards, but they must work ground up to create scorecards based on the specific mission of their work group or "team."

The focus of this chapter is teams at the first level. Collaborations within organizations and across time zones, however, can span various levels. The models in this chapter work for an ongoing team with a mission. Teams with one-shot goals are addressed in Chapter 17 under "Collaborative Goals."

LEARNING OBJECTIVES

After studying this chapter, you should be able to achieve the following:

1. Design a first-level team scorecard.
2. Execute a 10-step method for creating a first-level team scorecard.
3. Learn how a first-level team scorecard can be translated into three report formats:
   - Metric reports
   - Metric scorecards linked to corporate strategy
   - Metric to action tool
4. Learn how to reduce an overall metric scorecard into a single index.
5. Learn how to translate metrics into contingency lines.
6. Understand nonlinear associations between metric outcomes and organizational effectiveness.

This chapter will present a step-by-step process for creating a first-level team scorecard. Two extended examples will be used to demonstrate the scorecard creation process. A manufacturing example is used to describe how to create a basic scorecard and an engineering example will be used to describe the process for reducing scorecards into an overall index.

Technique: Creating a First-Level Scorecard

Who is responsible for creating first-level team scorecards? Ad hoc committees tasked with designing metrics for entire organizations. Managers who have vice presidents breathing down their necks. Right-minded leads whose managers don't seem to have time to create metrics, but they know they are needed anyway. Consultants designing metrics for clients (such as the highly esteemed and boundlessly imaginative Huwe Management Consulting). Basically, team scorecards can be designed by anyone who wishes to measure team performance.

Let's begin with a few observations about the metaprocess (the process of the process) behind creating first-level scorecards. First, the first-level scorecard is basically an extension of the *basic metric model* of work performance presented in Chapter 2. The elements added to an actual team scorecard include (a) consideration of how the team goes about renewing its resources and (b) how the team contributes to overall organizational strategy.

Second, it would be nice to go through steps A through I of a *basic metric model*, but the application to work settings requires additional steps that will aid us when we present scorecards. These steps include checking that we are measuring the right variables, defining terms, ensuring advance scrutiny, and planning how to use a scorecard.

Third, you might be dejected to learn that this is a subjective activity. Each step requires an answer and often there is no "one right answer." For example, what do you use as a benchmark when setting goals? Previous history? A corporate benchmark? Even if you refer to something concrete, your answer still reflects a decision that is made subjectively.

Fourth, in a perfect world the process of creating a team performance scorecard would be linear and we could proceed in order, doing one step at a time. In reality, metric scorecard creation is an iterative process in which you are likely to find yourself going back and revising earlier steps.

Following is an overview of the steps to create a first-level scorecard. A completed example is provided in Table 6.1.

- **Step One: What is your reason for designing metrics (motive)?**
- **Step Two: What is your scope?**
- **Step Three: What is your level of analysis?**
- **Step Four: Make sure that you are measuring the right variables.**
- **Step Five: Define your terms.**
- **Step Six: Advance Scrutiny—What criteria must your metrics meet?**
- **Step Seven: Complete the scorecard.**
- **Step Eight: Round out your team scorecard.**
- **Step Nine: Scrutiny.**
- **Step Ten: Use the scorecard (translate metrics to action).**

In the spirit of creating a learning organization that documents its processes, you are encouraged to sit down at your computer or pull out a pad of paper and begin on the right track: document your decisions on each of the following process steps as you go along. This can be written into a "statement of method" that is not necessarily a part of future Power Point presentations, but rather is on hand to answer any kind of procedural questions that arise when giving presentations.

Step One: What is your reason for designing metrics (motive)?

This book is written with one motive in mind, using metrics to improve performance. Most managers, however, have complementary motives such as monitoring employees, providing recognition, and so forth (see Chapter 1 for a more-detailed list of motives). It is important to label these at the outset.

Manufacturer Running Example: This first-level manager's plant manufactures many parts, but the main batches consist of bolts and fasteners. His motives are to monitor and improve team performance as well as support corporate total quality management (TQM) and lean manufacturing activities.

Step Two: What is your scope?

If you were a vice president for Fisher Broadcasting, you might develop a set of metrics for all of your radio stations, but you would not think of applying the metrics to your television operations. The Boeing Company might develop a set of metrics for its commercial airplane operation, but use an entirely different set of metrics for its Integrated Defense Systems. The basic question of scope is, "Who will these metrics apply to?" If you are a vice president in a company with geographic departmentation, your metrics may apply only to your people in a certain part of the country. If you are a first-level manager, the metrics may apply only to your direct reports. The scope is spelled out when you write in the name of the team for which you are developing a given scorecard.

Manufacturing Running Example. The first-level manager is developing a scorecard for his seven direct reports, mindful that his work could go on to be used by other managers at his "bolts and fasteners" plant. However, he also is aware that his metrics might be senseless outside of his company's plants.

Step Three: What is your level of analysis?

The **level of analysis** is a specification of what counts as the object we are observing when measuring attributes: individual, team, department, organization, and so forth. If you spelled out the scope of your metrics, the level of analysis is likely to follow logically. For example, the first-level manager creating metrics for his own direct reports is working at the team (or "group") level of analysis. In this chapter, we are strictly considering the case of metrics that are designed for one manager's work team. In practice, a given team might follow the classical prescriptions of four to seven employees in the "span of control" or strive to be a "flat" organization where there is a 1:30 ratio between managers and employees. Although employees are often borrowed from other organizations, a rule of thumb is for a manager to consider his team to consist of all the people for whom he does performance appraisals.

Manufacturing Running Example. The scope is this manager's direct reports, so the level of analysis is a first-level team.

Step Four: Make sure that you are measuring the right variables.

It cannot be stated enough: Metrics are not about objects, they are about attributes. For first-level work teams, we begin by considering their deliverables: what products or services do they produce? Alternatively, we could consider their processes or functions, but this will lead us to the same path: the deliverables that are the outcome of the processes or functions.

The *basic metric model* applied to work performance (Chapter 2) leads us to consider performance on each key deliverable as key team attributes and three subdimensions to describe each deliverable: quality, quantity, and efficiency. Systems theory (Chapter 3) and a concern for an organization's strategic renewal (Agarwal & Helfat, 2009) would lead us to consider two other attributes: renewal and strategic contribution.

A cautionary note fits at this point. If you plan to "increase" efficiency, be sure that you have plans to reallocate the resources you save. For example, if you increase cycle time, does that mean that machines then sit idle? If you reduce the number of hours its takes workers to complete a task, what do the workers do with their leftover time? Increased efficiency does not pay if it means underutilization.

Manufacturer Running Example. This manager wants to measure quantity, quality, efficiency, employee cross-training, employee commitment, and safety.

He has chosen cross-training as a renewal variable because downtime is costly in his plant. He has chosen employee commitment because turnover is an industry problem. He might have chosen just-in-time flow of resources to support a lean initiative but decided this would be measured at a higher level within the company's enterprise resource planning (ERP) system.

Step Five: Define your terms.

If a manager hopes to develop valid measures for any given variable, the starting place is to provide a theoretical definition for each variable. Theoretical (or "conceptual") definitions will later be linked to "operationalizations." An **operational definition** is defining something in terms of how it will be measured. The clearest way to establish validity is to ensure that conceptual and operational definitions match (Cronbach & Meehl, 1955).

This book sets forth basic definitions for each scorecard attribute. **Quantity** is the amount of work that gets completed. **Quality** is a reflection of how well work is done from the perspective of the relevant customer or inspector. If your purpose for measuring quality is control, then all aspects must be measured. If your goal is to identify what brings in customers, then the key is to find the few key quality attributes that differentiate performance. **Efficiency** is how well a system uses inputs to achieve its outputs. **Renewal** is the state of the employees and physical resources that reflects short- and long-term capacity to maintain an ongoing system. In reference to team performance, we would conceptually define **employee renewal** as the state of employees that reflects capacity to maintain an ongoing system. Building from the idea that organizations must be ambidextrous, exploiting the present and exploring the future (O'Reilly & Tushman, 2004), **strategic contribution** reflects efforts to support the strategic initiatives that are designed to carry the organization into the future. Conceptually defined at the first level, **team strategic contribution** is the team's efforts to support organizational strategic initiatives.

Manufacturer Running Example. Quantity of bolts and fasteners can be defined as the number that has passed inspection. (An alternate definition might be the number delivered to customers.) Quality of bolts and fasteners is the extent to which the bolts and fasteners conform to requirements specified by the various manufacturers. Efficiency is the number of resources that go into producing the bolts and fasteners as compared to the number of bolts and fasteners produced. Employee cross-training is the extent to which an employee is trained to complete more than one process. Employee commitment is the employee's intention to stay with the company. This company has designated "safety" as its top priority; team strategic contribution is the individual team's performance on that initiative.

Step Six: Advance Scrutiny—What criteria must your metrics meet?

Chapters 11 and 12 are filled with measurement issues and statistical issues to consider when creating metrics. Chapter 2 provided some helpful basic criteria that can be considered in advance:

- Measures should be reliable (consistent).
- Measures should be valid (measure what you think you're measuring).
- Measures should be feasible (it is easy to gather data).
- Measures should be logical (ethical, balanced, fit in your system).
- Measures should be actionable (employees can do something to influence results).
- Measures should be parsimonious (simple but relevant).
- Measures should be statistically sound (measures reflect variation that, if necessary, allow the results to be inferred to larger populations).

Obviously, you can add to this list. For example, some might consider whether a measure is "appropriate within a given corporate culture." Some people also are concerned about whether a metric causes someone to "lose face."

Manufacturing Running Example. We will keep scrutiny criteria in mind as we go forward in the measurement process. As just one example, it would be tempting to go with profit as the measure of efficiency. Would it be fair to hold the plant that is building the parts accountable for profit when the people in marketing set the prices? In this case, holding the manufacturing plant accountable for profit breaks the *actionable* criterion in that it holds them accountable for something controlled elsewhere. This also demonstrates why it is important to define terms. Earlier, it was stated that the manufacturing organization's efficiency was marked by how well they used inputs to produce outputs. Rather than use profit to measure efficiency, a manager would choose a metric such as "cost per part."

Step Seven: Complete the Scorecard.

Completing the scorecard for work teams begins with some basic level-setting questions that get at the outputs of your team: What is your team's mission? What are the key deliverables of your team? Once these are answered, continue the process of completing the rest of the team scorecard. Table 6.1 displays the answer to each question as applied to the running manufacturing example.

Step 7A: Identifying the Team Mission.

Coming up with a mission statement might be obvious to some teams and, conversely, might be an offsite exercise of frustration for others. The method that works well for designing metrics is to define the team's mission in this format:

To provide _____ products/services for _____ customers.

Step 7B: What deliverable are you measuring?

This step is important because it provides the level of abstraction at which you are working. Many teams might answer "but we provide hundreds of services." Frankly, if 40 people are providing hundreds of different services, then the services are so small or seldom repeated that it is not worth the hassle of coming up with measures for each and every one. The practical approach is to say, "Well, overall, what do you do?"

Table 6.1 Basic Metric Model Applied to a Manufacturing Example

Name of Team Being Measured: Manager X's Machine Operator Team

Mission: To Provide Bolts and Fasteners to a Variety of Automotive Manufacturers

Level of Analysis: First-Level Team

Example: Reason for Metrics	Attributes of the Object Being Measured	Dimensions	Behavior Metric (Measure/Unit)	Behavior Goal	Outcome Metric (Measure/Unit)	Outcome Goal
Improve performance	Bolts performance	Quantity	Extra break time: Minutes per day	0	Number of bolts per day	1,000
		Quality	% Checklists completed per day	100%	Number of defects per batch of 10,000	Less than 1
		Efficiency	Average employee overtime needed per batch of 10,000	5%	Cost per batch of 10,000	$26.40
	Fastener performance	Quantity	Extra break time: Minutes per day	0	Number of fasteners per day	1,000
		Quality	Checklists completed per day	100%	Number of defects per batch of 10,000	Less than 1

(Continued)

Table 6.1 Basic Metric Model Applied to a Manufacturing Example (Continued)

Example: Reason for Metrics	Attributes of the Object Being Measured Dimensions	Behavior Metric (Measure/Unit)	Behavior Goal	Outcome Metric (Measure/Unit)	Outcome Goal
	Efficiency	Average employee overtime needed per batch of 10,000	5%	Cost per batch of 10,000	$38.90
Employee	Training	% employees cross-trained to perform more than one process (checked quarterly)	100%	Commitment (1 to 5 employee measure administered annually)	Favorable rating by over 80% of the team
Safety	Training	Hours per year, per employee	5	Lost-time accidents per year, per team	0

Date of Scorecard Update: _____ Metric Owner: _____

If focusing on just one deliverable just does not seem to work, a technique that works well is to think of "about three" deliverables. It could be two or four, but if you get past four deliverables, you are making the measurement become more complex than the work itself.

Teams may have problems conceptualizing their products or services as "deliverables." One way to think of it is to say, "If we were to take what you do and put it in a box, what is it that you give others?" For some, it is a computer program. For others, it is a report. In a service organization, it may be answers to questions on a phone call. The essential idea is "What do you deliver to a customer?" Alternatively, "What do they get from you?"

Step 7C: Identify metrics for all attributes.

This book uses the *basic metric model* presented in Chapter 2. The model is written from the perspective of the reader who, left to right, wants to see how behaviors result in outcomes. However, once you write in the motive and deliverables, you are likely to complete the outcome variables and go back to derive the behavioral variables. The important thing is not the order in which you fill in the blanks, or even that you do fill in all the blanks. The important use of this model is that you consider important coupling of elements for any given scorecard:

- Behaviors and outcome metrics are both considered.
- Goals are considered with metrics.
- A measurement unit is specified with each metric.
- Key attributes and dimensions are considered.

An important variation is to consider whether you need quality metrics for each deliverable or whether one overall quality metric applies to your team. In the manufacturing example (see Table 6.1), you would keep a separate quality measure for each product. In contrast, consider the case of a technical support team. They might take two or three broad categories of phone calls. The team's overall quality, however, might be measured by an overall "customer satisfaction" survey. In this case, "quality" would be a major dimension or "attribute" of the object being measured and appear in the same column with "renewal" and "strategic contribution." In the manufacturing example, quality is treated as a subdimension for each deliverable.

Having problems "coming up with" metrics? You are not alone. Three approaches may be useful at this juncture: the intuitive approach, the use of crib sheets, and propose and attack.

Intuitive Approach

The intuitive approach begins with a focus on the team that is in your scope. In reference to that team, ask a manager or person creating metrics "How is that team doing in terms of variable X?" For example, how is this work group doing in terms of productivity? If you say, "Great?" you then ask, "Why?" If you say, "Poorly," you say, "Why?" The typical answer yields an indicator, and the indicator can then be translated into a metric.

Crib Sheets

Using crib sheets simply means going to a list and choosing the metric you judge to be the best fit. Chapter 4 includes crib sheets that reflect various approaches to measuring productivity and quality. Crib sheets for organizational attributes are provided in Chapter 18.

Propose and Attack

This method involves simply proposing a metric and opening it to attack from others. The person doing the proposal is likely a consultant, someone who has nothing to lose politically, or simply someone whose skin is so thick that they grow scales. The point of this method is to invite criticism and generate brainstorming.

Step Eight: Round out the team scorecard.

Some companies want the overall corporate strategy to be reflected in the first-level scorecards used across their enterprise. For example, it is common for companies to measure safety at a team level. For an alternate example, many emphasize a "community" strategy in which employees are encouraged to do volunteer work. However, the measure of volunteer work appears on individual employee performance appraisals rather than on team scorecards.

At this step, ensure that your metrics are aligned with your corporate score-card and that they reflect all the attributes of your team that should be in the scorecard. This does not just mean the "dimensions" of performance (productivity and quality), but rather team attributes such as employee satisfaction, safety, innovation, or any other element of the corporate scorecard.

The balance of metrics is another key decision in any system. The following are some balances to consider:

- Past, Present, and Future metrics
- Long- and Short-term metrics
- Behavioral and Outcome metrics
- Productivity and Quality metrics
- Subjective and Objective metrics
- Direct and Indirect metrics (tangible and intangible referents)

Manufacturing Running Example. In a manufacturing environment, a likely additional attribute beyond productivity, quality, and employee dimensions is safety. Hence, metrics to reflect safety are added to the example in Table 6.1.

Step Nine: Scrutiny.

It is time to address Chapters 11 and 12, chapters containing the series of measurement and statistical issues that need to be considered when creating any measure. At the risk of sounding pessimistic, even when you have the best of intentions and have done your best to be careful, chances are that someone who did not happen to be on the metrics team will be closer to the work at hand and possibly have a better metric. The same goes for people who know how metrics can be "gamed." The prudent approach for managers or teams creating metric systems is to treat their metric scorecards as a "rough draft" and invite criticism from their team before considering the actual scorecard "official."

On the other hand, it is *not* recommended that you go to a team with a blank sheet. People are not trained to develop metrics, and it is not a feel-good group activity. Most agree that metrics are incredibly important and feel proud of the work they accomplish when they walk out of metrics meetings, but most also walk out with some form of headache or languor. (Not a joke.)

The scrutiny step is also a point a point of reflection. It is likely that scrutiny will send you back to revising metrics, just as coming up with metrics likely sent you back to reconsider how you defined your terms.

Finally, be ready for the dejection you will feel when you realize that metrics are never perfect. People will always be able to find exceptions and things that are missed. If your metrics cover 90% of the actual work, you will be doing well—or as well as can be done feasibly. You could go on and on discussing your metrics, but at some point you have to punt. There are many things to consider when creating metrics but don't let the rules become more important than the game.

Manufacturing Running Example. The plant manager reads Chapters 11 and 12 of *Metrics 2.0,* makes corrections, and takes the scorecard to his or her team. The team then offers input and "corrects" the work the manager has done.

Step Ten: Use the metrics.

The way that metrics will be used will depend on the implementation team's initial motive. Once metrics have been chosen, a system needs to be set up that will specify how the metrics will be gathered (most likely by computer), analyzed (also by computer), and presented. Meanwhile, metrics need to be packaged in at least three different ways—if, in fact, they are being used to improve performance:

- **Reports**. Metrics need to be translated into an ongoing scorecard that is used to track results, possibly creating a new form that reduces the metrics into an index.
- **Links to Strategy**. Metrics need to be visibly linked to overall strategy.
- **Engagement**. Scorecards need to be presented as "Metrics to Action" tools that encourage employees to participate in finding ways to improve performance.

Manufacturing Running Example. As shown in Table 6.2, the translation from a "Metric Scorecard" to a "Report Form" simply involves adding score columns. This basic example can be made more elaborate by adding in trends, visual graphs, dashboards, or elaborate interactive media.

Chapter 13 shows how columns can be added to make a "Linking Tool" in which employees can see how their team goals are reflected on an organizational

Table 6.2 First-Level Scorecard Translated into a Metric Report Form

Attribute	Dimensions	Behavior Metric (Measure/Unit)	Current Score	Behavior Goal	Outcome Metric (Measure/Unit)	Current Score	Outcome Goal
Bolt Performance	Quantity	Extra break time: Minutes per day	——	0	Number of bolts per day	——	1,000
	Quality	Checklists completed per day	——	100%	Number of defects per batch of 10,000	——	Less than 1
	Efficiency	Average employee overtime needed per batch of 10,000	——	5%	Cost per batch of 10,000	——	$26.40
Fastener Performance	Quantity	Extra break time: Minutes per day	——	0	Number of fasteners per day	——	1,000
	Quality	Checklists completed per day	——	100%	Number of defects per batch of 10,000	——	Less than 1
	Efficiency	Average employee overtime needed per batch of 10,000	——	5%	Cost per batch of 10,000	——	$38.90
Other: Employee	Training	% employees cross-trained to perform more than one process (checked quarterly)	——	100%	Commitment (1 to 5 employee measure administered annually)	——	Favorable ratings by over 80% of the team
Safety	Training	# of hours per year, per employee	——	5	# of lost time accidents per team	——	0

Date of Scorecard Update: _____   Scorecard owner: _____

scorecard. See Chapter 16 (Table 16.7) for an example of a linking tool. Chapter 13 also explains how a few items from this scorecard can be translated into a "Metrics to Action" tool. The "Metrics to Action" tool can be used to guide sessions in which employees are asked to brainstorm ideas on how to achieve the metric goals.

Concluding Remarks on Attributes: A Return to Parsimony

The process described in this chapter is systematic. It provides a logical path for considering all possible types of metrics and has you make the same considerations that scientists make when creating measures, including *both* behavioral and outcome measures, *both* metrics and goals, and quality from *both* a general perspective and a customer perspective, as well as consider major concepts, definitions, indexes, scrutiny criteria, and so forth. However, if you look at the scorecards used in research by Pritchard, Jones, Roth, Stuebing, & Ekeberg (1988) or look at scorecards in use by any first-level manager that you know, it is rare that they would have that many measures. In practice, we consider all of the elements of the scorecard and then go forward parsimoniously with the few metrics that do the best job of describing how our team is doing. Alternatively, we may choose to keep all of our metrics from the *basic metric model* but reduce them to a simpler index—a key conceptual topic we now consider.

Technique: Indexes and Contingency Lines

The example of engineers who design lighting for passenger trains will be used to describe two major topics (see Table 6.3). First, this example will demonstrate how a scorecard can be reduced to one overall index. Second, this example will be used to demonstrate the often nonlinear association between performance on a given variable and impact on overall organizational performance.

Before proceeding, we can use the engineering example in Table 6.3 to make three tangential, but important, points. First, the term "NA" is used in examples when the metrics are not applicable. This demonstrates how efficiency metrics often suffice for quantity metrics (and vice versa). Second, the engineering example also demonstrates how some output metrics also suffice for behavioral metrics. As an example, any metric that says "number of widgets completed" is referring both to an outcome and a behavior. Third, see whether you can find problems with the engineering example. Notice that this scorecard includes a "count" of drawings. However, a fundamental problem with count metrics is that one needs to specify the size of projects. Are we counting easy drawings? Or complex drawings? We might refer to this as the "fundamental" problem of count metrics.

To Index or Not to Index?

An **index** can be defined two ways. First, an index is an increment or unit that is used as a reference against the numbers that we choose to reflect attributes (e.g., the metric system). Second, an index is a composite set of scores based on a

Table 6.3 Example Metrics Scorecard Contents for a First-Level Engineering Team

Mission: To Provide Lighting Systems for Passenger Train Compartments

Date of Update: _____ Metric Owner: Manager X

Reason for Metrics	Work Behaviors (Deliverables)	Attributes	Behavior Metric (Measure/Unit)	Behavior Goal	Outcome Metric (Measure/Unit)	Outcome Goal
Improve Engineering Performance	Provide technical support	Quantity	Average total break time per day, per employee	Less than 30	Average number of minutes on hold (measured in monthly report)	Less than 2
		Quality	# of times patience is lost with a caller	0	Satisfaction survey score per month	9.9 out of a 10 rating
		Efficiency	(NA—metric does not make sense and is somewhat reflected in quantity metric)			

Design exit signs	Quantity	Number of drawings per month per team[1]	100	(NA)	
	Quality	% checklists completed per month	100%	# of drawings rejected for defects by customer	1 per 200
	Efficiency	Average number of designs completed per month, per employee	8	(NA—reflected in behavior metric)	
Design bathroom signs	Quantity	% drawing major milestones met per month	100	(NA—reflected in efficiency metric)	
	Quality	% checklists completed per month	100%	# of designs rejected for defects by customer (monthly)	1 per 200
	Efficiency	Average number of designs completed per month, per employee	4	(NA—reflected in behavior metric)	

(Continued)

Table 6.3 Example Metrics Scorecard Contents for a First-Level Engineering Team (Continued)

Reason for Metrics	Work Behaviors (Deliverables)	Attributes	Behavior Metric (Measure/Unit)	Behavior Goal	Outcome Metric (Measure/Unit)	Outcome Goal
	Design complex emergency systems	Quantity	% major milestones met (50 hours +)	100	(NA—outcome is reflected in behavioral metric)	
		Quality	% of lean processes adopted	100% at level 4 rating or higher	# of drawings rejected for defects by customer	1 per 200
		Efficiency	Average number of designs completed per month, per employee	2	(NA—outcome is reflected in behavioral metric)	
		Employee	# of hours per quarter	10	Satisfaction Score	Top Quartile of comparison companies
	Training hours per year	Safety	# of hours per year	5	Lost time accidents per month	0

summation of individual measures. Recent "dashboard" approaches provide an example of how a scorecard can be reduced down to a single index. Not only are indexes simple, but they are a way to weight and communicate priorities.

It is tempting to take the scores on different deliverables and translate them into a single index through simple weighting. For example:

10% Technical support
20% Exit signs
20% Bathroom signs
50% Emergency systems
100% Total

Some difficulties are immediately obvious. The manager might refute, "What do you mean by weighting or importance? Where do we spend the most of our time? What is the most important? What costs the most? What takes the most people?" Frankly, any of these methods can apply and this demonstrates how subjective it is when you create an index.

Another method for creating indexes that the author has found to be easier for managers was used by Pritchard, Weiss, Goode, and Jensen (1990). In this approach, managers developing metrics were asked to assign 100 "importance points" to the product or service that is the most "important." They were then asked to rate the importance of the products in reference to that 100 score. In fact, if another product seemed equally important, it was considered okay to weight an additional product with 100. The following is an example:

40 points, Technical support
80 points, Exit signs
80 points, Bathroom signs
100 points, Emergency signs

Table 6.4 Example Metric Scores to Translate into Contingency Lines

Importance Points	Metric	Goal	Current Raw Score
40	Customer satisfaction score for technical support	9.9	9.2
80	# of drawings rejected by customers	1 in 200	4
80	Average # of drawings per month, per employee, combined for exit signs and lavatory signs	8	6
100	% Major milestones met for emergency signs	100	60

A next step is to choose a few key metrics from your overall scorecard and use this reduced set as your system. Table 6.4 is an example using the importance point method.

So far, these weightings are important to give feedback to employees about where they should be putting their effort. Neither system will help us create an index, however, until we find a way to standardize the metrics in a way that scores can be added together. One way to standardize metrics and weight them by importance is to draw contingency lines that correspond to the effects of the metric outcomes on organizational performance (Pritchard et al., 1988). Coincidentally, the creation of contingency lines will demonstrate the next concept in this section, the nonlinear association between metric scores and organizational effectiveness.

To draw a contingency score, begin with the blank Figure 6.1 and complete the five steps. In each case, refer to the example metric scorecard presented in Table 6.5 and draw on Figure 6.1.

Steps to Complete the Contingency Line

Step 1. On the x-axis, write in the raw scores increments that are generally possible on your measure. For example, the survey assessing technical support might actually be a scale of 1 to 10, but for all practical purposes no one really gets below a 5. Write in increments of 5 to 10.

Step 2. Mark the spot that demonstrates how high your positive "importance" score is on the y-axis. Your y-axis can also be thought of as your "effectiveness" points. In this case, write in an X at the intersection of a 10 on the customer survey and 40 importance points.

Step 3. Decide what score on the x-axis is considered to be neutral, it neither particularly helps nor hinders the organization's effectiveness. In this case, we will mark a "7" as having 0 importance points.

Table 6.5 Overall Index Corresponding to Metric Scores and Contingency Lines

Importance Points	Metric	Goal	Current Raw Score	Effectiveness Score
40	Customer Satisfaction score for technical support	9.9	9.2	40
80	# of drawings rejected by customers	1 in 200	4	−50
80	Average # of drawings per month, per employee, combined for exit signs and lavatory signs	8	6	40
100	% Major milestones met for emergency signs	100	60	−45

Total Index Score: -15

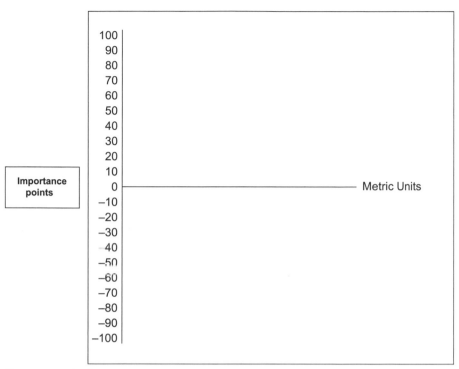

Figure 6.1 Blank Contingency Diagram

Figure 6.2 Technical Support Score Translated to a Contingency Line

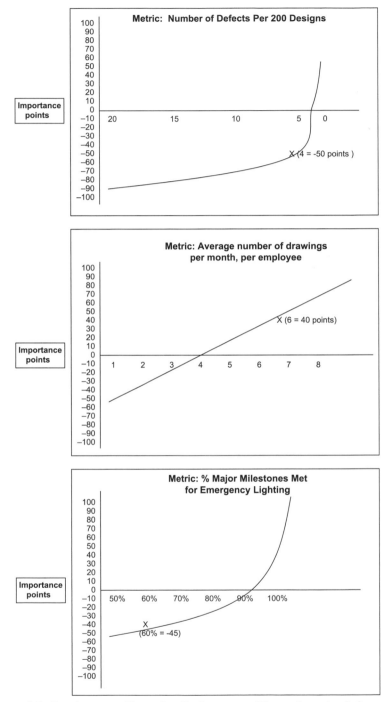

Figure 6.3 Contingency Lines for Performance Dimensions in Reference to Table 6.5

Step 4. Now, consider the damage that the lowest score could have on your company. At this point, consider the idea that a poor performance might actually have a bigger impact on the company that good performance. To demonstrate this, mark a satisfaction score of 5 as having −50 importance points.

Step 5. Now, draw in the line that connects the X marks and reflects the association between raw metric scores of the x-axis and effectiveness points in the y-axis. However, as you draw the line, consider the idea of diminishing returns. Make it so that the highest level of importance points, 40, is already achieved with a score of 9 and then levels off between 9 and 10.

Step 6. Compare Figures 6.1 and 6.2 to see if your lines match.

Figure 6.2 demonstrates the **nonlinear association between metric scores and organizational effectiveness**. That is, improvements in customer satisfaction do not create a straight increase in organizational effectiveness, but a nonlinear increase. The example also demonstrates visually how customer service scores reflect diminishing returns after a certain point (i.e., once the score is 9 or higher).

Now, let's put it all together. Drawing from the example in Table 6.4, translate the following metric scores into one overall rating. The first metric, Technical Support Customer Satisfaction Score, was already completed in Figure 6.2. Assume the unit of measurement is one month for each metric. The rest of the scores are plotted on Figure 6.3.

How did our technical support team do? Once we have plotted the contingency lines, we are now able to collapse the scores into a single index shown in Table 6.5. From the looks of this report, they spent a lot of effort in the technical support area but were falling short on the most important task, working on the emergency lighting system.

Critics will observe that at several points subjectivity enters into the creation of an index. For example, how should you weight it? What variables should be chosen? What attributes? What dimensions? And along with any metrics, what are the goals? How often should measures be taken? These questions reflect the subjective decisions that are made in the creation of any given index. Ironically, the part and parcel of metrics in general.

CHAPTER SUMMARY

This chapter presented a step-by-step process for creating first-level scorecards and included examples of scorecards for both a tangible manufacturing product and a less tangible engineering product. The engineering example also demonstrated two significant metric processes: a method for communicating metrics in the form of contingency lines and a method for translating a scorecard into an index. Contingency lines vary on a standardized scale of −100 to +100 and demonstrate how performance on a metric may have a nonlinear association with organizational outcomes.

REFERENCES

Agarwal, R., & Helfat, C. E. (2009). Strategic renewal of organizations. *Organization Science, 20*, 281–293.

Cronbach, L. J., & Meehl, P. E. (1955). Construct validity in psychological tests. *Psychological Bulletin, 52*, 281–302.

O'Reilly, C. A., & Tushman, M. L. (2004, April). The ambidexterous organization. *Harvard Business Review, 82*(4), 72–81.

Pritchard, R. D., Jones, S. D., Roth, P. L., Stuebing, K. K., & Ekeberg, S. E. (1988). Effects of group feedback, goal setting, and incentives on organizational productivity. *Journal of Applied Psychology, 73*, 337–358.

Pritchard, R. D., Jones, S. D., Roth, P. L., Stuebing, K. K., & Ekeberg, S. E. (1989). The evaluations of an integrated approach to measuring organizational productivity. *Personnel Psychology, 42*, 69–115.

Pritchard, R. D., Weiss, L. G., Goode, A. H., & Jensen, L. A. (1990). Measuring organizational productivity with ProMES. *National Productivity Review, 9*, 257–271.

7 DEPARTMENTAL SCORECARDS

There is an old adage about two bricklayers. You ask one bricklayer, "What are you doing?" He says, "Laying bricks." You ask the next bricklayer, "What are you doing?" He says, "Building a cathedral."

Is it as simple as that? Does the accountant doing payroll understand how his performance is linked to the organization's overall vision of being "The greatest innovator of product X the world has ever seen?" He might see how surfing the Web caused him to goof up a bunch of checks, but how does that relate to some lofty corporate vision? Even if the company has a balanced scorecard that taps operational efficiency, is it clear how the actions of one individual team are linked to the overall performance of a company?

Some directors would rather cut their arm off than be forced to look at their belly buttons. They are pressured by a blizzard of metrics from different teams below and a hail of demands from executives above. They are asked to somehow reduce a complex organization into a meaningful set of numbers. Often, the result is a set of metrics pulled together for no reason other than creating nonsense reports that nobody reads.

However, the challenge of departmental metrics is worth it for managers charged with creating metric systems. If done right, departmental metrics provide an important conceptual link between first-level performance and overall corporate outcomes. We'd like for the bricklayer to see how the brick is one part of the cathedral, but it might have more meaning if the bricklayer knows that if he does not do a good job on this particular arch, the entire side of the building will fall.

CHAPTER OVERVIEW

From a systems perspective, a **department** is a small system that consists of an interlocked group of groups (Katz & Kahn, 1978). When creating scorecards for

---

LEARNING OBJECTIVES

After studying this chapter, you should be able to achieve the following:

1. Execute the basic process for creating a department scorecard.
2. Explain how a department scorecard provides the links between first-level scorecards and organizational scorecards.
3. Describe eight types of departmental performance attributes that yield different departmental scorecard models: *collection of first-level team scorecards, rolled-up first-level team scorecards, functional attributes, process attributes, ownership of organizational attributes, intermediate variables, initiative performance,* and *combinations*.
4. Locate crib sheets that give indicators for each type of departmental attribute.

---

first-level teams, we may consider a first-level group to be a system, but the same team can also be conceived as a subsystem of the larger department. From an accountability standpoint, departments usually are headed by a director, but also could be headed by a vice president or some middle manager who manages other managers.

Ethiraj and Levinthal (2009) mathematically demonstrated the need to push metrics down to the departmental level. They concluded that when organizational goals are in conflict (e.g., improve quality, global expansion), the organization does better on achieving both goals when different departments focus on the different goals (e.g., operations and marketing, respectively).

Just as the department is a midlevel unit of analysis between team and organization, departmental scorecards provide the link between high-level corporate scorecards and first-level worker action. One way to demonstrate these links is to use the engagement processes described in Chapter 13. Another is for directors and vice presidents to create their own departmental scorecards.

This chapter provides the steps for creating scorecards at the department-level of analysis. An expanded discussion about different types of departmental scorecards is included at Step Four because the different scorecard models correspond to different types of attributes that are measured. Different choices include (a) team metric collections, (b) rolled-up team metrics, (c) functional metrics, (d) process metrics, (e) organizational scorecard variables owned by the department, (f) intermediate variables, and (g) some combination of (a) through (f). This section also provides sets of indicators that can be used to measure each type of attribute.

As advised throughout this book, begin any metric creation process with a keypad or notepad to capture your thinking. Make sure to note the decision for each step of the scorecard creation process. This won't necessarily be part of any presentation or final scorecard, but the notes are invaluable for writing a statement of method. The statement of method is then accessible to answer questions about how you created your metrics.

Process for Creating Departmental Scorecards

The process for creating a department scorecard is basically the same as that for creating a team scorecard except that the attributes for describing an entire department might be different. The following is an overview of the steps for creating departmental scorecards:

- **Step One: What is your reason for designing metrics (motive)?**
- **Step Two: What is your scope?**
- **Step Three: What is your level of analysis?**
- **Step Four: Make sure that you are measuring the right variables.**
- **Step Five: Define your terms.**
- **Step Six: Advance Scrutiny—What criteria must your metrics meet?**
- **Step Seven: Complete the scorecard.**
- **Step Eight: Round out your team scorecard.**
- **Step Nine: Scrutiny.**
- **Step Ten: Use the scorecard (translate metrics to action).**

Step One: What is your reason for designing metrics (motive)?

All the reasons for developing team or organizational scorecards apply to departments (e.g., motivation, compensation decisions, monitoring organizations, accountability, and so forth). An additional reason is that departmental metrics perform a linking function. High-level corporate goals can be pushed down to the departmental level and, in turn, be pushed down to first-level teams or organizations. For example, a company that has just suffered from a strike may have a corporate-level initiative to raise worker morale. Directors might push down the initiative by having first-level managers include a "morale" variable in the strategy section of their scorecards. However, individual department heads also may be individually accountable for the morale numbers within their own departments.

Step Two: What is your scope?

Scope refers to the population to which your measures will apply. At this point, define your department. What teams will be included in your scorecard? For example, if it is engineering, is it engineering for the entire organization? Or is the vice president or director responsible for engineering only one strategic business unit?

Step Three: What is your level of analysis?

The **level of analysis** refers to the manner in which phenomena are grouped when measures are taken. Levels of analysis vary by (a) individual, (b) first-level team, (c) department, (d) organization, (e) division, or (f) company. In this case, we focus on the departmental level.

But what does "departmental" level mean? The easiest answer is to consider all of the teams a given director, senior manager, or vice president is responsible for and consider whether they are best conceived of as a (a) group of groups or (b) as a networked system. Are they united by a process, a product, a function, or combined into a matrix organization?

Step Four: Make sure that you are measuring the right variables.

From a metric standpoint, three types of departments vary by the manner in which roles are defined. This will affect your choice of variables.

1. Departments composed of first-level teams who all essentially do the same thing (e.g., 300 call-center employees broken down by 10 supervisors).
2. Organizations composed of first-level teams who do different things (e.g., the human resources (HR) department broken into training, compensation, benefits, planning, and safety).
3. Organizations composed of first-level teams who do interlocking processes (e.g., manufacturing organizations who build separate parts of an overall whole product).

Your type of department will have implications for the type of departmental metrics that you choose. In all, there are eight basic **departmental metric models**:

- Individual first-level scorecards for each team.
  ○ Attributes to measure: Quality, quantity, efficiency, renewal, and strategy.
- Roll-up: The same first-level scorecard is used for each team and scores are rolled up to create an overall score.
  ○ Attributes to measure: Quality, quantity, efficiency, renewal, and strategy.
- Select key functional metrics used to represent the entire organization.
  ○ Attributes to measure: Functional performance (e.g., engineering, logistics, etc.).
- Select process metrics that represent the overall organization.
  ○ Attributes to measure: Process metrics (time, quality, cost, or other efficiency metrics).
- Select the elements of the corporate scorecards that are owned by your department.
  ○ Attributes to measure: Elements of the organization scorecard (finance, operations, etc.). These departmental measures can be rolled up at the organization level.
- Select intermediate activities to which several departments contribute.
  ○ Attributes to measure: Performance on specific intermediate variables. For example, suppose a power company lists 40 key action items to attain their vision. One action item is to minimize outage time. Another action item is to draw world-class talent. The transmission and distribution department might be concerned with both items. The HR department would be concerned only with the second item.
- Select organizational initiatives to which you are expected to contribute.
  ○ Attributes to measure: Initiative performance (e.g., morale improvement, cost-cutting, lean process implementation, etc.).

- Some combination of the above, possibly including the addition of renewal and strategic contribution. The strategy variable would be added if none of the organizational initiatives are selected.

Chapter 16 provides examples of scorecards at all levels of analysis for an example company. An example scorecard for a Technical Services Department is shown in Table 16.4. The mission of this department is to provide technical services both to existing and new customers. The department has dedicated some first-level teams to product development and others (such as the example discussed in this chapter) to ongoing customer support.

Notice that the example scorecard in Table 16.4 has a mix of roll-up metrics (e.g., customer satisfaction, employee satisfaction, and duplicate service hours across operations) and reports from individual teams (products created for customer acquisition). The scorecard also has a mix of attributes, some basic scorecard elements (quality, efficiency, renewal) and one drawn from higher-level organizational action items (customer acquisition). The customer acquisition item obviously would appear in the scorecard for the company's sales organization as well, but this scorecard shows how a technical team might support that initiative with new products. The scorecard reflects the strategy to drive sales out of new products, not the reverse.

The departmental scorecard in Table 16.4 has one other notable feature: simplicity. This is a scorecard that highlights the focus of the department. It is likely that the director of several teams has hundreds of individual metrics at her disposal.

Chapter 16 also provides examples of how scorecards can be linked at various levels. Looking across the tables, you can see how the corporate scorecard (Table 16.5) feeds the departmental scorecard (Table 16.4), the departmental scorecard feeds the team scorecard (Table 16.3) and the team scorecard can even be pushed down to an individual level (Table 16.9) to feed the customized sections of a performance appraisal.

Collection of Individual First-Level Scorecards

The process for creating first-level scorecards is described in Chapter 6. Basically, any given team's performance is characterized by the following attributes: productivity (quality and efficiency), quality, renewal, and strategic contribution. If a given director's teams do extremely different tasks, then their scorecards cannot be combined into roll-up metrics. One approach is simply to collect the first-level scorecards.

Roll-up Metrics of First-Level Scorecards

A **roll-up** metric (also known as a "cascading" metric) is a measure at a higher level of analysis that is the simple sum of the same measure taken at lower levels of analysis. For example, hours of safety training can be measured for each employee and then rolled up as an overall measure of "average safety hours" for an entire team. In turn, a director could roll up weighted average safety hours for all first-level teams. Roll-up metrics first can be taken at the departmental level and then can be broken down by teams. For example, a director could know the average number of hours of safety training received by all individuals in an organization and then break down the numbers for each team.

Which of the following is **not** an example of a metric that can be rolled-up?

A. Average hours of safety training per employees
B. Costs per team
C. Numbers of drawings produced
D. Employee job satisfaction

The answer is C. Each manager can report hours of safety training, costs, and job satisfaction scores and directors can compute these hours as an overall statistic. The problem with the number of drawings, or for any quantity metric for that matter, is that the object being compared across teams must be standard. Hours, dollars, and scores on a satisfaction scale are the same measurement units. The number of drawings produced could refer to large projects in one department and small projects in another department and aggregating the measures may not make sense. An expanded discussion of roll-up metrics is provided as a special topic in Chapter 17.

Functional Metrics

Functions reflect a particular task performed by a grouping of people, such as engineering or HR. If you want to create your own functional metrics, the basic mental process begins with asking, "Who are your customers?" Bearing those customers in mind, the standard process to develop attributes and key performance indicators is to ask two key questions:

- Considering performance with customer X in the past month, how are we doing on function X?
- How do we know?

Rather than create new metrics, you can go to crib sheets. Chapter 18 provides detailed lists of various organizational performance indicators that can be translated into metrics. Several of these provide indicators for functional organizations. For example:

- Financial (accounting and finance departments)
- Employee—HR (human resources departments)
- Employee—Learning (organizational development departments)
- Operations and Processes: Quality (manufacturing departments)
- Operations and Processes: Productivity (manufacturing departments)

- Customer (marketing departments, customer service departments)
- Supplier (logistics departments)

Some basic metrics and indicators for other functional departments are as follows:

Accounting/Administrative

- Accuracy
- Automation (percent services automated)
- Budget deviation
- Collection period
- Complaints
- Costs (average per employee)
- Cross-trained employees (percent)
- Customer satisfaction
- Defects in billing and paycheck
- Internal customer satisfaction
- Milestones met
- Outsourcing cost/benefit
- Turnaround

Customer Service (See items of the Customer Satisfaction Surveys in Chapter 10.)

- Benchmarked consumer ratings
- Budget deviation
- Costs
- Cross-trained employees (percent)
- Customer satisfaction level
- First-call resolution
- Number of referrals
- Time to respond and repair
- Utilization—doing as much with resources as you can

Engineering

- Accuracy
- Budget deviation
- Changes (average costs per person)
- Completeness
- Conformance
- Costs (as a percent of sales)
- Cross-trained employees (percent)
- Customer satisfaction
- Defects
- Design releases (number)

- Milestones met
- Outsourcing
- Turnaround time
- Patents filed
- Revision requests (number or percent)
- Rework

Facilities (See also "Safety.")

- Asset and space utilization
- Budget deviation
- Complaints and number of responses per day
- Costs: Maintenance
- Cost: Utilities
- Cross-trained employees (percent)
- Employee satisfaction with facilities
- Empty desks versus overcrowded areas
- Preventive maintenance (percent completed on time)
- Recycling
- Turnaround time (work orders, response, and completion times)

Human Resources

- Absenteeism
- Compensation benchmarks to other companies
- Complaints
- Costs (per hire, per paycheck)
- Cross-trained employees (percent, both department and whole company)
- Employee survey results
- Grievances (number per year)
- Hiring (time to hire)
- Manager satisfaction with recruits
- Outsource costs
- Recruiting costs
- Recruiting turnaround (from need expressed to job filled)
- Percentage completed performance management
- Sick days
- Training (see metrics for Training departments below)
- Turnover (number, costs)

Information Support

- Backlog hours
- Budget deviation

- Costs (as a percent of sales)
- Cross-trained employees (percent)
- Customer ratings
- First-call resolution
- Milestones met
- System downtime

Manufacturing

- Accuracy
- Budget deviation
- Conformance
- Completeness
- Costs
- Cross-trained employees (percent)
- Defects
- Flexibility
- Milestones met
- ISO scoring
- Six Sigma scoring
- Turnaround time

Marketing

- Brand image (JD Powers rating)
- Budget deviation
- Channel
- Costs
  - Percent of sales/percent of new sales
  - Advertising costs
  - Agency costs
  - Distribution costs
  - Marketing department costs as a percent of sales
- Cross-trained employees (percent)
- Market share
- Milestones met
- Purchase intention
- Positive reports in press
- Sponsorships (local events and national events)
- Wallet share

Purchasing

- Budget deviation
- Costs

- Cross-trained employees (percent)
- Discounts (dollar value)
- Defective percent of purchases
- Forecasting accuracy
- Inventory costs
- Lead time
- Penalties
- Shortfalls
- Signatures (number needed to process)
- Turnaround
- Vendor turnover

Research and Development

- Costs
- Cross-trained employees (percent)
- Customer input
- Patents
- Prototypes
- Revenue from automation and process improvements
- Revenue from new sales
- Technology transfer

Safety

- Accidents (number, costs, type)
- Budget deviation
- Compensation claims
- Costs
- Cross-trained employees (percent)
- Percent checklists complete
- Percent training complete
- Security breaches

Training

- Costs
- Number trained
- Outcomes to bottom line
- Ratio (people served versus total population)
- Survey responses
- Test success rate
- Transfer

Sales

Behavior Measures

- Number of cold calls
- Number of requests for proposals (RFPs)
- Number of meetings
- Number of networking events attended
- Hours worked per week

Accomplishment Measures

- Ratio of pitches to sales
- Dollars billed
- Gross margin per project

Process Metrics

Processes are the steps taken to produce a service or product and may or may not involve more than one first-level team. For example, providing surgery is a process that spans many departments including administration, admitting, nursing, and surgical care. The following are basic steps to develop process metrics:

Step 4a: Define the product and customer.

Step 4b: Define core outcomes variables for customers (timeliness, quality, cost, product performance).

Step 4c: Define steps of the process flow across departments or work groups, noting that this can go across organizational boundaries.

Step 4d: Identify performance indicators for all of deliverables associated with each step (Step 4c) that influence key customer factors (Step 4b).

Step 4e: Translate indicators into metrics.

How do you know which processes to measure? You could go crazy trying to identify all the possible processes in a given team or organization. If you really want to split hairs, you could say that there is a "process" for turning off a computer. (I wish I could say that this was a made-up example!) One good approach is to identify all key deliverables and then note what processes are *needed* to get the product or service out the door. This includes both processes that do and do not exist, in which case your metrics project has the serendipitous effect of being a simultaneous push for process documentation.

As always, an alternative to creating metrics is to use a crib sheet. Generic metrics for processes include cycle time (quantity), quality, and costs (efficiency).

Chapter 18 presents an extended list of productivity and quality metrics that apply to processes.

Functional and process metrics naturally fit together (Fitz-enz, 2000) as the deliverables for many departments (functions) are the outcome of processes. For an example, "payroll" could be considered either a function or a process and be measured with cycle time, errors, and cost. Notice that we could have arrived at the same three dimensions from either the crib sheet for accounting functional metrics or from the list of common process metrics. The basic mantra of "time, cost, quality" applied to processes reflects the basic dimensions of "quantity, efficiency, quality" that reflect the productivity and quality of any team's work performance, whatever the level of analysis.

Elements of the Corporate Scorecard Translated to a Departmental Scorecard

Sometimes the corporate scorecard will reflect indicators that can directly be translated by departments into scorecards. For example, a marketing department would likely "own" the organizational scorecard's metrics for customer acquisition or market share. At least one other department, however, likely would be responsible for those measures as well (e.g., product development and market share). One argument for this method is that it builds in metrics that include future performance (either those in the corporate scorecard or initiative metrics). Additionally, departmental scorecards can include renewal and strategy variables in the same way that first-level scorecards can.

Initiative Performance

It is highly unlikely that a director would make an entire scorecard based on how well his department contributes to an initiative, even if it is a departmental initiative rather than corporate initiative. The typical practice would be for the director to add initiative items to a scorecard or create a separate "Metrics to Action" model.

Combination Scorecard

It is also possible to provide a departmental scorecard that derives metrics from functions, processes, corporate scorecards, and roll-up measures from first-level scorecards. This option was demonstrated earlier with the example shown in Chapter 16 (Table 16.4). As with all measures, the choice of metric depends on the nature of the deliverables being produced by the department.

Step Five: Define your terms.

Once you have decided on attributes to measure, it is extremely important to define your terms with words (conceptual and nominal definitions) before operationalizing the terms (defining terms according to how they will be measured). You would rather do it upfront than be put on the spot when giving a presentation. Chapter 4 provides expanded conceptual discussions for productivity, quality, and various employee variables. Definitions for processes, functions, or organizational variables will vary by context.

Step Six: Advance Scrutiny—What criteria must your metrics meet?

Now that you have selected your attributes and defined your terms, you are ready to begin choosing or creating metrics. As you do this, remember the following basic criteria (and recall the mnemonic from Chapter 2 for something you hate to look at as much as you hate measurement error: RVFLAPS).

- Reliability
- Validity
- Feasibility
- Logic
- Actionable
- Parsimony
- Statistically sound

Each topic is discussed at length in Chapters 11 and 12. For departmental scorecards, one topic warrants particular attention: Logic. It seems that vice presidents and directors hunger for roll-up metrics that often do not make sense. Special care needs to be taken to ensure that if you are adding up measures, you are in fact taking a count or average of something that is in a standardized unit. A dollar spent in one department is the same as a dollar spent in another department, but a project completed by one department may look nothing like a project completed by another department.

Step Seven: Complete the scorecard.

Once you have chosen the attributes (or variables) to measure, generating metrics basically involves choosing between a Basic Metric Model (Chapter 2) or a Metrics to Action Model (Chapter 13) and filling in the boxes.

Step Eight: Round out your team scorecard.

This step involves ensuring that your scorecard is aligned with the overall organizational scorecard. In case you did not do this earlier, be sure to examine the overall organizational scorecard to make sure that relevant company measures also appear in your departmental measures (e.g., safety or financial metrics).

As with team and organizational metrics, the balance of metrics is a key decision in any system. The following are some obvious balances to consider:

- Past, present, and future metrics
- Long- and short-term metrics (hard and soft metrics)
- Behavioral and outcome metrics
- Productivity and quality metrics
- Subjective and objective metrics
- Direct and indirect metrics (tangible and intangible referents)

Step Nine: Scrutiny.

Open the product of your work, the departmental scorecard, to scrutiny from others. This can be done by having the scorecard reviewed by a few key team members or by holding a large team meeting focused on improving the scorecard. At this point, you can use the checklists for measurement and statistics that are presented in Chapter 16.

Step Ten: Use the scorecard (translate metrics to action).

Chapter 13, "Engagement: Getting from Metrics to Action," expands on the various ways that you use scorecards once they are created. If the reason for creating the departmental scorecard is to improve performance, then at least three translations of your scorecard involve specific action:

- Use your scorecard to show how employee actions are linked to overall corporate strategy.
- Engage your employees to come up with ways to improve performance.
- Report results.

CHAPTER SUMMARY

Departmental scorecards provide a linking function between lower-level team scorecards and higher-level organizational scorecards. This chapter presented a step-by-step process for creating departmental scorecards with an expanded discussion about attributes to include. Eight departmental metric models were presented: combination of individual scorecards, roll-up measures, functional metrics, process metrics, corporate scorecard elements, intermediate activities, organizational initiatives, and combination scorecards.

REFERENCES

Ethiraj, S. K., & Levinthal, D. (2009). Hoping for A to Z while rewarding only A: Complex organizations and multiple goals. *Organization Science*, *20*, 4–21.

Fitz-enz, J. (2000). *The ROI of Human Capital*. New York: Amacom.

Katz, D., & Kahn, R. L. (1978). *The social psychology of organizations* (2nd ed.). New York: Wiley.

8 *ORGANIZATION SCORECARDS*

The organizational scorecard is the defining battle of the war. Performance appraisals, first-level team scorecards, and departmental scorecards all focus on a mission and vision that are articulated at the organizational level. The organizational scorecard is not just a rating system, it is the translation of the organization's vision into concrete results.

Getting the organizational scorecard right is a matter of art and balance. It is art because it requires strategy. It is balance because it involves getting all the key organizational attributes needed to reflect current performance as well as the future performance that will carry the organization into the future.

CHAPTER OVERVIEW

An individual manager or director can decide to create a scorecard and then get input from their employees on how to correct it. The task is not that complex. Creating an organizational scorecard is another story. It is a process that requires an entire management team to articulate a strategy as well as to create metrics.

The purpose of this chapter is to provide the context for lower-level scorecards by providing an overview of organizational scorecards. This chapter provides a discussion of key concepts, examples of different scorecard models, and scorecard balances. The chapter concludes with a high-level description of the process to create an organizational scorecard.

Conceptualization

Organizational scorecards are created for a strategic business unit. A **strategic business unit** has its own products, own customers, own distribution

---

LEARNING OBJECTIVES

After studying this chapter, you should be able to achieve the following:

1. Explain how the shift in world wealth from tangible to intangible assets led to a need for a new type of organizational scorecard.
2. Compare four models of organizational scorecards: *Balanced Scorecard, Baldrige criteria, stakeholders model,* and *combined model.*
3. Describe the basic dimensions of performance that are measured in organizational scorecards.
4. Describe the link between *strategy* and *scorecard.*
5. List six balances that need to be considered when scrutinizing organizational scorecards.
6. Give a high-level description of the process to create an organizational scorecard.

---

system, own production facilities, own financial performance measurement system, and own strategy (Kaplan & Norton, 1996). A company may consist of one or several strategic business units, meaning that the company may need one or several organizational scorecards.

Scorecards strive to measure both tangible and intangible assets. **Tangible assets** are physical properties owned by an organization such as buildings, materials, and machines. **Intangible assets** are elements of value that are not physical. For example, customer relationships, innovative services, operating processes, and intellectual capital of workers are all examples of intangible assets. A 2005 study by the World Bank reported that natural capital accounts for 5% of the world's wealth, produced capital for 18%, and intangible capital for 77% ("Our Intangible Riches," 2007).

Three types of metrics appear on every scorecard model: financial, business process, and customer. **Financial** metrics are traditionally focused on tangible assets; the exception is the recognition of the difference between "paper" value and market value. Some examples of financial metrics include Economic Value Added (EVA), which is Operating Profit − Taxes − Cost of Capital, and Tobin's Q, which is the ratio of market value to the cost of replacing the firm's assets.

Business process metrics refer to the execution of tasks that get tangible and intangible products out the door. Business process metrics are a close cousin of financial metrics in that they feed financial equations. For example, computing profit (a finance metric) requires process costs (a process metric).

Customer metrics reflect marketing efforts and mark the value of the company from variables oriented to the customer perspective. These variables can reflect marketing efforts, such as perceived product value or market share, or can reflect operational efforts to improve quality when quality is judged from the customer's perspective.

A growing body of research connects marketing metrics to financial outcomes. Which metrics are the most important? At least four asset metrics affect the value of a given firm: brand equity, customer satisfaction, customer equity (e.g., customer lifetime value [CLV]), and product quality. A set of four action metrics have been linked to shareholder value: advertising, price promotions (negative impact), distribution channels, and new products (Srinivasan & Hanssens, 2009). A study focused on the retail level connected the following marketing metrics to specific financial outcomes: brand value metrics, customer value metrics, word of mouth and referral, retention and acquisition metrics linked, cross-buying and up-buying, multichannel shopping metrics, and product return metrics (Petersen et al., 2009). Another model distinguished attitudinal, unobservable marketing metrics (e.g., customer satisfaction, service quality, loyalty, and intention to purchase) and behavioral, observable marketing metrics (e.g., acquisition, retention, cross-selling, and CLV (Gupta & Zeithaml, 2006). This last scheme distinctly connects satisfaction to firm performance measures (shareholder value, profit, Tobin's Q) and customer satisfaction is easily measured at all levels.

CLV is a particularly useful metric at the organizational level of analysis because it is used to predict future behavior. CLV is a function of revenues that a firm receives from a customer minus the costs for the firm to maintain the relationship with the customer (Borle, Singh, & Jain, 2009). The revenues of individual customers can be summed and predicted on the basis of past data: purchase timing, purchase amount, and customer lifetime with the firm (a reflection of the customer's defection to other firms).

How are scorecard categories related? This is an important question because if people have conflicting goals in different categories (e.g., reduce costs, improve quality), the result can be a freeze in performance. Ethiraj and Levinthal (2009) identified three effective methods for dealing with these possible conflicts: goal myopia, temporal differentiation, and spatial differentiation. **Goal myopia** is focusing on a single goal to guide action. They showed that focusing on a single goal dramatically improved performance; increasing the number of goals led to decreases in improvement to the point that eight goals put the organization back to the status quo. **Temporal differentiation** is changing the myopic goal over time, such as an emphasis on cost-cutting for some period of years, system integration for another, international expansion at another, and so forth. They concluded that temporal differentiation was helpful, but performance measures go down when goals are initially introduced. **Spatial differentiation** is dividing goals by departments. For example, operations focuses on cost-cutting and quality, and marketing focuses on market share. They found little difference between focusing on one or two goals at the department level and found that the presence of departmental goals made the organization scores go up in all areas. These departmental metrics likely reflect elements of the overall scorecard, process metrics, or functional metrics.

The problem of multiple goals is a fundamental problem of business strategy. Does a company want to be highest quality (e.g., Mercedes Benz)? Or lowest cost (Hyundai)? You can't be both. One way to thwart conflicting goals is to depict scorecard variables on a strategy map, a method advanced by Kaplan and Norton (2000). Another way is to create an index that weights scorecard categories (see Chapter 6).

Example strategy maps for Sky City Entertainment Group are shown in Figures 8.1 and 8.2. Sky City operates five casinos in New Zealand and Australia as well as restaurants, hotels, convention centers, and cinemas (Sky City Entertainment Group, 2009). In this particular business, surrounding communities are essential stakeholders because Sky City enjoys a monopoly nearly everywhere they operate casinos except Queenstown, New Zealand. It is considered "highly unlikely" that more casinos will ever be built in New Zealand, the country where Sky City earns roughly two-thirds of its revenue.

In December 2007, Nigel Morrison was named the new CEO of Sky City. He faced a series of strategic decisions that were the subject of an international case competition for business school students: Should they continue to focus on Australasia or expand into the Asian Pacific market? Should they be a gaming company or an entertainment company? Should they target family customers or high rollers?

The family strategy involved keeping the cinemas, upgrading facilities, and orienting marketing and training to family customers (see Figure 8.1). The high-roller strategy involved an asset sell-off and an entirely different program for marketing and training (see Figure 8.2). The key point is that the different strategies involve a completely different set of metrics. For example, the customer category would have a completely different set of items if oriented toward families rather than high rollers. The community metrics in the family strategy would mark efforts to provide family programs that would not exist in the high-roller strategy. Moreover, a stakeholder approach would trump a Balanced Scorecard approach because of the saliency of community metrics. Had it been a different company, such as Apple Computers, a combined approach would trump the stakeholder approach. Apple relies so heavily on innovation and product pipeline that these tactics would warrant adding a strategic section at the highest levels of organizational measurement. A "stakeholder" or "combined" approach reflects a scorecard that encompasses these possibilities.

Scorecard Models of Organizational Performance

Scorecard models are not only attempts to demonstrate the value of intangibles, but also methods to depict strategy. Four major models are discussed in this section: the Balanced Scorecard model (BSC), Baldrige criteria, a stakeholders model, and a combined model.

BSC Model

The BSC model was popularized by the book *The Balanced Scorecard* (Kaplan & Norton, 1996). This model requires that four dimensions of organizational performance need to be measured: financial, business process, employee learning, and

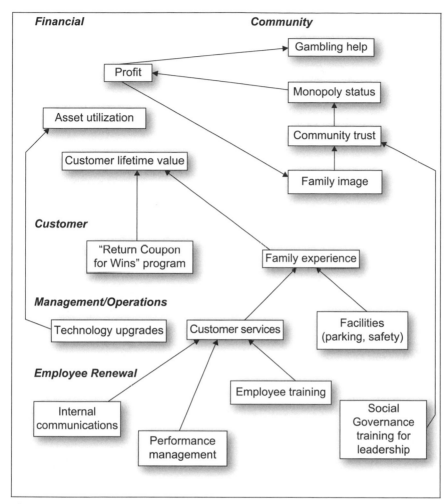

Figure 8.1 Strategy Map for Sky City Entertainment Group: Family Strategy
Source: © Ruth A. Huwe.

customer. A generic example of metrics in a BSC scorecard is shown in Table 8.1. Notably, this example includes metrics that could broken into "leading" and "lagging" categories. For example, profit is a lagging indicator and customer satisfaction is a leading indicator. In categories at lower levels, behavioral metrics are leading and outcome metrics are lagging.

More recently, Kaplan & Norton (2007) observed that uses of the scorecard have expanded into four key areas: translating the vision, communicating and linking, business planning, and feedback and learning. They also describe anecdotal efforts by companies to push down metrics to lower levels.

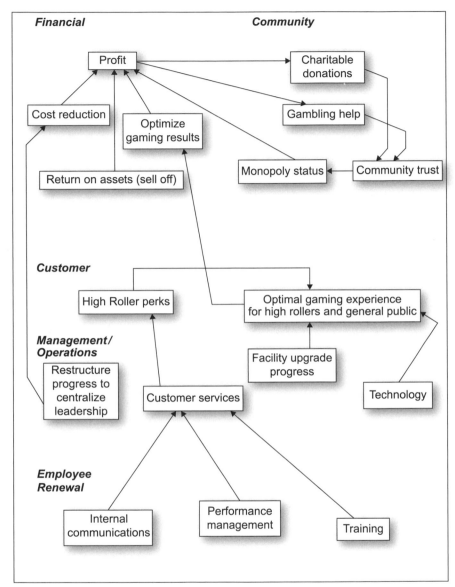

Figure 8.2 Strategy Map for Sky City: High-Roller Strategy
Source: ©Ruth A. Huwe.

Baldrige Criteria

The Baldrige criteria use a different set of scorecard categories. As shown in Table 8.2, Baldrige criteria include additional categories for leadership, strategic planning, and measurement. Rather than the BSC category for "growth and learning," the Baldrige criteria is closer to a stakeholder approach with "workforce outcomes."

Table 8.1 Generic Organization Scorecard

Generic Balanced Organizational Scorecard		
Dimension	Weight	Metrics/Indicators used for Index
Financial	40%	ROI
		EVA
		Revenue Growth
		Revenue Mix
		Profit
		Asset utilization
Customer	20%	Market Share
		Customer retention
		Customer acquisition
		Customer satisfaction
		Customer profitability
Operations	25%	Quality
		Cycle Time
		Adopt Best Practices
		Cost
Learning/People	10%	Satisfaction
		Turnover
		Absenteeism
		Training: Skill Inventory and Development Plans
Community	5%	Contributions
		Environmental compliance
		Ethics training
		Safety training
		Accidents
	100%	

Source: © Ruth A. Huwe.
Note: EVA = Economic Value Added; ROI = Return on Assets.

The associations between scorecard categories are also different on the Baldrige criteria. In the BSC model, associations between different metrics will vary from company to company and be shown in a strategy map. In the Baldrige criteria, each category is given a weight that adds to a total score. Baldrige categories are also conceived in system-theory terms with elements having cause-effect relations (see Chapter 3, Figure 3.2).

Stakeholders Model

Richard, Devinney, Yip, and Johnson (2009) argue that organizational performance be measured from the perspectives of all primary stakeholders:

Table 8.2 Baldrige Criteria

2009 Categories and Items	Point Values
I. Leadership	120
1.1 Senior Leadership	70
1.2 Governance and Social Responsibilities	50
II. Strategic Planning	85
2.1 Strategy Development	40
2.2 Strategy Deployment	45
III. Customer Focus	85
3.1 Customer Engagement	40
3.2 Voice of the Customer	45
IV. Measurement, Analysis, and Knowledge Management	90
4.1 Measurement, Analysis, and Improvement of Organizational Performance	45
4.2 Management of Information, Knowledge, and Information Technology	45
V. Workforce Focus	85
5.1 Workforce Engagement	45
5.2 Workforce Environment	40
VI. Process Management	85
6.1 Work Systems	35
6.2 Work Processes	50
VII. Results	450
7.1 Product Outcomes	100
7.2 Customer-Focused Outcomes	70
7.3 Financial and Market Outcomes	70
7.4 Workforce-focused Outcomes	70
7.5 Process Effectiveness Outcomes	70
7.6 Leadership Outcomes	70
TOTAL POINTS:	1,000

Source: NIST (National Institute of Standards and Technology). (2009). *Baldrige national quality program. Criteria for performance excellence.* Baldrige National Quality Program (pp. 7–22). Retrieved July 11, 2009, from http://www.baldrige.nist.gov/PDF_files/2009_2010_Business_Nonprofit_Criteria.pdf. Reprinted by Permission from the Baldrige National Quality Program.

managers, employees, suppliers, customers, stockholders, governments, and nongovernmental organizations (NGOs). Additionally, they conclude that measures must account for key performance indicators (KPI) that are internal to an organization (i.e., metrics at lower levels), the organization's environment, and management practice. They also echo Kaplan and Norton's (1996) call for balance across the short- and long-term measures.

Combined Model

As argued in Chapter 3, systems theory (Katz & Kahn, 1978; von Bertalanffy, 1968) and a necessity for strategic renewal (Agarwal & Helfat, 2009) lead to the addition of a strategy category on scorecards. To identify possible scorecard categories, combine the BSC dimensions, Baldrige dimensions, stakeholders, and strategic renewal to come up with the following choices: financial, business processes, employees, customer, community, ethics, stakeholders (e.g., community), and strategic contribution. A comparison of all models is shown in Table 8.3.

The role of strategic initiatives warrants comment. An **initiative** is a change program designed to improve an organization. Where do initiatives fit on scorecards? It is possible to add a line for specific initiatives, but another approach is to give them an entirely different scorecard (see Chapter 13). This is particularly true for initiatives sponsored by lower-level directors and managers who take on initiatives that are not appropriate for other segments of the organization. For example, consider a director of transmission and distribution at a power company who takes on an initiative to find any technological means to reduce the numbers of minutes that power is out each year. Would it make sense for the human resources department to adopt that initiative?

Balancing the Scorecard

Aside from balancing performance dimensions, at least six other balances need to be considered at the organizational level.

External versus Internal

Outcomes such as overall productivity need to be considered in tandem to internal processes such as overhead and resources.

Customer versus Overhead

Everyone wants higher quality and responsiveness, but at what cost? Customer ratings have to be considered in tandem to the costs that produce those ratings.

Past versus Future (lagging vs. leading)

Outcomes of the past are lagging variables whose effects are not known until a future point. For example, Return on Capital Employed (ROCE) is not known until it pays off. Customer satisfaction is not known until it results in repeat business. These measures need to be considered in tandem to leading variables

Table 8.3 Comparison of Scorecard Perspectives

BSC	Baldrige	Stakeholders	Combined
Business Process	Business Process (Internal and Organizational Outcomes)	Managers of processes	Processes
Customer	Customer	Customer	Customer
Learning & Growth	Workforce	Employees	Workforce
Financial	Financial	Shareholders	Financial
	Leader: Community	Community	Community
	Leaders: Ethics Measurement	Political Management	Ethics Management Renewal
		Other stakeholders	Other stakeholders
			Other strategic variables (e.g., Innovation, Globalization)

Source: ©Ruth A. Huwe.

that drive actions of the future, such as R&D (Research and Development) or CLV. Here is a succinct set of examples: past statistic (revenue), present statistic (sales), and future statistic (new business).

One approach to ensure attention to time factors is to include both behavioral and outcome metrics. Behavioral metrics gauge specific activities that lead to outcomes and tend to be oriented toward the present.

Past, present, and future are captured when scorecards include elements that reflect both current mission and future vision. For example, a team scorecard includes mission items (productivity and quality) as well as vision items (renewal and strategy).

This book includes both behavioral and outcome metrics on lower-level scorecards (first level and department) and calls for performance attributes to reflect both mission and vision. Still, if more emphasis is needed to get in the strategy and vision, a separate vision scorecard can be created (see Chapter 13).

A related temporal issue is choosing metrics based on organizational life-cycle stages: growth, sustain, and harvest. For example, financial metrics for the growth era might include growth rate (percent) in revenues. Financial metrics for the sustain era might include ROCE, operating income, or gross margin. Financial metrics for the harvest era might include Return on Investment (ROI) and EVA.

Objective versus Subjective

Would a company want *all* objective measures? Do they tell the story? But consider, would you want *all* subjective measures?

Diagnostic versus Strategic

Diagnostic measures can be viewed as those focused on your own organization. **Strategic measures** are metrics of competitive excellence.

Strengths and Weaknesses

Are you measuring only complaints but missing the customers you never had? Conversely, are you designing a self-serving scorecard that measures only strengths? Scorecards need to be scrutinized to ensure that they are not balanced one way or the other.

Steps to Creating a Balanced Scorecard

Who is responsible for creating an organizational scorecard? In general, this is a large project that requires a wide variety of participants: the leaders who need to articulate the vision, the information technology personnel who design the systems to gather the measures, the organization development staff or consultants who facilitate the process, the managers who translate the higher level numbers for their staff, and the employees who are expected to understand the numbers that mark the performance of their work. This is at a minimum. The following is a high-level description of the overall process:

- **Step One: Describe the organization.**
- **Step Two: Describe the company's mission, vision, and strategy.**
- **Step Three: Describe the company's strategy in terms of a strategy map.**
- **Step Four: Generate possible metrics for each of the dimensions of performance reflected in your strategy map.**
- **Step Five: Reduce your set of metrics to a list of 25 or less that make up a final scorecard.**
- **Step Six: Provide a visual link between vision, strategy, the scorecard, and action.**
- **Step Seven: Communicate the scorecard (Iterative with Step Eight).**
- **Step Eight: Align lower-order scorecards with the organizational scorecard.**

As with all scorecards, it is important that managers sit down at a keyboard or pull out a pad of paper and document decisions made at each step in the process. This can be written into a statement of method.

Step One: Describe the organization.

The Baldrige criteria (NIST, 2009) present a detailed method for providing an "overview" that includes a description of the workforce, major technologies, facilities, and so forth. Hoover's Online is an excellent source of general corporate information that also provides an excellent model for describing companies. The basics include the following:

- Brief history (years of service, merger activity)
- Logo
- Geographic location
- Publicly versus privately held
- Products and services
- Customers
- Main delivery mechanisms to customers
- Major competitors
- Size (employees, dollars)
- Recent financial performance
- Current news headlines

Step Two: Describe the company's mission, vision, and strategy.

In this step, provide a verbal description of the basic mission and vision of the company and strategy that the company should use to reach it. Notice that this is a prescriptive step. If it were a *descriptive step*, you would be describing the strategy as it is. As a *prescriptive step*, you are describing the strategy as you feel it "ought to be."

A **vision statement** is what a company hopes *to be*. The **mission statement** is the company's reason for existence, or what the company hopes *to do*. Notice that within a mission statement, you can tell both the company's service or product as well as its customers. Examples from CAIR (Council on American-Islamic Relations, 2006) are shown below:

> CAIR's vision is to be a leading advocate for justice and mutual understanding.
>
> CAIR's mission is to enhance understanding of Islam, encourage dialogue, protect civil liberties, empower American Muslims, and build coalitions that promote justice and mutual understanding. (2006, homepage)

The **strategy** is a reflection of *how* the organization plans to compete. A standard approach to strategy is to consider core competencies and a SWOT (strengths, weaknesses, opportunities, and threats) analysis. The following are just a few examples:

- Being a leader (or second to market) on some key technology
- Being a leader (or second to market) to take advantage of an upcoming societal trend
- Low-cost producer
- Market innovator

- High-end or customized product or service provider
- Focus on variables that make a difference in customer preference (as opposed to product attributes that are taken for granted)
- Leverage areas where you have competitive advantage

Step Three: Describe the company's strategy in terms of a strategy map.

This step involves the choice of scorecard models and showing the relationship between categories. In this book, I recommend considering all elements of the combined approach and mapping the association with a strategy map. A strategy map is recommended over the Baldrige criteria on the intuition that the actual importance of different scorecard categories will vary by company.

Step Four: Generate possible metrics for each of the dimensions of performance reflected in your strategy map.

Beyond Chapter 18 of this book, an excellent source for organizational metrics is *Keeping Score* (Brown, 1996). Additionally, Kaplan and Norton (1996) offer the following questions that are extremely helpful for triggering metrics:

FINANCIAL: "To succeed financially, how should we appear to our shareholders?" (p. 9).

BUSINESS PROCESS: "To satisfy our shareholders and customers, what business processes must we excel at?" (p. 9).

EMPLOYEE: "To achieve our vision, how will we sustain our ability to change and improve?" (p. 9).

CUSTOMER: "To achieve our vision, how should we appear to our customers?" (p. 9).

For other elements of a combined model, the following additional questions can be considered:

ETHICS: "What demonstrates our ethical standards?"

COMMUNITY: "What practices meet regulations or even enhance our contribution to our community?"

STAKEHOLDERS: "What key stakeholders have we missed that warrant scorecard status?"

STRATEGY: "Is there an element of our strategy that is so important that it warrants scorecard status?"

Step Five: Reduce your set of metrics to a list of 25 or less that make up a final scorecard. (Steps 5A, 5B, and 5C are iterative steps.)

Step 5A: Choose the best metrics.

Step 5B: Weight the scorecard categories (see Table 8.1).

Step 5C: If you must, cheat and make an index to keep the scorecard parsimonious.

Step Six: Provide a visual link between vision, strategy, the scorecard, and action.

Demonstrate the link between your high-level scorecard and the actions of individuals within the organization. For models on how scorecards translate into initiatives, see Chapter 13.

Step 6A: Write in your measures (metrics).

Step 6B: Decide on your targets (goals).

Step 6C: Decide which initiatives or activities support your goals.

Step Seven: Communicate the scorecard.

How do you get from high-level organizational scorecard to individual-level worker actions? First, you need to communicate your scorecard in a way that it reaches employees and *is internalized.* Making little laminated cards with logos and scores will go nowhere but the seat of the pants unless a full-scale effort is made to communicate the metric system. A wide variety of communication media and approaches are described in Chapter 13.

Step Eight: Align lower-order scorecards with the organizational scorecard.

Creating scorecards to push metrics down to lower levels is described in Chapter 5 (performance appraisal is the individual level of analysis), Chapter 6 (team scorecards are the group level of analysis), and Chapter 7 (scorecards at the departmental level of analysis).

CHAPTER SUMMARY

An organizational scorecard reflects the performance of a strategic business unit that has its own products, own customers, own distribution system, own production facilities, own financial performance measurement system, and own strategy. This chapter presented a high-level description of the process for creating an organizational scorecard. Four approaches were introduced: the Balanced Scorecard, Baldrige Criteria, a Stakeholders approach, and a Combined approach.

REFERENCES

Agarwal, R., & Helfat, C. E. (2009). Strategic renewal of organizations. *Organization Science, 20*, 281–293.

Borle, S., Singh, S. S., & Jain, D. C. (2009). Customer lifetime value measurement. *Management Science, 54*, 100–112.

Brown, M. G. (1996). *Keeping score.* New York: Amacom.

CAIR (Council on American-Islamic Relations). (2006, July). CAIR. Retrieved July 21, 2006, from http://www.cair-net.org/default.asp?Page=About.

Ethiraj, S. K., & Levinthal, D. (2009). Hoping for A to Z while rewarding only A: Complex organizations and multiple goals. *Organization Science, 20,* 4–21.

Gu, S. (2008). *Sky city entertainment group.* Case prepared for the Champions Trophy Case Competition 2008. Auckland, New Zealand: University of Auckland Business School.

Gupta, S., & Zeithaml, V. (2006). Customer metrics and their impact on financial performance. *Marketing Science, 25,* 718–739.

Kaplan, R. S., & Norton, D. P. (1996). *The balanced scorecard.* Boston, MA: Harvard Business School Press.

Kaplan, R. S., & Norton, D. P. (2000, September/October). Having trouble with your strategy? Then map it. *Harvard Business Review, 78*(5), 167–176.

Kaplan, R. S., & Norton, D. P. (2007, July-August). Using the balanced scorecard as a strategic management system. *Harvard Business Review, 85*(4), 150–161.

Katz, D., & Kahn, R. L. (1978). *The social psychology of organizations* (2nd ed.). New York: Wiley.

NIST (National Institute of Standards and Technology). (2009). *Baldrige national quality program: Criteria for performance excellence.* Baldrige National Quality Program. Retrieved July 11, 2009, from http://www.baldrige. nist.gov/PDF_files/2009_2010_Business_Nonprofit_Criteria.pdf.

"Our Intangible Riches." (2007, August). Growth Strategies. Retrieved September, 19, 2007, from http://findarticles.com/p/articles/mi_qa3908/is_200708/ ai_n19511507.

Petersen, J. A., McAlister, L., Reibstein, D. J., Winer, R. S., Kumar, V., & Atkinson, G. (2009). Choosing the right metrics to maximize profitability and shareholder value. *Journal of Retailing, 85,* 95–111.

Richard, P. J., Devinney, T. M., Yip, G. S., & Johnson, G. (2009). Measuring organizational performance: Towards methodological best practice. *Journal of Management, 35,* 718–804.

Sky City Entertainment Group. (2009). Home page. Retrieved July 11, 2009, from http://www.skycityentertainmentgroup.com/About-SKYCITY/Welcome.html.

Srinivasan, S., & Hanssens, D. M. (2009). Marketing and firm value: Metrics, methods, findings, and future directions. *Journal of Marketing Research, 46,* 293–312.

von Bertalanffy, L. (1968). *General systems theory* (Rev. ed.). New York: George Braziller.

Part Three
Surveys and Scale Construction

9 SCALE CONSTRUCTION

It starts to feel like armor: laptop, PowerPoint notes, memory stick. The battle-field is yet another conference room where you will reveal the results of your survey. What happens if someone in the audience knows what you're talking about? "Excuse me," she intones. "Exactly why did you choose those items?"

Because my survey is self-serving and designed to make me look good?

"Because . . ."

Because I let some consulting firm figure it out and didn't bother to watch what they were doing?

"Because . . ."

Because survey construction is some esoteric wasteland only pointy headed academics have to think about?

She continues, "And why did you put the items in the particular order that you chose? And why is it a scale of 1 to 3 instead of 1 to 5 like every other survey we use?"

If you choose to brazen it out, you would not be the first. Another option is to understand the fundamentals of scale construction.

CHAPTER OVERVIEW

This chapter begins with a basic vocabulary of concepts related to scale construction. As discussed below, the term "scale" has various definitions but essentially means a quantitative depiction of a phenomenon. The next sections describe specific scale construction activities: defining terms, writing scale items, and selecting rating scales. The chapter concludes with a step-by-step description of the scale construction process.

LEARNING OBJECTIVES

After studying this chapter, you should be able to achieve the following:

1. Identify terms that describe a *phenomenon*, including *concept, construct, conception, variable, attribute*, and *indicator*.
2. Know the difference between a *concept* and *construct*.
3. Describe the difference between a *measure*, a *psychometric instrument*, a *survey*, and a *scale*.
4. Know different types of definitions as they relate to measurement.
5. Perform all steps of a scientific definition process, including *conceptual definition, nominal definition, explication*, and *operationalization*.
6. Write a *scale item*, including a *declarative statement, ratings scale*, and *anchor*.
7. Describe the steps to scale construction.
8. Explain when you need to measure *intercoder reliability* and be able to judge whether this criterion has been met successfully.
9. Explain when you need to use *factor analysis* and be able to judge whether this criterion has been met successfully.
10. Explain when you need to use *reliability analysis* and be able to judge whether this criterion has been met successfully.
11. Explain when you need to use *power analysis*.

Conceptualization

Which of the following can be measured with a single count?

- You are a social scientist who wants to measure how 10th graders vary in terms of career aptitudes.
- You are an executive who wants to measure how customers perceive the quality of your company's products.
- You are an epidemiologist who wants to measure the number of people who have been infected by the H1N1 virus.
- You are a human resources manager who needs to measure job performance.

Only one of these phenomena manifests something that can be measured with a single count: the flu. Two of the items, the flu and job performance, reflect phenomena that can be observed. The other items, career aptitude and customer perception of service quality, require us to get inside the heads of people. For this, we need survey scales.

To understand the link between constructs and scale construction, consider the relationship between the terms presented in Figure 9.1.

A **phenomenon** is an occurrence, state, fact, or circumstance that is known through the senses. Some occurrences are similar to one another and, over time,

Measure	Psychometric Instrument		Survey	Scale	Anchor	Item
Variable	Construct	Concept	Conception		Attribute	Phenomenon

Figure 9.1. Scale Construction Concepts
Source: © Ruth A. Huwe.

we start to classify the occurrences as a certain type of phenomenon. For example, we might observe that a worldwide practice is for clowns to give out teddy bears. The Red Cross also gives out teddy bears. Police officers also have teddy bear drives. The occurrence that teddy bears provide comfort is a *phenomenon*.

A phenomenon is not to be confused with a concept. A **concept** is "a noun that stands for a class of objects: man, sex, aggression, verbal ability, social class, intelligence, and conformity are examples" (Kerlinger, 1979, p. 20). As shown in these examples, a concept may have either an object or a phenomenon as its referent. I have a concept of a teddy bear (object). I have a concept of teddy bears giving comfort (phenomenon).

Notice that the terms phenomenon and object appear to be interchangeable. A convention of this book is to refer to "objects" in scorecard chapters because it is easier to think of "teams" or "organizations" or "batches of parts" as objects with attributes. For mental constructs or occurrences such as those described by scales, the word "phenomenon" is used to signal the referent.

We can think of our brain as having file drawers for various concepts (Babbie, 2007). For example, consider the concept *compassion*. Inside that file is everything we ever heard about compassion. In one person's file, it might be individual conceptions such as "saw someone give money to a beggar." In another it might be "wept at a movie." In another, "a professor let a student turn a paper in late." Each of those conceptions adds up to a **concept**, which can also be taken as a family of conceptions.

A *construct* is a hypothetical category which possesses heuristic or interpretive value even if it does not purport to describe any observable reality (Gould & Kolb, 1964). Basically, a **construct** is a type of concept that is only known through definition.

An **attribute** is a facet of an object or phenomenon. Describing an attribute in measurable terms leads us to find indicators. An **indicator** is something that signals the presence or absence of attributes. For example, an indicator of love interest might be the number of "I'm thinking about you" phone calls per day.

A **variable** is a type of concept that labels attributes that take on different values. *My gender* is not a variable. *Team gender composition* is a variable if it changes over time.

As stated at the outset of this book, a measure is a set of rules for assigning numbers to reflect attributes of a given object. The term *metric* is used interchangeably with *measure*, but a clear metric includes the specification of a measurement unit. For example, we would consider the measure "hours of volunteer time" with the measurement unit "per person, per quarter" to create the metric "hours of volunteer time, per person, per quarter." A **survey** is a questionnaire. A **scale** is a type of survey that includes items that can be added together because they contain rating scales. A **rating scale** is a unit of measure that goes with individual survey items (e.g., a scale of 1 to 7). An **anchor** is the end of a scale that signifies a high and low point. A **psychometric instrument** is a type of scale that taps inward states (feelings, beliefs, attitudes, and values).

Scientific Definition Process

There are four general ways to define terms: (a) dictionary definition, (b) synonym, (c) antonym, or (d) use the word in a sentence. The scientific definition process includes five additional ways to define terms: (a) conceptual definition, (b) nominal definition, (c) explication, (d) operationalization, and (e) in terms of subdimensions.

A **conceptual definition** uses words to describe a concept and is usually drawn from research literature. A **nominal definition** is a working definition of a concept that is used in a specific context or study. If possible, we use a definition provided in previous research as our nominal definition because this allows us to compare results with extant data. Otherwise, we consider previous definitions along with our own research needs and advance our own definitions.

Suppose we described my physical appearance only in terms of nose size, and I was a crazed arsonist sought by the police. Would that attribute be enough to describe me to a police officer? We need enough attributes so that a phenomenon is described adequately enough to be recognized. The identification of attributes involves explication.

An **explication** is a designation of what will and will not be counted as a phenomenon. In practice, theses and dissertations have the editorial space for defining what does and does not "count as" a phenomenon, but journal articles and corporate studies almost never provide explication. However, the explication process is always necessary in scale construction because explication yields indicators and indicators yield measures.

An **operationalization** is a definition that describes a variable in terms of how it will be measured. Notice that the operational definition is the metric instrument. The whole act of operationalization *is* the act of creating a metric.

Subdimensions (or "dimensions") represent groupings of attributes that describe a phenomenon. We might describe a person in terms of "looks" and "personality." Within each category, many facets might be identified. Looks may include attributes such as eye color, hair color, weight, height, tan, and so forth. Personality might include attributes such as agreeableness, locus of control, and Machiavellianism. Looks and personality can be considered dimensions of "humans" or variables unto their own right. The personality traits of agreeableness, locus of control, and Machiavellianism may be considered dimensions of the "variable" personality or subdimensions of the "personality dimension" of humans. How these traits are classified depends on the abstraction at which you are considering terms.

Survey Items

A survey includes questions that seek information, including open questions, scale items, or some combination. A scale item consists only of closed-ended declarative statements that have corresponding rating scales. A **contingency question** is an item that depends on how the respondent answered a previous item. Typically, the contingent question is indented as in the following example.

Does this person routinely help coworkers? YES NO

> Which of the following are examples of the way that this person gives help to coworkers?
> _____ Gives computer training
> _____ Proofreads work
> _____ Critiques presentations

In the era of electronic surveys, it is possible to show contingency questions only if the respondent answered a certain way. For example, if the respondent answered NO to the first question (does not help coworkers), no examples of help would appear on the screen.

An **open-ended item** calls for a verbal response. For example, a supervisor might complete a scale about an individual's organizational citizenship behavior and then also respond to an open-ended question such as, "What are other ways that the individual provides help to coworkers?" This item is part of the survey but not part of the scale. A scale includes items that can be added together because they have rating scales.

Chapter 5 presented several types of rating scales in the context of writing performance appraisal items: Behaviorally Anchored Rating Scales (BARS), Behavior Observation Scales (BOS), Forced Distribution, Adjectival Anchors, Adjectival Anchors Combined with Numbers, and Relative Percentile. Additionally, Chapter 10 provides types of rating scales with anchors from customer service measurements, including the following: simple ranking (an ordinal method of 1st, 2nd, 3rd), importance expressed through weighting, or basic Likert scales.

Technique: Creating a Scale

This section presents a process for creating a scale that will serve as a metric for any given concept or construct. To demonstrate how we go from concept to measure, we begin with a running example of how to measure *ingratiation*. As with all processes, this book is limited by the linear nature of language. The process is set forth as a sequence but some steps are iterative. That is, you may need to go backward and redo steps before jumping forward.

The following is an overview of the basic steps to scale construction:

- **Step One: Define your reason for taking measures (motive).**
- **Step Two: What is your scope?**
- **Step Three: What is your unit of analysis?**
- **Step Four: Make sure you are measuring the right variables.**
- **Step Five: Define your terms.**
- **Step Six: Make sure all relevant attributes are reflected in your conceptual definition.**
- **Step Seven: Identify all possible indicators of your focus variable's attributes. (Steps Seven and Eight are done simultaneously.)**
- **Step Eight: Write the scale items.**
- **Step Nine: Reduce the list of items to those that go on the final scale.**
- **Step Ten: Prepare the final instrument.**
- **Step Eleven: Proofread the instrument.**
- **Step Twelve: Pilot test.**
- **Step Thirteen: Use your measure.**

Remember to document your decisions on each of the following process steps as you go along. This can be written into a "statement of method" that is not necessarily a part of future Power Point presentations, but rather is on hand to answer any kind of procedural questions that arise.

Step One: Define your reason for taking measures (motive).

Because it is geared toward managers, this book focuses on performance improvement as the typical motive for any metric, whether it is a scale metric or other metric. We proceed by looking at both the academic approach and business approach because the academic approach reflects the formal steps that would be taken by a research company, consulting firm, or anyone conducting a formal study.

In academia, there are two **justifications for scientific research**: practical application or contribution to theory. In turn, there are four basic **purposes for scientific theory**: description, explanation, prediction, or control. Whatever your justification or purpose, your investigation is then guided by either a hypothesis (or multiple hypotheses) and/or a research question (or multiple research questions). A **hypothesis** is a prediction about the relationship between two or more variables. A **research question** is an investigation about the relationship between two or more variables.

Ingratiation Running Example: Imagine that you are an informal "lead," a position in which you are expected to do day-to-day supervisory functions but are not given the power of a manager. You are working in a context in which your company has just been sold. A new manager is brought in and a scramble is on for your workers to protect their jobs. Unfortunately, the manager fires all of your good people and keeps only the ones who know how to "kiss up." It's a maddening phenomenon that is given a variety of loathsome labels. In academia, you would call it *ingratiation*. In business, we'd give it a more colorful label. (To class up the book, we'll stick with the academic label.)

Why would a manager care to measure ingratiation? To stop losing good workers. The purpose for the measure would be to help leads or managers detect ingratiation.

But why would an academic care to measure it? Let's say that in this case, the academic wanted to settle a question once and for all: Does ingratiation work? In this case, we might proceed with a hypothesis such as the following:

H1: Even if there is no difference in work performance between effective and ineffective ingratiators, effective ingratiators will get more promotions than ineffective ingratiators.

Step Two: What is your scope?

Consider the statistics that will be generated by your scale. What is the population to which these numbers will apply? Where will this be used? For your department? For other companies?

Ingratiation Running Example: Population in general.

Step Three: What is your unit of analysis?

What will your survey be measuring attributes about? Individuals? Groups? Departments? Organizations? Batches of parts? An object such as a car?

Ingratiation Running Example: Individual behavior.

Step Four: Make sure you are measuring the right variables.

Given your motive, what exactly is it you hope to measure?

Ingratiation Running Example: Given the motive, it isn't "ingratiation" we hope to measure. It's "seeing through" ingratiation or "effective ingratiation."

Step Five: Define your terms.

It is critical that you define your terms for several reasons. First, definitions guide the entire measurement process and will help you determine the attributes that are used to describe (and then measure) a variable. Second, defining terms forces you to consider the idea that your concept may have dimensions.

Ingratiation Running Example: Ingratiation.

Conceptual Definition. Ingratiation is formally defined as "an attempt by individuals to increase their attractiveness in the eyes of others" (Liden & Mitchell, 1988, p. 572). Ingratiation may be described as behaviors "ranging from subtle verbal or nonverbal positive reinforcement to more blatant formulas of 'apple polishing' or 'brown nosing'" (Schenck-Hamlin, Wiseman, & Georgacarakos, 1982, p. 95).

Nominal Definition. **Effective ingratiation** is nominally defined as ongoing ingratiation behavior where the actor's manipulative intent is not "seen through" by the target.

Explication. Ingratiation is differentiated from other persuasion strategies in that (a) it is illicitly designed (involves "manipulative intent") and depends on the concealment of ulterior motivation (Jones & Pittman, 1982), (b) involves enhancement of the target, and (c) evokes the target to attribute likable or attractive characteristics to the actor.

Operationalization. Effective ingratiation can be measured by having a boss and a coworker focus on a given target employee and complete a scale that asked how much the given employee exhibited ingratiation behaviors. If there is "no statistical difference" between the boss and coworker scores, the employee is "seen through" and classified as ineffective. However, if the coworker saw many more of the ingratiation behaviors than the boss, a difference that is statistically significant, then the ingratiation is counted as "effective." Hence, effective ingratiation is operationalized as the difference between supervisor and coworker measures of a target employee's ingratiation.

Dimensions. Ingratiation tactics fall into categories or "styles" such as "conformity" or "flattering" (Jones, 1964). The categories can be seen as dimensions of ingratiation or treated as separate variables. Considering dimensions may lead us to develop subscales for each type of ingratiation.

Iterative Step: If there are subdimensions and you are testing hypotheses, go back to ensure that your hypotheses still make sense.

Ingratiation Running Example: A boss may be able to see through "flattery" but not "agreement." Separate scales need to be created for each ingratiation style. New hypotheses should be written that treat each subdimension as a variable.

Step Six: Make sure all relevant attributes are reflected in your conceptual definition.

Generally, the attributes you identify will reflect aspects of an overall variable. For example, the entire premise of the book *Balanced Scorecard* is the idea that it is not enough to define a company's "performance" in terms of just "financial performance," but in terms of four major attributes. Others would point to the threat of gamed metrics and point out that productivity should not be measured without quality.

Ingratiation Running Example: Check that the definition includes manipulative intent, attribution of attractiveness, influence, and effectiveness (whether someone is seen through). In this case, we might redefine **effective ingratiation** as manipulative influence attempts that involve enhancing targets that are not seen through by the target.

Step Seven: Identify all possible indicators of your focus variable's attributes.

An **indicator** signals the presence or absence of an attribute. For example, saying "yes" to the question "Does my coworker always agree with our boss?" is an indicator of an the ingratiation behavior of "agreement."

What are all the indicators to reflect our phenomenon? This is the $64,000 question and when creating a scale measure, answering this question can take up the bulk of our work. *It is assumed that you did not find an excellent measure in previous research.*

Ask: Is there a previous measure that will suffice?

If there is a previous measure that will suffice, use it! Another informal (but frequently used) method for coming up with scale items is to have a group of students, maybe even grad students, simply brainstorm items. The classic method, however, is to follow formal steps of literature review, qualitative data gathering, content analysis, and a reliability check of the content analysis (Steps 7A, 7B, 7C, 7D below).

Step 7A: Conduct a literature review of previous conceptualizations and attributes studied.

Conduct a literature review to identify attributes of the variable that have previously been discovered. These attributes then will be translated into scale items.

Ingratiation Running Example: In this case, a literature review of 70 studies was conducted to identify related persuasion tactics, including ingratiation, compliance-gaining, persuasion, influence, and self-presentation research (Huwe, 1990). The following 27 categories were identified:

- Other enhancement (flattery)
- Conformity (agree)
- Self-degradation
- Instrumental dependency (remind them how powerful they are)
- Name dropping
- Change with the situation
- Favors
- Modesty
- Though manipulation (present an idea in a way that the supervisor thinks it is his or her own)
- Inflate task importance
- Boss importance (tell the boss he or she is important)
- Humble
- Friendly
- Pre-giving (giving gifts)
- Positive altercasting (liken the boss's behavior to those of a high-status person)
- Amount of talk (better listener than talker)
- Commonality (things in common)
- Openly likes (comment on how much you like the boss)
- Language manipulation (match the boss's, not use foul language)
- Infrequency of interruption
- Smiling
- Laughs (laugh at jokes even when they are not funny)

- Questioning (ask a lot of pointless questions)
- Vocal agreements
- Exclusion of negatives (never call attention the boss's weaknesses)
- Attentive when conversing

The indicators were translated into 36 scale items. The items were administered to 238 working undergraduate and graduate business students. A factor analysis of their responses reduced the list to 22 items. Factor analysis techniques are described in fuller detail under Step Nine.

Step 7B: Do a qualitative study to identify possible indicators.

Use open-ended questions to ask a group of subjects to describe all the ways they have experienced a given phenomenon. Basically, have the respondents brainstorm for you or give you an example that will be one of a collection of examples.

Ingratiation Running Example: The initial 238 respondents also completed an open-ended survey. They were asked to describe an instance of successful ingratiation and an instance of unsuccessful ingratiation.

Step 7C: Conduct a content analysis that identifies categories of indicators.

This step is a reduction. From all the hundreds of responses that you gathered in your qualitative study (Step 7B), your responses need to be reduced to a set of categories. It should be that the categories are **mutually exclusive** in that one item does not fit in more than one category, and they should be **exhaustive** so that nearly all of your items will fit in your categories. However, it seems there are always some haywire responses so, in practice, a "miscellaneous" category generally is used for stray items.

Ingratiation Running Example: The qualitative study in Step 7B yielded hundreds of responses. Three coders classified all of this open-ended data into different categories. The tactics can be thought of as conceptions or lower-order attributes, and the categories of tactics can be thought of as dimensions or a higher-order attribute. The resulting categories of higher-order attributes were somewhat different from those already uncovered in the literature review:

- Nice demeanor (friendly to others)
- Commonalities (choosing communication topics the boss is interested in)
- Agrees
- Change with the situation
- Idle talk
- Socializes
- Backstabber (takes credit for others' work)
- Favors (small tasks, menial tasks)
- Self-enhancer (attempt to appear intelligent, seek special recognition)
- Boss seeking (try to get more face time with the boss, go to the boss with every little problem)

These categories were translated into 15 scale items.

Step 7D: Check the reliability of the content analysis.

In actual corporate practice, sometimes just one person does the content analysis. In academic research, the standards are a bit stricter. Two or three people (often graduate students) work separately from each other and do a content analysis in which they identify the categories that they see.

Intercoder reliability is a statistic that compares the consistency with which various **coders** (people who classify data into category) do their work. An example is Cohen's Kappa. Page and Iwata (1986) provide an excellent description for conducting this analysis. As a rule of thumb, 0.60 is considered acceptable for exploratory research and 0.80 generally is accepted across social science disciplines.

Ingratiation Running Example: Cohen's Kappa was taken as the indicator of intercoder reliability across three coders. Reliability was only accepted if Kappa equaled 0.60 or higher.

Step Eight: Write the scale items.

As much as you can, when writing the scale items, use the raw language of the people who will answer the scale. Be sure to write different versions of the scale for different respondents (e.g., observers versus self-ratings, supervisors versus coworkers, etc.). Also decide whether you want a pen-and-paper survey or an electronic survey. Then, perform two iterative steps: write the items and choose a rating scale.

Step 8A. Write the items. (8A and 8B are iterative.)

Write the closed-ended statements that you wish to use as items on your scale.

Ingratiation Running Example: The following are example scale items. These examples include rating scales.

Your coworker tends to stress things he/she has in common with your boss.
        Strongly Disagree   1 2 3 4 5 Strongly Agree

Your coworker is inattentive when conversing with the boss. (NEGATIVE ITEM)
        Strongly Disagree   1 2 3 4 5 Strongly Agree

Step 8B: Select the rating scale for your items.

At least eight issues need to be considered when selecting the rating scale for your items.

Step 8B1. Decision:

Level of measurement. Notice what happens when you plug in the rating scales for the following items:

My coworker flatters the boss.

YES   NO

Compared to others, my coworker agrees with the boss.

LOW   MEDIUM   HIGH

My coworker makes a flakey effort to laugh at my boss's jokes.

DISAGREE   1 – 2 – 3 – 4 – 5 – 6 – 7   AGREE

My boss expresses disagreement with our boss.

NEVER   0   1   2   3   4   5   6   7   8   9   10   ALWAYS

Mathematically, it would be nonsense to add the answers to these items together, particularly because they are at different levels of measurement (nominal, ordinal, interval, and ratio). If you intend to combine items, all items must have the same scale.

Step 8B2. Decision:

Do you put the "good" side of the scale to the left or to the right? This is a matter of preference. The author likes to put the "good" side on the right because English language speakers read from left to right.

Step 8B3. Decision:

How many points are in the scale—5, 6, or 7? The points on the scale must distinguish things that people can remember. For example, could people count the number of times someone flatters the boss? Not likely. Can they agree or disagree on a person's tendency to make flattering comments. Probably so.

Step 8B4. Decision:

How many numbers on the scale? Recent evidence shows that on scales of 1 to 5, people will not choose "5" because it is socially undesirable to choose an "extreme" answer (Kuncel & Tellegen, 2009). One solution is to go to a 7- or 9-point scale. You might also consider other scales used by the company for whom the survey is being conducted such as their employee survey. Aligning your scale with other scales used by the company allows for future comparisons of data.

Step 8B5. Decision:

Do you want an odd or even number on the rating scale? An even number such as a rating of 1 to 6 forces the respondent to be positive or negative, not allowing for a neutral position.

Step 8B6. Decision:

Are your items worded at a particular level of analysis? The **level of analysis** refers to the manner in which phenomena are grouped when measures are taken. For example, is the respondent being asked about the ingratiation of a particular coworker? A particular coworker-supervisor dyad? Is the measure about a team? Notice that this changes the wording of items. For example, in the case of the ingratiation scale, three versions had to be written: one for the focal person (possible ingratiator), one for the coworker, and one for the boss. Item content was about what occurred between supervisor-subordinate dyads.

Step 8B7. Decision:

What type of rating scale to use? A combination adjectival and numerical rating scale was chosen to measure ingratiation:

Strongly Disagree	Mildly Disagree	Neutral	Mildly Agree	Strongly Agree
1	2	3	4	5

Step 8B8. Decision:

Which items should be negatively worded? The item "Your coworker is inattentive when conversing with the boss" is negatively worded for an ingratiation scale. This catches people who are starting to answer out of habit rather than attention to items. You would later program the computer so that 1 = 5 and 2 = 4 to reverse your negative wording.

Once you have made a decision about your rating scale, proofread and rewrite the items to ensure that they make sense with your scale.

Step Nine: Reduce the list of items that will go on the final scale.

Four statistical techniques are used to reduce the list of items that will go on the final scale: factor analysis, reliability analysis, validity check, and a run of descriptive statistics to test for normality.

Step 9A. Conduct a factor analysis.

Factor analysis is a statistical technique that identifies key underlying dimensions or subscales of your variable. That is, the factor analysis will tell you if you are measuring one variable or actually several "styles" or "types" of the same phenomenon that each represent a different variable.

The details of factor analysis are beyond the scope of this volume, but one of the best guides is the documentation that comes with the Statistics Package for Social Sciences (SPSS) software (Norusis, 1993). SPSS is a commonly used statistics program that goes beyond the scope of Excel. The most common alternates are SAS and SYSTAT. The availability of these programs depends on your discipline or the standard chosen by your company.

Two "rules of thumb" are worth mentioning here. First, how do you choose your number of factors? Second, how do you choose which items "load" on a factor? First, conduct a "scree" test, typically accepting dimensions that reflect an Eigenvalue of 1 or higher. Second, select items on the basis of how high they load on one factor as compared with their loading on another factor. One technique is to select items where their primary loading (biggest loading) was 0.6

on one factor and no higher than 0.4 on another or if the primary loading was 0.5 on one factor and no higher than 0.3 on another.

What happens to the items that do not load on any factor? They are excluded. This is how a factor analysis reduces items.

How many people do you need? Again, there are two rules of thumb: 10 times the number of scale items (e.g., a 30-item scale would need 300 people for the pilot test) or a minimum of 200.

Ingratiation Running Example: The 22 items from the literature review items (Step 7A) and the 15 items from the qualitative analysis (Step 7B) were combined into a 37-item scale that was administered to a different set of 118 respondents. Note that this sample is small and that an astute statistician would have some hurdles to clear to show that it was acceptable to proceed.

Identifying factors with Eigenvalues greater than 1 yielded a four-factor solution. Accepting items that loaded 0.6 on one factor but no higher than 0.4 on another *or* that loaded 0.5 on one factor and no higher than 0.3 on another, yielded 19 items. The final scale had four dimensions that reflected ingratiation styles: other enhancement (12 items), conformity (5 items), the lack of conformity (2 items), and modesty (2 items). The dimensions were labeled to reflect the items that loaded on a given factor. The factor analysis results are shown in Table 9.1.

Step 9B. Conduct a reliability analysis.

Reliability analysis is a statistical technique that assesses the consistency with which your items measure the category or "dimension" they are supposed to reflect. Reliability can be compared to consistency as with a bathroom scale—is it the same when you stand on it again? Just as you can goof with the bathroom scale by leaning or taking off your watch and jewelry, the consistency of scale items can be messed up by flaws in the items wording.

The most common reliability statistic is Cronbach's alpha. A rule of thumb is that 0.80 or higher is considered very reliable for a research scale, though alphas as low as 0.60 are accepted for exploratory research.

The alpha statistic is also going to be sensitive to the number of scale items. The more items you have, the easier it is to "blend in" a bum item and to obtain a higher alpha.

An excellent test provided in statistics packages tells you the reliability of a given scale if an item was deleted. In this manner, you can identify and delete items that drag down the overall reliability of items in a given scale or subscale.

To have the shortest scale possible, you want at least two items to reflect each dimension or factor of your variable. The two items can then be correlated to demonstrate reliability.

Ingratiation Running Example: After the factor analysis, 19 items were loaded on four factors. Each factor's items were considered a subscale and a reliability analysis was done on each grouping reflecting "active enhancement," "active conformity," "passive conformity," and "modesty." For exploratory research,

Cronbach's alpha had to be 0.60 or higher for items to be retained in the final survey.

Step 9C. Conduct a validity check.

Validity is the extent to which you are measuring what you think you are measuring. One way to establish validity is to correlate your scale's scores to scores

Table 9.1. Factor Analysis of Ingratiation Items

Item	Factor 1	Factor 2	Factor 3	Factor 4
Favors	0.81634*			
CWST	0.78729*			
Pques	0.77992*			
Ndrop	0.76912*			
CWS	0.74687*			
Power	0.74343*			
Jokes	0.68150*			
Brains	0.67759*			
Bseek	0.67251*			
Arrog	−0.67120		0.41942	
Nice	0.62511*			
Liking	0.62199			0.41258
Flatter	0.59851			0.41054
Listen	−0.53224*			
Flatter2	0.52056			0.36163
Self-en	0.50452*			
Ptalk	0.37334			
Favors2		0.66878*		
Friendly2		0.63966*		
Agree		0.57294*		
Common2		0.54352	−0.40891	
Sbseek		0.50915		
Agree2		0.49025		
Lang/com		0.46274		
Common		0.42827		
Weakness	−0.34876		0.67198*	
Opinion			0.66133*	
Critic			0.56622	0.37129
Modesty				0.59734*
Praise			−0.42599	0.54801
Smile				0.52080
Humble				0.50782*

Source: © Ruth A. Huwe.
Note: $N = 118$.
*Denotes items used in subscale construction.

on another scale that should be *related*. A common validity statistic would be the Pearson correlation ($r =$). Another way to identify validity is to check to see whether subjects responded in the predicted pattern when given negative items. For a detailed validity discussion, see Chapter 11.

Ingratiation Running Example: As an example, the ingratiation subscale of "active enhancement" was positively (but not highly) correlated to "emotional openness" ($r = 0.26$, $p < 0.01$). Negative items loaded negatively on the appropriate factors.

Step 9D. Check the normality of the items.

The normality of items can be checked through analysis of descriptive statistics. To be thorough, test each moment of the distribution: central tendency, dispersion, skewness, and kurtosis. An expanded discussion is presented in Chapter 12.

Ingratiation Running Example: Descriptive statistics were examined for all 19 items of the final ingratiation scale. All items met criteria for normality.

Step Ten: Prepare the final instrument.

This step involves careful proofreading of your instrument and translating it into the format that will be presented to respondents.

At this point, you also may want to consider the ordering of your items. Questions about the order of items begin with the distinction of global items about an overall object versus specific items about attributes. An **assimilation effect** occurs when global items are put after a series of specific items and then tendency is for there to be a higher score on the global items. It is called an assimilation effect because people are summarizing (or assimilating) the specific questions that came before the global question. The **contrast effect** occurs when a general question is placed at the beginning of a survey, and then specific items are contrasted against the overall question, leading to a lower rating of the specific attribute (DeMoranville & Bienstock, 2003).

The final format of the instrument typically includes six parts:

- Demographics
- Information about ethics
- Instructions
- Scale and items
- Next steps
- Participant thanks

Demographics. The demographics may come at the beginning or at the end, but the instrument definitely should have some way to identify respondents. This could range from just having a box for a code number to asking for a collection of "demographic" information. The following are typical demographics included in a scale:

- Age
- Ethnicity
- Religious preference
- Occupation
- Industry
- Education level
- Gender
- Marital status
- Geographic location
- Income level

Information about Ethics. Typical information about ethics includes whether the scale is confidential, voluntary, and how information will be used (e.g., will people reading results know you?). If there are concerns about confidentiality, a useful approach is simply to describe the steps that will be taken to protect the respondent's anonymity, including a statement of exactly who will and who will not see the scale.

Instructions. Instructions must be written at the lowest level possible. Assume nothing. As an example, if you ask a question that asks "Yes" or "No" and has two bubbles, direct them that they should check in the bubbles. The instructions generally provide respondents with a purpose for taking the test and directions on how to proceed. It is also a courtesy to tell people how long you think it will take them to do the survey.

Scales and Items. Survey items should be coupled with the rating scales with every glance of the eye. The scale should be written prominently on every page that the respondent is seeing. One way on electronic scales is to have the scale in a banner at the top of every page.

Next Steps. It is important that the respondent then knows what to do with the scale they have just completed. Whether it is to send it to a particular address or to press a button on a Web site, every instruction must be spelled out.

Participant Thanks. Finally, thank people for their participation. In fact, sometimes you will reward people for taking a survey (e.g., their name is put in a lottery to win a prize). If this is the case, you should tell them about their reward up front.

Ingratiation Running Example: All elements were included in the final instrument.

Step Eleven: Proofread the instrument.

This seems obvious but it is not a step to skip to skip (ha ha). At this point, you know a great deal about the subject you are measuring but the layperson taking the measure does not. It is also possible, as with any writing process, that you simply will miss errors. If you are in a business environment, it is particularly important to have people who are "natives" read your instrument and correct any overly scientific verbiage you may have accidentally inserted. Business readers must then convince you to insert verbiage that fits their particular culture. The goal is to write items that sound as natural as possible to the people who are responding to them.

Ingratiation Running Example: A thesis committee of three professors proofread the scale.

Step Twelve: Pilot test.

This single word "pilot" is the best piece of measurement advice anyone will ever give you. Pilot studies can be a "hold-back" sample, a technique in which you have the first 10 or 20 subjects complete a survey, make minor corrections, and then continue to submit the survey. In this case, you may or may not keep the data depending on whether the corrections were minor or major. Alternatively, the pilot involves giving the survey to a small set of subjects as a ministudy. Corrections are made on the basis of the study.

Step Thirteen: Use your measure (to test your hypotheses).

In a business context, you can now use your scale as a measure for a metric. If you wish to use your measure to reflect a larger population of people, you will need to conduct a *power analysis*. For example, if you surveyed 30 employees and took their attitudes to reflect that of a 300-employee organization, you would have to conduct a power analysis to assess whether those 30 people were sufficient. Power analysis is discussed at length in Chapter 12.

In academia, you would use your measure to test hypotheses. This involves both power analysis and hypothesis tests. Two categories of statistics are used for hypothesis tests: (a) tests of association and (b) tests of difference. Various types of statistics are also discussed in Chapter 12.

Ingratiation Running Example: In this case, power analysis revealed that there were a sufficient number of respondents, despite 118 being too few subjects to conduct a normal factor analysis. The main hypothesis was supported. For those subjects who had been promoted within the previous two years, coworkers saw a significantly greater amount of ingratiation than the target supervisors ($t = 4.4$, $p < 0.001$ for active enhancement, $t = 2.3$, $p < 0.05$ for active conformity). For those who had not been promoted within the previous two years, supervisors "saw through" the ingratiation in that the amount of ingratiation they perceived was not significantly different than the amount perceived by coworkers ($t = 1.46$, NS for active enhancement, $t = 0.69$, NS for active conformity). No differences were identified in the performance level between subjects who had been promoted and those who had not been promoted.

Retrofitting Hypotheses

Could the researcher have gone back and rewritten the hypotheses to include questions that they knew would be supported by results? The answer is NO! You cannot go back and rewrite hypotheses when they do not turn out how you like.

Retroduction is a serious ethical breach. If the results guide you to consider other statistics tests, you can report additional tests under the topic of "post hoc analysis."

CHAPTER SUMMARY

The chapter presented a vocabulary of measurement terms associated with scale construction. The discussion of surveys and scales included examples of several types of rating scales: simple ranking, forced distribution, numerical anchors, adjectival anchors, and combinations of numerical and adjectival anchors. This chapter also included a description of the full scale construction process with the running example of an ingratiation scale.

REFERENCES

Babbie, E. (2007). *The practice of social research* (11th ed.). Belmont, CA: Wadsworth.

DeMoranville, C. W., & Bienstock, C. C. (2003). Question order effects in measuring service quality. *International Journal of Research in Marketing, 20,* 217–231.

Gould, J., & Kolb, W. L. (1964). *A dictionary of the social sciences.* New York: Macmillan.

Huwe, R. A. (1990). Ingratiation success as a function of supervisor communication style and communication competence: Scale construction and pilot analysis. Masters Thesis, San Diego State University.

Jones, E. E. (1964). *Ingratiation: A social psychological analysis.* New York: Appleton.

Jones, E. E., & Pittman, T. S. (1982). Toward a general theory of strategic self-presentation. In J. Suls (Ed.), *Psychological perspectives on the self* (pp. 231–262). Hillsdale, NJ: Lawrence Erlbaum.

Kerlinger, F. N. (1979). *Behavioral research: A conceptual approach.* New York: Holt, Rinehart, & Winston.

Kuncel, N. R., & Tellegen, A. (2009). A conceptual and empirical reexamination of the measurement of the social desirability of items: Implications for detecting desirable response style and scale development. *Personnel Psychology, 62,* 201–238.

Liden, R. C., & Mitchell, T. R. (1988). Ingratiatory behaviors in organizational settings. *Academy of Management Review, 13,* 572–587.

Norusis, M. J. (1993). *SPSS for windows advanced statistics release 6.0.* Chicago, IL: SPSS Inc.

Page, T. J., & Iwata, B. A. (1986). Interobserver agreement. In A. Poling & R. W. Fuqua (Eds.), *Research methods in applied behavior analysis* (pp. 99–126). New York: Plenum.

Schenck-Hamlin, C., Wiseman, R. L., & Georgacarakos, G. N. (1982). A model of properties of compliance-gaining strategies. *Communication Quarterly, 30,* 92–100.

10   *CUSTOMER SURVEYS*

You are stuck. STUCK. Until you get your new computer up and running. No matter what you do, you get an error message. ERROR. ERROR. ERROR. As only a desperate person would, you begrudgingly accept that you will be nailed $60 per hour and pick up the phone to call technical support. And so it begins . . .

"Welcome to Company X. To better assist you, please key in your ID code at the tone." #$*@! If I knew the ID code, I wouldn't be calling! "Please choose from the following set of menu options. . . ." You hit a number and wait 20 minutes. Can you do some work while you wait? No, because the lame music they play is interrupted every 15 minutes with some pronouncement about why you should be trying to do this on the Web. Finally a human voice. "I'm sorry, that's handled by a different department. Please call . . ."

It is hard to overstate the importance of customer service. For sales, it can mean the deciding factor between gaining and losing accounts. For operations, it can mean avoiding rejects and or driving up costs. For virtually any given internal customer, poor service can mean bottlenecks, delays, and fines.

But what counts as excellent customer service is a matter of perception, requiring us to get inside the heads of people. It is possible to hold focus groups and conduct interviews, but the quickest and cheapest approach is to create a scale. Although scales are discussed at length in the previous chapter, the need for customer service scales cuts across so many scorecards that the topic warrants a separate chapter.

CHAPTER OVERVIEW

Customer satisfaction data are particularly useful not only because they yield results, but also because respondents can proactively yield a brainstorm of new

---

LEARNING OBJECTIVES

After studying this chapter, you should be able to achieve the following:

1. Identify different *types* of customers.
2. Understand how a customer service *scale* is a portion of an overall customer survey.
3. Describe the difference between a *product* and *service*, including prototypical features of each.
4. Define major customer service variables, including *purchase intention, purchase behavior, customer attitude, perceived product quality, perceived service quality, customer satisfaction, service value,* and *sacrifice.*
5. Understand the quarrel between the SERVQUAL and the SERVPERF customer service measures.
6. List a general set of *attributes* used to describe customer service.
7. Describe several types of *rating scales* popularly used for customer service measurement.
8. Execute the process for creating a customer service survey that includes development of a customer service scale measure.

---

ideas for products. Customer satisfaction also affects key organizational outcomes, including customer lifetime value (Borle, Singh, & Jain, 2008) and then firm value (Srinisvasan & Hanssens, 2009). At the first level, customer surveys may be the one metric for understanding internal customer satisfaction.

This chapter will discuss three topics associated with customer perceptions. First, key concepts are introduced to give a vocabulary of terms associated with customer service. While the measure of product quality was a main topic of Chapter 4, this chapter will delineate the measure of service quality. The chapter concludes with a step-by-step process for creating a customer survey that is both quantitative and qualitative.

Conceptualization

Consider the relationship between the terms shown in Figure 10.1. Which are subsets of which? Which is in reference to what? Which is an indicator of the other? Which are dependent variables?

Quality

There are many ways to define quality. First and from the Japanese philosophy, quality is "zero defects" or "doing it right the first time" (Parasuraman, Zeithaml, & Berry, 1985). Second, quality can be conceived as "conformance to requirements." Third, quality can be operationalized through an individual's rating. Fourth and also from the individual's perspective, quality can be judged

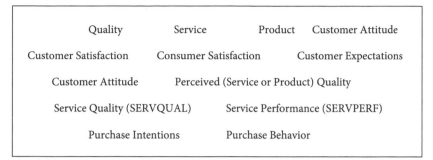

| Quality | Service | Product | Customer Attitude |

Figure 10.1. Concepts Related to Customer Service

as a gap between expectations and performance. Fifth, quality can be viewed as fitness for use. Sixth, quality can be defined in terms of loss avoidance (for a full discussion, see Reeves & Bednar, 1994).

Metrics of quality perceptions rate two types of referents: a product or service. In general, a **product** involves a tangible output and a **service** involves both a product and its delivery. However, many products are a mix of service and product (e.g., gas station service and gas, software and tech support lines, airplanes and follow-up service). One study gave the following clarification (Bowen, Siehl, & Schneider, 1989):

Prototypical Service

- Intangible output
- Customized output
- Customer participation
- Simultaneity of production and consumption
- Labor intensive

Prototypical Product

- Tangible output
- Standardized output
- Technical core buffered from the customer
- Inventory of goods consumed at a later point in time
- Capital intensive

Service quality is an evaluation from a customer (customer attitude) and is in reference to a *phenomenon*. A **phenomenon** is an occurrence, state, fact, or circumstance that is known through the senses. **Product quality** is an evaluation about a tangible product and is in reference to an *object*. Different approaches to measuring product quality are discussed in Chapter 4.

A **scale** is a type of survey that includes items that can be added together. However, if you go to the trouble of administering a scale, you may as well add additional survey items that gain important customer data. Hence, the pragmatic position here is that a customer service scale is part of an overall customer survey. A **survey** is a questionnaire that seeks information, scaled or otherwise.

Brown (1996) provides a useful typology of three types of customers:

1. *Users*: Employees in other functions who use the products and/or services provided by the support functions.
2. *Stakeholders*: Shareholders, bosses, corporate exectuives, and others who care about the overall health of the organization.
3. *Others Like Us*: Business unit or location support function personnel who provide similar products and services. (p. 72)

Internal customers are *users* and *others like us*. Stakeholders could be either external or internal. **External customers** can be conceived as distributors, end-users of products, and so forth.

Purchase intention is a prediction about the probability that someone will purchase a product in the future. **Purchase behavior** is the actual execution of a product or service transaction.

Tying the Other Variables Together. *Customer attitude* encompasses both consumer satisfaction and perceived service quality. **Perceived product quality** is an individual's long-run overall evaluation of a product and **perceived service quality** is an individual's long-run overall evaluation of a service (Cronin & Taylor, 1992; 1994). Both concepts stem from a comparison of what people feel service firms should offer versus their perception of firms when they provide the service (Parasuraman, Zeithaml, & Berry, 1988). **Consumer satisfaction** and **customer satisfaction** are interchangeable terms (e.g., Danaher & Haddrell, 1996) and can be conceived in three ways. First, customer satisfaction can be a *relationship-specific* construct. For example, industrial suppliers may rate their distributors in measures that reflect satisfaction with their relationship. Second, customer satisfaction can be a *transaction-specific* construct (Parasuraman et al., 1988). For example, consumers rate a specific product purchase. Third, customer satisfaction can be viewed as a *confirmation or disconfirmation of prior expectation*. **Expectations** reflect what a customer thinks about a product or service prior to experience with the product or service.

Along with customer attitude, another variable that influences behavioral intentions is perceived **service value**, reflecting a "get versus give" or "net gain" evaluation by consumers. A related (but not identical) variable sometimes considered is **sacrifice**, what one sacrifices or gives up to acquire a service (Brady et al., 2005).

At first glance, it would also appear that **customer attitude variables** (customer satisfaction, perceived product quality, and perceived service quality) and **service value** would be dependent variables, as those variables seem like something businesses would hope to improve. In fact, they are considered moderators of what happens between a customer having an "expectation" about a product or service and the customer's future "purchase behavior."

Marketing journals include debates about how to measure customer service. Pulling from these articles (Brady et al., 2005; Cronin & Taylor, 1992, Parasuraman et al., 1985; Parasuraman et al., 1988; Parasuramn, Zeithaml, & Berry, 1994), the following is a portrait of the customer experience:

1. Individuals have customer expectations.
2. Customer service is provided. (Alternate: A product is experienced.)
3. Transaction experience leads to satisfaction or dissatisfaction. The individual's experience with the service is reflected in the individual's customer attitude of consumer or customer satisfaction (an immediate transaction-based perception).
4. Consumer or customer satisfaction then influences an individual's rating of perceived service quality (an ongoing evaluation).
5. Perceived service quality then influences purchase intentions.
6. Purchase intentions then influence purchase behavior.

The bottom line question is as follows: "Is it that customer attitude is a function of the product performance? Or is it the gap between expectation and service performance as it was experienced?" Research evidence supports the former (Bolton & Drew, 1991; Cronin & Taylor, 1992) and this greatly simplifies the whole model. Rather than draw up measures of all of these variables, the person creating the measure can look at how number 3 (satisfaction in reference to a given transaction) affects number 6 (purchase behavior).

Measuring attitudes toward a given transaction is facilitated by two major measures: the quality measure SERVQUAL (Parasuraman et al., 1985; 1988; 1994) versus the satisfaction with performance measure SERVPERF (Cronin & Taylor, 1992). The SERVQUAL was first conceptualized in 1985 (Parasuraman et al., 1985), and the seminal article presenting the instrument was published in 1988. Both measures include the same customer satisfaction attributes (e.g., empathy, responsiveness) but vary by scaling (expectations met-not met versus agree-disagree), reflecting a generic set of customer service attributes that can be used across all service industries (Coulthard, 2004).

A search in the Social Science Citation Index demonstrated that more than 700 articles had cited the seminal SERVQUAL publication by 2006. There is considerable evidence that the SERVQUAL is both reliable and valid (Jiang, Klein, & Crampton, 2000). Though less dominant than the SERVQUAL, a European alternative the INDSAT has been cited in more than 100 articles (Homburg & Bettina, 2001).

Table 10.1 presents attributes of customer satisfaction as measured on the SERVPERF/SERVQUAL instruments. In practice, I have found that teams reduce this to the few items that seem most relevant. This is particularly true when measuring the satisfaction of internal customers.

Whichever approach you use, an important practice in scale construction is to add a global item to the scale. A **global item** is a judgment about an overall phenomenon, not just its attributes. An example of a global item would be,

Table 10.1 SERVQUAL Attributes of Service Quality

Reliability

1. Providing services as promised.
2. Dependability in handling customers' service problems.
3. Performing services right the first time.
4. Providing services at the promised time.
5. Maintaining error-free records.

Responsiveness

6. Keeping customers informed about when services will be performed.
7. Prompt service to customers.
8. Willingness to help customers.
9. Readiness to respond to customer's requests.

Assurance

10. Employees who instill confidence in customers.
11. Making customers feel safe in their transactions.
12. Employees who are consistently courteous.
13. Employees who have the knowledge to answer customer questions.

Empathy

14. Giving customers individual attention.
15. Employees who deal with customers in a caring fashion.
16. Having customer's best interest at heart.
17. Employees who understand the needs of their customers.
18. Convenient business hours.

Tangibles

19. Modern equipment
20. Visually appealing facilities
21. Employees who have a neat, professional appearance
22. Visually appealing materials associated with the service.

Source: Parasuraman, A., Zeithaml, V., & Berry, L. L. (1991). Refinement and reassessment of the SERVQUAL scale. Journal of Retailing, 67, 420–450. Reprinted with Permission by Elsevier.

"How would you rate your overall satisfaction with service quality?" A global item can later be correlated to the rest of the scale to establish the scale's convergent validity.

Types of Rating Scales

Although customer satisfaction appears to be the most important driver of purchasing behavior, managers may be interested in several variables associated with customer perceptions: value, importance, expectations, and satisfaction. Just as performance appraisal is a subject matter with specific types of rating scales, standard formats are associated with the measure of customer service.

Comparison and Importance Anchors

Sometimes, the goal is to have the respondents identify the attributes of service that are the most *important* to them. For example:

Very   1—2—3—4—5—6—7   Very
Unimportant   Important
_____ 1. The staff is courteous at all times.

Observe that either the "Expectations Met" or "Satisfaction" scales can be varied according to level of measurement. The following are examples:

Ordinal:
Choose one of the following: Expectations Met 1 Expectations Not Met 0

Interval:
Expectations Not Met   1   2   3   4   5   6   7   Expectations Met

Ratio:
Not Met   0   10   20   30   40   50   60   70   80   90   100   Met

Ordinal:
Choose one of the following: Satisfied   1   Dissatisfied   0

Interval:
Dissatisfied   1   2   3   4   5   6   7   Satisfied

Ratio:
Completely   Completely
Dissatisfied   0   10   20   30   40   50   60   70   80   90   100   Satisfied

The conceptualization section presented various attributes that can be translated into survey items. This section presented a variety of rating scales. Taken together, the survey items and rating scales make up the heart of the scale. However, the whole process of customer service scale construction includes the set of decisions that need to be made when creating any metric. The next section lays out this process for the specific case of measuring service performance.

Technique: Process to Create a Customer Service Scale

Chapter 9 presented a complete scientific process for creating survey scales. This section provides a simple method for creating a service performance scale that capitalizes on previous customer service research. In addition, a running example for an internal software team is provided.

As you do when creating any scorecard or scale, sit down at a keyboard or pull out a pad of paper and begin on the right track: document your decisions on each of the following process steps. These notes can be written into a "statement of method" that is not necessarily a part of future Power Point presentations, but is on hand to answer any kind of procedural questions that arise.

Step One: Define your reason for taking measures (motive).

An array of reasons for measuring customer perceptions was discussed at the outset of this chapter. Beyond performance improvement, customer surveys provide valuable product and service information.

Software Team Running Example: Internal customers for a software team. The motive is to improve performance and to identify new services that could be offered.

Step Two: What is your scope?

Articulate which customers will be measured with the scale. Alternatively, you can ask "if we draw statistical inferences from these survey results, who will be the population to which we infer our findings?"

Customers generally are segmented according to meaningful characteristics: age groups, occupations, new customers, geographic regions, and so forth. For example, one study demonstrated that dimensions of customer service (in this case, a banking setting in which dimensions included corporate image, innovativeness, physical and staff service, pricing, and convenience) were different for *business* customers and *individual* customers. In fact, only four dimensions were significant to the business customers (Athanassopoulos, 2000).

Software Team Running Example: Internal customers of a software team. The survey will be used to describe the service of one department that serves internal customers from many other departments.

Step Three: Decide the unit of analysis.

The **unit of analysis** is a specification of what counts as the object we are observing when measuring attributes. For example, a team is the referent and unit of analysis for a team scorecard. We measure attributes of a team such as productivity and quality. For another example, if we were creating a survey about product quality, the product would be the referent and unit of analysis. We may designate the unit of analysis as a single product or a batch of products. In the case of customer service, our scale is about a phenomenon. We ask, "What happened during a service experience?" Do we take a measure after a single transaction? Do we measure the ongoing service of a department over a period of time? The unit of analysis needs to be identified in the instrument's instructions.

The unit of analysis should not be confused with the respondent. In the case of any psychometric instrument, the measure is completed by individuals (Fornell, Johnson, Anderson, Cha, & Bryant, 1996).

Software Team Running Example: Internal customers of a software team. The previous month's service is measured. The scale's opening instructions include verbiage such as, "The purpose of this scale is to measure the perform-ance of Team X. Please think of your interactions with this team in the past month as you rate them on the following items."

Step Four: Make sure that you are measuring the right variables.

The customer service variables depicted in Figure 10.2 and the host of motives listed at Step One demonstrate that several important variables could be meas-ured when creating a customer service scale.

Software Team Running Example: Internal customers of a software team. The team realizes that they also want to know the importance placed on various attributes of their services. Given this, the measure will focus on potential *inno-vations*, overall *perceived service quality*, and *importance of service attributes*.

Step Five: Define your terms.

Each term you hope to measure must be defined.

Software Team Running Example: **Perceived service quality** is an individual's long-run overall evaluation of service experience. **Importance of service attrib-utes** are characteristics of the service experience that stand out in the respond-ent's mind. **Innovation** is defined here as new uses for the team's services.

Step Six: Make sure all relevant attributes are reflected in your conceptual definition.

This step triggers you to consider whether your definition includes everything it should.

Software Team Running Example: Internal customers of a software team. In this case, "service experience" is a broad descriptor for perceived service quality. Other definitions might have broken the variable into dimensions such as serv-ice and delivery. In this case, definitions will be kept as defined previously.

Step Seven: Identify all possible indicators of your focus variable's attributes. (Steps Seven and Eight are done simultaneously.)

This step can require an entire study to identify indicators, depending on your answer to Step 7A.

Step 7A: Is there a previous measure that will suffice?

Blessedly, the SERVQUAL provides a list of attributes than can be taken to reflect customer service (See Table 10.1.). In cases where there is no existing scale, the researcher must go through the set of Steps 7A1, 7A2, 7A3, 7A4. An example for those steps is provided in Chapter 9.

Step 7A1:

Conduct a literature review of previous conceptualizations and attributes studied.

Introduction. The purpose of this scale is to measure the performance of Team X. Completion of this survey is voluntary and confidential.

Instructions. For this first part, please think of your interactions with this team in the past month as you rate them on the following items. In the blank, write in the number 1, 2, 3, 4, or 5 that best reflects your response on the following scale:

DISSATISFIED 1 2 3 4 5 SATISFIED

_____ 1. **Reliability.** Consistency of performance and dependability.

_____ 2. **Reliability.** Getting things right the first time.

_____ 3. **Responsiveness.** Timeliness of service.

_____ 4. **Competence.** Skill and knowledge to perform the service.

_____ 5. **Access.** Ease of contact.

_____ 6. **Courtesy.** Politeness of contact personnel.

_____ 7. **Communication.** Keep customers informed in a language level they can understand.

_____ 8. **Credibility.** Belief that the department has the customer's best interests at heart; trustworthiness, believability, and honesty.

_____ 9. **Security.** The manner in which this department handles my information with an appropriate level of confidentiality.

_____ 10. **Understanding/Knowing the Customer.** Making an effort to understand the customer's specific requirements.

_____ 11. **Understanding/Knowing the Customer.** Makes an effort to provide individualized attention.

_____ 12. **Tangibles:** Physical evidence of the service; physical facilities; appearances.

Overall, what do you think of service from Team X in the past month?
Poor 1 2 3 4 5 Excellent

What makes you give this rating? What part of their service is particularly important to you? What needs improvement?

_____

What additional services would you like to see offered by Team X? _____

Figure 10.2. Example Items and Rating Scale.

Step 7A2:

Do a qualitative study to identify possible indicators.

Step Seven 7A3:

Conduct a content analysis that identifies categories of indicators.

Step Seven 7A4:

Check the reliability of the content analysis.

Step Eight: Write the scale items.

This step involves both the selection of the rating scale and selection of items. It is typically an iterative step in that you have to go back and make sure that the wording of the items makes sense with your chosen scale.

Step 8A: Write the items.

Step 8B: Select your rating scale.

As discussed in Chapter 9, there are several things to consider when selecting the rating scale. As discussed earlier in this chapter, there are also several scale options that are specific to customer service measurement.

Software Team Running Example: Internal customers of a software team. Inspired by the SERVQUAL, items were written to reflect perceived service quality of the internal software team. The items in Figure 10.2 were written to reflect service quality, hence the dissatisfied to satisfied anchors.

You may notice a trick in the items shown in Figure 10.2. The name of the attribute being measured is bolded. Why not? It is just one more way to communicate to the respondent precisely what you hope to measure. Anything you can do to add accuracy will pay off with a scale that is more reliable and valid.

In addition to the scale, a global item was added to measure an overall perception of service, and two other items were included to tap importance and innovation.

Step Nine: Reduce the list of items to those that go on the final scale.

In practice, the SERVQUAL can be seen as a starting place. For example, the items in Figure 10.2 have some SERVQUAL attributes but not all. You also can add attributes that are important in a given setting. This is not the formal scientific approach involving Steps 7A1, 7A2, 7A3, and 7A4, but it is practical.

Had the SERVQUAL not been available and an original instrument created, reducing items would involve the following additional steps:

Step 9A: Conduct a factor analysis.

Step 9B: Conduct a reliability analysis.

Step 9C: Conduct a validity check.

Step 9D: Check the normality of the items.

Instructions for completing Steps 9A, 9B, 9C, and 9D are provided in Chapter 9.

Step Ten: Prepare the final instrument.

There are six main parts of any given instrument:

- Demographics
- Information about ethics
- Instructions

- Scale and items
- Next steps
- Participant thanks

Software Team Running Example: Internal customers of a software team. The example shown in Figure 10.3 includes ethics information, instructions, the scale, and additional items. Demographics could come at the end (or beginning). The example in Figure 10.3 includes "Demographics, "Next Steps" and "Thanks."

Step Eleven: Proofread the scales.

Make sure to have another set of eyes proofread the scales.

Step Twelve: Pilot test.

If you did not do a ministudy in the previous step, it behooves you to have a small number of people complete the survey before administering it on a large scale. Do some statistical runs such as those in Steps 9A, 9B, 9C, and 9D to identify any bum items.

Step Thirteen: Use your measure.

What to do with the results? The scale portion will need to be added together. Some like to report the frequencies such as "What percentage of people scored a 4 or 5?" This is a reference to favorable results. Another way to crunch the results is to take the average item scores, either summing the scores together for subdimensions (reliability, responsiveness, assurance, empathy, and tangibles) or looking at performance on each individual item. Final results can be presented as an individual report or can be fed into metric scorecards developed elsewhere.

Now, just a few questions about you. We remind you that your answers will be treated confidentially.

Age: _____   Gender: M F Occupation: _____

(Optional) Annual Income:
Under 20k _____   21-50k _____   51-100k _____   100+ k _____

(Optional) Ethnicity
Caucasian: ____ Latino: ____ African American: ____ Asian: ____ Other: ____

Thank you for your participation!

When finished, please hit the send button and your results will be forwarded to _____.

Figure 10.3. Example Ending of a Survey

Software Team Running Example: Internal customers of a software team. The software team's manager can use the scale ratings as a measure of quality in his or her team's first-level team scorecard.

CHAPTER SUMMARY

This chapter presented a vocabulary of terms associated with the measure of quality and service. A step-by-step process was introduced to demonstrate how the process of creating a customer survey can be greatly simplified by drawing from the SERVQUAL measure. This chapter also presented an additional set of rating scales that can be used in surveys: importance anchors, expectations, agree-disagree, and dissatisfied-satisfied.

REFERENCES

Athanassopoulos, A. D. (2000). Customer satisfaction cues to support market segmentation and explain switching behavior. *Journal of Business Research*, *47*, 191–207.

Bolton, R. N., & Drew, J. H. (1991). A multi-stage model of customers' assessments of service quality and value. *Journal of Consumer Research*, *17*, 375–384.

Borle, S., Singh, S. S., & Jain, D. C. (2008). Customer lifetime value measurement. *Management Science*, *54*, 100–112.

Bowen, D. E., Siehl, C., & Schneider, B. (1989). A framework for analyzing customer service orientations in manufacturing. *Academy of Management Review*, *14*, 75–95.

Brady, M. K., Knight Jr., G. A., Cronin, J. J., Tomas, G., Hult, M., & Keillor, B. D. (2005). Removing the contextual lens: A multinational, multi-setting comparison of service evaluation models. *Journal of Retailing*, *81*(3), 215–230.

Brown, M. G. (1996). *Keeping score*. New York: Productivity Press.

Coulthard, L. J. M. (2004). Measuring service quality: A review and critique of research using SERVQUAL. *International Journal of Market Research*, *46*, 479–497.

Cronin, J. J., & Taylor, S. A. (1992). Measuring service quality: A reexamination and extension. *Journal of Marketing*, *56*, 55–68.

Cronin, J. J., & Taylor, S. A. (1994). SERVPERF versus SERVQUAL: reconciling performance-based and perceptions-minus-expectations measurement of service quality. *Journal of Marketing*, *58*, 125–31.

Danaher, P. J., & Haddrell, V. (1996). A comparison of question scales used for measuring customer satisfaction. *International Journal of Service Industry Management*, *7*, 4–12.

Fornell, C., Johnson, M. D., Anderson, E. W., Cha, J., & Bryant B. E. (1996, October). The American customer satisfaction index: Nature, purpose, and findings. *Journal of Marketing*, *60*, 7–18.

Homburg, C., & Bettina, R. (2001). Customer satisfaction in industrial markets: Dimensional and multiple role issues. *Journal of Business Research, 52,* 15–33.

Jiang, J. J., Klein, G., & Crampton, S. M. (2000). A note on SERVQUAL reliability and validity in information system service quality measurement. *Decision Sciences, 31,* 725–744.

Parasuraman, A., Zeithaml, V. A., & Berry, L. L. (1985). A conceptual model of service quality and its implications for future research. *Journal of Marketing, 49,* 41–50.

Parasuraman, A., Zeithaml, V. A., & Berry, L. L. (1988). SERVQUAL: A multiple-item scale for measuring consumer perceptions of service quality. *Journal of Retailing, 64,* 12–40.

Parasuraman, A., Zeithaml, V., & Berry, L. L. (1991). Refinement and reassessment of the SERVQUAL scale. *Journal of Retailing, 67,* 420–450.

Parasuraman, A., Zeithaml, V., & Berry, L. (1994). Reassessment of expectations as a comparison standard in measuring service quality: Implications for further research. *Journal of Marketing, 58,* 111–124.

Reeves, C. A., & Bednar, D. A. (1994). Defining quality: Alternatives and implications. *Academy of Management Review, 19,* 419–446.

Srinisvasan, S., & Hanssens, D. M. (2009). Marketing and firm value: Metrics, methods, findings, and future directions. *Journal of Marketing Research, 46,* 293–312.

Part Four
Scrutiny of Metrics

11 *MEASUREMENT ISSUES*

How do you think it goes when managers present new metric scorecards to the rank and file? Will they explode into hearty praise? Will they remark upon the "Validity of it all! The Parsimony!"

If you expected this, you would be deluded.

When it comes down to it, scorecards are used to judge people. This means threat and a defensive reaction is a natural human response. Chances are that people are not going to be looking for the positive features, such as the fairness, feasibility, or balance. People are poised to throw rocks, criticize you, and declare your metrics to be lame.

They will be looking for mistakes.

Hopefully, the mistakes are unnecessary because you will catch them first. This chapter and the one that follows are oriented toward scrutiny, giving managers the means to critique their own scorecards before presenting them to others.

CHAPTER OVERVIEW

For typical managers, the problem is not "coming up" with metrics but choosing from the overwhelming number of metrics that are already embedded in company systems. Scrutiny is a core competency for the manager in charge of metrics, whether it is the ability to (a) scrutinize the metrics you are creating or (b) scrutinize preexisting metrics in a way that helps you choose the right ones.

Measurement issues have been reduced to seven criteria for metrics: validity, reliability, feasibility, logic, actionable, parsimony, and statistical soundness. Chapter 12 is devoted to the issue of statistical soundness and all other issues are described in this chapter. The discussion for each concept will include

---

LEARNING OBJECTIVES

After studying this chapter, you should be able to achieve the following:

1. Recognize criteria for judging metrics and metric scorecards: *validity, reliability, feasibility, logic, actionable, parsimony,* and *statistical soundness.*
2. Describe seven major types of validity: *content, construct, convergent, divergent, predictive, face,* and *ecological* and identify methods for establishing each type of validity.
3. Define *reliability* and describe major types of reliability: general reliability of a scale, intercoder reliability, split-half reliability, and test-retest reliability.
4. Describe how the *reliability* of a measure is established.
5. Define what is meant by *roll-up* metrics.
6. Define *parsimony* and understand how an *index* can be used to achieve a parsimonious set of metrics.
7. Know what to do with missing measurements.
8. Know when to include open-ended questions to create metrics.
9. Describe the tradeoff between *accuracy* and *precision.*
10. Describe the fundamental problem with count metrics.
11. Identify both advantages and disadvantages associated with anecdotal data.
12. Know the risks associated with making scorecards public.
13. Understand the importance of making your metric creation process a "double-loop" process.

---

definitions (see boldface terms) followed by an example and key measurement issues. Additionally, for each concept, two questions will be answered:

- What is the relevance for business metrics?
- How does one establish whether the measure meets a particular criterion?

This chapter also addresses miscellaneous measurement questions that arise.

Validity

Validity is the extent to which scores on measures reflect true differences in attributes of the objects the scores are meant to represent rather than differences arising from error or some random factor (Nunnally, 1978). To better understand this, think of what would happen if you were to measure weight with a ruler. Height with a scale? Questions of validity center on whether your measure corresponds to the nature of the phenomenon you are measuring. Basically, you are asking, "Are you measuring what you think you are measuring?"

Weight with a ruler? Height with a scale? It seems like people in business could not really make measures that stupid, right? But recall in Chapter 1 in which the efficiency expert thought that time on the phone was a valid measure of worker productivity.

There are seven major types of validity to consider: content, construct, convergent, divergent, predictive, face, and ecological. **Content validity** is the extent to which a measure adequately reflects all the relevant aspects of a concept that it is meant to measure. Put another way, the measure should adequately "sample" the "domain of content" that represents the concept. For example, consider measurement of an individual's job satisfaction and suppose that the individual works at a horrid plant with an overbearing boss and disgraceful company policies—but the pay is good. If your job satisfaction measure asked only about pay, it would lack content validity.

How much content is enough? You could go on and on with various attributes of an individual's job and at some point have to reduce the various attributes into dimensions. For example, the most common scale of job satisfaction, the Job Description Index (JDI), measures five different facets of job satisfaction: supervision, work, pay, promotion, and coworkers (Smith, Kendall, & Hulin, 1969).

What is the relevance for business metrics? Content validity is a criterion to consider in many business situations, including exams to test training, customer service surveys, performance appraisals, or scorecards. The question for exams is whether they adequately reflect all of the training. The question for customer service surveys is whether they reflect all relevant aspects of customer service. For performance appraisals, the question is whether they judge all relevant aspects of an individual's job. As applied to scorecards, the question is whether the chosen dimensions reflect all key relevant attributes of performance.

One guideline is to begin with the mission or organization's vision. It is possible for a team to create metrics without knowing the company vision, but the corporate scorecard (which hopefully reflects a strategy and vision) will give guidelines on what attributes should be considered important to a team. It also will give values that instruct teams how to weight various metrics on their scorecards in the case that they later hope to make an index.

Another issue related to content validity is whether you measure something on which you are performing well. As an example, I have owned Toyota cars for years and have never seen my temperature gauge go above the midpoint. Would this mean that I should go without a temperature gauge? Of course not. The choice of attributes to include depends on the importance of the ongoing performance of whatever you measure: work teams, cars, and so forth. Alternatively, if you are constructing a customer satisfaction survey, the metric that never varies might simply be a metric that wastes time because it does not differentiate what customers would buy. In this case, you would measure only the variables that cause fluctuations in customer ratings.

How does one establish content validity? Content validity is established two ways. First, specify the procedures you used to create your measure, particularly demonstrating that you selected from all possible logical contents. Second, when deciding dimensions to consider for a scale, use Cohen's Kappa statistic to demonstrate that more than one person thought that possible contents were properly categorized. Kappa is a measure of intercoder reliability. Finally, when creating metric reports and initial scorecards, be sure to have a statement of method on hand for questions about how you created your metrics.

Construct validity is the extent to which a measure is measuring the concept it purports to measure. To understand the idea of construct validity, we begin by exploring, "What is a construct?" As stated by Nunnally (1978), "to the extent that a variable is abstract rather than concrete, we speak of it as being a **construct**. Such a variable is literally a construct in that it is something that scientists put together from their own imaginations, something that does not exist as an isolated, observable dimension of behavior" (p. 96). For example, intelligence, motivation, or job satisfaction cannot be seen with the naked eye. We know they exist, but we would have a tough time playing out these constructs in a charades game if we weren't allowed to use some sort of letter trick.

To the extent that a variable is more abstract, it is more difficult to validate. As an example, a concrete variable is "time to order raw materials." The measure is a straightforward observation of how much time it takes from the time an order is received until the time when raw materials are ordered. You can argue about whose clock to use, but the method of measurement is not going to have much of an impact on results. For concrete variables, you have relatively few choices of how to go about measurement. As in the "time to order raw materials" variable, it's pretty clear that it's going to involve a clock (and hopefully some clear definitions about what counts as "customer order received" and "raw materials ordered").

But consider abstract concepts such as intelligence, stress, or job satisfaction. Just defining the *intelligence* construct spurs unlimited debate in schools across the country.

What is the relevance for business metrics? Strictly speaking, any time we create an index (e.g., Customer Satisfaction Index) or a scale (e.g., Job Satisfaction Index), we are using constructs. Additionally, this will boil down to whether your audience believes that your indicators actually represent the variable you purport to measure. For example, does "Milestones Met" actually reflect productivity?

How does one establish construct validity? Construct validity basically is established by providing a theoretical description of the object you wish to measure (i.e., define it), specifying how you will measure it, and then demonstrating the correspondence between the measure and the concept (Cronbach & Meehl, 1955). For example, suppose you conceptualized productivity as both quantity and efficiency, and then specified that you would measure it through "number of defects." Is there correspondence between your definition and your measure? Defects measure something important, quality, but the measure of defects does not represent productivity.

One other aspect of construct validity is the demonstration that you do not have dimensions that, in turn, reflect constructs in their own right. An example by Nunnally is whether you developed a measure of anxiety but then discovered two distinct types of anxiety. Other relevant examples include conceptualizing productivity as having two dimensions (quantity and efficiency) or performance as having two dimensions (quality and productivity). Using the defects measure would be akin to using a ruler to measure weight.

Convergent validity is the extent to which a measure of a given attribute "converges with" or matches measures of attributes that are logically, positively related to the measure. As an example, most Internet dating services rest on the assumption that the attribute of "attraction" and "similarity" may not be the same thing, but the two variables would be expected to have a positive correlation. For a business example, consider the concept of "efficiency" and the concept of "worker utilization." We would expect these concepts to be positively correlated, but in fact they are not the same thing. We establish convergent validity of one variable by correlating it to a variable in the expectation that the correlation will be positive. For divergent validity, we expect just the opposite: a negative correlation.

Divergent validity is the extent to which a measure of a given attribute "diverges with" or *does not* match measures of attributes that are logically, negatively related to the measure. For example, Internet dating services appear to assume that "education differences" have a negative correlation to "attraction," in which the wider the gap between two people, the less the relationship is expected to work out. Back to the business example, we expect that worker "stress" would be negatively correlated to "job satisfaction."

What is the relevance for business metrics? In practice, it is unlikely that people are going to quarrel over whether your Job Satisfaction Index is actually correlating with your productivity measure, and so forth. However, it is likely to raise red flags if variables expected to be positively or negatively correlated are not. For example, efficiency should be positively but not perfectly correlated to quantity of work completed.

How do we establish convergent and divergent validity? Correlate a variable to another variable and see whether it has the expected association—that is, positive for convergent validity and negative for divergent validity.

Predictive validity is the extent to which a measure predicts what it should predict. For example, do Scholastic Achievement Test (SAT) scores actually predict school performance later in life? In business, do your chosen metrics actually predict business outcomes?

There are three types of predictive validity. First, **postdiction** is whether this current measure applies to the past. For example, can current tests detect a mistake made in the past? **Concurrent** validity is whether the current measure applies to your current state. For example, does your quality measure reflect current quality performance? **Predictive validity** is whether your measure applies to the future. For example, does quality predict key variables such as return sales? Cronbach and Meehl (1955) observed that both concurrent and predictive validity are "criterion-oriented" in that you basically are using one measure to predict another criterion measure, and if the criterion happens to occur at a future point in time, it is taken to be predictive validity. If the focus measure and criterion occur essentially at the same time, it is considered concurrent.

What is the relevance for business metrics? The most important link is that we hope metrics about behavior will predict metrics about outcomes. Do measures of research and development (R&D) now predict future predictions of market share? Do measures of lean implementations now predict increases in productivity?

How does one establish predictive validity? The typical way to establish predictive validity is to correlate scores on two measures, your metric of focus and the metric you hope that your metric predicts. For example: Correlating Graduate Management Admission Test (GMAT) scores with actual grades earned while completing a masters of business administration. This correlation is known as a validity coefficient.

Face validity is the extent to which a measure, on its face, looks like what it is supposed to measure. For example, consider the example of using odometer readings for police performance. Does that look like a good measure of police performance? On the other hand, we are likely to look at items on the SERVQUAL measure of customer satisfaction (Parasuraman, Zeithaml, & Berry, 1991) and think, "Hmmm, ease of contact, reliability, competence . . . yes, that *looks like* it reflects the construct of customer service."

What is the relevance for business metrics? Questions of face validity are most central when choosing indicators to reflect any given attribute. Any time you present a scorecard survey to an audience, people can question whether your scorecard categories actually reflect high performance.

How does one establish face validity? This is the most informal of all the forms of validity. We simply look at a metric and ask whether it makes sense.

Ecological validity is the extent to which results of a given measure created in one context will hold up in other contexts. The typical question of ecological validity is whether a measure used in a laboratory would hold up in the real-world setting. For example, we might be able to measure pupil dilation as a measure of comprehension in a laboratory setting, but could we use that in a corporate training context?

What is the relevance for business metrics? The most likely application of this issue is when some team is being used to "pilot test" or "experiment with" a new program. If that team is in some way a unique case that is unlike any other team in the company, then it is not likely that findings within that team will generalize.

How does one establish ecological validity? Argue that the setting in which your metrics were created or used matches the context in which the metrics will be applied.

Validity and Processes Presented in This Book

Process steps can protect against measurement problems. For example, one step in scorecard creation calls for asking a team to scrutinize scorecards; this is to support face validity. For another example, content validity is aided at four steps: identify terms, make sure you are measuring the right variables, advance scrutiny, and construct explication. Each process in this book has been written with an eye toward establishing each type of validity. As well, the processes in this text were designed to hold up against other forms of scrutiny, which are considered next.

Reliability

Reliability refers to consistency, predictability, and dependability. For example, if we can predict someone will show up on time, we consider the person "reliable." If the person is not consistent in when he shows up or cannot be predicted to behave in a certain way, we consider the person to be unreliable (Kerlinger, 1979). The **reliability** of a measure is the extent to which the measure can be repeated and get the same results. Cohen (1977) observed that anything that introduces error, be it observational carelessness or dirty test-tubes, detracts from reliability.

What is the relevance for business metrics? Reliability is an important consideration for any metric and any survey scale. When presenting metric reports, you might be questioned as to whether trends reflect actual trends or possible reliability problems with your measures, such as a variation that is due to error.

How do we establish reliability? Cronbach's Alpha is the statistic used to assess the reliability of a survey and is based on "both the average correlation among items (the internal consistency) and the number of items" (Nunnally, 1978, p. 230). A rule of thumb is to consider a survey to be reliable if Cronbach's Alpha is 0.80 or greater, with a little flexibility for exploratory measures for which 0.60 or higher is acceptable.

Aside from consistency, several other types of reliability correspond to methods for establishing reliability. **Intercoder reliability** reflects the extent to which two or more people make the same measurement judgments as they classify observations into categories. Cohen's Kappa is a statistic that reflects intercoder reliability and the same acceptability scores apply: 0.80 or higher is excellent, 0.60 or higher acceptable only for exploratory purposes. **Split-half reliability** is a test of whether one half of a test or survey correlates to the other half of a test or survey. **Test-retest reliability** is determined by a test or survey taken by the same person twice to see whether scores are consistent over time. The reliability of a statistic is demonstrated by the **confidence interval**, which is the range of scores we expect a statistic to be between in case it wavers due to error.

Feasibility

Feasibility is the extent to which measures can be attained in a practical manner. The concept implies many things. First, feasibility implies that the act of gathering metric data is not overly expensive or time consuming. Second, feasibility implies that data can be gathered in a manner that is ethical. Third, feasibility implies that data can be gathered quickly enough that they actually can be used before a task is done again. Fourth, feasibility implies that enough data actually can be obtained to reflect the population you wish to describe.

Response rate bias occurs when only a portion of those given a measure in fact complete the measure. In a sense, the response rate bias is a testimony that scores on a metric cannot be obtained feasibly.

Another issue related to the feasibility of measures is the medium that is used to gather data. One study directly assessed the differences in findings between phone, e-mail, and mail surveys. Few differences were found except that the e-mail surveys appeared to have slightly better predictive validity (Coderre, Matthieu, & St. Laurent, 2004). It might seem that computerized metrics always would be the best option, but this is not necessarily the case. If you set aside meeting time for paper surveys or questionnaires, you have a captive audience and possibly a higher return rate.

What is the relevance for business metrics? Metrics that are not feasible should be selected against in the first place. For example, open-ended questions may be rich with data but they require a great investment in time for analysis. Is it worth it?

How do we establish that a measure is feasible? Do everything you can to make the data as easy to gather as possible, using automation unless it hurts the return rate. Also, the hassle of gathering metrics underscores the need to identify people who are responsible for gathering and reporting data.

Acceptable response rates vary widely from context to context. In corporate contexts in which a truly random sample has been attained, you might insist on more than 90%. In studies of divorce, you might accept 20%.

Logic

Sometimes, you just have to ask "Is this measure just plain stupid?" Aside from standard issues, such as reliability or validity, issues that fall under the heading of sheer logic include ethics, the balance of metrics, and appropriate applications of metrics.

Ethics

There are many ethical considerations. Does the metric involve sharing of data that should be kept confidential? Is it against the law to formulate a metric a certain way? Does this metric cause pain (aside from basic ego bruising for poor results)?

Balance

Deciding how to balance metrics is a key decision when creating a scorecard at any level. Chapter 8 presents organizational models that force a balance (e.g., the Balanced Scorecard, the stakeholder model, and the combined approach). Some of the decisions considered previously in this book include the balance between (a) long- and short-term metrics, (b) behavior and outcome metrics, and (c) metrics that reflect the past, present, and future.

Application

Two basic concerns are associated with applicability: can you use the same metric across settings and can metrics be "rolled up?" It may seem that metrics such as "costs" fit across different departments, divisions, or any unit of analysis. However, scorecards are meant to reflect strategy. If one unit has a different strategy than another unit, then they need different scorecards.

A related issue is the concept of an aggregate or "roll-up" measure. A **"roll-up" measure** is a measure at a higher level of analysis that is arrived at by adding all the individual elements within that level of analysis onto the same measure. To illustrate, if we wanted to measure revenue per employee, each manager could report this statistic to the department head, each department head could add up the number from all managers, and the vice president could add up this number from each department head. The vice president's result would be the same as if he or she simply added the revenue per employee for each individual employee. The problem is that elements can be rolled up only if the units of analysis are identical in size. For example, one dollar is the same as another dollar and costs can be rolled up. However, number of engineering releases across different teams cannot (typically) be simply counted and added up across teams because each release varies in size.

What is the relevance for business metrics? Ethical issues should be considered for all metrics. The question of balance is particularly important for scorecards (hence, the idea of BSC models). Issues to do with applicability are a concern only if you wish to use your scorecard across various settings.

How do we establish that metrics are logical? As with the judgment of face validity, there is no mathematical answer to this question. The judgment that a metric is "logical" requires active scrutiny and common sense.

Actionable

An **actionable** metric is one in which people can do something to influence results. The opposite is a metric where people are powerless to influence outcomes on their metric score. For example, you don't want to create a metric on work output for one team when the output is completely depending on inputs from another team.

What is the relevance for business metrics? Every metric must be actionable.

How do we establish this measurement criterion has been met? Common sense and knowledge of the organizational context.

Parsimony

A basic tenet of scientific method is **parsimony**, explaining the greatest amount with the fewest variables. The quest for parsimony is the same as the quest for simplicity.

What is the relevance for business metrics? A central issue is the number of metrics to include in a scorecard. At what point is a variable important enough to warrant a metric? If it accounts for 5% of our work? If it accounts for 10%? For teams, this book reduces the number of variables to consider by linking them to deliverables. For departments, this reduction is achieved by linking measures to team scorecards, functional measures, or process measures. Conversely, Chapter 18 presents a parsimony nightmare as it provides a basic collection of possible metrics that could be considered.

At the organizational level, experts recommend that CEOs should track 15 to 20 measures and other managers should shoot for 12 (Brown, 1996). For human memory and what teams can remember, we may recall the magic number seven plus or minus two that guides how phone numbers are grouped. A typical human brain can only process a series of five to nine concepts without difficulty.

An index can aid the quest for parsimony. It reduces the number of measures that any one human has to take in. It also gains the advantage of weighting, in which case someone considers priorities when creating the index and thereby makes it more accurate than a simple sum of measures. Unfortunately, the creation of an index involves several points where subjective judgments are made (e.g., the choice of weights and variables to include).

A number of issues influence the number of metrics to include. One issue is whether you seek to focus on *attributes* or *variability*. For example, in the performance appraisal context there are threshold competencies (essential characteristics everyone needs to be minimally effective) and differentiating competencies (factors that distinguish superior from average performers) (Spencer & Spencer, 1993). The threshold competencies correspond to focusing on attributes. The differentiating competencies focus on variability.

The variability approach is taken by the Gallup organization in their "Big 12" employee survey items. They note that they could measure the extent to which people are satisfied with their pay, but people at all organizations—high and low performing—are concerned with that variable. Instead, they focus on the variables that distinguish the high performers from the low performers (Buckingham & Coffman, 1999).

A similar but slightly different issue pertains to "hygiene" variables. Do you measure things that are taken for granted? For example, would you measure if you have clean bathrooms when it is expected they will always be that way? A related issue mentioned previously is whether you should include metrics to measure what you are already doing well.

How do we establish this measurement criterion has been met? There is no one statistic for "parsimony." A rule of thumb may be that if you have a few metrics that account for 90% of your productivity, and no one additional variable accounts for the remaining 10%, then you have done a practical job of identifying key variables. In a perfect world, we would explain 100% of variables. For some metrics, such as accounting, this would be the goal. For others, such as quality or productivity, it is mostly fantasy.

Statistical Soundness

Chapter 12 is devoted to this subject. A checklist of key questions is provided in Chapter 16. This checklist basically asks whether you have made mathematical mistakes in your choice of variables or in your computations.

Miscellaneous Metric Issues

Still more! Several miscellaneous metric issues do not fit neatly into categories discussed earlier.

What do you do about missing measurements?
Even though managers are often confronted with an overwhelming number of metric choices, it is estimated that 20% (Kaplan & Norton, 1996) to 50% (Brown, 1996) of measurements will be missing when creating balanced scorecards. Plan on needing to create methods for gathering metrics and initiating new procedures (e.g., changing computer codes, making individuals responsible for tracking metrics, and so forth). Scorecards should identify **metric owners**, people who are responsible for gathering and reporting metrics.

Another problem is when people fail to fill in scale items. For some scales, this is a very serious loss because if the scale is used in a multivariate analysis, it can render the respondent's entire survey useless. However, the question of how you fill in the blank will always be related to one issue: "Am I making an inference that is appropriate?" In other words, can I really guess what would go into the blank? One technique is to fill the blank with the average of other scores on the subscale, though others would argue that you have to leave it blank and sacrifice the data when necessary.

What if some people answer all measures with some bias—same score, high scores, and so forth?
A defense against this is to reverse items in the scale construction process.

How long does it take to see the effects of interventions?
In their study of 308 U.K. manufacturing firms, Birdi et al. (2008) found that productivity improvements from empowerment took from 1 to 4 years. For team-working, productivity improvements weren't evident for 6 to 9 years after implementation. Birdi et al. (2008) also speculated the effects of some practices (e.g., automation, just-in-time manufacturing) may be suppressed because almost all of the competition are using the same technique.

Should I include both closed- and open-ended questions?
Include open-ended items when you want to learn the "why" behind quantitative responses. Additionally, you include open-ended measures when you suspect there are important attributes that you do not yet know to measure.

What is the tradeoff between accuracy and precision?
The more accurate your measure, the less precise your measure. For example, suppose I asked you "how many almonds did you eat last week?" You might be able to estimate "0" or "about a dozen?" If I asked for the precise number, you might say "Well, let's say 20," but that number is likely to be inaccurate. In general, the more precise, the less accurate and vice versa.

Is there a priming effect?
Another source of error is the priming effect. This occurs when any information is given before other forms of subjective data collection. For example, in customer service surveys using the SERVQUAL, it has been demonstrated that the scores given on the first couple of items (e.g., a 4 on a scale of 1 to 5) will influence the top scores given on the rest of the items (Coulthard, 2004).

How does unit size pose a problem? Why can't I use "count" metrics?
If products or services are the same, you can make a metric by simply counting up "how much" work was done. For example, if you had the number of machine parts manufactured or a number of 60-minute massage sessions provided, you could make a simple count.

The problem is that you cannot just add up the number of products or services that vary in size. One solution is to make rough categories, classify, and then take counts. For example, you could categorize the parts as "noncomplex, complex" or group them into categories based on number of minutes (or seconds/hours/days) to produce and then take counts.

Another solution is to use "milestones met" to create a metric, but then you face the issue "How big are the milestones?" Imagine if you did a count of milestones met and found out that you met 10 of the 12 milestones reflected on a given Gantt chart. But what if the two that you missed were "100-hour" projects and the ones met were "10-hour" projects? If you weighted this metric by hours, you now would have a metric that would be less gamed. Is it perfect yet? You would need some kind of measure of the "accuracy" of forecasts made by the people who make the hour projections.

Are both the "scope" and "unit of analysis" clearly distinguished?

Often, these two concepts are the same. The **scope** is the population to which you will infer your numbers to represent. It may be that your scope is just the team you measured. It may be that you take this team's total to represent the performance of all teams within a given region, or industry, or whatever boundary you define. The **unit of analysis** is the number of objects you are observing when taking a given measure. For example, do we measure the output of an individual and mark a score? Or do we measure the output of an entire team and mark a score for the team's total? Steps 2 and 3 of both the team or department scorecard and scale construction process consider the scope and unit of analysis, respectively.

In general, do you consider "anecdotal reports" to be data?

Anecdotal reports, success stories, and failure stories may not be in the form of data, but they should be included in reports of performance. The anecdotes may be describing a phenomenon that was not quite measurable but was, in fact, an important change in the way the organization functioned. Often, implementations in any given system begin with a "story" of how something was shown to work "at one's own company."

Incidentally, the hardened statistician fresh out of college might be somewhat surprised to find that anecdotal data are acceptable at all. The world of academia rests on formal study and summarized findings. In business, things are simply different. As noted by Kaplan and Norton (1996), anecdotal reports can be an important source of information that is available long before variability on a metric can be detected.

Should scorecards be public?

If your scorecard is public, your strategy is public. The advantage, however, is that the more public your scorecard, the more likely your employees will know it and be influenced by it.

Do you have a double loop? Is there something in your measurement system that triggers you to update your metrics? Is there something that documents how you came up with your metrics?

Double loop refers to the "meta" of what you are doing, the task about your task. In the case of metrics, this means documenting the process for how you came up with your metrics (a warning stressed at the outset of every process section) and including a blank on your scorecard that triggers you to update your metrics.

Why would I ever use a pen-and-paper survey? Given that we are in an electronic age and given the horrendous task of data input, why would I ever use paper?
This is a question of validity. Suppose you hand out a paper survey at the end of a meeting. You now have a captive audience and nearly everyone completes the survey. If you send it electronically, you only get a fraction of the respondents. Which results are more valid? The approach that yields the greater response rate.

CHAPTER SUMMARY

This chapter described several criteria for judging metrics: validity, reliability, feasibility, logic, actionable, and parsimony. Additional issues were then considered, and all issues are summarized in a checklist at the end of Chapter 16.

REFERENCES

Birdi, K., Clegg, C., Patterson, M., Robinson, A., Stride, C. B., Wall, T. D., et al. (2008). The impact of human resource and operational management practices on company practices on productivity: A longitudinal review. *Personnel Psychology, 61,* 467–501.

Brown, M. G. (1996). *Keeping score: Using the right metrics to drive world-class performance.* New York: Productivity Press.

Buckingham, M., & Coffman, C. (1999). *First break all the rules.* New York: Simon & Schuster.

Coderre, F., Mathieu, A., & St. Laurent, N. (2004). Comparison of the quality of qualitative data obtained through telephone, postal and e-mail surveys. *International Journal of Market Research, 46,* 347–358.

Cohen, J. (1977). *Statistical power analysis for the behavioral sciences* (Rev. ed.). New York: Academic.

Coulthard, L. J. M. (2004). Measuring service quality: A review and critique of research using SERVQUAL. *International Journal of Market Research, 46,* 479–497.

Cronbach, L. J., & Meehl, P. E. (1955). Construct validity in psychological tests. *Psychological Bulletin, 52,* 281–302.

Kaplan, R. S., & Norton, D. P. (1996). *The balanced scorecard: Translating strategy into action.* Boston, MA: Harvard Business School Press.

Kerlinger, F. N. (1979). *Behavioral research: A conceptual approach.* New York: Holt, Rinehart, & Winston.

Nunnally, J. C. (1978). *Psychometric theory.* New York: McGraw-Hill.

Parasuraman, A., Zeithaml, V., & Berry, L. L. (1991). Refinement and reassessment of the SERVQUAL scale. *Journal of Retailing, 67,* 420–450.

Smith, P. C., Kendall, L. M., & Hulin, C. L. (1969). *The measurement of satisfaction in work and retirement.* Chicago, IL: Rand McNally.

Spencer, L. M., & Spencer, S. M. (1993). *Competence at work: Models for superior performance.* New York: Wiley.

12 STATISTICS PRIMER

Creating a metric system can present a minefield of decisions. Decision: Choose a unit of analysis. Decision: Define your terms. Decision: Select your scope. Decision: Choose your measure. Decision: Choose your measurement unit. Even if you make the right decisions, it can all blow up from one crucial misstep: the wrong statistic for combining scores.

This book arms you with checklists and process steps to shield you from making key mistakes when creating metrics. Along these lines, this chapter culminates in a checklist of statistics issues that are summarized in Chapter 16.

Perhaps you have never studied statistics. In that case, this chapter will give you a basic foundation. Perhaps you are a manager or business major who took a required quantitative method class, tried to erase the class from your memory, and are now confronted with the sorry news that creating metrics requires you to remember it all. For you, this chapter will serve as a review.

CHAPTER OVERVIEW

The topics in this chapter shift between basic foundations of knowledge that are needed to understand statistical arguments and the rhetorical claims that are made to justify statistical inferences. Thus, this chapter takes the form of a primer that unfolds as follows:

- Conceptualization
- Statistical Inference (claim that Type One Error is not committed)
- Four Moments of a Distribution (claim that a sample is normal)
- Levels of Measurement
- Types of Statistics
- Power Analysis (claim that Type II Error is not committed)
- Sampling Methods (claim that a sample is representative)

LEARNING OBJECTIVES

After reading this chapter, you should be able to achieve the following:

1. Explain how *statistics* are a form of *rhetoric* that provides a language of scientific argument.
2. Differentiate the terms *sample, population,* and *census.*
3. Differentiate *statistics, parameters, inferential statistics,* and *descriptive statistics.*
4. Understand the relationship between a *research hypothesis, null hypothesis, Type One Error,* and *Type Two Error.*
5. Describe a *frequency, mean, deviation, sum of squares, variance,* and *standard deviation.*
6. Know how the *four moments of a distribution* can be used as criteria to argue that a given sample is normal.
7. Describe the four levels of measurement: *nominal, ordinal, interval,* and *ratio.*
8. Identify different types of statistics according to whether they are a measure of *difference* or *association* between populations.
9. Calculate power analysis in a way that tells you the number of subjects or objects you need when gathering data.
10. Understand the four ingredients of any given power analysis equation: *effect size, alpha criterion, beta criterion,* and *sample size.*
11. Know methods of sampling that can be used to argue that a sample is *representative.*
12. Understand the four ingredients of any given power analysis equation: *effect size, alpha criterion, beta criterion,* and *sample size.*
13. Know the difference between various types of associations: *correlation, causal, mediator,* and *moderator.*

The chapter concludes with a discussion about statistical associations that have relevance for business metrics. A checklist of statistical issues is provided in Chapter 16.

Conceptualization

Consider the terms in Figure 12.1. How are they related?

A **statistic** is a number used to reflect a summary of numerical data (Kerlinger, 1979). A **datum** (plural: data) is a numerical or verbal description of an observation that has been recorded. For example, the numbers 6, 4, 5 are data that reflect numbers of defects in three batches of parts. We can summarize that data into a single statistic. If the statistic we choose is the "average," then the summary is 5.

Statistic	Parameter	Descriptive	Population	Alpha
	Data	Sample	Census	
	Type One Error		Type Two Error	
	N	n	Meta-Analysis	

Figure 12.1. Concepts from Statistics
Source: © Ruth A. Huwe.

A **descriptive statistic** is a number that summarizes an attribute of a given sample. In the previous paragraph, the descriptive statistic is the average and it summarizes the attribute of "defects." When a statistic describing a sample is then projected to represent a larger population, we often continue to call it a "statistic," but the proper term is "parameter." A **parameter** is a statistic used to describe attributes of a larger population. For example, if we used that average of 5 defects to represent the number of defects per process in the entire plant (including those we have not measured), then the number 5 becomes a parameter.

What rhetoric do we use to persuade you that numbers can be extrapolated from a small sample to a larger population? We begin our argument with the claim that a **sample** is a group of objects that we observe and those objects are a subset of the larger population. A **population** is larger group of objects to which we will make inferences. The symbol n is used to represent the number of observations in a sample and N is used to represent the number of observations across an entire study. The objects might be people, things, or whatever we define as our unit of analysis. For example, we may conduct stress tests on a sample of parts that reflect the larger population of parts, rather than conduct stress tests on every member of the population of parts.

Statistical inferences are predictions about larger populations based on samples. **Inferential statistics** are numbers that reflect a summary of data that we expect to represent attributes of a population of objects. Note than in inferential statistics, however, the data are based on observations of a sample. We do not have to make an inference when there is no difference between the sample and the population; in these cases, we have a census. A **census** is a body of data that reflects observations made on every object in the population.

An important part of the rhetoric that gets people to agree with our statistical inferences involves predicting the error of our answers. **Error** is the extent to which we expect our statistical inferences to be incorrect. Two types of error are associated with the two types of hypotheses. **Type One Error** is proclaiming an association between variables when none exists. It is the mistake of *accepting* a research hypothesis when you should not. It is also referred to as an "alpha error" because of the statistic that is used to reflect this type of error. **Alpha** is a preset criterion that you arbitrarily decide before crunching data to reflect how much of a chance you are willing to take that you make Type One Error. For example, you decide on an alpha of $p < .01$, roughly meaning the chance that your result is a mistake is less than 1 in 100. The convention in social sciences (including the science of organizational behavior that is used to guide metrics for work teams) is alpha = .05. We express the chance of error as follows: $p < .05$.

A **Type Two Error** occurs when you overlook an association, proclaiming no relationship existed between two variables when in fact you missed an association. In other words, a phenomenon *does* exist but you were unable to capture it because, basically, you did not have the power to look hard enough. It is not unlike being unable to see a spec of lint because the power of the lens on your glasses was too weak. For another example, you may not be able to detect a phenomenon if you ask only 5 people, but you might detect it if you have the resources to ask 50 people. Type Two Error is associated with *rejecting* a research hypothesis when you should not have rejected it. Type Two Error is also referred to as "beta error" because beta is a statistic that is used to reflect the chance that you have made this error. The standard in social sciences is for beta = 0.20 or lower, corresponding to power of 0.80 or higher (Beta = 1 − Power). This could be written beta = 0.20, but power analysis is rarely reported. Cohen (1992) argues that power of 0.80 is a reasonable criterion to set it as corresponds to ratio of 0.20 beta error to 05 alpha error, making it a 4:1 chance to you commit Type Two Error rather than Type One Error.

Sometimes, you will have to declare a conclusion to a hypothesis but also proclaim that you are suspicious that you made a statistical error. It is much more serious to make a Type One Error rather than a Type Two Error. Hence, if you must "err" one way or another,[1] choose a Type Two Error.

As you might suspect, the chances of making an error are decreased if we have a larger sample size. Some studies attempt to get the biggest sample possible by conducting a meta-analysis (see Chapter 1).

Statistical Inference: The Mental Leap from Samples to Populations

Imagine that you are walking around a lake and see a tiny little bird fluffing in a nearby mud puddle, a cute little thing still with some of its fuzzy underhair. You might think, "My gosh that's a small little thing. Look at its little gullet. I bet it only weighs about 2 ounces."

Now suppose that someone started to weigh all of these birds around the lake. Would you expect that they'd all weigh the exact same weight? Of course not. Let's say the first one weighs 2.1 ounces. You continue this process with more and more birds. One weighs 2.3 ounces. Another scrawny one weighs 1.8 ounces.

Now, given just what you know so far about these little birds, what do you suppose are the chances that one will weigh 0.5 of an ounce? Or weigh 5 ounces?

Table 12.1. Example Frequencies

Employee Name	Score
Jane Doe	7
Nancy Plum	8
John Jones	7
Samuel Hamilton	8
Adam Trask	6
Dagney Taggart	9
Howard Roark	9
Leopold Bloom	8
Jebediah Smith	10
Dinah Dilal	8

Our frequencies would look like this:

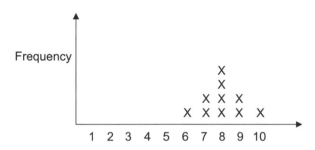

Source: © Ruth A. Huwe.

We don't expect to find any of these birds weighing in at 2 pounds.

Now let us switch from birds to other objects we may wish to study, in this case, humans. We might expect grown people to weigh 80 or 400 pounds, but not 8 or 8,000 pounds. And we know there are some average numbers and that the people around 80 pounds are fewer than, say, those who weigh 150, just as those who weigh 400 are fewer than those who weigh 150. The world works in a normal distribution, with most phenomena falling at middle-range numbers, and the rest fanning out into lower and lower frequencies of occurrence.

Decades ago, statisticians calculated the chances that numbers would fan out in certain patterns. These computations provide the basic knowledge about the world that allows us to make the wide variety of inferences that make up probability theory: the normal distribution. To describe this distribution, we begin with a central concept, *frequencies,* and proceed with an extended example.

A **frequency** is the number of observations recorded for a given score. Imagine that we have a worker satisfaction rating system in which we were given scores on a scale of 1 to 10 (see Table 12.1).

But our next task is to extrapolate from our sample to what we might think our distribution would look like in a population that is out in the world. In the 1920s, Sir Ronald Aylmer Fisher redirected the focus of statistics to the task of describing the nature of populations. In that period, he calculated the statistics tables that now are the foundations of computer statistics programs and reference sections of statistics textbooks. With his calculations, we can make the following intellectual leap: that the proportions of a "normal" population will be as shown in Figure 12.2.

But what does the "1.00" or "1.96" mean? Those are hypothetical units we call **standard deviations,** standardized units of numerical deviation from a mean. Standard deviations reflect how most numbers are near average (or near the mean) and extreme cases are fewer in number. If we were describing a sample, the symbol we can use for standard deviation is *s* or SD (we will go with the latter symbol since it is clearer). If we wish to describe the standard deviation of a larger population, we use the symbol σ.

Obviously, what counts as "1.00" or a standard deviation unit will be different for different samples. Of the birds at the outset of this section, the average weight might be 2 ounces, but we expect that 68% might be between 0.2 ounces above and below the mean (one SD = 0.2 ounces). Of the humans, the average might be 150, but we expect that 68% might fall between 40 pounds above and 40 pounds below (one SD = 40 pounds).

So far, we have considered several concepts, including individual scores, frequencies, means, variance, and standard deviation. The following is a summary of statistic symbols you can expect to see in metrics:

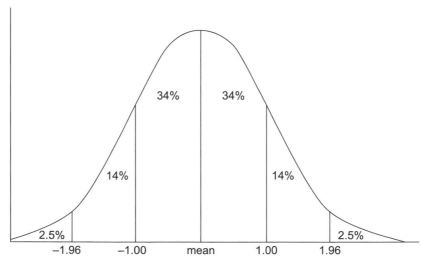

Figure 12.2. Example of a Normal Distribution

n = number of objects in a sample

N = number of objects in a population

SD = standard deviation of a sample

σ = standard deviation of a population

x̄ = mean

μ = mean of a population

s^2 = variance

SS = Sum of Squares

s = standard error (a sampling statistic that is the square root of SD)

x_i = an individual score (reflecting an observation)

All of Fisher's inferences rest on one fundamental assumption: you can only use a sample to make inferences if the sample has a *normal* distribution. The language of statistics provides us with an argument to establish that a given sample is normal, an argument that involves a consideration of the four moments of a distribution.

Four Moments of a Distribution

The four moments of the distribution are ways to categorize statistics that describe samples: central tendency, dispersion, skewness, and kurtosis. Each "moment" refers to the level of exponent associated with each formula in the category as shown below.

Moment One:

$$\textbf{Mean} = \sum_{i=1}^{n} \frac{Xi}{n}$$

Moment Two:

$$\textbf{SD} = \sqrt{\frac{\sum_{i=1}^{n}(X - \bar{X})^2}{n-1}} \quad S^2 = \frac{\sum_{i=1}^{n}(X_i - \bar{X})^2}{n-1}$$

Moment Three:

$$\textbf{Skewness} = \frac{\sum_{i=1}^{n}\left[(Xi - \bar{X})/SD\bar{X}\right]^3}{n-1}$$

Moment Four:

$$\textbf{Kurtosis} = \frac{\sum_{i=1}^{n}\left[(Xi - \bar{X})/SD\right]^4}{n-1} - 3$$

If each of the four moments meets a certain criterion, a claim can be made that a distribution (sample or population) is "normal" and the knowledge shown in Fisher's statistics tables can be used to make predictions.

First Moment: Central Tendency

Central tendency is the extent to which scores of a distribution are gathered about the middle. Three statistics reflect central tendency: the mean, median, and mode. The **mean** is the average. The **median** is the frequency midpoint of the distribution, the point at which half the scores fall higher and half the scores fall lower. The **mode** is the most frequent score.

A **criterion for normality** is the language that science gives us to argue that a given sample is normal. *A criterion for normality* at the first moment is that the mean, median, and mode must be roughly equal.

All things considered, you typically would use the mean to describe the center of a distribution. If the mean, mode, and median are not equal, then you must choose the most appropriate statistic. One consideration is whether the average is "pulled" by **outliers**, scores that are unusually higher or lower than the mean. A real-world example is when you try to describe the "average" net worth of people in Washington State. At one point during the peak of the dot-com craze, this figure was around $300,000. Can you imagine? Turns out, the numbers were pulled to the high-end by Microsoft millionaires. Also noteworthy: Bill Gates would be in that data set. In this case, it would be more appropriate to go with the median.

For an example in which the mode is the statistic of choice, suppose you conducted a study in which you wanted to know the "average" or "central" number of sexual partners that people prefer over their lifetime. The average might be several, but most likely the mode will represent the most typical case: 1 (McBurney, Zapp, & Streeter, 2005).

Another technique for dealing with outliers is to "trim" the data, removing lowest 20% and highest 20%. For example, the following data set (2, 2, 2, 3, 3, 6, 6, 6, 7, 21, 41) would be changed to (2, 3, 3, 6, 6, 6, 7). The mean in the first set is 9, in the second set it is 4.71 (Erceg-Hurn & Mirosevich, 2008).

Application to Business Metrics. The practitioner has to decide which statistic does the best job of describing central tendency of the metric under consideration. A final scrutiny issue concerns how you report statistics of central tendency. Central tendency statistics should always be reported along with measures of dispersion, to which we now turn.

Second Moment: Dispersion

Dispersion is the extent to which scores are spread out across a distribution of possible scores. Two statistics can be used to describe dispersion: standard deviation and variance. In many cases, however, a simple first-level indicator, the range, will suffice. The **range** is the difference between the lowest and highest scores in a distribution.

A criterion for normality for the second moment is whether the standard deviation or variance is sufficiently large to reflect that numbers are spread across the entire range of possible numbers. If you have a scale of 1 to 7 and no one gives a score lower than a 5, you have a problem. Another point of scrutiny associated with the second moment concerns whether the variances or standard deviations for two different samples are equal. If the ratio between one sample's standard deviation and another sample's standard deviation is not "1," then you are in violation of the standard that two samples for comparison have "homogeneity of variance." It would be like comparing the scores given by one supervisor who gives everyone a 4 and another supervisor who gives a full range of scores. If there is "heterogeneity of variance," it is also a cue that one of the samples does not have a normal distribution.

What happens if your sample is not normal? Some would argue that classic parametric techniques such as a student's *t* test or Analysis of Variance (ANOVA) are "robust," meaning the techniques are resistant to Type One Errors. *Robust statistics* are resistant both to Type One and Type Two Errors. Older methods to fix the data set would be to use a logarithmic transformation or to take the square root of the data. Beyond trimming data, a modern method is to compute windsorized variance. This means reordering the data set from lowest to highest, removing the lowest and highest 20%, and replacing data at the highest end of the data set with the lowest score. For example, the data set (1, 5, 6, 7, 8, 9, 10, 12, 14, 18, 28) would be trimmed to (6, 7, 8, 9, 10, 12, 14) and then changed to (6, 6, 6, 7, 8, 9, 10, 12, 14, 14, 14). Still another method is to compute an ANOVA-type statistic as based on a ranking of data. Original scores across all data samples are converted into ranks and resulting means are treated the same as in regular ANOVA (Ecreg-Hurn & Mirosevich, 2008, provide expanded examples for each of these techniques).

Application to Business Metrics. If you are working with small teams, it is probably rare to have a true normal distribution. For example, you often will see people change productivity charts from a range of "0 to 100" to "50 to 100," because that is where the scores actually fall. On the other hand, if you look at any situation in which you are doing destructive sampling, such as doing stress tests on a sample of parts that reflect a larger population, then you should be concerned if you do not have a normal distribution, because your ultimate goal is to characterize an entire population on the basis of the few parts that you just sampled.

The problem of variation is also related to ceiling effects. For metrics, one kind of ceiling effect occurs when items are not sufficiently difficult, all subjects score high, and comparisons cannot be made.

Another common problem related to metrics and dispersion concerns performance appraisal. Walden (2003) made the point that although the majority of people are average performers, a star computer programmer can produce at a magnitude 10 times that of the average performers, and the poor performers actually can produce negative results. Alternatively, we all know supervisors who cannot imagine giving a performance appraisal score less than a 4. Yet the typical measure claims that scores disperse over a full range of 1 to 5.

Third Moment: Skewness

Skewness refers to the lopsidedness of the distribution. Figure 12.3 demonstrates examples of positive, negative, and symmetrical (no) skews.

A criterion for normality associated with the third moment is that the skewness should be between −1.00 and 1.00.

Application to Business Metrics. As alluded to earlier, skewness is a problem in performance ratings when supervisors skew ratings at high or low ends. Another key problem related to metrics and skewness is evident in customer service ratings, for which the common tendency is for negative skew (Danaher & Haddrell, 1996).

Fourth Moment: Kurtosis

Kurtosis refers to the peaked or flatness of a distribution. Figure 12.4 depicts types of kurtosis. Another possibility is a bimodal distribution for which the sample is characterized by two bubbles.

A criterion for normality is that scores fall between −1.00 and 1.00. The more positive the distribution, the more peaked the kurtosis statistic and the more flat the distribution, the more negative the kurtosis. If the kurtosis score does not fall between −1.00 and 1.00, the sample cannot be used to generalize to a larger population unless you subject it to a mathematical transformation.

Application to Business Metrics. One problem related to kurtosis occurs when supervisors are ordered to give forced distributions and only reward the "top 10%" or punish a "bottom 25%" and so forth. In fact, many times, teams really are peaked because they all are good (or average) at what they do.

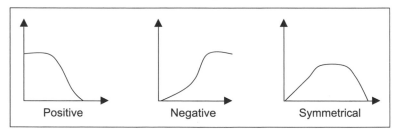

Figure 12.3. Types of Skew

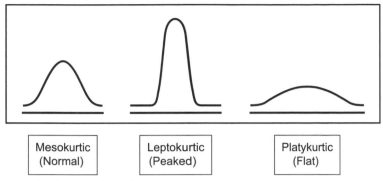

| Mesokurtic (Normal) | Leptokurtic (Peaked) | Platykurtic (Flat) |

Figure 12.4. Types of Kurtosis

Four Moments: What Do You Report?

At a minimum, when reporting results, you should include mean, standard deviation, and the shape of distributions (Levine, Weber, Park, & Hullett, 2008). When reporting scale measures, you also should report the number of items on the scale. For example, if one group had a mean of 2.8 and another group a mean of 3.5, there may be a significant difference, but you would have a different finding if it were a 7-point scale rather than a 5-point scale.

Levels of Measurement

Level of measurement is the level of precision at which we measure a variable and is based on the relationship between the attributes used to describe that variable. There are four standard levels of measurement: nominal, ordinal, interval, and ratio.

Nominal: An object's attributes can be described as being in one category or another, but no mathematical relationship exists between the categories. That is, one category is not necessarily higher or lower than another.

Ordinal: An object's attributes can be described as being in one category or another and some categories are higher or lower than others. However, the distance between the categories is not necessarily the same.

Interval: An object's attributes can be described as being in one category or another and some categories are higher or lower than others. However, the distance between categories does have meaning and is considered to be equal.

Ratio: An object's attributes can be described in categories that go higher and lower in equally appearing intervals and there is a rational zero.

Nominal and ordinal levels of measurement are referred to as "dichotomous" because they put responses into "categories." Interval and ratio levels of measurement are referred to as "continuous." The following are examples of the same phenomenon, love, being measured at different levels of measurement:

Nominal level:
Item: Do you love me?
YES/NO
Ordinal level:
Item: What is your level of love for me?
Low   High
Interval level:
Item: How much do you love me?
Very little   1   2   3   4   5   A lot
Ratio level:
Item: How much do you love me?
Number of female flicks attended in last year? _____

A visual representation of levels of measurement is provided in Table 12.2. Another example of different levels is the nerdiness scale introduced in Chapter 2.

The $64,000 Question: How Do You Choose Your Level of Measurement?

First and foremost, the level of measurement depends on the nature of the phenomenon being measured. For example, if you wanted to measure "Amount of Communication," it would make sense to go with a rational level measure (corresponding to an actual zero that exists in reality) and ask, "How many minutes did you talk?" Alternatively, you could go with a Likert scale, such as "Not Talkative 1 2 3 4 5 6 7 Talkative." It seems like the choice of the former would be obvious, except for that pesky little tradeoff made in science between accuracy and precision (see Chapter 11, "Miscellaneous Metric Issues").

A couple of judgment calls are specific to interval measures. For example, how many scale points should be used, 1 to 5? Or, 1 to 10? A rule of thumb is seven plus or minus two (Coulthard, 2004). Another approach is to align the scale with other scales used at a company (e.g., if the employee survey is a 1 to 5 scale, that is what executives will later understand).

Table 12.2. Levels of Measurement by Attribute Description

	Object's Attributes Can Be Categorized	Attributes are Higher or Lower	Intervals Between Attributes are Relatively Equal	The Object Can Be Described as Having a Rational Zero Value
Nominal	X			
Ordinal	X	X		
Interval	X	X	X	
Ratio	X	X	X	X

Source: ©Ruth A. Huwe.

One more issue for interval measures is whether you want an even or odd number of scale points. An even number of scale points forces people to give a favorable or unfavorable opinion. An odd number of scale points will allow people to give a neutral answer.

Types of Statistics

An **independent variable** is a variable that produces change in other variables; it is the causal variable. A **dependent variable** is a variable that "depends upon" another variable for its effect; it is the effect. You can select the correct statistic for solving any problem based on knowing (a) the type of statistic test (difference or association), (b) which variables are independent and dependent, and (c) levels of measurement for all variables.

Statistics That Test Differences

T-test: Dichotomous independent variable, one continuous dependent variable that is described as a mean (e.g., test whether an average score of two work groups is significantly different).

ANOVA: Dichotomous independent variable, one continuous dependent variable that is described as a mean (e.g., test whether an average score of three or more work groups is significantly different).

MANOVA: Dichotomous independent variable, multiple continuous dependent variables that is described as a mean (e.g., use several indicators of productivity and compare three or more work groups).

Statistics That Test Associations

Correlation: Two variables are continuous, and neither is designated as dependent or independent (e.g., the extent to which one customer satisfaction scale covaries with another customer satisfaction scale).

Biserial Correlation: One variable is dichotomous, and the other variable is continuous (e.g., correlate a pass-fail rate proportion to measures of test scores).

Rho: Correlation between two sets of ranks (e.g., two supervisors rank the same 20 employees and you test for intercoder reliability).

Simple Regression: One independent variable is continuous, and one dependent variable is continuous (e.g., Graduate Record Examination [GRE] scores are used to predict grade point average [GPA]).

Multiple Regression: One dependent variable is continuous, and multiple independent variables are continuous (e.g., a formula of GRE and GPA is used to predict how much money one will make).

Logit Regression: One dependent variable is continuous; some multiple independent variables are continuous and some are ordinal (e.g., marketing research that mixes scaled survey items and yes/no items).

Multiple Discriminant Analysis: Multiple independent variables are continuous, and one dependent variable is dichotomous. The independent variables are likely to be scores (e.g., several variables together such as GPA and GRE will predict whether or not one will drop out).

Log-linear Analysis: The independent and dependent variables both are categorical (e.g., whether marriage, money, and children will predict, yes or no, if one is happy or unhappy).

Canonical Correlation: Multiple independent variables are continuous, and multiple dependent variables are continuous (e.g., employee survey results where clusters of demographic intercorrelations and clusters of satisfaction intercorrelations are considered together).

Mix

Chi Square: One summed dependent variable is continuous, and one independent variable is categorical (e.g., how many customers choose one of three different models).

Formulae for several statistics are provided in Table 12.3. Computation of these techniques is beyond the scope of this chapter and, frankly, beyond most people. Typically, these calculations are point and click selections in statistics packages such as SAS, SYSTAT, or SPSS.

Power Analysis

Let us imagine that you have developed a fantastic customer service measure. It is open-ended and gathers rich information, but takes quite a long time to complete. It also takes money to process and crunch the data. In a perfect world, you would like to survey *all* of your customers and see what they think. But this is impractical, so you decide only to survey a subset of your customers. But how many is enough? This is a question for power analysis.

Power analysis tells you the probability that a statistical test of a sample will reflect the population the test is meant to reflect. The statistic used to judge a test of statistical power is beta, which ranges from 0 to 1.00. For example, suppose you expect there to be a 0.23 correlation between efficiency and skill utilization of workers. Given the way you went about gathering data to observe this correlation, your beta = 0.60 and power = 0.40. This means that there is only a 2:5 chance that you will find a correlation around 0.23 *even if the 0.23 correlation exists in reality*. Recall that Type Two Error is when you "overlook" a finding that exists in reality. Tests of power analysis are tests of Type Two Error.

Three key factors influence the power of any statistical test:[2]

- The preset alpha criterion chosen by the researcher
- The effect size, where the bigger the effect the easier to detect its existence
- Reliability

Table 12.3. ES Indexes and Their Values for Small, Medium, and Large Effects

Test	ES Index	Effect Size		
		Small	Medium	Large
1. m_A vs. m_B for independent means	$d = \dfrac{mA - mB}{\sigma}$	0.20	0.50	0.80
2. Significance of product-moment r	r	0.10	0.30	0.50
3. r_A vs. r_B for independent rs	$q = z_A - z_B$ where $z =$ Fisher's z	0.10	0.30	0.50
4. $P = 0.5$ and the sign test	$g = P - .50$	0.05	0.15	0.25
5. P_A vs. P_B for independent proportions	$h = \varnothing_A - \varnothing_B$ where $\varnothing =$ arcsine transformation	0.20	0.50	0.80
6. Chi-square for goodness of fit and contingency	$w = \sqrt{\displaystyle\sum_{i=1}^{k} \dfrac{(P1i - P0i)2}{P0i}}$	0.10	0.30	0.50
7. One-way analysis of variance	$f = \dfrac{\sigma m}{\sigma}$	0.10	0.25	0.40
8. Multiple and multiple partial correlation	$f^2 = \dfrac{R^2}{1 - R^2}$	0.02	0.15	0.35

Source: Cohen, J. (1992). A power primer. *Psychological Bulletin, 112,* p. 157. Reprinted with permission by the American Psychological Association.
Note: ES = population effect size.

Table 12.4. N for Small, Medium, and Large ES at Power = 0.80 for Alpha = 0.01, 0.05, and 0.10

Test	0.01			0.05			0.10		
	Sm	Med	Lg	Sm	Med	Lg	Sm	Med	Lg
1. Mean dif	586	95	38	393	64	26	310	50	20
2. Sig r	1,163	125	41	783	85	28	617	68	22
3. r dif	2,339	263	96	1,573	177	66	1,240	140	52
4. $P = .5$	1,165	127	44	783	85	30	616	67	23
5. P dif	584	93	36	392	63	25	309	49	19
6. x^2									
1df	1,168	130	38	785	87	26	618	69	25
2df	1,388	154	56	964	107	39	771	86	31
3df	1,546	172	62	1,090	121	44	880	98	35
4df	1,675	186	67	1,194	133	48	968	108	39
5df	1,787	199	71	1,293	143	51	1,045	116	42
6df	1,887	210	75	1,362	151	54	1,113	124	45
7. ANOVA									
2g^a	586	95	38	393	64	26	310	50	20
3g^a	464	76	30	322	52	21	258	41	17
4g^a	388	63	25	274	45	18	221	36	15
5g^a	336	55	22	240	39	16	193	32	13
6g^a	299	49	20	215	35	14	174	28	12
7g^a	271	44	18	195	32	13	159	26	11
8. Mult R									
2k^b	698	97	45	481	67	30			
3k^b	780	108	50	547	76	34			
4k^b	841	118	55	599	84	38			
5k^b	901	126	59	645	91	42			
6k^b	953	134	63	686	97	45			
7k^b	998	141	66	726	102	48			
8k^b	1,039	147	69	757	107	50			

Source: Cohen, J. (1992). A power primer. *Psychological Bulletin, 112,* p. 158 Reprinted with permission by the American Psychological Association.
Note: ES = population effect size, Sm = small, Med = medium, Lg = large, diff = difference, ANOVA = analysis of variance. Tests numbered as in Table 12.1.
a. Number of groups.
b. Number of independent variables.

The reliability of a test will be demonstrated by sample size. Hence, any computation of power comes down to knowing four variables that are interlocked—thus, if you know scores of three, the other score is given:

alpha criterion   effect size   sample size   power (beta)

The following tables enable us to calculate the effect size for any given statistical test of our choosing when beta = 0.80 (a common level to accept). Table 12.3 gives the estimated effect sizes for various statistics and we can compare those to our metric. For example, suppose we wanted to see if employees really approve of a new company policy. We suspect they will strongly favor it because 80% approved in the past and only 20% disapproved.

Effect sizes are generally labeled with rules of thumb. For example, Cohen (1992) labeled small ($r = 0.10$), medium ($r = 0.30$) and large ($r = 0.50$). As pointed out by Levine et al. (2008), this can vary by literature. They note that where average effect sizes in sex differences can be $r = 0.12$, average effect sizes in studies of identical twins might be more like $r = 0.80$. A 0.30 correlation may be weak in one discipline and strong in another.

Basically, the table arms us with the ability to answer two of the most common questions related to power analysis:

1. How large of a sample do we need to detect this difference?
2. Did we have enough power to detect a difference in opinion?

The first question is done at the point at which you design a study or metric. If 80% of the employees approved the policy (and 20% disapprove), we want accuracy with an alpha level of 0.05 and power = 0.80, then the second table tells us that we would need to sample only 30 employees to detect this difference. How so? Table 12.3 tells us that for a proportion equation (Formula 4 in Tables 12.3 and 12.4 because the percentages come from one single population) we should calculate P - .50 for effect size. Table 12.3 then tells us that anything over 0.25 is a big difference that reflects a strong effect. We find 30 on Table 12.4 under a large effect for .05. If we had suspected a small effect such as 48% to 52% disapproval, we would need 783 subjects to detect a significant difference ($p < 0.05$) with sufficient power (beta = 0.80).

A key point: Notice that we were armed with three of the four power variables when we referred to Tables 12.3 and 12.4. The tables provided the score on the fourth variable. It is not unlike a recipe.

The second power question is assessed once you have gathered data. Suppose you found a .30 difference, a large effect for a proportion equation (Formula 4 in Tables 12.3 and 12.4). Suppose you preset your alpha criterion at 0.01 rather than 0.05, and had sampled 30 subjects. You now want to find the power of your test. The second table would say that you needed to ask 44 employees. You would have to survey 14 more employees or would have to admit that you do not have the power to detect results.

Many people find the next statement rather amazing. In the previous example in which the power table told you that you needed to sample only 44 employees, those 44 employees could represent a population of 500 or 5,000. How can that be? The catch is that the data used to represent a larger population actually reflect that larger population, and the only way to establish that is to use methods that involve random sampling. It is possibly harder to sample 5,000 rather than 500.

Sampling Methods

Representativeness is the scientific criterion that a sample actually reflects a larger population. An accepted practice to establish representativeness is to demonstrate that a sample is random. A **random sample** is one in which every member of the population could potentially be chosen. It is tougher to randomly sample from a population of 5,000 than 500, but if your power analysis told you that you needed only, say, n = 44, then a sample of 44 could reflect the entire 5,000.

In business, you could figure out how to program your computer to generate a random list. Another way to increase power is to expand the confidence interval to accept a wider margin of error.

There are many approaches to sampling. A *convenience, haphazard,* or *fortuitous* sample is based on whatever happens to be an easy data source (e.g., college sophomores, bored employees, etc.). *Expert choice* is when experts pick "typical" or "representative" specimens. *Quota sampling* is when efforts are taken to make subgroups within a sample reflect subgroups in the population, such as having a sample with the same proportion of males and females as that found in the population about which you will be making inferences. Finally, *sampling of mobile populations* involves "capture-tag-recapture" methods such as those used in wildlife studies (Kish, 1965). Convenience, expert choice, quota sampling, and sampling of mobile populations are different *types* of sampling, but they are not necessarily methods of random sampling.

Common Questions

For business metrics, there are two points at which questions of power analysis are generally raised. First, people want to know how many people are needed for a given survey. Second, people want to know how many parts need to be tested to reflect defects in a larger population.

Survey Question. It is common for companies to conduct employee surveys on a scale of 1 to 5 such as follows:

1	2	3	4	5
Poor	Below Average	Average	Good	Excellent

The frequencies of scores in the two higher "favorable" categories are then reported. How do we process this? One way is to compare our numbers to benchmark companies. We might ask a question such as "Is having 67% of the score fall on 4 or 5 significantly worse than the benchmark company having 70% of their scores fall on 4 or 5?" In this case, we would use Statistic 5 on Cohen's list (see Table 12.4).

The sample size issue also haunts us. What if we just want a description of the opinions within our own company, and we do not want to go to the expense of surveying every single employee? How many is enough? We use the four power analysis ingredients described earlier and compare our results to Tables 12.3 and 12.4.

Defect Question. Another question arises when we test batches of an object that must be destroyed. For example, if we find 6 defects per 1,000 parts in a tested sample, how could we extrapolate that to mean there are 6 defects per 1,000 parts in a product batch of 1,000,000? In this case, the confidence interval would reflect our power. The wider the confidence interval, the greater our chance of making a mistake. For example, if we say that 68% of our parts will have between 4 and 8 defects, we also might say that 95% will have been 2 and 10 defects. This demonstrates the tradeoff between accuracy and precision, as well as the loss of accuracy when we increase our power to describe objects.

Associations: Correlation, Causality, Moderating, and Mediating

In this section, four concepts that describe associations are presented because of their particular relevance for business statistics: *correlation*, *causality*, *moderating*, and *mediating*.

Correlation

A **correlation** reflects the *extent* to which numbers reflecting two different variables "vary together." The symbol for a correlation is r and r can range from -1.00 to $+1.00$. A negative correlation means that as one number goes up, the other goes down and vice versa. A positive correlation means that numbers "vary together," both go up or both go down.

Causality

One issue related to correlation is that people confuse a "correlation" between two variables to mean that one variable "causes" the other. In fact, to be able to claim **causality**, three conditions must be in place:

- Correlation
- Time order, one variable comes before the other
- Lack of "spurious" or alternate causes

For a business example of spurious correlation, consider the finding that companies who have a higher proportion of female executives have a higher return on investment. Is this because women cause profits? Or would this be because the kind of company that is progressive enough to have more women is also the type of "better" company that would have higher profits?

Moderating

A **moderator variable** is a third variable that comes between two other variables to "moderate" or alter the way two variables are associated. A moderator can be a categorical variable (e.g., sex, gender, race, class) or continuous variable (e.g., level of information). A moderator can affect the direction or strength of association.

We can test your understanding with a common example. The contingency table in Table 12.5 demonstrates results from a typical goal-setting study. First, consider what is reported inside the cell. What kind of number? Second, if feedback and goal setting have an interaction effect, which cell do we expect to have the highest score?

What goes into the cell is your dependent variable, most typically "task performance." If an interaction effect were present, we would expect the highest score to occur in Cell 3. If feedback had a main effect, we would expect that average of Cells 1, 2, and 3 to be significantly higher than the average of Cells 4, 5, and 6. If we expect goal setting to have a main effect, we would expect the average of Cells 3 and 6 to be significantly greater than the average of Cells 2 and 5.

Mediating

A **mediator variable** is a third variable that comes between two other variables and must be present for the independent variable to have an effect on the dependent variable. An example of a mediator is "perceived injustice." A supervisor may be unfair, but the employee's satisfaction will not be affected unless the supervisor is perceived as unfair.

In the language of causality, a mediator is similar to being **necessary**, "a condition that *must* [sic] be present for the effect to follow" (Babbie, 2007, p. 93).

Table 12.5. Contingency Table with Goal-Setting Examples

	No Goals	"Do Your Best" Goal	Specific Goal
Feedback	(Cell 1)	(Cell 2)	(Cell 3)
No Feedback	(Cell 4)	(Cell 5)	(Cell 6)

Source: ©Ruth A. Huwe.

Table 12.6. Example of Mediator Effects

	Linker	Nonlinker	Average
Informative feedback	0% productivity increase	10% productivity increase	5%
Uninformative feedback	0% productivity increase	0% productivity increase	0%
Average	0%	5%	

Source: ©Ruth A. Huwe.

This can be contrasted to a sufficient cause. Galileo Galilei (1564–1642) can be credited with an excellent definition of **sufficient** cause as "that and no other is to be called cause, at the presence of which the effect always follows, and at whose removal the effect disappears" (qtd. in Hage & Meeker, 1988, p. 4). A mathematical depiction of a mediating effect is shown in Table 12.6.

As shown in Table 12.6, network status as a linker or nonlinker mediates the effects of informative feedback on productivity. In other words, informative feedback had an effect *only* if the subject was a nonlinker.

CHAPTER SUMMARY

This chapter began by laying a conceptual foundation, defining statistical terms, and showing how concepts are related. The chapter then provided a basic primer on key statistical issues: statistical inference and potential for Type I and Type II Error, four moments of a distribution to establish sample normality, levels of measurement, types of statistics and formulae, power analysis, sampling methods, and the distinction between mediating and moderating variables.

NOTES

1. Get it? "Err." "Error."
2. Very strictly speaking, a fourth factor that influences power is whether you choose to conduct a one- or two-tailed test of significance. Following Cohen (1977), one-tail tests are discouraged. Moreover, business practitioners rarely make these distinctions. However, if it is of particular importance to you, making a test one-tailed is simply doubling your alpha level. For example, if you did say $p < 0.05$ if there is a "difference," you now would say $p < 0.10$ that variable A will be higher (or lower) than B. However, if the reverse happens—that is, B is lower than A—then you have no power to detect a difference.

206 / *Metrics 2.0*

REFERENCES

Babbie, E. (2007). *The practice of social research* (11th ed.). Belmont, CA: Wadsworth.

Cohen, J. (1977). *Statistical power for the behavioral sciences.* New York: Academic.

Cohen, J. (1992). A power primer. *Psychological Bulletin, 112,* 155–159.

Coulthard, L. J. M. (2004). Measuring service quality: A review and critique of research using SERVQUAL. *International Journal of Market Research, 46,* 479–497.

Danaher, P. J., & Haddrell, V. (1996). A comparison of question scales used for measuring customer satisfaction. *International Journal of Service Industry Management, 7,* 4.

Ecreg-Hurn, D. M., & Mirosevich, V. M. (2008). Modern robust statistical methods. *American Psychologist, 63,* 591–601.

Hage, J., & Meeker, B. F. (1988). *Social causality.* Boston, MA: Unwin Hyman.

Kerlinger, F. N. (1979). *Behavioral research: A conceptual approach.* New York: Holt, Rinehart, & Winston.

Kish, L. (1965). *Survey sampling.* New York: Wiley.

Levine, T. R., Weber, R., Park, H. S., & Hullett, C. R. (2008). A communication researchers' guide to null hypothesis significance testing and alternatives. *Human Communication Research, 34,* 188–209.

McBurney, D. H., Zapp, D. J., & Streeter, S. A. (2005). Preference of sexual partners: Tails of distributions and tales of mating systems. *Evolution and Human Behavior, 26,* 271–278.

Walden, D. (2003). Getting the most out of technologists. *Center for Quality of Management Journal, 11*(2), 13–21.

Part Five
Using Metrics

13 ENGAGEMENT: GETTING FROM METRICS TO ACTION

OFFSITE DISEASE

(OFF-SIT DI-ZEZ)

1. The tendency for leaders and teams to create goals at offsite meetings and then forget about them as soon as they get back to work.
2. Teams that create elaborate metric scorecards and then never do anything with them.

Offsite disease. You know it when you see it. A bunch of key company players get together in some nice resort or location outside the office, trap each other in the same room for days on end, and force each other to get some planning done. Great goals are made! Great visions are articulated! Good intentions are beamed! Everyone means to go back with a new zest! And . . .

Nothing happens.

Teams creating metric systems are now entering the deepest part of the jungle: navigating to a cure for offsite disease. Accountability in the form of metrics seems to be one answer, but an even better answer is to engage employees to improve scores in ways management could never conjure on their own.

CHAPTER OVERVIEW

Variously known as "employee involvement," "empowerment," or "employee participation," the concept of "engagement" has achieved buzz term status. Originally conceptualized as the opposite of burnout, **engagement** is vigor and dedication directed toward a job (Salanova & Schaufeli, 2008) and is strongly correlated to satisfaction (Wefald & Downey, 2009). **Disengagement** occurs

---

LEARNING OBJECTIVES

After reading this chapter, you should be able to achieve the following:

1. Understand why it is important for managers to learn how to leverage employee engagement.
2. Engage employees to make the link between metrics and actions.
3. Engage employees to make the link between change initiatives and actions.
4. Generate tools to make the link between metrics and change initiatives.
5. Demonstrate to employees how actions reported on lower-level individual scorecards are lined up to objectives stated on higher-level organizational scorecards.
6. Translate a metric scorecard into a complete metric report.
7. Identify the points of action involved in getting out metric reports.
8. Understand how a scientific model can be used to guide contents of a metric report.
9. List various ways to gather metric data.
10. List comparisons that can be made to communicate metric results more effectively.
11. List various media that can be used to relay metric results.
12. Describe techniques for describing results visually.

---

when employees distance themselves and experience negative attitudes toward work (Demerouti, Bakker, Nachreiner, & Schaufeli, 2001, p. 501). **Empowerment** is defined as "passing considerable responsibility for operational management to individuals or teams (rather than keeping all decision-making at the managerial level)" (Birdi et al., 2008, p. 480). Engaging employees in metric scorecards involves both the increased energy required of engagement and the delegated decision making required of empowerment.

Research shows that empowerment at the individual level produces favorable outcomes at the organizational level. A study of 308 U.K. manufacturing firms compared the effects of three psychological interventions (empowerment, training, and teamwork) and four operational interventions (Total Quality Management [TQM], just-in-time, advanced manufacturing technology, and supply chain partnering). Only empowerment and training had main effects on productivity, with a gain of nearly 7% value added per employee from empowerment (Birdi et al., 2008). Another study introducing the Job Demands-Resources (JD-R) framework showed that where exhaustion was a function of **job demands** (sustained physical and mental strain), disengagement was a function of **job resources** (social support, job control, performance feedback) (Demerouti et al., 2001). Building on the JD-R framework, another study showed job resources did not result in proactive behavior unless employees were engaged (Salanova & Schaufeli, 2008).

Arguments for engagement can be made from other perspectives as well. First, according to a tenet of socio-technical systems (STS), if you want to know the best way to achieve an outcome, get ideas from people who actually do the job (Emery & Trist, 1965). Second, open systems are characterized by equifinality, the property that many paths can be taken to achieve the same outcome (Katz & Kahn, 1978). Employees are important sources of innovation for identifying new means to achieve results. Third, TQM calls for continuous improvement (Ahire, Landeros, & Golhar, 1995). Again, employees are intellectual resources for identifying the means for improvement. Fourth, **engagement interventions** involve employees in a variety of activities, particularly goal setting, setting up plans for achieving goals, and general group decision making. Participation in goal setting improves both self-efficacy and task strategy development (Latham, 2007). Fifth, at some point, it falls on leaders to *articulate* the organization's mission and vision. But once this "view from the top" is pieced together, a mechanism still is needed to link higher-level organizational goals to the level at which team members actually are doing the work. Engagement interventions are a means for doing so.

Long-standing data from consensus decision-making research attest to the importance of engagement and empowerment as evidenced by the superiority of collaborative decisions. A typical study demonstrates that, given the correct task, it is rare that even the highest-performing individual can make a better decision than a group (Watson, Michaelsen, & Sharp, 1991). In a study of 222 project teams who were engaged in consequential problem solving, the groups outperformed the most proficient member 97% of the time and 40% of the process gains were attributed to synergy rather than the average or most knowledgeable group member scores (Michaelsen, Watson, & Black, 1989). Other research shows that groups do not necessarily perform better than the brightest individuals, but consistently perform better than the group average (e.g., Burleson, Levine, & Sampter, 1984; Hill, 1982; Libby, Trotman, & Zimmer, 1987).

This chapter begins with three methods for engaging employees (Engagement Tools): a Metrics to Action tool and two types of initiative scorecards. The chapter next uses a linking tool to show the connection between high-level scorecards and individual-level activities. The focus then turns to methods for presenting scorecard reports.

Engagement Tools

This section describes three ways to use metrics to facilitate engagement. Each technique requires translating metric scorecards into different formats: linking metrics to action, linking metrics to initiatives, and links across scorecards.

Linking Metrics to Action

A **Metrics to Action tool** is any tool that leaves a "fill in" section for writing in the actual *actions* that are used to improve a metric. A manager can pick and choose a few key metrics from a first-level, department, or organization scorecard and plug the examples into the dimensions and metrics section. However, the choice of goal and actions to achieve the goal is left blank. The team is invited to brainstorm actions as well as give input about the goals and metrics. A generic outline is provided in Table 13.1 and an example is shown in Chapter 16 (Table 16.6).

The Metrics to Action tool is purposefully accompanied with a team agenda. This is to drive home the point that this is a participative activity. The following is an example:

Team Agenda for Presenting *Metrics to Action* Tools
1. **Describe the process for employees—who did what.**
2. **Describe the purpose of the scorecard.**
3. **Review the metrics and goals associated with each focus of measurement.**
4. **Ask the team to improve the metrics and goals (if they see fit).**
5. **Engage the team to figure out the following:**
   HOW to achieve the goals?
   WHO will do what?
   HOW will you find time and budget?
   Is this up to the individuals or should the team find a way?
   WHO will track the metrics?

It is recommended that, at a minimum, leaders take responsibility to articulate the referents (their vision and mission elements) and at least advance ideas about metrics and possibly goals. If the employees were left to think up their own

Table 13.1 Metrics to Action Tool

Team Name: _____   Date of Update: _____

Team Mission or Vision: _____

Attribute	Metric (Measure/Unit)	Goal	Short-Term Actions to Improve	Long-Term Actions to Improve
XXX	XXX			
XXX	XXX			
XXX	XXX			
Scorecard updated: ____				

Source: © Ruth A. Huwe.

metrics and goals (without any metrics training), the likely results are chaos, bickering, or gaming. Nothing stops the manager, however, from presenting a metric scorecard as "tentative" and asking the employees to correct it.

Key double-loop questions also can be added to the manager's agenda when presenting this tool:

- How did we develop these metrics?
- When will these be updated?
- How will we deliver performance data?
- What kinds of rewards will there be upon goal attainment?
- How will data on these metrics be used?

Metrics for Initiatives

Organizational survival depends on setting goals that lead organizations to make changes that enable them adapt to their environment. **Initiatives** and **change programs** are synonymous as both terms refer to initiatives undertaken to bring about a different way of doing things. An initiative could be an effort to improve ongoing performance or can signal a new facet for measurement. For example, a change program could be an innovation initiative that supports a first-to-market strategy or could be an initiative to improve productivity by 50%. The essential point is that the programs involve *change* and doing something other than business as usual. Two models for using metrics to aid initiatives are now presented.

Team by Activity Matrix A team by activity matrix is shown in Table 13.2. Managers can create 2 × 2 matrices as tools in many ways. This example happens to have three features. First, the unit of analysis down the side of the matrix is a

Table 13.2 Team by Activity Matrix

	Six Sigma	ISO 9000	Engagement	Teaming	Baldrige	TQM
Team A	1	2	3	2	4	5
Team B	1	3	2	3	3	1
Team C	5	4	3	5	4	2
Team D	1	2	5	5	4	2

Source: © Ruth A. Huwe.
Note: ISO = International Organization for Standardization; TQM = Total Quality Management.
Key:
1 = Unaware
2 = Aware
3 = Implementation has begun
4 = Fully implemented
5 = Model for others

group of teams. This could be plants, organizations, or any unit of analysis. Second, improvement activities that are common to the teams are described across the top. Third, the measures inside the matrix happen to be the extent to which the various teams have been engaged in the improvement activity.

This tool is excellent in many ways; two particularly useful features are that it not only provides a metric for progress, but also provides both a communication mechanism and recognition. As a communication tool, this matrix shows a person "who is doing well" within one's own organization and unique corporate culture. In this example, suppose you are manager of Team A and you need help on Six Sigma. Who do you call? According to Table 13.2, you would contact the manager of Team C.

Initiative Scorecards Where does vision come from? Some organizations have mechanisms for gaining input from employees, but ultimately vision is articulated during an offsite meeting that involves senior leaders. The standard approach is to accompany a vision statement with bullets. A **vision bullet** is a statement that identifies either a value associated with the vision or an intermediate goal that should be met to achieve the vision. The vision bullet may or may not trigger a change program.

The following is an example of a Microsoft vision statement about collaboration with the Philadelphia school district:

> Rooted in the vision of an empowered community where learning is continuous, relevant, and adaptive, the School of the Future will:
>
> - Create a replicable model that improves student achievement through holistic reform of secondary education
> - Apply research and development to generate educational practices, creating an environment involving all members, igniting them to take a passionate, personal responsibility for learning and inspiring a commitment to active citizenship
> - Incorporate best of class technology solutions in all appropriate aspects of the learning community including curriculum delivery, community collaboration, back-office support and content creation, dissemination and assessment. (Microsoft, n.d.)

Rather than include lines about the vision within the organizational scorecard, sometimes a company will create what will be called here a **Vision Scorecard**, that is, a separate scorecard for achievement of the vision and its bullets. For example, the Philadelphia School District's ongoing scorecard is likely to include metrics about how many students are served and how many tests are passed. The three bullets can be taken as goals to guide initiatives that need to be taken to ensure that the school can function in the future. In this case, the bullets respectively concern holistic reform, incorporating research and development into educational practices, and incorporating technology solutions. As shown in Table 13.3, translating the vision and bullets simply means plugging the bullets in as dimensions on a Metrics to Action Tool.

Table 13.3 Initiative Scorecard Based on Vision Bullets

Team Name: _____ Date of Update: _____

(Scorecard) Dimension	Metric (Measure/ Unit)	Goal	Short-Term Action	Long-Term Action
Objective: Holistic Reform				
Objective: Incorporate R&D into curriculum				
Objective: Incorporate technology solutions into curriculum				

People responsible for collecting metrics: _____
Date of scorecard update: _____
Source: ©Ruth A. Huwe.
Note: R&D = research and development.

Another approach is to decide on an initiative and then look to standard indicators used to mark achievement of the initiative with standard indicators rather than bullets. For example, suppose you had an "Innovation" initiative. You could take the exact scorecard from Table 13.3 and change the scorecard dimensions to reflect standard indicators such as "Cost Savings," "Patents," "Industry Awards," and "Break-even Time."

Linking Tools

Three types of links are associated with scorecards. First, as shown in the previous section, you can link a lower-level scorecard to an initiative. Second, using a "linking tool," you can add columns to a given scorecard to show the links between that scorecard and either overall organizational scorecard categories or to initiatives. An example linking tool is shown in Chapter 16 (see Table 16.7). Finally, you can visually see the links between different scorecards as they line up across levels of analysis. For example, Chapter 16 shows the entire cascade of how an organizational scorecard (see Table 16.5) flows into a departmental scorecard (see Table 16.4) into a team scorecard (see Table 16.3) and finally into an individual's scorecard (see Table 16.9) that can be translated into the performance appraisal.

Scorecard Reports

Although many feedback, motivation, and engagement techniques require translations of metric scorecards, an *essential* translation is the metric report that hopefully will influence performance. This section includes tips and methods for three key points of action that are associated with creating metric reports: gathering metric data, analyzing metrics, and disseminating reports.

Gathering Metric Data

Most companies have computer systems to track data, variously called "Enterprise Resource Planning System," "Management Information System," the "Human Resources Information System," or whatever other catchy acronym they have been given by the people who created a customized system for a given company. There are two key points to be made about these systems:

- Use them. Automate data gathering as much as possible.
- Define accountability. If you decide that a given metric is to be used to judge performance, be sure to identify *who* is responsible for gathering the data.

Beyond company computer systems, following are several additional sources of data (Brown, 1996):

- Web-based data
- Surveys
- Focus groups
- Automation (customized computer programs)
- Surveys
- Checklists
- Inspection
- Analysis
- Purchased from outside source
- Observation
- Lab testing
- Mystery shopping
- Counting in general
- E-mail count
- Critics (e.g., food critics)

Analyzing Metrics

Hopefully the company computer system will crunch data for you, typically giving descriptive statistics. If you are creating surveys, you will need a high-powered statistics package such as SPSS, SAS, or SYSTAT. For the most part, an Excel spreadsheet will meet most of your statistical needs. Chapter 12 provides an entire primer on statistical analyses.

Disseminating Reports

Just as statistics are a form of rhetoric, metrics are a form of feedback, a report. The dissemination of metric reports involves several key steps:

- Audience analysis
- Content selection
- Choice of media to disseminate the report

Audience Analysis Any presentation always begins with audience analysis. In this case, there are several options:

- Senior management
- Board of directors
- Public
- Employees
- Suppliers
- Partners
- Collaborators
- Customers
- Government
- Donors (for nonprofits)
- Others

Once the audience is identified, an important step is to identify any template to which the audience is accustomed. In the best case, the organization will have a consistent format. Not only is it easier to process a known format, but also consistent reports are easier to compare.

Content Selection Following the format of scientific method will help you "not forget" key pieces of information that need to be relayed. As with the outline of any given research article, the following elements should be incorporated into your report:

- Justification
- Definitions of terms (hypothesis explanation in scientific studies)
- Method
- Results
- Discussion in lay terms
- Limitations
- Future implications

Justification. The justification section of a scientific document provides the significance of a topic. In the case of metrics, this section would demonstrate the link between your scorecard and higher organizational outcomes or lower personal outcomes.

Definition of terms. Both conceptual and operational definitions of variables reflected in metrics were specified during both the scorecard and scale construction processes specified in this book. As well, all processes in this book begin with the warning that you should document your thinking as you go. This thinking should be captured in a method statement (see Method next paragraph) and available to anyone tasked with presenting metric reports. For audiences who are not "face to face," the method section can be presented as a footnote that people can access if they have questions. Sometimes, however, definitions may be so tricky that you will want to include them in the main metric report.

Method. At the point at which metrics were created (either the creation of surveys or scorecards), you are cautioned to document your process as you go. This documentation can be used to make a methodology statement that includes all the key steps such as motive, conceptualization of terms, operations that specify how things will be measured, and a demonstration that you considered potential problems. At a minimum, potential problems to scrutinize upfront include reliability of your measure, validity, feasibility, logic, actionability, parsimony, and statistical soundness.

Results. Your reports should include the names of your metric, score, variability of the score, and trends (cf. Brown, 1996).

Discussion in lay terms. Just as scientific articles include a "layman" section that describes results in a meaningful manner, your metric presentation should use at least two methods to make your results meaningful to the audience: comparisons and visual demonstrations.

Aside from goals, a variety of comparisons can be made to render metrics meaningful to any given audience:

- Historical data
- Current scores compared to future goals and action plans
- Comparisons to your competitors
- Comparisons to your industry
- Trends
- Cause-effect relationships
- Correlations to scorecard outcomes (e.g., revenue or savings)
- Correlations to competitive performance
- Correlations to help determine root causes
- Correlations to help set priorities
- Electronic versus bricks and mortar
- Market segments
- Individual average
- World class/Top quartile

- Industry rankings
- Benchmark: corporate average
- Benchmark: corporate best
- Domestic versus international
- Individual best

You should follow the scientific practice of reporting a score with variation. Also as with science, if special circumstances affect the score (e.g., the events of September 11, 2001), you would include that narrative in the report. You might make a special point of writing it onto the report as a footnote rather than just mentioning it in passing because people often miss meetings and only receive written reports.

Another important point about results is the explanation behind the processes used to gather them. A large body of research concerning organizational justice implies that employees will perceive a system as fairer when results are presented with an explanation about how the results were obtained (Colquitt, Conlon, Wesson, Porter, & Ng, 2001).

Limitations. This is the point at which the presenter brings up limitations (better you do it before it comes up in questions). One broad category of limitations is inability to gather data.

W. Edwards Deming (1994) has called for examining common causes of variation and separating special cases to understand the action to take. Along this vein, scorecard reports can be accompanied with an "explanation" section as part of the "limitations" section. For example, numbers might be skewed from some natural disaster, an event such as Hurricane Katrina.

Future implications. Future implications should address both substance of the metric reports and process. The substance of the report implies the results: the good and bad. The strengths should be discussed both in terms of recognition and opportunities that these strengths imply. The weaknesses should be approached in a problem-solving manner (rather than accusing manner) with an eye toward learning innovations that will not only fix the problem but also make the products, services, and employees better than before. The audience should know when the next report will be available so employees are inspired by a timeframe for improvement.

Choice of Media to Disseminate the Report Assuming you have developed your metric contents (metrics to action tools, initiative scorecards, links to strategy, and reports of results), you still need to consider the *manner* in which this information is disseminated. At a minimum, your choice of medium will depend on purpose and audience. The following are some options:

- Posters
- Trinkets with corporate messages
- Power Point presentations

- Breakfast meeting (or any lure with food)
- Calendars
- One-on-one meetings
- Individual mailing
- Webinars or Webcasts
- CD-ROMs
- E-mail
- Brochures or booklets
- Banners
- Town meetings
- Newsletters
- Orientation seminar
- Training
- Intranet
  ○ Log-in screen
  ○ CEO message
  ○ Frequently asked questions (FAQ)
- Agendas (within meetings)
- Interactive Web sites
- Telephone distribution lists
- Test employee knowledge (e.g., Web)
- Video transmissions
- Other

CHAPTER SUMMARY

This chapter presented three key tools for using metrics to engage employees: the Metrics to Action tool, the Team by Activity Matrix, and Initiative Scorecards. This chapter also described key action items associated with metrics: gathering metric data, analyzing metric data, and disseminating metric data. The dissemination discussion included a scientific outline for presenting metric reports that assures managers that they will not forget key contents.

REFERENCES

Ahire, S., Landeros, R., & Golhar, D. (1995). Total quality management: A literature review and an agenda for future research. *Production and Operations Management, 4*, 277–307.

Birdi, K., Clegg, C., Patterson, M., Robinson, A., Stride, C. B, Wall, T. D., et al. (2008). The impact of human resource and operational management practices on company practices on productivity: A longitudinal review. *Personnel Psychology, 61*, 467–501.

Brown, M. G. (1996). *Keeping score*. New York: Productivity Inc.

Burleson, B. R., Levine, B. J., & Sampter, W. (1984). Decision-making procedure and decision quality. *Human Communication Research, 10,* 557–574.

Colquitt, J. A., Conlon, D. E., Wesson, M. J., Porter, C., & Ng, K. Y. (2001). Justice at the millennium: A meta-analysis of 25 years of organizational justice research. *Journal of Applied Psychology, 86,* 425–445.

Demerouti, E., Bakker, A. B., Nachreiner, F., & Schaufeli, W. B. (2001). The job demands-resources model of burnout. *Journal of Applied Psychology, 86,* 499–512.

Deming, W. E. (1994). *The new economics for industry, government, education* (2nd. ed.). Cambridge, MA: Massachusetts Institute of Technology.

Emery, F. E., & Trist, E. (1965). The causal texture of organizational environments. *Human Relations, 18,* 21–32.

Hill, G. W. (1982). Group versus individual performance: Are N+1 heads better than one? *Psychological Bulletin, 91,* 517–539.

Katz, D., & Kahn, R. L. (1978). *The social psychology of organizations* (2nd ed.). New York: Wiley.

Latham, G. P. (2007). *Work motivation.* Thousand Oaks, CA: Sage.

Libby, R., Trotman, K. T., & Zimmer, I., (1987). Member variation, recognition of expertise, and group performance. *Journal of Applied Psychology, 72,* 81–87.

Michaelsen, L. K., Watson, W. E., & Black, R. H. (1989). A realistic test of individual versus group consensus decision making. *Journal of Applied Psychology, 74,* 834–839.

Microsoft. (n.d.) Building the school district of the future. Retrieved December 18, 2007, from http://download.microsoft.com/download/2/a/a/2aa67f06-08c3-478e-babf-9e9290a34f62/SOFVision.doc.

Salanova, M., & Schaufeli, W. B. (2008). A cross-national study of work engagement as a mediator between job resources and proactive behavior. *International Journal of Human Resource Management, 19,* 116–131.

Watson, W. E., Michaelsen, L. K., & Sharp, W. (1991). Member competence, group interaction, and group decision making: A longitudinal study. *Journal of Applied Psychology, 76,* 803–809.

Wefald, A. J., & Downey, R. G. (2009). Construct dimensionality of engagement and its relation with satisfaction. *Journal of Psychology, 143,* 91–111.

14 *METRICS AS FEEDBACK*

*To a team or manager implementing a metric system, the organization develop-
ment department can seem like Sirens. There they are, singing the praises of
change programs, lulling you into the false sense that the task of coming up with
metrics can be delegated away as part of some larger performance management
system.*

*It is true that metrics do feed the beast, the overall performance management
system. Hopefully, the goals of a team are easily transferred to an individual's
performance appraisal and, hopefully, ongoing metric reports do fold into annual
reports.*

*However, one element of a performance appraisal system is personal between
managers and employees and cannot be pushed off to human resources:
coaching.*

*Presenting metrics as a sole form of feedback would be like eating the right fats
only to ignore proteins and carbohydrates. Metrics are but one of many forms of
feedback and should not be used in isolation. The goal of this chapter is to present a method for incorporating metrics with other types of feedback contents.*

CHAPTER OVERVIEW

This chapter begins with definitions of key terms associated with feedback in
business contexts. A historical review of feedback research is then presented to
demonstrate how conceptual milestones still influence how feedback is provided
in the 21st century. To underscore the importance of various types of feedback

---

LEARNING OBJECTIVES

After studying this chapter, you should be able to achieve the following:

1. Describe the three types of feedback that comprise performance management systems.
2. Differentiate positive and negative feedback.
3. Differentiate affective and cognitive feedback effects.
4. Compare goal-setting theory and systems theory depictions of feedback as a "gap."
5. Distinguish the major methods of conceptualizing feedback: knowledge of results, knowledge of performance, and feedback intervention.
6. Explain how feedback became a prominent topic in the science of organizational behavior.
7. Understand the nature of feedback effects on performance.
8. Give the research-based answers to the following questions about feedback execution:
   - Should feedback be positive or negative?
   - Who should give feedback?
   - How often should you give feedback?
   - How do you make feedback consistent?
   - What do you include in feedback contents?
   - What are criteria for effective feedback?
   - How do you make feedback more informative?
   - Should feedback be given in public or private?
9. Translate academic knowledge on feedback effects into a practical technique.

---

contents, the nature of feedback effects will be quantified. A practical list of feedback principles is then given for coaches and managers, and the chapter concludes with a simple technique that pulls together lists of feedback research findings, contents, and prescriptions.

Conceptualization

The term *feedback* is used in many ways. In systems theory, feedback is conceived as information about outputs that is returned as input. In electronics, feedback might be a loud noise from putting a microphone too close to a speaker. In a communication model, feedback is conceived as a listener's ongoing response to a message. In each case, feedback has some sort of "return" or "response" element. **Feedback** is nominally defined here as task-related information given with the purpose of improving performance.

A comment on the potentially destructive nature of feedback is warranted. Consider this question, which the author has asked students on many occasions: Is there ever a case when it is okay to raise your voice when giving negative feedback? It is likely that your impulse is to say, "Never! It is unprofessional to raise your voice in any work context." But if I ask this question of masters of business administration students, generally a hand shoots up that quickly affirms, "Yes." And that person is usually from the military. More answers will trickle in.

"Well, if it is the only way to get through to the person."

"If *every other means* has been exhausted and the person is just thick."

"Imagine an emergency room where it's a matter of life and death."

"What if it is in the corporate culture to yell, like, aren't we always hearing stories about yelling at Microsoft?"

Notice that in each of these cases, the feedback is still constructive because it is getting through.

We can think of *destructive* feedback in two ways. First, it may be destructive because the way it is delivered engenders defensiveness and has no impact. Second, feedback may be destructive because it actually hurts performance. In either case, it has to do with the content or the manner in which the feedback is given.

So imagine that we go to all the trouble to get highly informative metric data and then it has no impact because we didn't know how to deliver it? The study of metric delivery is the study of feedback delivery. The goal of this chapter is to harness what is known about feedback to make our metrics as effective as possible.

Feedback and Contemporary Performance Management Systems

In the 21st century, it would be difficult to find a *Fortune* 500 company that does not have a performance management system. In general, these systems contain three types of feedback:

- Coaching
- Metrics
- Performance appraisal

The three types of feedback can be distinguished by three dimensions: formality, frequency, and level of analysis. **Coaching** is informal feedback generally given orally rather than in writing. Variously known as "atta boys" or "informal feedback," coaching is relatively ongoing as it could be daily, weekly, monthly, or quarterly, and it is focused on individuals.

Metrics are known as performance management feedback. Metrics take the form of scorecard updates, reports, trend lines, sales data, and so forth. Metrics are generally formal in that they are in writing and they are (hopefully) ongoing. Metrics are possible at the individual level of analysis, such as daily reports given to sales personnel in retail operation, but they primarily are reported at higher levels of analysis: group, department, organization, industry, national, or global.

Performance appraisals (also known as an "evaluation," "summary," and "review") summarize an individual's performance at the end of a relatively long period of time, and typically are given on an annual basis. The terms "summary" and "review" are more politically correct in that they do not have the "judgmental" connotations of the words "evaluate" or "appraise."

Performance appraisals are formal in that they are written and part of a record. Ironically, they are conducted at the individual level of analysis and then linked to compensation rewards; this is ironic because most companies claim to want their people to work as a "team" and yet their rewarded metric is at the individual level of analysis.

Performance management systems are the combination of all three types of feedback. The ideal is that performance summaries contain "No Surprises!" This assumes that the annual appraisal is a "summary" because ongoing feedback preceded it.

History of Feedback Research

The history of feedback research can be summarized by describing five conceptual milestones that influence how feedback is practiced in the 21st century. First, feedback was distinguished as positive versus negative. Second, feedback effects were distinguished in terms of being cognitive and affective. Third, conceiving of feedback as a "gap" led to explanations for how feedback effects occur. Fourth, quarrels emerged over definitions of feedback. Fifth, goal-setting theory made feedback a standard concept in every motivation textbook.

A *first milestone* was the distinction of a feedback sign being "positive" or "negative," beginning with experiments in the early 20th century that examined how "knowledge of results" (KR) affected performance (e.g., Arps, 1920; Jones, 1910). Thorndike's Law of Effect equated positive feedback to "reinforcement" and negative feedback to "punishment" (Thorndike, 1913). However, a feedback sign does not just mean "positive" or "negative" as in a dichotomous variable. In metrics, a feedback sign can be considered a continuous variable as with higher grades being "more positive," not just "positive."

A *second milestone* came with the division of cognitive (or "thinking") and affective (or "emotional") feedback effects. Ammons's (1956) influential review solidified this trend when he conceptualized feedback effects as having to do with learning and motivation. This dichotomy would stick in future research such as in Nadler's (1979) review when he described feedback in terms of its "directive function" (cognitive) and its "incentive function" (affective). Kluger, Lewinsohn, and Aiello (1994) later divided the affective domain in two dimensions: pleasantness (valence of the emotion) and arousal (strength of the emotion).

A *third milestone* in feedback research came with the conceptualization of feedback as a "gap" between an actual and desired result. According to goal-setting theory, feedback gives information about the gap between a *performance result* and a *goal*. The gap then triggers task strategy development (Locke & Latham, 1990). According to system theory, the gap of focus is between the *performance result* and a *standard*. The gap then triggers action (Ashford & Cummings, 1983; Kernan & Lord, 1990; Kluger & DeNisi, 1996). Another major motivation theory, social cognitive theory, acknowledges that people are influenced by both the foresight of goals (feedforward) and the hindsight of shortfalls (feedback). Both feedforward and feedback reflect gaps that influence self-regulation.

The systems theory explanation of the gap concept is to think of a thermometer as providing "feedback" about heat to a furnace system. The thermometer tells what the "actual" temperature is and then compares the "actual" to the "expected," the expected being the temperature set by some human. The feedback is the "gap" between actual performance and expected performance, and the feedback (or "gap") triggers the mechanism's action to reduce the gap.

Results from one study can be used to demonstrate how a systems theory explanation plays out in a feedback study (Kluger, Lewinsohn, & Aiello, 1994). These researchers used grades to represent feedback. They hypothesized that there would be a linear association between feedback sign and pleasantness, meaning that the more positive the feedback, the more pleasant it was perceived to be. They also hypothesized that there would be a curvilinear association between performance "gap" (actual grades and expected grades) and action levels. The idea is that if there is an extremely negative gap, grades far below what is expected, the gap would trigger action. A minimal gap would lead to minimal action. A large positive gap, however, would also trigger action and arousal. Why? The typical explanation is that an extremely big performance gap (performing well over what is expected) leads one to reset goals to a higher level (Latham, 2007). In this scenario, if the student receives grades much higher than expected, the student will reset goals.

Here is an example of how the high, favorable performance gap might play out in another setting. Suppose I am feeling terrible as I am hiking a 3,000-foot mountain with a heavy pack. My initial goal is to make it up the mountain, but I start coming up with feeble excuses about why I should turn around. However, I look at my watch and note that my time is well ahead of the fitness level needed to climb a 14,000+ mountain like Mt. Rainier. I'm doing well! Really well! Suddenly I'm motivated. And I decide to do what? Not only finish the climb, but try to beat the time that it would take to make it up Mt. Rainier (a much harder goal considering that the initial goal was simply to make it up the mountain). Am I motivated because of some strategy I was given on how to make it up the hill? Nah. It's sheer emotion, the thrill of the possibility of achievement. The effect is affective.

Coincidentally, could negative feedback or task strategy information have worked in the climbing example? Suppose someone said, "Look, you're going really slow. [Negative feedback.] It's obvious that you're straining your muscles. Why don't you do the limp step?" The person then demonstrates the limp step, a technique that dramatically saves muscle strength. [Task-strategy information.] Would the negative feedback about the limp step have an impact on performance? Indeed, but in this case, I would argue that the effect is mostly cognitive.

This example plays out over and over in our lives, particularly in situations in which high performance is unexpected. For example, what happens when we weigh ourselves and we lose more weight than expected? We now try to be *really* good. What happens when children learn they are doing much better than anticipated in a class? Now they *really* try. But the reverse is also true. What happens when the employee learns he is "just average." He plods along. What happens when he finds out he is failing miserably? He shapes up!

Debates about the role of cognition and affect, or "logic and emotion," go back to the ancient times of Aristotle in his distinctions between *logos* and *pathos* (Cooper, 1932) and to the contemporary moans of the person in love with someone who is "all wrong for me logically." The ongoing debate of feedback effects on affect versus cognition is beyond the point of this book except the essential point: feedback affects both cognition and emotion. Feedback can take the form of KR (metrics) as well as many kinds of information about task performance.

A *fourth milestone* in feedback research stems from the definition of feedback. In an early review, Ammons (1956) regarded feedback as "knowledge of performance" (KP). Locke and Latham (1990) argue that feedback is just KR. In their famous statement, they said "Few concepts in psychology have been written about more uncritically and incorrectly than that of feedback . . . Actually, feedback is only information, that is, data, and as such has no necessary consequences at all" (p. 224). Kluger and DeNisi (1996) note that telling someone that they type 100 words per minute is KR but telling them "you do not use your thumb for typing" is a feedback intervention (FI). This book considers KR as one of but many concepts within the KP or FI definitions of feedback.

A *fifth milestone* in feedback research was the emerging prominence of goal-setting theory, a standard theory included in every major organizational behavior textbook. Locke and Latham (1990) observed that more than 500 studies in eight countries representing more than 40,000 subjects had provided overwhelming support to the theory by the time their book was published. Goal-setting theory has led to a huge body of research that establishes that KR (a.k.a. feedback, a.k.a. metrics) leads to an increase in performance.

Clearly, feedback is more powerful if coupled with goals. If I tell you, "You took 20 minutes to complete that task," what does that mean? But if I say, "You took 20 minutes, and your goal was to finish in less than 30 minutes," that means something. All scorecards in this book call for coupling metrics with goals. As well, this book advocates providing a logical rationale for goals, such as the benchmarks the goals are based on.

For most of the 20th century, feedback research was focused on "prescriptions" and tests of the conditions in which feedback could be made more effective. One intrepid doctoral student reported that by 1990 there were at least 123 different prescriptions or "rules" for giving effective feedback in existing research literature (Roberts, 1990). These studies led to the sorts of "do" and "don't" guidelines found in standard supervisor manuals (and in this chapter) to this day.

The blizzard of studies conducted in the 20th century led to the possibility of meta-analyses to test for the overall effectiveness of feedback described earlier. This research allows us to expand on the nature of feedback effects.

Nature of Feedback Effects

When you are on your job, how long can you go without seeing your boss? A day? A month? If you see your boss every day, you are likely affected by the knowledge that he is aware of how well you are doing. Even if you do not see your boss, you may be aware of him monitoring you through some sort of metric system.

But imagine the situation in which you rarely see your boss and there is no system in place. Would you still continue to perform?

You are likely thinking, "Of course! I am a professional." Sure, but are you performing *extra tasks beyond what is expected of you*? **Feedback effects** are *additional* improvements in performance that are inspired by receiving feedback and are beyond how you would have performed without the feedback.

A recent study demonstrated the power of metrics as feedback. This study compared the effects of "text" feedback versus those who received "numeric/normative" feedback that gave numbers and quantitative data on how they did in comparison to others. The subjects were leaders who received "360" feedback from bosses, direct reports, and peers. Not only did they react more favorably to numeric feedback, positive responses were associated with future development needs. Those who responded negatively had a larger number of development needs post-feedback (Atwater & Brett, 2006).

Several reviews provide strong evidence for the impact of feedback on performance (Balcazar, Hopkins, & Suarez, 1986; Kopelman, 1982; Nadler, 1979). One review found that feedback led to positive performance results in all 27 studies evaluated (Kopelman, 1982). Following a more stringent criterion of "consistent" results (impacting every subject within a treatment condition), another review showed that feedback shaped behavior in the desired direction in 41% of the studies (Balcazar, Hopkins, & Suarez, 1986).

Meta-analyses also document feedback effects (Guzzo, Jette, & Katzell, 1985; Stajkovic & Luthans, 1998). Kluger and DeNisi (1996) assessed 131 studies and found that feedback interventions had a relatively large effect on performance ($d = 0.41$) but also reported that in 38% of the studies they reviewed, feedback effects were negative. They underscored the point that the effectiveness of feedback depends on the way it is presented.

Two other meta-analyses have examined the effects of feedback from different sources. One study examined 24 longitudinal studies that compared 360 feedback (Smither, London, & Reilly, 2005). Feedback effects on performance were generally statistically significant but very small. The results showed that 19 of 21 effect sizes were positive for direct report feedback, 6 of 7 effect sizes were positive for peer feedback, 8 of 10 effect sizes were positive for supervisory feedback, and only 6 of 11 effect sizes were positive for self-feedback. Another meta-analysis reported that both direct report and peer feedback accounted for a significant amount of variation in objective measures (e.g., product, profit) that was "above and beyond" other sources of variation (Conway, Lombardo, & Sanders, 2001).

A widely influential study by Pritchard, Jones, Roth, Stuebing, and Ekeberg (1988) used the contingency line method described in Chapter 6 and compared effects from feedback alone, feedback plus goals, and feedback plus goals plus incentives. This study is particularly relevant because feedback was given in the form of metrics. Results showed that feedback improved productivity 50% over baseline, adding goal-setting improved productivity 75% over baseline, but incentives improved productivity only 1% over baseline.

The Pritchard study is surprising in that it appears that incentives seem to have no significant impact on performance. What gives? Is this to say that incentives have no impact? One meta-analysis showed that the effects of incentives were far more variable than even feedback effects (Guzzo, Jette, & Katzell, 1985). In many cases, incentives had a negative impact on productivity. This underscores the point that just as there is an art to delivering feedback, there is art behind any motivational technique—even rewarding with money.

Practitioner Technique: What Feedback Contents to Include?

Principles of feedback delivery reflect findings in academic "prescription" research and the contents one typically finds in the performance management chapter of a first-level supervisor training manual. Several principles will now be described.

Should feedback be positive or negative? Both common sense and theory would imply that you should give both positive and negative feedback. Operant psychology generally points to the power of positive reinforcement, but this does not mean that negative feedback (or "punishment") is ineffective. Systems theory would explain that negative feedback would trigger a person to take action to close the gap (Katz & Kahn, 1978). Goal-setting theory would say that one outcome of positive feedback is resetting goals to a higher level (Latham, 2007). Recent research shows that feedback is more likely to be "accepted" if it is positive (Bell & Arthur, 2008).

As it happens, feedback research that compares the effects of positive and negative messages is split. One review concluded that positive comments are more powerful (Balcazar, Hopkins, & Suarez, 1986), but another study found negative contents are more powerful when directed toward groups (Mesch, Farh, & Podsakoff, 1994).

It is obvious that both positive and negative feedback influence behavior, the point here is to remember to give the positive feedback. This returns us to an essential question of metrics: do you want to create metrics for something you do well? The answer is "yes" if that variable concerns something that is important to your mission or vision.

A final way to stress the need for positive feedback is to consider the example of small children. Have you ever had to babysit? If you are smart, you figured out early on that it is much easier to say "Oh Good!" when the child does something well rather than focus on the negative and say "Don't." If you focus on the negative, your life becomes a series of "Don't Don't Don'ts." The same principles apply to adults in that it is easier for them to build on strengths rather than learn entirely new behaviors.

Who should give feedback? Five key sources of feedback were identified decades ago: the company, the supervisor, coworkers, particular tasks, and the worker's own feelings and ideas (Grellor & Herold, 1975). Since then, there has been an explosion of 360 feedback that adds upward, customer, and supplier information as potentially important sources. As described earlier, it appears that within the 360 context supervisory and upward feedback is the most effective and self-appraisal is relatively ineffective (Smither, London, & Reilly, 2005). Those studies, however, are focused specifically on managerial work performance. Other types of self-generated feedback (e.g., checklists or feedback from tasks) have been shown to improve performance (Balcazar et al., 1986; Grellor, 1980).

Will feedback across sources be in agreement? As discussed under performance appraisals, the correlation between self-ratings and supervisory ratings is still low with self-ratings being more lenient (Heidemeier & Moser, 2009). In their review of this research, Latham, Almost, Mann, and Moore (2005) observed that different populations such as *peers* and *subordinates* observe different actual behaviors in different contexts, hence perfect agreement is not likely.

One study examined how demographic differences across feedback senders affected reactions to performance feedback (Geddes & Konrad, 2003). This study included 180 nonsupervisory employees from an organization that represents more than 120 nationalities. They found that employees reacted more favorably to negative feedback from managers who were white and unfavorably to negative feedback from women. They also found that employees reacted more unfavorably to negative feedback from same-race managers.

How often should you give feedback? The oft-cited mantra "the more feedback, the better" deserves qualifications. First, giving individuals more feedback than they are able to process can have a negative effect (Ilgen, Fisher, & Taylor, 1979). Second, according to the concept of diminishing returns, giving too much feedback may not be worth the manager's effort. Balcazar et al. (1986) reported that although most experiments focus on feedback on a daily basis, there were no differences in consistent effects across daily and weekly conditions. The effects of feedback fell off, however, when only given monthly.

Another oft-cited mantra is that feedback should be given "ASAP!" That is, you should get feedback to people as soon after they complete a task or meet a milestone as possible. This makes intuitive sense. We all can probably remember papers that we wrote for which the teacher took so long to return the assignment that we forgot the learning points. However, there are also exceptions where providing immediate feedback can distract. For example, one study demonstrated that constantly giving KR feedback during a golf-putting task actually hurt the golfer's ability concentrate on the task (Butki & Hoffman, 2003). Another basic example comes from the radio industry. It is a general practice that program directors should not criticize disc jockeys while they are on air but rather wait until they are off shift. The idea is to avoid psychologically throwing disc jockeys while they are still on the air.

All this said, it is still best to get feedback to people as soon as possible. Perhaps the most important frequency issue is better termed a "timing" issue—that is, it is critical to get feedback to a person before she does the same task again. For example, if you have to do a certain type of report, your supervisor needs to get you feedback on the first report before you do the second report. In the case of metrics, you would want to know your January sales data as early into February as possible. What happens if you do not get it until mid-February? Think of how utility companies (or any company) give you a bill involving variable consumption. If there is a lag time between the end of the service (say your electricity usage) and when you receive the bill, the bill does not have the metric effect where you want to say "Oh, I'm going to save this next month" because you are already into the next month—and blowing it!

How do you make feedback consistent? We have all had the experience where someone (a boss, a teacher, a coach) has told us that we are doing well one day and then says that we need to improve the next day—and the whole time, we were doing the task the same way! Why would it be good one day and not another? A similar example is when we compare notes with our peers and find out that our boss told one of us that we were doing well, the other we were doing poorly, and in fact, we did things the same. What is behind this inconsistency?

There are many pet theories on the subject, but when the author asks this question of college students, the answer is pretty consistent: managers are told that they have to give feedback and they feel they have to say "something." Couple this with the notion that they think that for it to be "feedback" it has to be "negative," they literally start making things up. Again, they have to say *something*.

One way to battle the inconsistency is to remember to give both positive as well as negative feedback. Another solution is even more basic: standards. The manager needs to decide on a set of standards for performance and then apply them (consistently) across situations. For example, consider the task of writing a report and the following ratings:

EXCEEDED EXPECTATIONS

MET EXPECATIONS

DID NOT MEET EXPECTATIONS

What does this mean? If the manager defines standards that go with the ratings, then it is easier to apply them consistently:

EXCEEDED EXPECTATIONS: No errors, extra analysis.

MET EXPECTATIONS: 3–5 errors, expected analysis.

DID NOT MEET EXPECTATIONS: Many errors, little analysis.

Incidentally, standards are not necessarily quantitative, but they often take that form.

If feedback is in the form of metrics, it seems that this would lead the manager to have more consistency, right? Not necessarily. Standards applied to metrics often come in the form of goals. We can imagine the situation where we completed 20 widgets one day and the boss said, "Great." Another day we completed 20 widgets and the boss said, "Work on improving your speed." What? If the boss only has metrics (quantitative feedback) but no "goals" or standards to compare the metrics, there is still room for inconsistency to arise. But if standards are specified (hopefully *a priori*) then there is little room for misinterpretation or inconsistency.

What do you include in feedback contents? Scorecards and survey results, metrics, are powerful feedback contents, but feedback is more than KR. As an example, process feedback relays "information about the manner in which an individual implements a work strategy" (Earley, Northcraft, Lee, & Lituchy, 1990, p.88). We could question whether process feedback has a bigger effect than outcome feedback, but at the end of the day, who cares? The effects of feedback contents have been shown to be additive. For example, giving people information about processes does not take away from the impact of information about outcomes—both contents improve performance.

The following different types of feedback contents have documented effects:

- Metrics (Brown, 1996)
- Process feedback (Earley et al., 1990)
- Praise (specific compliments) (Kim & Hamner, 1976)
- Mistakes (Hobson, 1986; Larson, 1989)

- Tell if the job is done correctly or incorrectly (Fedor, Buckley, & Eder, 1990)
- Strengths and weaknesses (Fedor et al., 1990)
- Information about performance from other sources (Fedor et al., 1990)
- Counseling (comments to deal with emotional aspects of reactions) (Roberts, 1990)
- Reasons for not meeting goals (Ashford, 1986)
- Feedback in relation to career progression (Burke, Weitzel, & Weir; 1978)
- Information about the performance of peers (Liden & Mitchell, 1985)
- Causal feedback (provide attributions for results) (Liden, Ferris, & Dienesch, 1988)
- Information about market conditions (Earley, Wojnarski, & Prest, 1987)
- Information about critical task behaviors (Stajkovic & Luthans, 2003)
- Information about what may be the better sequencing of behaviors, and what dynamic complexities where sequencing might need to change (Stajkovic & Luthans, 2003)
- Rewards attached to outcomes (Bobko & Colella, 1994)
- Expectancy for success (Bobko & Colella, 1994)
- Valence attached to standards (Bobko & Colella, 1994)
- Conflict with other standards (Bobko & Colella, 1994)
- Rationale for standards (Bobko & Colella, 1994)
- Difficulty of standards (Bobko & Colella, 1994)

How do you make feedback more informative? Most of us can think of a time when an authority figure (teacher, boss, coach) went on and on about something we did wrong—and we already had felt horrible in the first place. Going on and on about it did little more than rub salt in our wounds. Was it even worth their breath?

This gives us pause to consider a variable that has been seemingly lost in the swirl of feedback research: the idea that feedback should be *informative*. Classic information theory (Ritchie, 1991; Shannon, 1949) leads us to consider two message qualities that will improve the information value of feedback: novelty and relevance.

Novelty is content not already known to a receiver. This gets at the idea that feedback should be something that the employee does not "already know." In the work performance context, **relevance** means that feedback has some importance to a particular individual's job or interests. Consider this idea (as the author did for her doctoral dissertation): what kind of information is something that employees do not already know but is definitely relevant to them? Metrics. If a manager designs a metric system for employee performance, the employees could not possibly know it because the metrics did not already exist. If the metrics are about *their* performance, however, the metrics are obviously relevant to them. Metrics are contents that meet the informativeness criteria of being novel and relevant.

Should feedback be given in public or private? Studies have shown that public feedback is more effective than private feedback (e.g., McCuddy & Griggs, 1984; Quillitch, 1975; 1978), but one review reported that public feedback effects are generally confounded with other feedback cues (Nordstrom, Lorenzi, & Hall, 1991). In a review of "consistent" feedback effects, Balcazar et al. (1986) reported no differences between public and private feedback.

Two qualifications are warranted: one cultural and one that has to do with the nature of metrics. The knee-jerk reaction of American students is to say that positive feedback should be given in public and negative feedback should be given in private. But consider collectivist Asian cultures where "the nail that sticks up gets hammered down." Being singled out for positive behavior could be downright painful. It is reasonable to expect that people from some cultures—or just some people—would find it embarrassing to receive positive feedback in public.

In the case of metrics, if the results concern team performance then they have to be given in public. But if they concern individual performance comparisons, managers should think carefully about whether it is worth it to give them in public or private.

Practitioner Technique: How to Deliver Feedback

A typical manager is likely to be overwhelmed with the all the feedback prescriptions and contents one is expected to remember. This material is reduced into one simple technique that was first developed by long-time leadership professor Robert T. Woodworth from the Foster School of Business at the University of Washington and that has been refined over the past 15 years in highly stimulating and exceedingly valuable corporate training courses (offered by your faithful author).

The Woodworth method begins by distinguishing *content* and *delivery*. Content concerns the words and numbers that go into a feedback message. Delivery concerns the channels through which the messages are delivered.

Content. We begin with an essential question: What are criteria for effective feedback contents? Drawing loosely from information theory (Ritchie, 1991; Shannon, 1949), the practical answer is this:

- It is useful.
- It is important.

How do you make feedback contents **useful**? The following is a list of suggestions:

- The person has to be able to do something about it.
- It is focused on a behavior, not the person.
- It is perceived as fair, not biased.

- It is factual.
- It is succinct, not overloading the person with information.
- It is feasible.
- It provides suggestions.
- It gives specific.
- It includes examples.

How do you relay the **importance** of your feedback message? Describe the *consequences* of the performance you are describing. The consequences can be positive or negative. The following are examples:

- Consequence on costs.
- Consequence on the team.
- Consequence on your relationship.
- Consequence on the budget.
- Consequences on turnover.
- Consequences for the company.
- Consequences on the individual whose performance is in question.
  - Performance appraisal
  - Termination
  - Promotion
  - Reputation
  - Pay

Putting it all together, the Woodworth technique for articulating feedback that is useful and important uses the following format:

Feedback Format:

Behavior
  Specific Example (or Metrics/Standard)
    Consequences
      Suggestions for Future Improvement

To demonstrate with qualitative feedback, let us take an individual's performance and the common example of writing a report. The feedback might be something like this, "Something you need to work on is report accuracy. You have been forgetting to include confidence intervals. This makes the whole team look bad because the reports come from our department. Maybe use a statistics checklist when you do your proofreading."

Now to demonstrate with quantitative feedback (metrics), let us take a team's performance and the common example of milestones met. The metrics might be delivered something like this: "Let's look at milestones met. Last month we met 98% of our milestones."

STOP. At this point, notice that we do not know if this is good or bad. The metrics need to be coupled with a standard (or goal) in order to be interpreted. We continue with the example in full: "Let's look at milestones met. Last month we met 98% of our milestones, which means that 2% of our customers did not get their materials in time. We are shooting for a 0.001 of 1% error rate! The consequence is that we risk losing customers. One of the reasons we missed the milestones is because the Help Desk got overloaded, and this is something we can work on."

Delivery. Throughout this text, we have emphasized the creation of "scorecards" to relay metrics and observe that there are a wide variety of other channels for delivering feedback, including posters, Power Point, phone, video, and meetings (see Chapter 13 for a complete list). However, not only are metrics often delivered face to face, but these feedback sessions also present opportunities to relay the many other forms of feedback contents discussed in this chapter.

Delivering positive feedback does not take great skill, but delivering negative feedback can be true art. The key to getting negative feedback across is that you do so in a manner that does not engender defensiveness. Defensiveness occurs when individuals anticipate threat and is associated with defensive listening, literally the shutting out of information (Eadie, 1982; Gibb, 1961). How to overcome it?

The following is a list of several feedback delivery strategies. Be warned that if you try to parrot some technique from a management book that is not natural for you, your feedback message could come out like a bunch of psycho babble. The key is to choose a technique that fits the way you talk.

- Couple a positive and a negative, or give a positive-negative-positive sequence.
- Begin with a question—ask the receiver(s) how they feel they did.
- Describe the way you prepared your feedback.
- Frame your information as a "learning" situation.
- Use an analogy.
- "I do this, too . . ."
- Acknowledge situational factors that contributed to poor performance.
- Compare the person's behavior to the behavior of others.
- Note that the individual's intentions appeared to be positive.
- Make an inspirational statement of confidence.

CHAPTER SUMMARY

This chapter described the evolution of feedback research in terms of five conceptual milestones. First, feedback can be positive or negative. Second, feedback effects can be described as cognitive and/or affective. Third, feedback can be thought of as information about a gap between results and either a goal (goal-setting theory) or a standard (systems theory). Fourth, definitions of feedback vary from knowledge of results (KR), knowledge of performance (KP), and feedback interventions (FI). Fifth, goal-setting theory confirms feedback effects as do many meta-analyses considered in this book. This chapter concluded with practical feedback techniques that managers can use.

REFERENCES

Ammons, R. B. (1956). Effects of knowledge of performance: A survey and tentative theoretical formulation. *Journal of General Psychology, 54*, 279–299.

Arps, G. F. (1920). Work with knowledge of results versus work without knowledge of results. *Psychological Monographs, 28*, 1–41.

Ashford, S. J. (1986). Feedback-seeking in individual adaptation: A resource perspective. *Academy of Management Journal, 29*, 465–487.

Ashford, S. J., & Cummings, L. L. (1983). Feedback as an individual resource: Personal strategies of creating information. *Organizational Behavior and Human Decision Performance, 32*, 370–398.

Atwater, L., & Brett, J. (2006). Feedback format: Does it influence managers' reactions to feedback? *Journal of Occupational and Organizational Psychology, 79*, 517–532.

Balcazar, F., Hopkins, B. L., & Suarez, Y. (1986). A critical, objective review of performance feedback. *Journal of Organizational Behavior Management, 7*, 65–89.

Bell, S. T., & Arthur, W. (2008). Feedback acceptance in developmental assessment centers: The role of feedback message, participant personality, and affective response to the feedback session. *Journal of Organizational Behavior, 29*, 681–703.

Bobko, P., & Colella, A. (1994). Employee reactions to performance standards: A review and research propositions. *Personnel Psychology, 47*, 1–26.

Brown, M. G. (1996). *Keeping score: Using the right metrics to drive world-class performance*. New York: Quality Resources.

Burke, R. J., Weiztel, W. F., & Weir, T. (1978). Characteristics of effective employee performance review and development interviews: Replication and extension. *Personnel Psychology, 31*, 903–919.

Butki, B. D., & Hoffman, S. J., (2003). Effects of reducing frequency of intrinsic knowledge of results on the learning of a motor skill. *Perceptual and Motor Skills, 97*, 569–580.

Conway, J. M., Lombardo, K., & Sanders, K. C. (2001). A meta-analysis of incremental validity and nomological networks for subordinate and peer ratings. *Human Performance, 14*, 267–303.

Cooper, L. (1932). *The rhetoric of Aristotle*. London: Prentice-Hall.

Eadie, W. F. (1982). Defensive communication revisited: A critical examination of Gibb's theory. *Southern Speech Communication Journal, 47*, 163–177.

Earley, P. C., Northcraft, G. B., Lee, C., & Lituchy, T. R. (1990). Impact of process and outcome feedback on the relation of goal setting to task performance. *Academy of Management Journal, 33*, 87–105.

Earley, P. C., Wojnarski, P., & Prest, W. (1987). Task planning and energy expanded: Exploration of how goals influence performance. *Journal of Applied Psychology, 72*, 107–114.

Fedor, D. B., Buckley, M. R., & Eder, R. W. (1990). Measuring subordinate perceptions of supervisor feedback intentions: Some unsettling results. *Educational and Psychological Measurement, 50*, 73–89.

Geddes, D., & Konrad, A. (2003). Demographic differences and reactions to performance feedback. *Human Relations, 12*, 1485–1513.

Gibb, J. R. (1961). Defensive communication. *Journal of Communication, 11*, 141–148.

Grellor, M. (1980). Evaluation of feedback sources as a function of role and organizational level. *Journal of Applied Psychology, 65*, 24–27.

Grellor, M., & Herold, D. (1975). Sources of feedback: A preliminary investigation. *Organizational Behavior and Human Performance, 13*, 244–256.

Guzzo, R. A., Jette, R. D., & Katzell, R. A. (1985). The effects of psychologically based intervention programs on worker productivity: A meta-analysis. *Personnel Psychology, 38*, 275–291.

Heidemeier, H., & Moser, K. (2009). Self-other agreement in job performance rating: A Mcta-analytic test of a performance model. *Journal of Applied Psychology, 94*, 353–370.

Hobson, C. J. (1986). Factors affecting the frequency, timing, and sign of informal supervisor feedback to subordinates in a simulated work setting. *Multivariate Behavioral Research, 21*, 187–200.

Ilgen, D. R., Fisher, C. D., & Taylor, M. S. (1979). Consequences of individual feedback on performance. *Journal of Applied Psychology, 64*, 359–371.

Jones, G. M. (1910). Experiments on the reproduction of distance as influenced by suggestions of ability and inability. *Psychological Review, 17*, 269–278.

Katz, D., & Kahn, R. L. (1978). *The social psychology of organizations* (2nd ed.). New York: Wiley.

Kernan, M. C., & Lord, R. G. (1990). Effects of valence, expectancies, and goal-performance discrepancies in single and multiple goal environments. *Journal of Applied Psychology, 75*, 194–203.

Kim, J. S., & Hamner, W. C. (1976). Effect of performance feedback and goal setting on productivity and satisfaction in an organizational setting. *Journal of Applied Psychology, 61*, 48–57.

Kluger, A. N., & DeNisi, A. (1996). The effects of feedback interventions on performance: A historical review, a meta-analysis, and a preliminary feedback intervention theory. *Psychological Bulletin, 119*, 254–284.

Kluger, A. N., Lewinsohn, S., & Aiello, J. (1994). The influence of feedback on mood: Linear effects of pleasantness and curvilinear effects on arousal. *Organizational Behavior and Human Decision Processes, 60*, 276–299.

Kopelman, R. E. (1982). Improving productivity through objective feedback: A review of the evidence. *National Productivity Review, 2*, 43–55.

Larson, J. R. (1989). The dynamic interplay between employees' feedback-seeking strategies and supervisors' delivery of performance feedback. *Academy of Management Review, 14*, 408–422.

Latham, G. P. (2007). *Work motivation.* Thousand Oaks, CA: Sage.

Latham, G. P., Almost, J., Mann, S., & Moore, C. (2005). New developments in performance management. *Organizational Dynamics, 34*, 77–87.

Liden, R. C., Ferris, G. R., & Dienesch, R. M. (1988). The influence of causal feedback on subordinate reactions and behavior. *Group and Organization Studies, 13*, 348–373.

Liden, R. C., & Mitchell, T. R. (1985). Reactions to feedback: The role of attributions. *Academy of Management Journal, 28*, 291–308.

Locke, E. A., & Latham, G. P. (1990). *A theory of goal setting and task performance.* Englewood Cliffs, NJ: Prentice Hall.

McCuddy, M. K., & Griggs, M. H. (1984). Goal setting and feedback in the management of a professional department: A case study. *Journal of Organizational Behavior Management, 7*, 53–65.

Mesch, D. J., Farh, J., & Podsakoff, P. M. (1994). Effects of feedback sign on group goal setting, strategies, and performance. *Group and Organization Management, 19*, 309–333.

Nadler, D. A. (1979). The effect of feedback on task group behavior: A review of the experimental research. *Organizational Behavior and Human Performance, 23*, 309–338.

Nordstrom, R., Lorenzi, P., & Hall, R. V. (1991). A review or public posting of performance feedback in work settings. *Journal of Organizational Behavior Management, 11*(2), 101–123.

Pritchard, R. D., Jones, S. D., Roth, P. L., Stuebing, K. K., & Ekeberg, S. E. (1988). Effects of group feedback, goal setting, and incentives on organizational productivity. *Journal of Applied Psychology, 73*, 337–358.

Quillitch, H. R. (1975). A comparison of three staff-management procedures. *Journal of Applied Behavior Analysis, 8*, 59–66.

Quillitch, H. R. (1978). Using a simple feedback procedure to reinforce the submission of written suggestions by mental health employees. *Journal of Organizational Behavior Management, 1*, 155–163.

Ritchie, L. D. (1991). *Information: Communication concepts 2.* Newbury Park, CA: Sage.

Roberts, G. E. (1990 The influence of participation, goal setting, feedback, and acceptance on measures of performance appraisal system effectiveness). Unpublished doctoral dissertation, University of Pittsburgh.

Shannon, C. E. (1949). *A mathematical theory of communication.* Urbana: University of Illinois Press.

Smither, J. W., London, M., & Reilly, R. R. (2005). Does performance improve following multisource feedback? A theoretical model, meta-analysis, and review of empirical findings. *Personnel Psychology, 58*, 33–66.

Stajkovic, A. D., & Luthans, F. (1998). Self-efficacy and work-related performance: A meta-analysis. *Psychological Bulletin, 124*, 240–261.

Stajkovic, A. D., & Luthans, F. (2003). Behavioral management and task performance in organizations: Conceptual background, meta-analysis, and test of alternative models. *Personnel Psychology, 56*, 155–194.

Thorndike, E. L. (1913). *Educational psychology. volume I: The original nature of man.* New York: Columbia University.

15 *METRICS AND MOTIVATION*

Metric feedback is important, but it is just one of many types of feedback. And then feedback is just one of the seemingly endless types of motivation techniques.

Yet, consider the wasted effort if we develop beautiful metrics only to infuse a sense of job insecurity throughout the workplace. Or what if we have beautiful metrics but the reward system is so messed up that no one tries anyway? Or what happens when employees simply think all of our practices are unfair?

Navigating through the sea of best practices and motivation techniques may seem daunting, but there is a compass: motivation theories. Motivation theories not only describe what accounts for metric outcomes, such as productivity and satisfaction, but they point us to basic questions that we ask when presenting metrics or any other type of motivation intervention.

CHAPTER OVERVIEW

This chapter begins with key concepts related to motivation. A brief history of motivation research is given and then four categories of major motivation theories are described. Each discussion focuses on "outcomes" or real-world results associated with practices based on each theory and concludes with example questions that can be used by managers who wish to "audit" the extent to which motivation practices are being used in their organizations. As with any scale item, these open-ended items can be translated into quantitative items on an as-needed basis. The questions also enable the reader to see the practical issues addressed by each theory.

Key Motivation Concepts

The variables in Figure 15.1 are associated with motivation. Can you guess how these variables can be grouped together?

LEARNING OBJECTIVES

After studying this chapter, you should be able to achieve the following:

1. Understand why managers implementing metrics need to link metrics to broader feedback and motivation practices.
2. Define *motivation*.
3. Identify and define major dependent variables used to measure motivation effects: task performance, job satisfaction, organizational commitment, productivity, and withdrawal.
4. Personalize theories of motivation, understanding how everyday techniques you use to motivate yourself and others are reflected in concepts from motivation theory.
5. Identify four categories of motivation theories: needs-based theories, theories comparing intrinsic and extrinsic motivation, job content models and theories, and cognitive theories.
6. Describe the major concepts, outcomes, and managerial practices associated with Maslow's Hierarchy of Needs.
7. Describe the major concepts, outcomes, and managerial practices associated with theories that compare intrinsic and extrinsic motivation: Cognitive Evaluation Theory, Self-Determination Theory, Reinforcement Theory, Behavior Modification, Motivation-Hygiene Theory, and Expectancy Theory.
8. Describe the major concepts, outcomes, and managerial practices associated with job content models and theories: the work characteristics models and person-environment fit.
9. Describe the major concepts, outcomes, and managerial practices associated with cognitive theories: Social Learning Theory, Social Cognitive Theory, Self-Efficacy Theory, Goal-Setting Theory, and Theories of Equity and Justice.
10. Conduct a "motivation audit" that assesses the extent to which known scientific principles of motivation are being conducted in your own work group or organization.

Before turning to definitions, let's consider the connection between concepts. *Direction, effort,* and *persistence* are definitional ingredients of motivation. *Ability, resources,* and *motivation* are drivers of job performance. How do we measure motivation? That is, what do you take as dependent variables? You can measure the definitional elements (*direction, effort,* or *persistence*), attitudinal outcomes (*job satisfaction, organizational commitment*), or behavioral outcomes (*job performance, turnover,* and *absenteeism*).

What do managers cull from motivation research? The practices that favorably influence the motivation outcomes. For example, what leads to increased

Direction	Effort		Persistence	Ability	Resources
Motivation	Job Performance		Job Satisfaction	Fairness	
Organizational Commitment			OCB		
Withdrawal	Metrics				Dissatisfacti on

Figure 15.1 Motivation Concepts
Source: © Ruth A. Huwe.
Note: OCB = organization citizenship behaviors.

job satisfaction? Effectively delivered feedback (metrics) for one. But for others, a whole host of motivational practices should be used alongside metrics: meeting employees' needs, treating people fairly, setting goals effectively, and so forth. These topics are the main independent variables of motivation research. An **independent variable** is a variable that reflects a "cause," whereas a **dependent variable** is a variable that reflects an "effect."

Motivation generally is defined as internal processes that are manifested as the direction, effort, and persistence of effort toward completing a task or attaining a goal (Ford, 1992; Latham, 2007). **Direction** is how focused an individual is when working on a task. **Effort** is how hard an individual works on a task. **Persistence** is how long an individual continues to expend effort toward completing a given task.

Job performance is an individual's overall contribution to an organization and consists of task performance, counterproductive behaviors (or lack thereof), and organizational citizenship behaviors. **Task performance** is how well an individual performs duties associated with his role in an organization. You would hope researchers would include productivity and quality in this measure, but that is not necessarily the case. **Organization citizenship behaviors (OCBs)** are extrarole, discretionary behaviors that reflect a contribution to an organization. Basically, it means going beyond the job description. **Counterproductive behaviors** include the wide variety of ways an individual can hurt an organization. Examples would be psychological withdrawal (e.g., Internet surfing when you should work) or all-out sabotage.

Job satisfaction is a subjective evaluation about "the feelings a worker has about his job" (Smith, Kendall, & Hulin, 1969, p. 100). Job satisfaction can be conceived and measured in two general ways. First, job satisfaction is a "global" concept referring to how one feels about the overall job (Tett & Meyer, 1993) and can be measured by the "Job in General" scale (Ironson, Smith, Brannick, & Paul, 1989). Second, job satisfaction can be viewed in terms of various "facets" or "aspects" of one's job: supervision, work, pay, promotion, and coworkers. These facets are reflected in the most famous job satisfaction measure, the Job Descriptive Index (JDI) (Price & Mueller, 1986). Kinicki, McKee-Ryan, Schriesheim, and Carson (2002) conducted a meta-analysis that compared various facets of job satisfaction with various motivational outcomes. The strongest correlation was a positive correlation between satisfaction with supervision and OCBs (corrected $r = 0.45$, $p < 0.01$) and a negative correlation between satisfaction with work and intention to leave (corrected $r = -0.50$, $p < 0.01$).

There are three types of organizational commitment: affective, continuance, and normative. **Affective commitment** refers to an individual's emotional identification with an organization. **Continuance commitment** refers to one's intention to stay with an organization because leaving is not a favorable option. **Normative commitment** denotes one's willingness to stay with an organization out of moral obligation (Tett & Meyer, 1993). In a meta-analysis of 152 studies, Kinicki, McKee-Ryan, Schriesheim, and Carson (2002) reported a moderate to strong correlation between job satisfaction and organizational commitment ($r = 0.44$, $p < 0.001$), demonstrating that the constructs are similar but not the same.

The correlation between attitudinal and behavior outcomes has raised a debate for decades. In a meta-analysis of 74 studies, Iaffaldano and Muchinsky (1985) reported a low correlation between job satisfaction and job performance ($r = 0.17$, $p < 0.05$). More recently, a meta-analysis described the job satisfaction–job performance relationship as "largely spurious" as the effect could be eliminated largely by personality variables, locus of control, and particularly organization-based self-esteem (Bowling, 2007). A different meta-analysis, however, studied overall job attitude (job satisfaction and organizational commitment) for effects on general behavioral criteria combined (absenteeism, turnover, focal performance, contextual performance, and lateness). The researchers found that the attitudinal variables were strong predictors of the behavioral variables (Harrison, Newman & Roth, 2006).

In a related vein, one meta-analysis looked at the effects of employee attitudes on customer perceptions. Combining 28 studies, Brown and Lam (2008) found that employee satisfaction had a moderate association with customer satisfaction ($r = 0.25$, $p < 0.05$) and customer perceptions of service quality ($r = 0.29$, $p < 0.05$). They found the association was even stronger when services were more personal (e.g., medical) than object-oriented (e.g., mechanic), and were stronger for one-shot services (e.g., the person at an espresso stand by the side of a highway) versus services involving longer-term relationships (Brown & Lam, 2008). For managers, the upshot of these studies is that attitudinal variables are important whether or not you could build statistical cases to discard them.

Motivation is also associated with many negative outcomes. At an extreme, **learned helplessness** is a depressing condition in which individuals perceived no connection between their own actions and environmental outcomes. **Withdrawal** includes absenteeism, turnover, neglect, and general withdrawal behaviors (Podsakoff, LePine, & LePine, 2007).

Historical Overview

Until the mid-1850s, the study of motivation was more speculation and philosophy. In 1879, Wilhelm Wundt created the first scientific psychological laboratory in Germany. William James then established the first laboratory at Harvard in 1890. A major question in this era centered on the role of consciousness. James was influenced by contemporaries such as Sigmund Freud and Ivan Pavlov. Freud was famous for many things, including his theory of unconscious processes, the development of psychoanalysis, and the depiction of sexual desire as a primary motivational force. Pavlov won the 1904 prize for studying "Centrifugal Nerves of the Heart" but is most famous for his dog experiments that depicted learning on a physiological level. James felt that motivation could be known consciously through introspection and that learning was physiologically manifested by changes in nerve paths of the brain.

Carl Jung also addressed the debate over conscious forces as he advanced the idea of the **collective unconscious**, a reservoir of what is known as a species. His most famous works were published in the early 1900s.

Early questions of consciousness may sound far-fetched until you consider current efforts to map the brain and marketing strategies that are targeted to the unconscious. Recent research on goal-setting theory has shown how human performance can be affected by "subconscious priming," indirect messages such as exposure to words in a poster or simple pictures (Shantz & Latham, 2009). The development of the Dreamliner airplane at Boeing is greatly influenced by G. Clotaire Rapaille. Based on the idea of a collective unconscious, Dr. Rapaille conducts studies to identify what appeals across people from a given culture (Rapaille, 2001).

In psychology, motivation evolved from classical conditioning of Pavlov's dog to John B. Watson's behaviorist notion that stimulus-response was a law-like relationship, and on to B. F. Skinner's operant conditioning. These notions gave to motivation the "carrot and stick" flair that conceived of humans as motivated solely for financial gain. This conception would dominate the era of "scientific management" in the early 1900s.

One important figure in scientific management was Frederick Winslow Taylor. He began his work on efficiency at Bethlehem Steel Works by designing a method for the design of shovels that allowed people to work all day, reducing the number of people needed from 500 to 140. This would portend later fame for time and motion studies that basically improved methods for treating humans as machine parts. Beginning in the late 1890s, Taylor focused on all methods to improve productivity, including both work design and incentive practices. In 1911, he published his most famous work, *Principles of Scientific Management*.

Another important figure of the time was French industrialist Henri Fayol (1916/1949). He described the functions of a manager in terms of leading, planning, organizing, commanding, coordinating, and controlling. Although the phrase "command and control" is now treated with derision, it was standard in Fayol's time.

But during this period, there were some sparks of humanity. James' successor at Harvard, Hugo Munsterberg, would signal a shift in 1913 when he would interview workers about the "mental starvation" they faced at their jobs. This evolved into a major intellectual turning point that underscored the need for general motivation techniques, not just numbers in isolation.

The 1930s saw the publication of the Hawthorne experiments. For example, one study examined the effects of lighting on worker productivity. The researchers found that when they raised lighting levels, productivity improved. When they lowered lighting levels, productivity improved. In fact, when lights were lowered nearly to "moonlight" levels, productivity improved. What happened? They finally concluded that the shift in productivity was due to the human presence of the researcher (Mayo, 1933). The shift from viewing work as "humans" rather than "cogs" marks the transition to what is known as the "human relations" era.

Another intellectual milestone in organization behavior was the publication of Douglas MacGregor's *Human Side of Enterprise* (1960), a book published at the height of the human relations era that is still influential in the 21st century. MacGregor popularized the notion of Theory X and Theory Y. Theory X managers view humans as lazy avoiders of responsibility who need to be forced to do their work. Theory Y managers viewed humans as seekers of responsibility who consider work as natural as play. Theory X conceives of workers as needing coercive forces to be motivated, to be lured by a carrot or punished by a stick. Theory X marks the "old school," pre-human-relations thinking that managers need to use "command and control."

As the 21st century brought a shift from the industrial era to the information age, researchers began observing the changes in demographics in terms of diversity and education. According to the U.S. Department of Education's National Center for Education Statistics (2004), the percentage of 10th graders who aspire to go to college rose 21% (to 80%). Of poor families (those earning less than $35,377), 1 in 17 could expect to have a bachelor's degree by age 24. For those from wealthy families (those earning more than $85,000), the odds were 1 in 2. The U.S. Information Agency (1997) reported that "More than 60% of Americans now work in jobs that involve the handling of information and a high school diploma is seldom adequate for such work" (p. 3).

The workforce at the dawn of the 21st century has little resemblance to the "cogs" at the start of the 20th century, and neither do the jobs nor the motivational techniques. Older models focused on needs have met the test of time, while newer models emerged to consider the role of cognition and worker-environment fit. To summarize theories into techniques managers can actually use in concert with metrics, this chapter considers four categories of motivation theories.

Major Motivation Theories and Models

Think back to the last time you had to motivate yourself to do something. Maybe you had a sports goal such as climbing a mountain, running a marathon, or doing a long bike ride. Maybe you had a temptation goal, trying not to have that extra drink, dessert, cigarette, or coffee. Maybe you had an intellectual goal such as successfully completing an executive masters of business administration degree, conducting a study, or writing a book. Or maybe you're just trying to get through your regular work day. What exactly is it that motivates *you*? When you're in the middle of that exercise routine, staring down that chocolate, or facing a stack of papers to read, what is it that keeps you going? What do you say to yourself?

STOP. Do not continue until you have reflected on this question personally:

What motivates *you*?

If you're like most students who have been assigned to answer this question, your answer was something like the following:

- I will make my family proud.
- I will face public humiliation if I fail.
- I need to do this to ensure my financial security.
- I have to finish for the sense of achievement.
- I want the money.
- I want to beat my competition.
- I want to get it over with.

You may be surprised to learn that practically any answer you come up with has, in some way or another, been studied as an independent variable in motivation research. This body of literature can be used not only to identify ways for you to motivate yourself but, more importantly for this book, as ways for managers and leaders to motivate others to improve their scores on metric reports.

Human Needs

Maslow's Hierarchy of Needs (Maslow, 1954) emphasizes that humans have different *types* of needs and that there is a *hierarchy* of needs. In the order in which they must be met, the following are the six types of needs (Koltko-Rivera, 2006):

1. *Physiological* needs for shelter, thirst, hunger, and other bodily needs.
2. *Safety* needs for security and protection from harm.
3. *Social* needs for affection, friendship, and belongingness.
4. *Esteem* needs for both internal (our own self-respect) and external factors (recognition and status).
5. *Self-actualization* needs for growth and fulfilling one's potential.
6. *Self-transcendence* needs for a special cognitive activity "Being-cognition" or "B-cognition," experiences one feels at times of peak experiences, such as emotional experiences involving nature, aesthetic experiences, or mystical experiences.

The least familiar to readers, Maslow's "B-cognition" is also marked by a need to transcend one's own self or ego needs and be unified with and in service to forces beyond oneself.

The hierarchy notion is the idea that we will not be concerned about a higher level of needs until the current level is met. For example, we would not be concerned about maximizing our full potential if we can't put food on the table.

It seems we can never escape the concept of Maslow's Hierarchy of Needs. One survey cited Maslow as the 10th most eminent psychologist of the 20th century (Haggbloom et al., 2002).[1] His ideas are taught in speech and marketing classes for people designing persuasive appeals, in organizational behavior and management classes to describe people, and as a standard topic in child and adult education, psychology, and sociology (Benson & Dundis, 2003). But just when you think you are sick of Maslow, consider this:

Earlier, you were asked to consider what motivates you. How many items on your list appear on Maslow's hierarchy? If you mentioned anything to do with letting down teams or making your family proud, you were motivated by social needs. If you mentioned something to do with achievement or goals, you were addressing self-actualization needs. If you mentioned anything to do with security, you were describing safety needs.

Outcome Effects. How do Maslow's needs correlate to variables such as productivity and satisfaction? There is no major body of studies that makes these connections. Instead, studies assume that people have needs that need to be met (e.g., Rhoades & Eisenberger, 2002) and that they take meeting needs as an end unto itself.

Measurement. The *Need Satisfaction Questionnaire* (Porter, 1961) is an attempt to measure Maslow's concepts, but a later review concluded that this survey does not actually reflect the hierarchy (Dyer & Schwab, 1982). Another approach is to write a survey item about individual needs such as security (e.g., Zyberg & Berry, 2005). The following are example questions this theory would evoke:

1. Are people in your company worried about job security?
2. Does your company foster opportunities for employees to get to know one another? How would you describe the social atmosphere?

Another major "needs" theory is McClelland's Theory of Needs (1961), which originally focused on needs for power, achievement, and affiliation. Although the need for power adds to Maslow's list, this theory was skipped in this chapter because it is oriented more toward employee selection than performance improvement.

Intrinsic and Extrinsic Motivation

Intrinsic motivation is the urge to do a task because of an interest level in the task itself and because of the satisfaction one receives from the act of performing a task (Deci, 1975). **Extrinsic motivation** is the urge to do a task because performance results in some external contingency such as a reward (Gagne & Deci, 2005). A set of theories can be grouped by their orientation toward intrinsic or extrinsic rewards. Theories focused on *intrinsic versus extrinsic* motivators include cognitive evaluation theory and self-determination theory. Theories focused on *external* motivators include reinforcement theory and behavior modification. Theories focused on *intrinsic and extrinsic* motivators include motivation-hygiene theory and expectancy theory.

Intrinsic versus Extrinsic: Cognitive Evaluation Theory (CET). It would seem that the idea of intrinsic and extrinsic motivators would open an arsenal of techniques that managers could use to improve productivity and satisfaction. Why not make work fun? (Intrinsic) And provide recognition? (Intrinsic) And give bonuses? (Extrinsic) And praise? (Extrinsic). The original thinking was that intrinsic and extrinsic variables can be "added" together to increase motivation. This was a seemingly simple idea that eventually would lead to tremendous controversy and debate.

A first objection to "adding" intrinsic and extrinsic techniques was the idea that *tangible, extrinsic rewards could undermine intrinsic motivation*. The basic reasoning was something like, "If a kid enjoys a book but then is told he *has* to read the book to get a grade, the kid will no longer want to read the book." By 1999, a CET meta-analysis summarized 128 laboratory studies demonstrating that although positive feedback enhanced intrinsic motivation, linking performance to extrinsic factors (e.g., rewards, deadlines) detracted from intrinsic motivation (Deci, Koestner, & Ryan, 1999).

CET is controversial. For example, one popular way to measure intrinsic motivation is to measure whether people continue to do a task when they are not rewarded. However, there is a big difference between the child sitting in a lab who has nothing else to do but continue some word puzzles and the employee in a company who would be asked to continue working for no pay. In defense, another example would be using CET to get a gang out of your neighborhood. If you approach the gang and offer to pay them, they continue to hang out. If you then remove the pay, will they continue to hang out?

The idea that extrinsic reinforcers can undermine motivation has not been completely thrown out, just reformulated in self-determination theory (Gagnes & Deci, 2005). From this perspective, the greater the autonomy associated with extrinsic rewards, the greater the chance that the task remains intrinsically motivating. Self-determination theory holds that humans have three needs that fulfill intrinsic motivation: autonomy, relatedness, and competence. Greguras and Diefendorff (2009) emphasize that needs must be essential and universal. Taking their example, self-determination theory would not take "need for a high salary" to be a "need" because it is neither essential nor universal.

Outcome Effects. Intrinsic motivation is taken to be a dependent variable that a manager pursues in the same way that one pursues job satisfaction. Extrinsic motivators are measured through the use of "reinforcers" or "rewards" for performance; these are discussed below under reinforcement theory.

Measures. In a field setting such as the workplace, a "self-report" approach to the measure of intrinsic motivation would be pursued. A manager could ask the following questions:

1. Is your job enjoyable? What makes it enjoyable? What detracts from enjoyment?
2. Do you look forward to your job? Why or why not?

Extrinsic Reinforcers: Reinforcement Theory. Reinforcement theory is focused on extrinsic motivation, asking what types of "rewards" or "reinforcers" influence performance and satisfaction. To *increase* a behavior such as an employee's effort at a task, we administer one of two consequences to the employee:

Positive reinforcement is following the employee's response with something that is pleasant and rewarding (e.g., praise, money, time off, and so forth).

Negative reinforcement is following the employee's response by removing something is unpleasant (e.g., stop looking over their shoulder, stop mandatory overtime).

To *decrease* a behavior such as an employee's tardiness or rudeness, we administer one of two other methods for shaping behavior:

Punishment involves administering something that is unpleasant to the employee (e.g., humiliation in front of others, a lower score on a performance appraisal).

Extinction involves eliminating any reinforcer that is bringing about a behavior (e.g., stop praising, fine the employee, take away time off privileges, and so forth).

Outcome Effects. In a meta-analysis of 72 studies, Stajkovic and Luthans (2003) demonstrated the percentage of improvement in performance associated with three types of reinforcement: money (23%), feedback (10%), and social recognition (17%). Social recognition included promotion, pay raise, and transfer to better assignments. The results also showed that the three reinforcers had synergistic effects such that use of all three techniques had a 21% greater effect on performance than an additive model. The study builds on an all-field-study meta-analysis by Locke, Feren, McCaleb, Shaw, and Denny (1980) that found pay incentives increased performance by an average of 30%. Yet another meta-analysis also found that financial incentives enhanced performance and concluded that the idea of incentives detracting from performance should obtain "myth" status (Jenkins, Mitra, Gupta, & Shaw, 1998).

Measurement. Specific questions to measure the use of reinforcers include the following:

1. Are you satisfied with your level of pay?
2. Is your pay specifically linked to performing well?

Extrinsic Reinforcers: Behavior Modification. Luthans (1973) described the following steps to behavior modification:

- Identify behavior (how do you define the behavior?)
  - o Behaviors must be observable, measurable, task-related, critical to the task
- Measure behavior (what are the metrics that mark the behavior?)
  - o Use direct observation, time-sampling, archival data, historical data
- Analyze behavior (does it match goals?)
  - o Analyze functional consequences, behavioral contingencies
- Contingently intervene in behavior (did you couple rewards with behavior?)
  - o Develop the intervention based on organizational context (industry, structure, size, processes, technology) and apply as positive reinforcement (financial, nonfinancial, social, combination)
- Evaluate employee task-related behaviors aimed at performance improvement (did this work?)
  - o Measure to see if this worked: YES/NO. If Yes, maintain the modification with schedules of reinforcement (continuous or intermittent).

A meta-analysis of 19 studies showed behavior modification is associated with a powerful 17% improvement in performance (Strajkovic & Luthans, 1998).

Measurement. Behavior modification includes several motivational techniques (expectations, metrics, feedback, goal-setting, contingent reward, and various types of rewards). Specific questions to tap these practices are as follows:

1. Are expectations clearly defined for people at your company? What could be improved?
2. Are goals given to you in terms of behaviors or output? For example: A behavior goal is to "eat less than 2,000 calories a day." An outcome goal is to "lose 20 pounds."
3. Are rewards or feedback only given when goals are met? Or given at other times?

Extrinsic and Intrinsic: Motivation-Hygiene Theory. Frederic Herzberg's motivation hygiene theory challenges the idea that there is a continuum between dissatisfaction to satisfaction, arguing that satisfaction and dissatisfaction are conceptually distinct (Herzberg, Mausner, & Synderman, 1959).

Herzberg (2003) refers to **dissatisfiers** as extrinsic, environmental factors, wryly observing,

> Ask workers what makes them unhappy at work, and you'll hear about an annoying boss, a low salary, an uncomfortable work space, or stupid rules. Managed badly, environmental factors make people miserable, and they can certainly be demotivating. But even if managed brilliantly, they don't motivate anybody to work much harder or smarter. (p. 87)

On the other hand, he refers to **satisfiers** as intrinsic, job factors, continuing "People are motivated, instead, by interesting work, challenge, and increasing responsibility" (2003, p. 87).

The following are top satisfiers (Herzberg, Mausner, & Synderman, 1959):

- Achievement
- Recognition for achievement
- Work itself
- Responsibility
- Advancement possibility

The following are top dissatisfiers:

- Company administration
- Supervision-technical
- Salary
- Interpersonal relations-supervision
- Working conditions

Outcome Effects. Over 50 replications have established this theory as one of the most replicated in industrial psychology (Grigaliunas & Herzberg, 1971). Herzberg's theory was used to advance the concept of **job enrichment**, expanding the tasks within a given job to increase the person's responsibility. He pointedly distinguished this concept from **job enlargement**, expanding the variety of skills but at the same skill level. In their meta-analysis of field studies, Locke et al. (1980) found that job enrichment increased performance by 9% to 17%.

Measurement. Herzberg's theory identified key motivators that can be translated into items that tap the presence or absence of motivational factors.

1. Do you feel there is room for advancement at your organization? Is the path to "moving up" clear? Why or why not?
2. Does your company have ridiculous policies that impede your effectiveness?

Intrinsic and Extrinsic: Expectancy Theory. Expectancy theory was originally referred to as "VIE" theory and was advanced by Vroom (1964) in his book

Work and Motivation. The goal of this theory is to predict motivation as a function of three major independent variables: valence, instrumentality, and expectancy. **Instrumentality** is the extent to which one's performance outcome is linked to one's reward outcome. **Expectancy** originally was defined as the subjective probability that an action or effort will lead to performance, but in practice, it was measured as the relation or correlation between action and outcome. **Valence** is the value that a given individual places on a given reward. It is posited that rewards will be valued differently by different people. For examples of these concepts together, consider the student who we motivate to study. Will the student study hard if she does not have the "expectancy" that effort will result in a high grade? Even if she does get a high grade, does she believe the grade will be "instrumental" to her getting a good job out of college? Is a good job out of college a reward that has "valence" or value to her in particular, or does she really plan to be a stay-at-home parent?

Outcome Effects. van Eerde & Thierry (1996) conducted a meta-analysis of 77 studies that examined expectancy models and work-related criteria. They found the VIE variables more strongly related to effort and turnover than to overall performance.

Measurement. Expectancy theory leads to important questions that are not directly covered in other motivation theories. The following are examples:

1. Are there features of your job or workplace where you can try very hard but it does not show in your performance? If so, why is that?
2. Does management make an effort to tailor rewards according to individual preferences? For example, some people like time off. Others would prefer bonuses. Others yet would prefer social events. Is there an effort to make these matches to various preferences?

Job Content Models and Theories

In a sense, Herzberg's motivation-hygiene theory gets at work-design variables when it asks about responsibility, company policies, work itself, and working conditions. Vroom's expectancy theory also gets at work design when it asks about the extent to which a job is designed so that effort results in performance. However, other theories sidestep the concern for the "intrinsic motivation" construct and directly focus on features of the job. These theories and research areas include the job characteristics model, work-design studies, and person-job fit research.

Job Characteristics Model and Work Design. Hackman and Oldham's (1976) job characteristics model gives five concepts for describing motivational characteristics of a job. **Skill variety** is the extent to which workers get to use a variety of skills. **Task identity** is the extent to which people can see how their task contributes to a larger whole. **Task significance** is the extent to which the job has an impact on the lives of others. **Autonomy** is the freedom and discretion people get in choosing ways to perform their jobs. **Feedback** is from the job itself, that is, the extent to which individuals get knowledge about how well they did. A meta-analysis of nearly 200 job characteristic studies established the link between these variables and motivation (Fried & Ferris, 1987).

One meta-analysis expanded the model from "job design" to "work design" and assessed variables from 259 studies. *Social characteristics* of the job included interdependence, feedback from others, social support, and interaction outside the organization. These phenomena especially aided worker stress, burnout, job satisfaction, and organizational commitment. In particular, feedback improved performance and reduced role ambiguity. *Work context* characteristics included physical demands, work conditions, and ergonomics. These variables particularly affected stress as well as satisfaction. Additional *motivational characteristics* of jobs included task variety (as opposed to skill variety), information processing, and job complexity. These variables also had a positive effect on job satisfaction (Humphrey, Nahrgang, & Morgeson, 2007).

Outcome Effects. Although work-design variables are correlated to attitudinal and behavioral outcomes just discussed, some qualifications are warranted. Job characteristic studies show that the effects of job design are moderated by growth need, such that high-growth-need individuals are more affected by feedback, autonomy, and other job characteristics (Fried & Ferris, 1987; Loher, Noe, Moeller, & Fitzgerald, 1985). Humphrey, Nahrgang, and Morgeson (2007) found work-design characteristics to be moderated by "experienced meaningfulness." For example, a variety of tasks will not yield increases in satisfaction if you're switching from washing knives to forks to spoons. Finally, studies in this vein have shown workers to be demoralized when jobs were stripped of these motivational characteristics, such as in lean manufacturing implementations (Jackson & Martin, 1996; Parker, 2003).

Measurement. The job characteristics have been translated into the Job Diagnostic Survey (JDS) (Hackman & Oldham, 1975), the Job Characteristics Inventory (JCI) (Sims, Szilagyi, & Keller, 1976), or a more recent Work-Design Questionnaire (Morgeson & Humphrey, 2006). Open-ended questions associated with this theory would be as follows:

1. Are jobs at your company designed in a way that people get to use a variety of skills? Which jobs have high skill variety? Which jobs could use improvement?
2. Are jobs designed in a way that people understand the entire process they are working on, start to finish?

Person-Environment Fit

This research looks at several types of matches: person-job (PJ) fit, person-vocation (PV) fit, person-organization (PO) fit, person-group fit (PG), and person-supervisor fit (PS). **Person-job fit** "is broadly defined as the compatibility between an individual and a work environment that occurs when their characteristics are well matched" (Kristof-Brown, Zimmerman, & Johnson, 2005, p. 281).

Outcome Effects. In a meta-analysis of 172 studies, PJ fit and PO fit had strong, positive correlations to job satisfaction and organizational commitment. In this meta-analysis, only person-supervisor fit had a substantive correlation to overall performance ($r = 0.33$, $p < 0.01$) (Kristof-Brown et al., 2005).

More recently, Greguras and Diefendorff (2009) found that person-group fit affected relatedness need fulfillment, but it did not affect job performance. Demands-abilities fit (job fit) predicted needs for competence, but it did not have a direct effect on job performance. Competence, however, was associated with improved job performance.

Measurement. General questions of fit between environment and employee would be as follows:

1. Is there an effort to make sure that individual employees are well-matched to your *organization*? If so, how? Can you think of examples where there are mismatches?
2. Is there a way to detect when people do not fit into specific *work groups*? In the case of mismatches between people and groups, is there a quick process to get people to groups where they are a better fit?

Cognitive Theories of Motivation

As covered in Chapter 3, systems theory would predict that individuals intuitively compare their performance to a "standard" of performance and assess whether there is a "gap." The gap then triggers their choice of action. In a sense, cognitive theories of motivation are all about gaps. *Bandura's* cognitive theories argue that people seek to reduce gaps between performance and externally provided goals, but also between performance and one's internal sets of standards. *Goal-setting theory* looks at the gap between performance and an external goal. *Equity and Procedural Justice* theories look at the gap between what one receives and what they perceive others to receive. Each major theory is now described in turn.

Albert Bandura's Cognitive Theories: Social Learning Theory and Social Cognitive Theory. Albert Bandura received his doctorate in 1952, a time when "behaviorism" was the going trend in psychology. Behaviorist theories proceed on the assumption that one's environment causes one's behavior. In this thinking, we act to attain rewards or avoid punishments and the only data worth counting is what we observe objectively. Bandura, sometimes considered the father of cognitive psychology, found behaviorism simplistic and dove into the subjective, unobservable world of "cognition." He emphasized that how we *think* influences our **self-regulation**, the control of our own behavior. Before turning to regulation of work behavior and general motivation, Bandura first did the work for which he remains the most famous: social learning theory (Haggbloom et al., 2002).

Bandura began with a focus on the aggression of children and gained psychology textbook fame for his series of bobo dolls studies (Bandura & Walters, 1963). These experiments involved making a film of a woman beating up a clown doll and then showing the movie to kindergartners. The children were then given similar dolls to play with. Results showed that the children, in turn, imitated the woman's behavior. Later variations in the studies included showing rewards or punishment for how models treated the bobo dolls. Bandura summarized that we *learn* (or "acquire") behaviors socially but our subsequent imitative performance is motivated by rewards. He finally published his seminal text on social learning theory in 1977 (Bandura, 1977).

Social learning theory has direct implications for managers. For example, the idea that one can "lead by example" is based on the premise of social learning. Another direct application is that sometimes people don't believe they can perform a certain task until they see someone else do it. It is not just seeing someone else do the task that teaches them how to do it, but it motivates them to believe "if they can do it, I can as well."

In the mid-1980s, Bandura (1986) developed the theory that would make him a staple of organizational behavior textbooks: social cognitive theory. The term "social" credits that much of human thought and action is social in origin. The term "cognitive" credits that thought processes influence emotion, motivation, and action. The basic idea is that before humans are motivated to choose to engage in an action, they make a mental assessment about whether their effort will result in performance. This is a judgment of **self-efficacy**, an individual's personal judgment about "how well one can execute courses of action required to deal with prospective situations" (Bandura, 1982, p. 122). In other words, self-efficacy is not ability, but your *belief* in your ability.

Outcome Effects. Bandura and Locke (2003) cite nine meta-analyses demonstrating the power of self-efficacy effects. In a meta-analysis of 114 laboratory and field studies involving more than 20,000 subjects, Stajkovic and Luthans (1998) reported a significant, positive association between self-efficacy and performance (adjusted to account for sample size outliers and extreme values, $r = 0.38$). They recalculated these results and results from other meta-analyses to demonstrate the comparative power of various motivational effects to improve performance: self-efficacy (28% increase), goal-setting (10.39% increase), feedback (13.6% increase), and behavior modification (17% increase).

Measures. Bandura has stressed that no one scale can measure self-efficacy as it is specific to particular contexts (Latham & Pinder, 2005). For example, I may have self-efficacy when it comes to my ability to do a math problem but not when it comes to my ability to fix a car. Other concepts from his various theories provide highly relevant questions for managers not directly addressed by other theories.

1. Are people in your company provided with role models? Do you have a formal mentoring system?
2. Do managers make an effort to build your confidence? In your work setting, what contributes to your confidence and ability to perform your tasks? What takes away from it?

Goal-Setting Theory. Goal-setting theory (Latham and Locke, 1979; Locke & Latham, 1990) is the most dominant theory in the motivation field with more than 1,000 articles in a little over 30 years (Mitchell & Daniels, 2003). A **goal** refers to the completion of an activity or a level on a measure. In goal-setting research, *feedback* is defined as "knowledge of results" (KR), typically referring to specific quantitative scores on a measure. In other words, goals and metrics are basically inseparable.

Just as there is "constructive" and "destructive" feedback, there are "effective" and "ineffective" goals. There is a basic theorem of goal-setting theory: hard, specific goals (if accepted) will lead to increased performance (Locke & Latham, 1990). Corollaries to the theory add that feedback is a necessary (but not sufficient) condition for goal-setting effects (Erez, 1977) and that self-efficacy enhances goal-setting effects (Latham, 2007). Other evidence shows that *learning* goals should be differentiated from *performance* goals. Giving people hard goals when they are in the process of learning a complex task can actually detract from potential performance (Kanfer & Ackerman, 1989).

This book has stressed that *outcome* metrics and goals should be coupled with *behavioral* metrics and goals. Goal-setting research on distal versus proximal goals provides indirect support for this mandate. A **distal goal** is a more "distant" or longer-term goal such as an annual sales goal. A **proximal goal** is a more "proximate" or intermediate goal used to reach a distal goal such as a weekly sales goal. Research supports the idea that proximal goals enhance goal-setting effects. For example, one study found that people who set proximal (daily) weight goals lost more weight than people who set distal (weekly) weight goals (Bandura & Simon, 1977). Students who set proximal goals for the outcomes of individual study sessions have also been shown to have better outcomes on year-end exams than students with more distal goals (Morgan, 1985).

Most goal-setting research focuses on a single task. As discussed in Chapter 7, employees often are confronted by multiple goals that may be in conflict (Ethiraj & Levinthal, 2009). If one conceives of a "focal" goal and "other" goals, how is it that individuals prioritize their efforts? For metrics, this becomes a question of which measures people will focus on when trying to improve. Possible reactions include to step up effort, to abandon effort on the focal goal, to switch effort to other goals, or to coast toward the goal. In an impressive series of studies, Louro, Pieters, and Zeelenberg (2007) demonstrated three factors that influenced effort: positive emotions stemming from prior success, negative emotions stemming from prior failure, and effects when goal achievement is close or distant. If the focal goal is distant, positive emotions lead people to step up effort on the focal goal, whereas negative emotions lead people to rechannel energy toward other goals. If the focal goal is close, positive emotions lead people to coast and rechannel energy toward other goals, whereas negative emotions lead people to step up effort on the focal goal. However, the expectancy of success mediates both the emotional and proximity effects. Effort is highest toward the focal goal if expectancies are intermediate. If expectancy of success is extremely low or extremely high, people are likely to shift effort to intermediate goals.

For metrics, there are several implications. First, managers need to watch for conditions that lead to coasting ("don't stop now!") or cheer against negative emotions ("just because you did poorly in the past does not mean you should give up now!"). Second, indexes such as those in Chapter 6 can be used to provide information about how goals should be weighted. Third, if the overall goals are competing, they can be shifted between departments as in Chapter 7.

How hard should goals be? Some interpret a hard goal as one that "stretches" people. Another approach is to set the goal where it can only be reached by 10% of participants (Wood & Bandura, 1989). This practice originates in the competency model of performance measurement, where superior performance is statistically defined at one standard deviation above the average, a level typically achieved by 1 in 10 in a work situation (Spencer & Spencer, 1993).

Aside from the 1 in 10 prescription, Chapter 13 presents a variety of comparisons that can be used in metric presentations (e.g., historical data, benchmarks, and so forth.)

In some situations do you use an arbitrary "just improve" goal? Some would argue that this might be appropriate when you are starting something new and absolutely no data are available on which to base your goals.

For managers, an important goal-setting question is, "Who sets goals, the boss or the employee?" Although self-set goals would seem to be effective for commitment or "buy-in" purposes, the concern is that the level of goals might be lower if they are self-set and whether the goal triggers **task strategies**, that is, an individual's strategy for achieving a goal. One series of studies found that if managers gave a goal and gave an extensive rationale for goal level, there would be very little difference than if goals were "participatively" set in a rushed meeting in which employees had little time to discuss how to reach the goal. The effects varied by whether the goal-setting process triggered task strategies. Most of all, the actual performance effects in either situation were more affected by goal *level* (Latham, 2007).

Finally, a widely taught method for remembering goal-setting principles is the mnemonic SMART. The letters vary depending on who teaches it, but the link to goal-setting principles can easily be seen below:

SMART

- **S**pecific (goal specificity)
- **M**easurable (feedback in the form of metrics)

- Version 1: **A**ctionable (goal commitment, self-efficacy)
- Version 2: **A**ttainable (goal difficulty, goal commitment, self-efficacy)
- **R**easonable (goal difficulty, goal commitment, self-efficacy)
- **R**ealistic (goal difficulty, goal commitment, self-efficacy)
- **T**imely (feedback reports)
- **T**angible (same as Actionable, goal commitment, self-efficacy)

Outcome Effects. There is overwhelming evidence for the power of goals. One meta-analysis focused only on goals in work settings and found they improved performance by nearly a full standard deviation (O'Leary-Kelly, Martocchio, & Frink, 1994). Another meta-analysis estimated the effect at 0.75 standard deviations (confidence interval 0.57 to 0.93) (Guzzo, Jette, & Katzell, 1985). Wood, Mento, and Locke (1987) conducted a meta-analysis of 125 studies that manipulated task complexity to examine how this affected goal-setting effects. Goal-setting effects were strongest for simple tasks such as reaction time or brainstorming ($d = 0.76$) and weaker but still substantive for more complex tasks such as science and engineering work, faculty research productivity, and business game simulations ($d = 0.42$).

Measures. Some logical measurement questions directly follow goal-setting principles:

1. Do your managers set reasonable goals? Or do efforts to provide "stretch" goals sometimes come off as crazy goals that people ignore? Or possibly, do managers veer the other way and set goals that are too easy? Can you think of specific examples?
2. When setting goals, do managers provide the rationale for why they set the numbers they choose? For example, they might set a goal to perform at a certain level and compare it to some industry standard to demonstrate that the goal is justified.

Equity Theory and Procedural Justice. Imagine if you worked at Microsoft in its dot-com, stock-option-granting heyday and found out that the person in the next cube over *who does the same work as you* negotiated 10 times the stock options that you did. Would you be demoralized? To the point that your performance would be affected? Perhaps you are enough of a professional that your performance on required tasks would not be affected, but would you be willing to do voluntary tasks on your own time? These are the questions addressed by equity and justice theories.

Equity is a principle of reward allocation in which one receives rewards based on how much one contributes. Alternate allocation principles are **equality** (everyone gets an equal reward), **need** (you get how much you need), and **tenure** (your reward depends on how long you have been here). Human toil over fairness of allocation goes back to biblical times (Matthew: 20). The basic proposition of equity theory (Adams, 1965) is that if people perceive inequity, they will be dissatisfied on the job. In equity theory, satisfaction (or lack thereof) is a focal outcome variable.

Perceived equity depends on how we compare the amount we contribute to other standards. The following are some basic comparisons we might make:

- Self (input to output)
- Self to others in organization
- Self to others in occupation
- Self to others in position
- Self to others with same education level
- Self to people in your country

A development in equity theory is the development of a trait measure in which individuals are classified as either "Benevolents" who are tolerant of undercompensation, "Equity Sensitives" who prefer equity norms, or "Entitleds" who are tolerant of overcompensation (Huseman, Hatfield, & Miles, 1985). The typical research question is whether overcompensation and undercompsenation vary as a function of personality variables. Research has demonstrated that "Entitleds" place a higher emphasis on tangible outcomes such as pay and "Benevolents" place a higher value on intrinsic outcomes such as values (King, Miles, & Day, 1993).

The effects of fairness on motivation are studied in research on organizational justice. There are four major types of justice: distributive, procedural, interpersonal, and informational. **Distributive justice** refers to the perception that resource allocations are fair. **Procedural justice** refers to the perception that procedures used to decide resource allocation are fair. Interactional justice has two components: interpersonal and intractional. **Interpersonal justice** is based on the perception that the individual was treated with respect on an interpersonal basis. **Informational justice** is the perception that one receives adequate information about allocation decisions. Some consider that there are only three categories of justice because they consider **interactional justice** as a general category that includes interpersonal and informational justice.

Outcome Effects. In a meta-analysis of 45 studies that compared both facets of OCB and types of justice, Fassina, Jones, and Uggerslev (2008) found relatively strong intercorrelations among the three types of justice (ranging from 0.43 between interactional and distributive justice, 0.56 between procedural and distributive justice, and 0.51 between procedural and interactional justice). This pattern of results is similar to those found in the meta-analysis by Colquitt, Conlon, Wesson, Porter, and Ng (2001). Another meta-analysis examined 190 studies with a total of 64,757 subjects and compared distributive, procedural, and "interactional" justice (Cohen-Charash & Spector, 2001). This study added the insights that justice perceptions did not vary as a function of perceiver demographics (gender, race, and age). More recently, the types of justice were collapsed into the idea of "overall justice," and not only was this found to be a better predictor for behavioral outcomes, but also overall justice mediated effects of individual types of justice (Ambrose & Schminke, 2009). For example, you might be unhappy with the procedures used if asked specifically, but this would not affect your performance unless you generally assessed the organization as unfair.

Measures. The "overall justice" scale used in the Ambrose and Schminke (2009) study had excellent psychometric properties and has the strongest association with actual outcomes. Both equity theory and justice concepts yield yet another set of questions for managers assessing their motivational practices. The following are examples:

1. Does it seem that some people in your company are unfairly overpaid while others are underpaid? Without naming names, can you give examples?
2. Do people receive explanations from management about how raises are given?
3. How are people told about pay increases? In person? On the paycheck? If it is in person, would you say that your manager treats you with politeness during salary discussions? Respect? Display the proper amount of emotion?

CHAPTER SUMMARY

This chapter presented concepts to define motivation and to distinguish types of motivation effects. Four categories of motivation theories were then reviewed: needs-based theories, theories comparing intrinsic and extrinsic effects, job-based theories, and cognitive theories. Each review included a basic description of concepts, outcomes of research generated by the theory, and questions that could be drawn from the theory to create a practical motivation audit.

NOTES

1. Other psychologists on the "Most Eminent" list and their eponym:
   - B. F. Skinner (Skinnerian)
   - Jean Piaget (Piagetian)
   - Sigmund Freud (Freudian)
   - Albert Bandura (Bandura's Social Learning Theory)
   - Leon Festinger (Festinger's Cognitive Dissonance Theory)
   - Carl R. Rogers (Rogerian therapy)
   - Stanley Schacter (Schacter's affiliation studies)
   - Neal E. Miller (Anxiety, biofeedback)
   - Edward Thorndike (Thorndike's puzzle box)
   - Abraham Maslow (Maslow's Hierarchy of Needs)

REFERENCES

Adams, J. S. (1965). Inequity in social exchange. In L. Berkowitz (Ed.), *Advances in experimental social psychology* (Vol. 2, pp. 267–299). New York: Academic Press.

Ambrose, M. L., & Schminke, M. (2009). The role of overall justice judgments in organizational justice research: A test of mediation. *Journal of Applied Psychology, 94*, 491–500.

Bandura, A. (1977). *Social learning theory.* Englewood Cliffs, NJ: Prentice Hall.

Bandura, A. (1982). Self-efficacy mechanism in human agency. *American Psychologist, 37*, 122–147.

Bandura, A. (1986). *Social foundations of thought and action: A social cognitive theory.* Englewood Cliffs, NJ: Prentice-Hall.

Bandura, A. (1997). *Self-efficacy: The exercise of control.* New York: W. H. Freeman.

Bandura, A., & Locke, E. A. (2003). Negative self-efficacy and goals revisited. *Journal of Applied Psychology, 88*, 87–99.

Bandura, A., & Simon, K. M. (1977). The role of proximal intentions in self-regulation of refractory behavior. *Cognitive Therapy and Research, 1*, 177–193.

Bandura, A., & Walters, R. H. (1963). *Social learning and personality development.* New York: Holt, Rinehart, & Winston.

Benson, S. G., & Dundis, S. P. (2003). Understanding and motivating health care employees: Integrating Maslow's hierarchy of needs, training, and technology. *Journal of Nursing Management, 11*, 315–320.

Bowling, N. A. (2007). Is the job satisfaction-job performance relationship spurious? A meta-analytic examination. *Journal of Vocational Behavior, 71*, 167–185.

Brown, S. P., & Lam, S. K. (2008). A meta-analysis of relationships linking employee satisfaction to customer responses. *Journal of Retailing, 84*, 243–255.

Cohen-Charash, Y., & Spector, P. E. (2001). The role of justice in organizations: A meta-analysis. *Organizational Behavior and Human Decision Processes, 86*, 278–321.

Colquitt, J. A., Conlon, D. E., Wesson, M. J., Porter, C., & Ng, K. Y. (2001). Justice at the millennium: A meta-analysis of 25 years of organizational justice research. *Journal of Applied Psychology, 86*, 425–445.

Deci, E. L. (1975). *Intrinsic motivation.* New York: Plenum.

Deci, E. L., Koestner, R., & Ryan, R. M. (1999). A meta-analytic review of experiments examining the effects of extrinsic rewards on motivation. *Psychological Bulletin, 125*, 627–668.

Dyer, L., & Schwab, D. (1982). Personnel/human resource management research. In T. Kochan, D. Mitchell, & L. Dyer, (Eds.), *Industrial relations research in the 1970s: Review and appraisal* (pp. 187–220). Madison, WI: Industrial Relations Research Association.

Erez, A. (1977). Feedback: A necessary condition for the goal setting-performance relationship. *Journal of Applied Psychology, 62,* 624–627.

Ethiraj, S. K., & Levinthal, D. (2009). Hoping for A to Z while rewarding only A: Complex organizations and multiple goals. *Organization Science, 20,* 4–21.

Fassina, N. E., Jones, D. A., & Uggerslev, K. L. (2008). Relationship clean-up time: Using meta-analysis and path analysis to clarify relationships among job satisfaction, perceived fairness, and citizenship behaviors. *Journal of Management, 34,* 161–188.

Fayol, H. (1949). *Industrial and general administration* (Constance Storrs, Trans.). London: Pitman House. (Original work published 1916).

Ford, M. E. (1992). *Motivating humans: goals, emotions, and personal agency beliefs.* Newbury Park, CA: Sage.

Fried, Y., & Ferris, G. R. (1987). The validity of the job characteristics model: A review and meta-analysis. *Personnel Psychology, 40,* 287–332.

Gagne, M., & Deci, E. L. (2005). Self-determination theory and work motivation. *Journal of Organizational Behavior, 26,* 331–362.

Greguras, G. J., & Diefendorff, J. M. (2009). Different fits satisfy different needs: Linking person-environment fit to employee commitment and performance using self-determination theory. *Journal of Applied Psychology, 94,* 465–477.

Grigaliunas, B. S., & Herzberg, F. (1971). Relevancy in the test of motivator-hygiene theory. *Journal of Applied Psychology, 55,* 73–79.

Guzzo, R. A., Jette, R. D., & Katzell, R. A. (1985). The effects of psychologically based intervention programs on worker productivity: A meta-analysis. *Personnel Psychology, 38,* 275–291.

Hackman, J. R., & Oldham, G. R. (1975). Development of the job diagnostic survey. *Journal of Applied Psychology, 60,* 159–170.

Hackman, J. R., & Oldham, G. R. (1976). Motivation through the design of work: Test of a theory. *Organizational Behavior and Human Performance, 16,* 250–279.

Haggbloom, S. J., Warnick, R., Warnick, J. E., Yarbrough, G. L., Borecky, C. M., Powell, J. L., et al. (2002). The 100 most eminent psychologists of the 20th century. *Review of General Psychology, 6,* 139–152.

Harrison, D. A., Newman, D. A., & Roth, P. L. (2006). How important are job attitudes? Meta-analytic comparisons of integrative behavioral outcomes and time sequences. *Academy of Management Journal, 49,* 305–325.

Herzberg, F. (2003, January). One more time: How do you motivate employees? *Harvard Business Review, 81*(1), 87–96. (Reprint from 1968.)

Herzberg, F., Mausner, B., & Synderman, B. B. (1959). *Motivation to work* (2nd ed.). New York: Wiley.

Humphrey, S. E., Nahrgang, J. D., & Morgeson, F. P. (2007). Integrating motivational, social, and contextual work design features: A meta-analytic summary and theoretical extension of work design literature. *Journal of Applied Psychology, 92,* 1332–1356.

Huseman, R. C., Hatfield, J. D., & Miles, E. W. (1985). Test for individual perceptions of job equity: Some preliminary findings. *Perceptual and Motor Skills, 61,* 1055–1064.

Iaffaldano, M. T., & Muchinsky, P. M. (1985). Job satisfaction and performance: A meta-analysis. *Psychological Bulletin, 97,* 251–273.

Ironson, G. H., Smith, P. C., Brannick, M. T., & Paul, K. B. (1989). Construction of a job in general scale: A comparison of global, composite, and specific measures. *Journal of Applied Psychology, 74,* 193–200.

Jackson, P. R., & Martin, R. (1996). Impact of just-in-time job content, employee attitudes, and well-being: A longitudinal study. *Ergonomics, 39,* 1–16.

Jenkins Jr., D. G., Mitra, A., Gupta, N., & Shaw, J. D. (1998). Are financial incentives related to performance? A meta-analytic review of empirical research. *Journal of Applied Psychology, 83,* 777–787.

Kanfer, R., & Ackerman, P. L. (1989). Motivation and cognitive abilities: An integrative/aptitude treatment interaction approach to skill acquisition. *Journal of Applied Psychology, 74,* 951–956.

King, W. C., Miles, E. W., & Day, D. D. (1993). A test and refinement of the equity sensitivity construct. *Journal of Organizational Behavior, 14,* 301–317.

Kinicki, A. J., McKee-Ryan, F. M., Schriesheim, C. A., & Carson, K. P. (2002). Assessing the construct validity of the Job Descriptive Index: A review and meta-analysis. *Journal of Applied Psychology, 87,* 14–32.

Koltko-Rivera, M. E. (2006). Rediscovering the later version of Maslow's hierarchy of needs: Self-transcendence and opportunities for theory, research, and unification. *Review of General Psychology, 10,* 302–317.

Kristof-Brown, A. L., Zimmerman, R. D., & Johnson, E. C. (2005). Consequences of individuals' fit at work: A meta-analysis of person-job, person-organization, person-group, and person-supervisor fit. *Personnel Psychology, 58,* 281–342.

Latham, G. P. (2007). *Work motivation.* Thousand Oaks, CA: Sage.

Latham, G. P., & Locke, E. A. (1979). Goal setting: A motivational technique that works. *Organizational Dynamics, 8,* 68–80.

Latham, G. P., & Pinder, C. C. (2005). Work motivation theory and research at the dawn of the twenty-first century. *Annual Review of Psychology, 56,* 485–516.

Locke, E. A., Feren, D. B., McCaleb, V. M., Shaw, K. N., & Denny, A. T. (1980). The relative effectiveness of four ways of motivating employee performance. In K. D. Duncan, M. M. Gruenberg, & D. Wallis (Eds.), *Changes in Working Life* (pp. 363–388). New York: Wiley.

Locke, E. A., & Latham, G. P. (1990). *A theory of goal setting and task performance.* Englewood Cliffs, NJ: Prentice Hall.

Loher, B. T., Noe, R. A., Moeller, N. L., Fitzgerald, M. P. (1985). A meta-analysis of the relation of job characteristics to job satisfaction. *Journal of Applied Psychology, 70,* 280–289.

Louro, M. J., Pieters, R., & Zeelenberg, M. (2007). Dynamics of multiple-goal pursuit. *Journal of Personality and Social Psychology, 93,* 174–193.

Luthans, F. (1973). *Organizational behavior.* New York: McGraw-Hill.

MacGregor, D. (1960). *The human side of enterprise.* New York: McGraw-Hill.

Maslow, A. (1954). *Motivation and personality.* New York: Harper & Row.

Mayo, E. (1933). *The human problems of an industrial organization.* New York: Macmillan.

McClelland, D. C. (1961). *The achieving society.* New York: Van Nostrand Reinhold.

Mitchell, T. R., & Daniels, D. (2003). In W. C. Borman, D. R. Ilgen, & R. J. Klimoski (Eds.), *Handbook of psychology: Industrial organizational psychology.* Motivation. (*Vol. 12*, pp. 225–254). New York: Wiley.

Morgan, M. (1985). Self-monitoring of attained goals in a private study. *Journal of Educational Psychology, 77,* 623–630.

Morgeson, F. P., & Humphrey, S. E. (2006). The Work Design Questionnaire (WDQ): Developing and validating a comprehensive measure for assessing job design and the nature of work. *Journal of Applied Psychology, 91,* 1321–1339.

O'Leary-Kelly, A. M., Martocchio, J. J., & Frink, D. D. (1994). A review of the influence of group goals on group-performance. *Academy of Management Journal, 37,* 1285–1301.

Parker, S. K. (2003). The longitudinal effects of lean production on employee outcomes and the mediating role of work characteristics. *Journal of Applied Psychology, 88,* 620–634.

Podsakoff, N. P., LePine, J. A., & LePine, M. A. (2007). Attitudes, turnover intentions, turnover, and withdrawal behavior: A meta-analysis. *Journal of Applied Psychology, 92,* 438–454.

Porter, L. W. (1961). A study of perceived need satisfaction in bottom and middle management jobs. *Journal of Applied Psychology, 45,* 1–10.

Price, J. L., & Mueller, C. W. (1986). Handbook of organizational measurement. Marshfield, MA: Pittman.

Rapaille, G. C. (2001). *Seven secrets of marketing in a multicultural world.* Provo, UT: Executive Excellence Pub.

Rhoades, L., & Eisenberger, R. (2002). Perceived organizational support: A review of the literature. *Journal of Applied Psychology, 87,* 698–714.

Shantz, A., & Latham, G. P. (2009). An exploratory field experiment of the effect of subconscious and conscious goals on employee performance. *Organizational Behavior and Human Decision Processes, 109,* 9–17.

Sims, H. P., Szilagyi, A. D., & Keller, R. T. (1976). The measurement of job characteristics. *Academy of Management Journal, 19,* 196–212.

Smith, P. C., Kendall, L., & Hulin, C. L. (1969). *The measurement of satisfaction in work and retirement.* Chicago, IL: Rand McNally.

Spencer, L. M., & Spencer, S. M. (1993). *Competence at work: Models for superior performance.* New York: Wiley.

Stajkovic, A. D., & Luthans, F. (1998). Self-efficacy and work-related performance: A meta-analysis. *Psychological Bulletin, 124,* 240–261.

Stajkovic, A. D., & Luthans, F. (2003). Behavioral management and task performance in organizations: Conceptual background, meta-analysis, and test of alternative models. *Personnel Psychology, 56,* 155–194.

Tett, R. P., & Meyer, J. P. (1993). Job satisfaction, organizational commitment, turnover intention, and turnover: Path analyses based on meta-analytic findings. *Personnel Psychology, 46,* 259–293.

U.S. Department of Education, National Center for Education Statistics. (2004). The condition of education 2004. Retrieved December 9, 2007, from http://nces.ed.gov/pubs2004/2004077.pdf.

U.S. Information Agency. (1997). Portrait of the USA. Chapter six: A diverse educational system. Retrieved June 30, 2006, from http://usinfo.state.gov/usa/infousa/facts/factover/ch6.htm.

van Eerde, W., & Thierry, H. (1996). Vroom's expectancy models and work-related criteria: A meta-analysis. *Journal of Applied Psychology, 81*, 575–586.

Vroom, V. H. (1964). *Work and motivation*. New York: Wiley.

Wood, R. E., & Bandura, A. (1989). Impact of conceptions of ability on self-regulatory mechanisms and complex decision-making. *Journal of Personality and Social Psychology, 56*, 407–415.

Wood, R. E., Mento, A. J., & Locke, E. A. (1987). Task complexity as a moderator of goal effects: A meta-analysis. *Journal of Applied Psychology, 72*, 416–425.

Zyberg, L., & Berry, D. M. (2005). Gender and students' vocational choices in entering the field of nursing. *Nursing Outlook, 53*(4), 193–198.

16   *PUTTING IT ALL TOGETHER*

Creating a metric system is a journey that takes you through a minefield of deci-
sions that are fraught with the potential for gaming, petty agendas, and demoral-
izing outcomes. Alternatively, it could be one of the most rewarding and
motivating endeavors a manager can experience.

   How can you avoid mistakes? Chart the course. Proceed systematically, writing
down the turns on the map as you go. The overall product should be a system
that shows how all the scorecards fit together and how motivation practices are
in place to complement the scorecards. It begins and ends with a system, not just
system theory but an entire metric system.

CHAPTER OVERVIEW

   This chapter summarizes the entire activity of creating a metric system as a
series of decisions that are made. Who makes these decisions? It could be a
complex negotiation between union and management, an extensive off-site series with key managers, or a cross-functional team. Regardless, each piece of
the system requires a conversation.

   This chapter is written for people who are tasked with facilitating the meetings in which metrics are created. In the spirit of guiding conversations, this
chapter summarizes metric decisions that have been discussed at length elsewhere in the text.

   To provide a running example, this chapter will describe possible metrics for
a real company. The company's name and factual details are changed to protect
the company's anonymity. The company will be referred to as Dashboard
Incorporated (Dashboard).

   Dashboard was founded in the late 1990s. Their headquarters are in the
United States and they have regional offices in Dublin and Melbourne. They

---

LEARNING OBJECTIVES

After studying this chapter, you should be able to achieve the following:

1. Facilitate team meetings where coleaders decide how to create a metric system.
2. Cross-reference chapters in this text to provide relevant models and instructions for creating pieces of metric systems.

---

have fewer than 500 employees and they are privately held. Their customers are marketing research firms.

Dashboard's primary service is to provide research panels and associated technologies. A research panel represents millions of potential respondents who complete marketing surveys. In Dashboard's case, they have developed a respondent base in more than 100 countries.

In a sense, Dashboard takes the content of this book to the next level. You may be a manager or consultant who has used this book to come up with metrics needed to judge the performance of a given team or company. But how do you gather the data on those metrics? Suppose you created a customer service survey. Using a pen-and-paper method would be antiquated when you can use an online method that can track clicks and process data automatically. Dashboard can provide the programming that translates those contents into interactive online surveys. They can then automate data gathering, process the data, and deliver results in a variety of technology-enabled report formats including dashboards.

Dashboard makes it to the lists of fast-growing technology firms. Their growth is driven by major acquisitions and expanded product lines. Not surprisingly, their metrics reflect a strategy to include the elements one would expect from a company that, itself, processes metrics: orientation to *customer* satisfaction, *productivity* in all processes and regions, a *financial* eye on investment returns, *employee* satisfaction, and special attention to strategic measures of *growth* and *integration*.

This chapter also presents an example first-level scorecard for Dashboard. The specific team was a generic "Service Bureau" team. Bureaus are groups of professionals, typically technical, who can be contracted to complete various services. In this case, the service bureau was a group who programmed online surveys.

Decision: What is the social unit/level of analysis for which you would like to make a scorecard?

The choice of social unit will give the level of scorecard you wish to make. As shown in Table 16.1, this book has included several types of scorecards,

Table 16.1 Scorecard Attributes and Dimensions

First-Level Teams	Departments (Possible Attributes)	Organization
Quality	Functional metrics	Processes
Quantity (Productivity)	Process metrics	Customer
Efficiency (Productivity)	Roll-up first-level metrics	Workforce
Renewal	Adapted corporate	Financial
Strategy	metrics	Community
		Ethics
		Management
		Renewal
		Other stakeholders
		Other strategic variables (e.g., innovation, globalization)

Collaborations	Initiatives/Vision	Initiatives/General
Progress	Bullet in vision statement (Objective)	Combination of other scorecard dimensions
Quality	Bullet in vision statement (Objective)	or metrics
Efficiency	Bullet in vision statement (Objective)	
Other key attribute		

Source: © Ruth A. Huwe.

including ones for first-level teams (Chapter 6), Departments (Chapter 7), Organizations (Chapter 8), Collaborations (Chapter 17), and Initiatives (Chapter 13). Once the decision is made on the type of scorecards, the various attributes can be used to describe the unit's performance.

Dashboard Running Example: A first-level scorecard will be designed for the "Service Bureau Team" that is part of the global operations department.

As described in Chapter 7, departmental scorecards have various attribute combinations such as individual first-level scorecards for each team, roll-up metrics, functional metrics, process metrics, elements of the corporate scorecard owned by your department, performance on intermediate activities, organizational initiatives, or some combination.

Table 16.2 Comparison of Metric Process Steps

First-Level Scorecard Steps	Organizational Scorecard Broad Steps	Survey Steps
1. Reason for metrics.	1. Describe the organization.	1. Reason for metrics.
2. What is your scope?	2. Describe the company's mission, vision, and strategy.	2. What is your scope?
3. What is your level of analysis?	3. Describe the company's strategy in terms of a strategy map.	3. What is your unit of analysis?
4. Make sure that you are measuring the right variables.	4. Generate possible metrics for each of the main variables on the strategy map.	4. Make sure that you are measuring the right variables.
5. Define your terms.	5. Reduce your set of metrics to a list of 25 or less.	5. Define your terms.
6. Advance Scrutiny: What criteria must your metrics meet?	6. Provide a visual link between vision, strategy, metrics, and action.	6. Make sure all attributes are included within your definitions of concepts.
7. Complete the scorecard.	7. Communicate the scorecard.	7. Identify all possible indicators of your focus variable's attributes.
8. Round out the scorecard.	8. Align lower-order scorecards with the organizational scorecard.	8. Write the scale items.
9. Scrutiny.		9. Reduce the list of items to a parsimonious subset.
10. Use the scorecard (translate metrics to action).		10. Prepare the final instrument (includes scrutiny).
		11. Proofread instrument.
		12. Pilot test.
		13. Use the measure.

Source: © Ruth A. Huwe.

Dashboard Running Example: The operations department consists of first-level teams that do distinctly separate functions such as facilities, panel operations, service bureaus, and information technology operations. If we were to make a scorecard for the entire operations department, we would need to make a separate scorecard for each individual team.

Decision: What are your decisions on each step of the metric creation process?

The process for creating a scorecard can be conceived as filling in relevant blanks of a basic metric model presented in Chapter 2.

The type of scorecard or scale you choose to develop will determine your process steps. The processes for creating department, initiative, or collaboration scorecards are basically the same as those for creating a first-level team scorecard. As shown in Table 16.2, however, the processes for creating first-level team scorecards, organizational scorecards, or surveys are distinctly different.

Dashboard Running Example: For Dashboard, the process for creating the first-level scorecard is followed (steps are shown in Table 16.2 and described in Chapter 6). At the first level, the Dashboard Service Bureau Team scorecard is shown in Table 16.3. Notably, a manager or team cannot create a first-level team scorecard without some knowledge of higher-level scorecards. For this reason, a corresponding departmental scorecard is shown in Table 16.4 and an example organizational scorecard is shown in Table 16.5.

The Dashboard first-level team scorecard (see Table 16.3) demonstrates several metric exceptions mentioned in this book. For one, sometimes it does not make sense to include both a quantity metric and efficiency metric. If employees have no control over the number of survey projects coming in, punishing them for completing fewer projects is demoralizing and goes against the ultimate goal of improving performance. The Dashboard example demonstrates cases in which a behavioral metric is also an outcome metric, such as when measuring turn-around time. Finally, the mission for this team clearly demonstrates that they have three deliverables. Scorecards can be simpler and focused on just one.

Another metric issue shown in the Dashboard example is the problem of count metrics. This example demonstrates a case in which types of deliverables need to be categorized to make a fair count (in the programming department, sample setting projects are not comparable to full programming departments).

For a company growing at a breakneck pace, the focus variable for employee renewal is retention. As a side note, this company employs highly educated people who continually learn through the course of their work; hence, employee development is not emphasized. This is likely to change as the company size settles over time.

Finally, the scorecard reflects components of the strategy of the company that are relevant to this particular team. The first-level manager can do things to drive a company-wide effort to integrate services, but a manager of an operations department is not likely to have any control over the acquisitions that

Table 16.3 Basic Metric Model for First-Level Teams Applied to Dashboard Incorporated

Name of Team Being Measured: Service Bureau.

Mission: To Provide Survey Programming, Technical Support, and Data Processing for Market Research Firms.

Unit of Analysis: First-Level Team.

Attributes of the Object Being Measured	Dimensions	Behavior Metric (Measure/Unit)	Behavior Goal	Outcome Metric (Measure/Unit)	Outcome Goal
Programming (Deliverable = Surveys)	Quantity	Cross-sale queries (e.g., offer other DASHBOARD services) (%)	100%	Sample settings projects late (beyond changed deadlines) per week	Decrease X% over baseline
				Full programming projects late (beyond changed deadlines) per week	Decrease X% over baseline
	Quality			Customer Satisfaction Survey results in favorable range (5, 6, 7), per month (%)	100%
				No. of mistake e-mails per month	0
				No. of lost client to bad data (per quarter)	0
				No. of links not working, panelist complaints per month	0

	Efficiency	Average hours billed per Sample Setting projects (per month)	Decrease 50% in one year	DASHBOARD Revenue per billed hour (checked monthly)	X%
	Efficiency	Average hours billed per Full Programming projects (per month)	Decrease 50% in one year	DASHBOARD Revenue per billed hour (checked monthly)	X%
Technical Support	Quantity	Range of turnaround time (per week).	No outliers taking a disproportionate amount of time (beyond X hours)	Percentage of problems solved within 6 hours	100%
	Quality	Query scripts utilized (e.g., Have we satisfied all of your needs? Did we detect needs you had but did not realize?) (% past month)	100%	Customer satisfaction scores in positive range (5, 6, 7), checked monthly	100%
	Efficiency			Hours billed for idle time, checked monthly	0
Data Processing (Deliverable = Surveys processing)	Quantity	NA (continuous flow of work)			

(Continued)

Table 16.3 Basic Metric Model for First-Level Teams Applied to Dashboard Incorporated (Continued)

Attributes of the Object Being Measured	Dimensions	Behavior Metric (Measure/Unit)	Behavior Goal	Outcome Metric (Measure/Unit)	Outcome Goal
	Quality	Checklists complete per week (data cleaning for missed responses, mistakes, etc.) (%)	100%	Mistake e-mails from customers (past month)	0
	Efficiency	Same as outcome		Average turnover time between when the survey is complete versus when the survey is exported (checked monthly)	50% improvement over baseline
Renewal: Employee	Turnover	Recognition events per quarter	X	Employee Satisfaction (%) positive ratings (4 or 5)	90%
				Turnover per quarter	X%
Strategic Contribution: Integration	Integration	Individual performance forms that include goals to drive integrated behavior (per year) (%)	100%	Duplicate services across organizations, hours per quarter	0

Date of Update: January 2009   Scorecard owner: Manager X

Source: © Ruth A. Huwe.

Table 16.4 Example Departmental Scorecard Translated into a Linking Tool

Name of Department Being Measured: Technical Services.

Department Mission: To Provide Technical Support for New and Existing Services.

Attribute	Behavior Metric (Measure/Unit)	Behavior Goal	Outcome Metric (Measure/Unit)	Outcome Goal	Link to Organization Scorecard	Link to Initiatives
Process efficiency			Duplicate services across functions (Hours across departments, per quarter)	X hours	Operations, Financial	Integration
Process quality			Customer satisfaction scores 5, 6, 7 (per quarter) (%)	95%	Operations, Customer	
Customer Acquisition (metric from corporate scorecard owned by this department)			No. of new products created to generate leads for sales	Variable goals per team	Customer	Growth
Renewal (roll-up metric)	Average employee training hours per employee, per quarter	4	Employee satisfaction scores favorable (per quarter) (%)	90%	Employee	

Date of update: January 2009   Metric Owner: Director X

Source: ©Ruth A. Huwe.

Table 16.5 Example of an Organization Scorecard for Dashboard Incorporated

Dimension	Corporate Measures	Weights	Weight by Attribute
Employee	Employee skill inventory and personal development plans	1	6
	Turnover	4	
	Employee Satisfaction	1	
Processes	Quality: Customer satisfaction ratings favorable	3	25
	Quality: Problems solved in 6 hours	6	
	Cycle time: Lead Conversion Time	5	
	Costs: ROI by function and product) (marketing, panel, bureaus, software products)	5	
	Costs: Product expenses by percent of overall sales	1	
	Revenue per employee (overall, internal vs. vendor)	5	
Customer	Market share	14	22
	Customer retention	5	
	Customer acquisition (percent new customers)	3	
Financial	Cash flow	4	21
	Profit	1	
	Revenue mix	5	
	ROI	8	
	EVA	3	
Integration	Adoption of best practices	1	6
	Revenue by integrated products	5	
Growth	Sales growth	20	20
			100%

Date of Update: January 2009   Scorecard Owner: Officer X
Source: © Ruth A. Huwe.
Note: EVA = Earned Value Added; ROI = Return on Investment.

drive the growth strategy. On the other hand, a scorecard in the finance department most likely would include both a growth and integration component.

Dashboard Running Example: The organization-level scorecard is kept simple and does not include behavioral items. These come later when the scorecard is translated into engagement tools.

The choice of dimensions on the Dashboard organizational scorecard was not driven by the formal articulation of a strategy map. Instead, this scorecard includes relevant dimensions from the *combined model* of organizational scorecards described in Chapter 8.

At the high level of an organization scorecard, the detail that differentiates a measure from a metric, the measurement unit, is left to those reporting results. Also, some items given a 1% weight are simply given a low weight because the metric is partially covered in other measures. Why include the measure? To drive behavior.

Decision: Do you need to develop surveys to measure quality?

Many approaches to quality measurement were discussed in Chapter 4. Because quality is often conceived as being in the eyes of a customer, however, measuring quality often requires that companies construct their own scales (Chapters 9 and 10).

Dashhoard Running Example: A Generic Customer Survey is shown on the following pages. Dashboard should probably choose the agree-disagree set of anchors. Items reflect attributes similar to the SERVQUAL measure described in Chapter 10, but irrelevant items are tossed out. For example, items concerning most of the "tangibles" were not likely to be a fit for a company with online services. Another detail is that the recommended *global* item is attached to the survey as well as an open-ended item that allows customers to give qualitative input. The reason for customer satisfaction scaling, global items, and open-ended items is discussed at length in Chapter 9.

Decision: How will you implement your scorecard?

Once you have created the scorecard, there are four ways to use it. First, use a Metrics to Action tool to demonstrate the link between metrics and action. Engage employees to come up with the actions and invite them to improve the goals or metrics. Second, if applicable, link the metrics to initiatives. Third, show employees how their lower-level actions cascade up to have effects at the organizational level. This cascade effect involves adding columns to scorecards to show how first-level scorecards are linked to categories on organizational scorecards. Fourth, present the actual Team Scorecard Reports.

Dashboard Running Example: The following pages include Dashboard examples of each translation: Metrics to Action (see Table 16.6), linking to corporate scorecard categories and to initiatives (see Table 16.7), and reporting (see Table 16.8). These three scorecards essentially include elements from the previous scorecards. Notice that the engagement scorecard (see Table 16.6) gives metrics but not the actions to improve. This scorecard is presented to employees with two objectives in mind: improve the metrics and identify actions to achieve the goals. Also it is likely that this overall table would be reduced to a few key improvement areas, such as the generic Metrics to Action tool provided in Chapter 13 (see Table 13.1).

Box 16.1. Generic Customer Service Survey for Dashboard Software Products

The following set of statements relate to your feelings about Dashboard software products and services. For each statement, please show the extent to which you believe Dashboard products and services have the feature described by the following statements.

1—2—3—4—5—6—7

STRONGLY   STRONGLY
DISAGREE   AGREE

_____ 1. DASHBOARD provides services as promised.

_____ 2. DASHBOARD is dependable in handling customers' service problems.

_____ 3. DASHBOARD performs services right the first time.

_____ 4. DASHBOARD provides services at the promised time.

_____ 5. DASHBOARD maintains error-free records.

_____ 6. DASHBOARD keeps customers informed about when services will be performed.

_____ 7. DASHBOARD provides prompt service to customers.

_____ 8. DASHBOARD's staff display a willingness to help customers.

_____ 9. DASHBOARD's staff display a readiness to respond to customer's requests.

_____10. DASHBOARD's employees instill confidence in customers.

_____11. DASHBOARD makes customers feel safe in their transactions.

_____12. DASHBOARD employees are consistently courteous.

_____13. DASHBOARD employees have the knowledge to answer customer questions.

_____14. DASHBOARD gives customers individual attention.

_____15. DASHBOARD employees deal with customers in a caring fashion.

_____16. DASHBOARD has customer's best interest at heart.

_____17. DASHBOARD employees understand the needs of their customers.

_____18. DASHBOARD's business hours are convenient.

_____19. DASHBOARD web sites are visually appealing.

_____20. Overall, I am satisfied with the service provided by DASHBOARD.

_____21. I would purchase DASHBOARD products again.

_____22. I would recommend DASHBOARD to other businesses.

What could DASHBOARD do to improve service to you?

_____

What did DASHBOARD do that was particularly helpful?

_____

Table 16.6 Metrics-to-Action[1] Tool Applied to an Organizational Scorecard (Dashboard Incorporated Example)

Dimension	Corporate Measures	Metric	Goal	Actions to Improve: Short Term (90 Days) Long Term
Employee	Employee skill inventory and personal development plans	% completed tools	100%	
	Turnover	%	x < 10%	
	Employee Satisfaction	% in favorable categories	90%	
Processes	Quality: Customer satisfaction ratings favorable	% in favorable categories	95%	
	Quality: Problems solved in 6 hours	% solved in 6 hours	96%	
	Cycle time: Lead Conversion Time	Average no. hours per small/large project	6 hours/3 days	
	Costs: ROI by function and product) (marketing, panel, bureaus, software products)	% - marketing % - panel % - bureaus % - software	20% increase over baseline	
	Costs: Product expenses by percent of overall sales	%	50% decrease over baseline	
	Revenue per employee (overall, internal vs. vendor)	Average %	NA	
Customer	Market share	%	30%	
	Customer retention	% intend to repeat (survey item)	100%	

(Continued)

Table 16.6 Metrics-to-Action[1] Tool Applied to an Organizational Scorecard (Dashboard Incorporated Example) (Continued)

Dimension	Corporate Measures	Metric	Goal	Actions to Improve: Short Term (90 Days) Long Term
	Customer acquisition (% new customers)	% of total customers	NA	
Financial	Cash flow	$	NA	
	Profit	$ by segment	NA	
	Revenue mix	$ by segment	40% software 30% panel 30% Bureau	
	ROI	$	NA	
	EVA	$	NA	
Integration	Adoption of best practices	Percent with 4 or higher ratings on Trotter Matrix	100%	
	Revenue by integrated products	$	40%	
Growth	Sales growth	%	50%	

Date of Update: January 2009   Scorecard Owner: Senior Manager X
Source: ©Ruth A. Huwe.
Note: EVA = Earned Value Added; ROI = Return on Investment.
1. All measurement units are annual on this particular corporate scorecard. Several figures NA (not available) to protect privacy.

Table 16.7 Linking Tool: First-Level Scorecard Linked to the Organizational Scorecard and to Initiatives

Attributes of the Object Being Measured	Dimensions	Outcome Metric (Measure/Unit)	Outcome Goal	Link to Corporate Scorecard	Corporate Initiatives
Programming (Deliverable = Surveys)	Quantity	Sample settings projects late (beyond changed deadlines) per week	Decrease X% over baseline	Processes	Lean principles
		Full programming projects late (beyond changed deadlines) per week	Decrease X% over baseline	Processes	
	Quality	Customer Satisfaction Survey results in favorable range (5, 6, 7), per month (%)	100%	Processes	Six Sigma
		No. of mistake e-mails per month	0	Processes	
		No. of lost client to bad data (per quarter)	0	Customer	
		No. of links not working, panelist complaints per month	0	Customer	
	Efficiency	DASHBOARD Revenue per billed hour (checked monthly)	X%	Processes	Lean principles
		DASHBOARD Revenue per billed hour (checked monthly)	X%	Processes	
Technical Support	Quantity	Number of problems solved within 6 hours	100%	Processes	
	Quality	Customer satisfaction scores in positive range (5, 6, 7), checked monthly	100%	Processes	Six Sigma
	Efficiency	Hours billed for idle time, checked monthly	0	Financial	Lean principles

(Continued)

Table 16.7 Linking Tool: First-Level Scorecard Linked to the Organizational Scorecard and to Initiatives (Continued)

Attributes of the Object Being Measured	Dimensions	Outcome Metric (Measure/Unit)	Outcome Goal	Link to Corporate Scorecard	Corporate Initiatives
Data Processing (Deliverable = Surveys processing)	Quantity	(NA—continuous flow)			
	Quality	Mistake e-mails from customers	0	Processes	Six Sigma
	Efficiency	Average turnover time between when the survey is complete versus when the survey is exported (checked monthly)	50% improvement over baseline	Processes	Lean principles
Employee	Turnover	Employee Satisfaction (%) positive ratings (4 or 5)	90%	Employee	Employee Recognition Initiative
		Turnover per quarter	X%	Employee	Employee Recognition Initiative
Integration	Integration	Individual performance forms that include goals to drive integrated behavior (per year) (%)	100%		Integration

Date of Update: January 2009
Source: ©Ruth A. Huwe.

Table 16.8 Team Scorecard Report

Attributes of the Object Being Measured	Dimensions	Data Responsibility	Outcome Metric (Measure/Unit)	Score/Trend	Outcome Goal
Programming (Deliverable = Surveys)	Quantity	John Q. ERP Technical Support	Sample settings projects late (beyond changed deadlines) per week	——	Decrease X% over baseline
		John Q.	Full programming projects late (beyond changed deadlines) per week	——	Decrease X% over baseline
	Quality	Mark F. Sales Manager	Customer Satisfaction Survey results in favorable range (5, 6, 7), per month (%)	——	100%
		Mark F.	No. of mistake e-mails per month	——	0
		Mark F.	No. of lost client to bad data (per quarter)	——	0
		Mark F.	No. of links not working, panelist complaints per month	——	0
	Efficiency	Sam M. Financial Manager	DASHBOARD Revenue per billed hour (checked monthly)	——	X%
		Sam M.	DASHBOARD Revenue per billed hour (checked monthly)	——	X%
Technical Support	Quantity	Mark F.	Number of problems solved within 6 hours	——	100%
	Quality	Mark F.	Customer satisfaction scores in positive range (5, 6, 7), checked monthly	——	100%
	Efficiency	John Q.	Hours billed for idle time, checked monthly	——	0

(Continued)

Table 16.8 Team Scorecard Report (Continued)

Attributes of the Object Being Measured	Dimensions	Data Responsibility	Outcome Metric (Measure/Unit)	Score/ Trend	Outcome Goal
Data Processing (Deliverable = Surveys processing)	Quantity		(NA – continuous flow)		
	Quality	Mark F.	Mistake e-mails from customers	———	0
	Efficiency	John Q.	Average turnover time between when the survey is complete versus when the survey is exported (checked monthly)		50% improvement over baseline
Employee	Turnover	Nancy M. of Human Resources	Employee Satisfaction (%) positive ratings (4 or 5)	———	90%
		Nancy M.	Turnover per quarter	———	X%
Strategic contribution	Integration	Ann D. of Organization Development	Duplicate services across functions (hours per quarter)	———	0

Date of Update: January 2009   Scorecard Owner: Manager X
Source: ©Ruth A. Huwe.

The linking tool (see Table 16.7) shows the relationship between initiatives and employee behavior. Initiatives bring together practices that pull together several key behaviors that are oriented in performance attributes (Six Sigma for quality, lean principles for productivity, and so forth). The challenge for companies is to focus on a few effective initiatives that have been proven to work. If companies try to push too many initiatives, they risk cynical "flavor of the month" responses by employees (not to mention information overload).

Table 16.8 is a straightforward report form. The key insert of this scorecard is the personnel responsible for gathering the data. Additionally, this scorecard can be presented to employees with ongoing ratings. The example shown in this text is content, a simple black-and-white table. This is precisely the type of form that a technology-based company (e.g., Dashboard) would translate into dashboards or other more visual presentations of interactive media.

Decision: How will you design your performance appraisal forms?

The process for creating a performance appraisal is described in Chapter 5. A list of possible contents is provided in Chapter 18.

Decision: How will you link your scorecard results to performance appraisals?

It is rare that companies drill down to the individual level, but the personal scorecard reflects how an individual worker's goals can be linked all the way up to corporate-level performance attributes. The basic steps are to plug the metrics from previous scorecards (corporate and team) into the metrics column and plug the appropriate goals from an individual's performance appraisal into the goals section. Table 16.9 presents a hypothetical example for a Dashboard employee.

Decision: What flaws do we have and how do we fix them?

Chapters 11 and 12 presented a range of measurement and statistical problems that can arise when creating metric systems. Other calls for scrutiny have been called out in various chapters, as warranted. The following provides a summary of issues that should be internalized as a mental check against metric mistakes. These lists can be used as checklists to scrutinize your work.

Measurement Issues: General Categories (Chapter 11)

- How was missing data handled?
- Were measures taken in a way that confidentiality was protected?
- Are measures ethical?
- Did they measure all relevant attributes? (content validity)
- Do efficiency gains need to be coupled with asset utilization metrics? (content validity)
- Are conceptual (word) definitions provided for key terms? (construct validity)
- Do the conceptual definitions match up to operational definitions? (construct validity)

Table 16.9 Example of a Personal Scorecard for a Service Bureau Employee at Dashboard Incorporated

Team: Service Bureau

Date: January 2007

DASHBOARD Employee: Hilda Z. Programmer

Team Metric	Corporate Performance Attribute	Score	Target/ Benchmark	Comparison (Possibly Shown with Visual Depiction)
Customer Satisfaction	Processes	80%	99%	52-week high: 85%
Time for Techni- cal Resolution	Processes	12 hour (average)	Less than 6	Previous month: 14 hours
Cross-reference Sales	Integration	40%	100%	Previous year: 0

Specific personal goals from performance appraisal:
1. Take a statistics class to enhance knowledge of what I am programming.
2. Develop a checklist to improve data processing turnaround.
3. Learn other operations to improve my ability to give leads on cross-sales.
Source: © Ruth A. Huwe.

- Have they considered whether this variable should be broken down into subdimensions? (construct validity)
- Does the way that this metric correlates to other metrics make sense? (convergent validity)
- Does this metric predict what it should? (predictive validity)
- Do these metrics make sense intuitively? (face validity)
- If this measure was invented elsewhere, does it really fit here? (ecological validity)
- Does this measure provide consistent results? (reliability)
- What is the confidence interval associated with scores on this measure? (reliability)
- Is this metric feasible? (feasibility)
- Is this metric ethical? (logic)
- Is this overall scorecard balanced? (logic)
  - Past, present, and future metrics
  - Long- and short-term metrics (hard and soft metrics)
  - Behavioral and outcome metrics
  - Productivity and quality metrics
  - Subjective and objective metrics
  - Direct and indirect metrics (tangible and intangible referents)

- Is this a roll-up metric that actually should not be rolled up? (logic)
- Can this metric be used across teams? (logic)
- Is this metric actionable? (actionable)
- Does this scorecard or survey include the most parsimonious set of variables possible? (parsimony)
- Does this index include obvious bias? In choice of weights? Variables included?
- Is the choice of labels appropriate? Is the choice of index appropriate?
- Is there a significant amount of data missing from this report?
- Are some people biased to respond a certain way? Particularly high or low?
- Are social desirability effects likely because of the way this measure was administered?
- Is there a halo effect associated with this measure?
- If this is a count metric? Is there a standardized unit size?
- Is the scope of this metric clear?
- Is the unit of analysis for this metric clear?
- Were anecdotal reports treated as data?
- Is this metric coupled with a goal?
- Should this metric or scorecard (and/or results) be publicly displayed?
- When was this set of metrics last updated?
- How did they come up with this metric?
- Is it clear who is responsible for updating this metric?

Statistics Issues (Chapter 12)

- Do they report the probability of error? And/or a confidence interval?
- Do the four moments of the distribution indicate that they have a normal sample? And, do they need a normal sample for the inferences they are making?
- Did they choose the right statistic for central tendency, the mean, mode, or median?
  - Is there sufficient variation?
  - What is the range?
  - If two samples are being compared, is there homogeneity of variance? $s_1^2/s_2^2 = 1$
  - Is the skew between -1.00 and $+1.00$?
  - Is the kurtosis between -1.00 and $+1.00$?
- Is this measured at the right level of measurement?
- Was there enough precision in the scales being used?
- Given the levels of measurement, did they choose the correct statistic for this analysis?
- Are they measuring at the right level of measurement?
- Is the tradeoff between accuracy and precision acceptable?

- Do they have enough statistical power to claim the results that they claim?
- Is the variation reported along with the mean?
- Did they report the probability of error?
- Do they have enough power to claim these results? Was their sample size big enough?
- Was this sample generated randomly?
- Is the association between two variables both statistically and substantively significant?

Surveys Only (Chapters 9)

- Did the survey include negatively worded items?
- Should this include both closed- and open-ended questions?
- Will people actually respond to this survey?
- What is Cronbach's Alpha? Is it over 0.80? How many scale items were there?
- Is there a validity coefficient reported?
- Does this survey reflect all the dimensions that it should?
- If parts of this survey were left blank, how was that handled?
- Should this include both open and closed questions?
- Is a priming effect associated with the order in which questions are asked, such that the first question influences the way the rest of the questions are answered?
- Was there an acceptable return rate?

Scorecards Issues for the Presentation of Results (Chapter 13)

- Does it show the link to corporate strategy?
- Does it show links to individual behavior, actions to improve?
- If relevant, does it show resources to support improvement efforts?
- Are the metrics clear?
- Are the results clear?
- Who completes the scorecard?
- Who is responsible for gathering data?
- Who are the scores in reference to?
- Is it simple or complex?
- Does it appeal both to visual and digital people?
- Does it show trends?
- Is there space for unusual events? A comment area?
- If relevant, are business cycles specified?
- Did they choose the right medium to communicate results?
- Does it include both behavior and outcome measures? (This is solved if you used the basic metric model in the first place or if you are asking

teams to come up with actions for outcome metrics, rather than specific behaviors)
- Does it include all the key topics called for by scientific method?
  - Justification
  - Definitions
  - Hypotheses (scientific reports)
  - Method
  - Results (shown with comparisons to render them meaningful)
  - Discussion
  - Limitations

Dashboard Running Example: This example will vary by the type of statistic. The major question for Dashboard is to decide how to break down their metrics: by product, by profit and loss, by region, or by vendor.

Decision: Which audiences will receive the reports?

Obvious audiences are senior management and employees. Chapter 13 provides a list of audiences to keep in mind when initially creating report systems.

Dashboard Running Example: Team leaders, senior management, the board of directors, and employees.

Decision: How will you gather data for reports?

Chapter 13 lists a variety of methods for gathering data. Two points warrant stressing: (a) that data gathering is automated as much as possible and (b) that there is clear accountability. Note that the scorecard in Table 16.7 includes a column for data responsibility. Responsibility is logically dictated by either method of gathering data or contents. For example, information on turnaround times is gained through the automation available in an enterprise resource planning system and gathering this data can be delegated to a technician. The content of financial information, however, is likely gathered by a finance manager.

Dashboard Running Example: Automation (computer), survey, checklists, focus groups, and mystery shopping.

Decision: What media will you use to communicate results in reports?

Power Point presentations and posters may seem to reign supreme, but a variety of creative options are listed in Chapter 13. Choice will depend on corporate culture.

Dashboard Running Example: With a presence in more than 100 countries and territories, Dashboard can rely on Power Point to present reports but must use transmissions such as Web-based access and video conferencing to generate reports.

Decision: How will you use metrics to motivate employees? What additional strategies will you use? (Chapter 15)

Chapter 15 presents a variety of motivational methods that can be tapped. At a minimum, you should consider strategies for delivering metrics as feedback and consider how you set the goals that accompany the metrics.

Three main types of feedback are evident in organizational settings: informal and ongoing, formal and ongoing, and formal and terminal. Scorecards reflect formal and ongoing feedback and performance appraisals reflect formal and terminal feedback. Chapter 14 provided a list of criteria for presenting effective feedback contents. For example, feedback is focused on the behavior and not the person. Chapter 14 also gave examples of feedback contents to relay consequences on others. For example, consequences could be described in terms of costs or reputation. Chapter 14 also provides a list of verbal strategies that are particularly useful for relaying negative feedback.

This text has stressed that goals accompany metrics to render them more powerful. Chapter 15 devotes an entire section to goal-setting. Although many use the SMART acronym, a scientifically based set of criteria for goals would be as follows:

- Specific for performance goals, encouragement on learning goals
- Difficult
- Accepted (not impossible, people accept the goal as important)
- Measurable
- Can be achieved (self-efficacy)
- Given with the rationale for the goal level

Goals are not the only way to communicate the power of a given metric. You can also use benchmarks, trends, and a wide variety of comparisons (see Chapter 13).

Decision: Who is responsible for metrics?

The quest goes far beyond a metric manager or team filling in the documents of this chapter. The human resources department needs to develop performance appraisal forms. The organization development department needs to work with senior management to implement initiatives and to train managers in motivation and feedback techniques. First-level and departmental managers need to be leaned on to create their own scorecards. And perhaps the biggest battle of all is that waged among members of the team creating the metric system as they negotiate the decisions laid out within this chapter and throughout this book.

CHAPTER SUMMARY

The chapter reframed the entire process of creating a metric system as a series of decisions that might be made by either a manager or a team charged with designing metrics. This chapter used an actual company as an example and demonstrated how scorecards can be created at all levels of analysis. This chapter also included checklists that consider potential mistakes described in other chapters: measurement issues, statistics issues, survey issues, and contents to consider when presenting results.

Part Six
Reference

17   SPECIAL TOPICS

Scorecards cover a lot of measurement ground. If you are capturing productivity, quality, measures of renewal, and strategic contribution, you are likely covering 90% of what matters.

But consider management innovations that have evolved since the 20th century. Employee surveys. Process measures. Tracking return on investment (ROI) for soft interventions. Activity-based accounting. There always will be new phenomena to measure and you cannot forget the nagging point: That which gets measured gets done. For this reason, there will always be additional metrics that go beyond major scorecard categories.

CHAPTER OVERVIEW

In the college course "Metrics for High Performance Work Teams," masters of business administration students are typically managers. Each year, I ask them to identify topics of special interest in their own places of employment. From year to year, the lists are never the same. It reminds us that as management practices, trends, and theories evolve, someone is going to cook up new things for us to worry about—and measure.

The following is a list of special topics in alphabetical order. Each topic is given a high-level description. Topics that require expertise from specific disciplines are accompanied with references for additional resources. This chapter concludes with a set of references that provides examples of how the SERVQUAL has been adapted to provide measures of customer service performance for a wide variety of industries.

Activity-Based Accounting

Activity-based accounting measures the costs for a process that spans different work groups or departments. The unit of analysis is the process, not a set of people. As an example, launching new products would involve adding costs for the following broad activities:

Production Costs + Test marketing + Reformulating the product

Accounting is beyond the scope of this textbook, but many resources provide detailed guidance (e.g., Glad & Becker, 1996; Hicks, 1999; Lewis, 1993).

Collaborations between Work Units

The following indicators can be used to create metrics to measure collaborations between work units:

- Special projects or collaborations (total number)
- Internal survey on teaming (measure if people feel supported by other departments)
- Gain-sharing level—degree to which the organization is entering team-based relationships with other business units, organizations, or customers
- Meeting invitations—number of times one team is invited by another to meetings
- Consulting—number of consulting requests
- Percent of teams with shared incentives
- Percent of time dedicated to special projects or collaborations
- Number of joint research projects
- Dotted-line relationships to other organizations
- Budget given from one team to another for services
- E-mails (number slotted to a special folder to track collaboration)

Collaborative Goals

Sometimes, companies bring together a variety of personnel—cross-functional teams, partnerships with other organizations, lead and manager pairs—who have some specific objective they wish to complete. The following is a set of steps for creating collaboration scorecards.

Step One: Identify the participants in your collaboration.

- Corporate
- Director
- Manager
- Lead
- Collaboration: Some mix?

Step Two: Write out your collaborative goal. In this step, figure out whether your goal is a one-shot project goal or an ongoing mission.

Format for a Project Collaboration:

To complete _____ by _____.
            (achievement/aspiration level)   (date)

Format for an Ongoing Collaboration:

To provide _____ to _____.
            (product/service)   (customer)

Step Three: Choose your scorecard model.

Project Model:

Collaborative Goal: _____

Progress indicator to measure the time between when you started and your goal date:
_____

Quality indicator to reflect how customers judge your final product: _____

Efficiency indicator to judge how you are working between the time when you started your project and your current status: _____

Other key attribute (e.g., innovativeness): _____

Ongoing Model:

Use the Basic Metric Model for Work Performance described in Chapter 2.

Step Four: Translate your work into a metric report form, Metrics to Action tool, or other format that triggers action. (See Chapter 13 for a variety of formats.)

Employee Survey: Gallup Twelve Items

It is beyond the scope of this textbook to discuss the design of employee surveys. If you have a large company, it is important that you benchmark your numbers with other companies; hence, you would be hiring an outside firm. If you have a small company, a down-and-dirty method is to obtain permission from the Gallup organization to use their 12-item survey.

The authors who summarized the Gallup work (Buckingham & Coffman, 1999) observed that they initially had questions about benefits, pay, senior management, and so forth, but those issues are important across companies and do not distinguish high and low performance. Their final 12 questions were the ones that distinguished companies who ranked high in productivity, profitability, customer satisfaction, and employee satisfaction. Items refer to a collection of motivation techniques: providing expectations, ensuring worker utilization, providing resources, supporting personal relationships, and so forth.

Intangibles: ROI of Interventions Computed

Managers increasingly are pressured to account for their spending, particularly since the economic jolt of 2008. ROI is a simple way to express how much value you receive for money spent. Whether computing ROI for a major innovation or for a soft-skill intervention, calculation of ROI begins with a simple cost-benefit analysis. For example, imagine that you set up a ride share program at your company. A rule of thumb is to accept 44 working weeks per year, though this can vary. The following is an example of benefits:

- 44 (weeks) × 1 (hour) × 60 (employees) × 75 (average billing rate per affected employee) = $198,000
- Cost of the program = $45,000
- A standard equation is [(Benefit-Cost)/Cost] × 100 = % ROI
- In this case, [(198,000-45,000)/45,000] × 100 = 340%

The following are some standard indicators to compute costs:

- Costs to create the intervention (in-house or outsourced)
- Planning costs
- Facilities
- Travel budget
- Users' salaries and benefits (costs to attend meetings or training) and possibly their lost billing time
- Overhead costs
- Cost of materials
- Evaluation costs

The following are tangible benefits associated with intangible interventions:

Financial

- Increased sales revenue
- Facility savings and profit
- Materials savings and profit
- Any increase in profit caused by the intervention
- Decrease in costs elsewhere in the organization

Human Capital

- Hours saved (pay)
- Additional billing hours for employees
- Fewer benefits paid out
- Cost of temporary and contract employees
- Cost of Turnover (Rule of Thumb): 6 months pay for nonexempt, one-year pay for managers (Fitz-enz, 2000)

- Cost of absenteeism (Compute revenue per full-time employee [FTE] per hour and divide in half, as you estimate they make up half their work.)

$$\frac{\text{Revenue per FTE per hour x 4\% absenteeism}}{2}$$

Intangibles: Measuring the Extremely Subjective

What do you do when you are forced to measure something that is intangible? Recall that a metric can be made for anything, even romantic love (Rubin, 1970). The problem is that you have to accept some level of subjectivity. Following are five approaches to measuring the subjective.

Logical Path. Link the intangible variable through the path of effects until it is finally linked to a tangible variable. For example, how do you quantify technology? Ultimately link it to financial outcomes. The following is an example of the logic:

- (INTANGIBLE) TECHNOLOGY CHANGE leads to increased PROCESS CONTROL leads to decreased COSTS leads to increased SALES leads to TANGIBLE (Revenue)

Checklist. Create a checklist or "to do" list of activities required to meet a goal and make a metric out of your list. You obtain a summary metric by computing the percentage of items completed. If 6 of 10 items are complete, you are "60% complete on your checklist." Yes, there is the unit size problem that some items on the list are bigger than others, but as discussed, the measurement of intangibles involves some levels of subjectivity. As stated, this is a down-and-dirty approach.

Overall Estimate. Estimate the percentage of a goal that is completed. This is as simple as it sounds:

- "What percent of the job/goal do you have completed?"

Yes, this can be gamed in that someone can claim to be halfway through when she has not even started. But what happens if they are completing this metric on a weekly basis? At some point, the lie catches up to her.

Worst Person. One technique is to fall back on the question, "Okay. Picture the worst person who ever did this task. What was it about him that made him *so* bad?" Alternatively, you can ask, "Who was the best person who ever did this task? What made him so good?" As an example, the author was nearly stumped when a student who owned a software company for making video games was trying to come up with metrics to judge his artists. How do you say that one artist is better than another? Quantitatively?

Open-Ended Items. Another occasion for measuring the truly intangible occurs when you are forced to use open-ended items, such as the discovery of product improvements or particular leadership problems. Conducting content analysis and computing intercoder reliability is beyond the scope of this text, but Page and Iwata (1986) give an excellent summary of the approach.

Process Metrics

Although the output of processes can be treated as a deliverable and measured in terms of productivity and quality, the very processes themselves can be the focus of measurement (Meyer, 1994). This is particularly true with reengineering efforts. The following are five hallmarks of reengineering (Davenport & Stoddard, 1994): (a) a clean slate, (b) cross-functional team coming together, (c) radical change in how things are done, (d) information technology as enabler, and (d) changes in human and organizational roles to accompany the material changes.

Step One: Specify the product to be measured and the customers.

- Product: Radio commercials
- Customer: Advertisers who purchase air-time

Step Two: Define what factors are critical for satisfying internal and external customers. For processes the following are typical:

- Time
- Cost
- Quality
- Product performance

Radio Running Example: At radio stations, costs are fixed for commercials unless outside help is called in, and in most cases, clients pay for outside help. Time is the difference between when a spot is purchased and it has to go on air. Sometimes there is little turnaround because that is a selling point of radio over television. Quality and product performance are difficult to verify. The commercial has to be approved by a client, but the correlation between the product and outcomes (sales) is nearly impossible to track.
Step Three: Map the cross-functional process steps used to deliver results. (See the Example in Figure 17.1.)
Step Four: Identify critical tasks and capabilities required to complete each process step. (See Figure 17.2.)

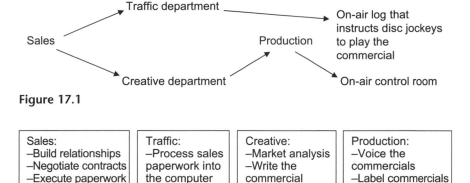

Figure 17.1

Sales: –Build relationships –Negotiate contracts –Execute paperwork	Traffic: –Process sales paperwork into the computer system	Creative: –Market analysis –Write the commercial –Maintain studios –Assign talent	Production: –Voice the commercials –Label commercials and deliver to the control room

Figure 17.2

Step Five: Identify indicators that track key tasks and capabilities (from Step Four) as they influence critical customer factors (from Step Two).

Sales:

- Dollars billed
- Turnaround time for paperwork
- Paperwork returns

Traffic:

- Number of errors

Creative:

- Percent of copy submissions approved by client
- Percent of commercials cut by each announcer as talent (optimal is a balance across announcers)
- On-time production

Production:

- Percent of commercials approved by client
- Accuracy of labeling

Step Six: Translate indicators into metrics (specifying who they apply to, how often they will be measured, etc.).

Some Points about the Radio Running Example

The radio example shows the internal metrics for a simple task (and includes a bit of fantasy, in that it is unlikely the sales people will care about a creative department's turnaround struggle if a hot sale is at stake). It is obvious that process metrics can become complex very quickly.

Project Management Metrics

At a minimum, the manager must define the goal, make a schedule, and estimate costs based on specifications. But how does one measure how "well" the project manager is doing? In general, projects can be described in four terms (Lewis, 1993):

- Cost (Total cost to do the project)
- Performance (What does a product do? How does it perform?)
- Time (Deadline)
- Scope (Magnitude of the project or job)

Cost

Most projects involve labor, materials, equipment, and other costs. The basic equation for costs is as follows:

$$C = f(P, T, S).$$

In other words, cost is a function of performance, time, and scope. Cost and Time are a U relationship. With Cost in the y-axis and Time in the x-axis, at some point, if a project takes too long, costs go up from inefficiency.

Performance

Performance is like a quality measure. When we conceive of projects as planned versus actual performance, then the focus on quality measures becomes a comparison of *specifications* and the *product as delivered*. Who is to judge this? Certainly there are empirical tests, but the perception of the customer is also critical.

How Do You Reduce Costs? Recall the equation: $C = f(P, T, S)$. One way to reduce costs is to extend time. Another way is to improve processes through improved efficiency or to reduce the scope of the project. You can focus on any variable in the equation to reduce costs.

Time or Scheduling

The key metric for scheduling is Milestones met versus Milestones not met. Unfortunately, this is just a tracking metric because different milestones vary in size. The final milestone is the critical one: whether your project meets the deadline.

It is helpful to consider events that can hold up a project and prepare a contingency for their occurrence. The following is a beginning list:

- Weather (earthquake)
- Working conditions
- Getting workers with necessary skills
- Absenteeism
- Management
- Economy

Scope

All the metrics in project management are sensitive to planned estimates (planned cost, planned deadline, and planned performance) and the scope of the project specifies the planning that drives all the other estimates. Scope is defined in the specifications up front.

Roll-up Metrics

Roll-up metrics are also referred to as "aggregate" or "cascading" metrics because of the manner in which data reflecting a common variable are combined. Roll-up metrics are actually a way to "gather" metric information. For example, imagine a vice president who wants to tackle his or her morale problems. If all employees are measured by a common metric (let's say a 1 to 5 scale), then the vice president can roll up metrics as shown in Table 17.1:

Meanwhile, the directors would have gotten the following type of scorecard from all of their managers. Just one scorecard is shown in Table 17.2. If the vice president wanted to pinpoint particular problems, he or she could actually just ask for an overall breakdown to the level of the individual manager as shown in Table 17.3.

Table 17.1 Vice President Scorecard

Vice President	Morale Rating	Number of Employees in Organization
Director 1	3	200
Director 2	4.2	300
Director 3	2.8	120

Source: © Ruth A. Huwe.

Table 17.2 Director Scorecard

Director	Morale Rating	Number of Employees in Manager Span of Control
Manager 1	2.8	80
Manager 2	3.2	80
Manager 3	3	40

Source: © Ruth A. Huwe.

Table 17.3 Vice President Scorecard Broken by Manager

Vice President	Morale Rating	Number of Employees
Director 1		
Manager 1	2.8	80
Manager 2	3.2	80
Manager 3	3	40
Director 2		
Manager 1	3.7	100
Manager 2	4	100
Manager 3	4.3	100
Director 3		
Manager 1	2.6	40
Manager 2	2.8	40
Manager 3	3.0	40

Source: ©Ruth A. Huwe.

Regardless, the individual directors would need to have gathered the data from their managers and sent it on up for the vice president to have it integrated. Although showing the vice president-by-manager breakdown might allow one to pinpoint where problems emerge, this goes against the point of "reducing" information because it is achieved in the simpler "vice president" scorecard.

There are restrictions on what can be rolled up. It is easy to roll up financial metrics or survey metrics such as those of a common 1 to 5 scale. However, what would happen if you tried to roll up "training metrics"? It might be that, from manager to manager, the number of skills to train would be varied. Or managers could game their listing of skills to make it look like more employees are cross-trained. Productivity is also an example of a metric that rarely can be rolled up. You cannot add up the total number of products produced by individual teams unless each team puts out the exact same product.

Safety Metrics

The Dupont Company has an outstanding reputation for safety performance and has developed a program that other companies can use. Their system presents a series of leading and lagging metrics that both prevent and quantify costs from safety problems (Cummings, 2009).

Lagging Metrics

A first set of lagging metrics is the quarterly tracking of safety incidents. The incidents are scored between 10 and 230 points into three categories (A, B, and C). The points are based on categories such as type of material released (flammability, toxicity, etc.), actual and potential size of release, degree of control at the site during an incident, involvement of lines of protection at the incident, actual and potential on-site impact (injuries, evacuation, etc.), actual and potential off-site impact, and actual monetary costs.

Leading Metrics

A first set of leading metrics includes audits that hopefully protect incidents in the first place. Dupont uses about 300 questions in a checklist. A second party conducts an annual review and the second party's work is reviewed by a third, external party. The unit of analysis includes 14 technical units as well as management.

A second set of leading metrics centers on measuring open and overdue recommendations. This metric also includes completion of action items and corrective action requests from the process safety management team.

A third set of leading metrics includes changes to the process safety management team. This includes updates and revisions to standards as well as changes within key personnel on the team.

Statistical Process Control

A basic premise to statistical process control is that process variation can be "controlled." For example, consider the process for creating radio commercials presented earlier (see "Process Metrics" earlier in this chapter). The steps involved an account executive submitting material for a commercial, a producer who wrote and produced the commercial, and then a client who approved the commercial. But suppose the writing was off? Would it be easier if you had the process "checked" earlier, at the point at which the commercial was written, rather than wait until the end of the process to find a final defect? And possibly miss air-time? This is the same process in manufacturing. Rather than wait for the entire product to be built, provide checks along the way that measure the "deviation" from what is expected at the checkpoint.

Seven basic charts are used to measure quality control: histogram, Pareto chart, check sheet, control chart, cause and effect diagram, flowchart, and scatter diagram. Although a basic idea is that processes have their own variation (rather than the "normal" distribution of other statistics), a control chart includes a process mean, an upper and lower warning limit 2 standard deviations above and below the mean, respectively, and an upper and lower control limit 3 standard deviations above and below the mean, respectively.

The amount of "how to" information on this topic is simply overwhelming and can be accessed through any search engine.

Supply Chain Metrics

Major categories of supply chain measures include a consideration of time, resource utilization, output, and flexibility. Box 17.1 summarizes a recent review of possible measures that identified 27 key performance indicators for the measure of supply chain management (Gunasekaran & Kobu, 2007).

Box 17.1. Key Performance Indicators for Supply Chain Management

- Accuracy of scheduling
- Bid management cycle time
- Capacity utilization
- Compliance to regulations
- Conformance to specifications
- Delivery reliability
- Forecasting accuracy
- Inventory costs
- Labor efficiency
- Lead time for procurement
- Lead time manufacturing
- Obsolescence cost
- Overhead cost
- Perceived quality
- Perceived value of product
- Process cycle time
- Product development time
- Product/service variety
- Production flexibility
- Return on investment
- Selling price
- Stock out cost
- Supply chain response time
- Transportation cost
- Value added
- Warranty cost

Source: Gunasekaran, A., & Kobu, B. (2007). Performance measures and metrics in logistics and supply chain management: A review of recent literature (1999-2004) for research and applications. *International Journal of Production Research, 45,* 2819–2840. Permission by Taylor and Francis.

Training Metrics

The most straightforward training metrics are "attendance" and cost per training hour. Unfortunately, attendance does not reflect learning. Moreover, if the trainer is "cheap," you just might be getting what you are paying for. Hence, the straightforward metrics are not the most common.

Four key attributes of training continue to be used most often in corporate contexts (Bennett, Edens, & Bell, 2003): reactions, learning, behavior, and results. Information theory (Ritchie, 1991) and the need for knowledge management provide three other relevant training metrics: novelty, relevance, and knowledge sharing.

Reaction is measured with self-reports—that is, the ratings given just after sessions that reflect attitudes toward the training program. Although used the most widely, reaction does not tend to correlate to the other attributes: amount learned, behavior change, or results produced.

Learning is typically measured by some sort of test, which can be completed with pen and paper or can be Web based. Not to be confused with job performance, learning is how much people learned from the training itself. Learning is considered to be a necessary but not sufficient condition for behavioral effects.

Behavior is measured by actual effects of job performance and typically is measured by supervisors or objective indicators. Self-reports of behavior change are possible, but they can be criticized as being subjective or even self-serving measures. Moreover, it is difficult to establish that changes in behavior are a result of training rather than environmental influences. A typical scientific design (pretest and posttest, control group and treatment group) is one way to establish a claim that training actually causes a change in behavior.

Results are measured by linking training and key variables on overall scorecards: costs, time savings, and so forth. The process of translating training into ROI is described earlier in this chapter under "Intangibles: Computing ROI."

An alternate approach is to conceive of training as "information transfer." According to Shannon and Weaver's classic "Mathematical Theory of Communication," information involves two elements (Ritchie, 1991): novelty and relevance. *Novelty* gets at the idea of whether you are learning something new. *Relevance* is whether the training you just received applies to your job. These questions can be included in reaction surveys.

Finally, current systems of knowledge management focus on leveraging knowledge, or *knowledge sharing*. A key question for trainers is asking how they will share their training. Will they do a brownbag session on the subject? Will they use the training contents for mentoring? A key question for reaction surveys is to ask, "Who will you tell about this class?" or "With whom will you share what you learned today?"

Translating Tools into Metrics

Sometimes, the very tools that managers use can be converted into metrics. For example, recall the "Team by Activity Matrix" tool presented in Chapter 13 (Table 13.2). This matrix showed the extent to which various teams were engaged in activities being promoted by the company. Teams were scored from 1 to 5, with 4 being fully implemented and 5 being a model for others. A director could convert this grid into a metric by counting all cells in which the scores were 4 or higher (meaning the programs were fully implemented). In this case, 8 of the 24 possible cells were 4 or higher, meaning that 33% of the programs were fully implemented.

Turnover Costs

A basic rule of thumb for computing turnover costs is to estimate them to be 50% of the annual salary of nonexempt employees, and 100% of the cost of exempt employees (Fitz-Enz, 2000). Turnover is extremely expensive because it includes recruiting costs, training costs, lost expertise, lost productivity, customer dissatisfaction, and so forth.

Web Site Metrics

The next section includes references for several studies that provide metrics for online services. Alternatively, the following are basic metrics used to judge Web sites:

- Milestones met
- Number of hits per year
- Number of return hits
- Number of downloads
- Number of clicks to complete a transaction
- Costs per distributor
- Number of units sold per distribution channel
- Level of documentation of site development
- Turnaround time on build-to-test sequence

Measures for Specific Industries

The following articles provide either measurement instruments or attributes. All of these articles refer to the SERVQUAL and many represent variations on its categories as applied to the specific business contexts of the users (e.g., Web sites, libraries, and manufacturing).

Airline Performance

Gursoy, D., Chen, M. H., & Kim, H. J. (2005). The US airlines relative positioning based on attributes of service quality. *Tourism Management, 26*, 57–67.

Bank Service

Aldlaigan, A. H., & Buttle, F. A. (2002). SYSTRA-SQ: A new measure of bank service quality. *International Journal of Service Industry Management, 13*, 362–381.

Han, S. L., & Baek, S. (2004). Antecedents an consequences of service quality in online banking: An application of the SERVQUAL instrument. *Advances in Consumer Research, 31*, 208–214.

Federal Government

Schay, B. W., et al. (2002). Using standardized outcome measures in the federal government. *Human Resource Management, 41,* 355–368.

Hospitals

Hiidenhovi, H., Nojonen, K., & Laippala, P. (2002). Measurement of outpatients' views of service quality in a Finnish university hospital. *Journal of Advanced Nursing, 38,* 59–67.

Lam, S. S. K. (1997). SERVQUAL: A tool for measuring patients' opinions of hospital service quality in Hong Kong. *Total Quality Management, 8,* 145–152.

Sower, V., Duffy, J., Kilbourne, W., Kohers, G., & Jones, P. (2001). The dimensions of service quality for hospitals: Development and use of the KQCAH scale. *Health Care Management Review, 26,* 47–59.

Vancampen, C., et al. (1995). Quality of care and patient satisfaction: A review of measuring instruments. *Medical Care Research and Review, 52,* 109–133.

Information Systems

Jiang, J. J., Klein, G., & Crampton, S. M. (2000). A note on SERVQUAL reliability and validity in information system service quality measurement, *Decision Sciences, 31,* 725–744.

Information Technology Consulting

Yoon, S., & Suh, H. (2004). Ensuring IT consulting SERVQUAL and user satisfaction: A modified measurement tool. *Information Systems Frontiers, 6,* 341–351.

Library Service

Roszkowski, M. J., Baky, J. S., & Jones, D. B. (2005). So which score on the LibQual plus (TM) tells me if library users are satisfied? *Library & Information Science Research, 27,* 424–439.

Manufacturing

Bowen, D. E., Siehl, C., & Schneider, B. (1989). A framework for analyzing customer service orientations in manufacturing. *Academy of Management Review, 14,* 75–95.

Portal Service Quality

Kuo, T., Lu, I-Y, Huang, C-H, & W, G-C. (2005). Measuring users' perceived portal service quality: An empirical study. *Total Quality Management & Business Excellence, 16,* 309–320.

Retail

Dabholkar, P. A., Thorpe, D. I., & Rentz, J.O. (1996). A measure of service quality for retailing stores: Scale development and validation. *Journal of the Academy of Marketing Science, 24*, 3–16.

Supply Chain Performance

Lai, K. H., Ngai, E. W. T., & Cheng, T. C. E. (2002). Measures for evaluating supply chain performance in transport logistics. *Transportation Research Part E-Logistics and Transportation Review, 38*, 439–456.

Tourism

Petrick, J. F. (2002). Development of a multi-dimensional scale for measuring the perceived value of a service. *Journal of Leisure Research, 34*, 119–134.

Travel Agency Services

Millan, A., & Esteban, A. (2004). Development of a multiple-item scale for measuring customer satisfaction in travel agencies services. *Tourism Management, 25*, 533–546.

Web Sites

Barnes, S. J., & Vidgen, R. (2001). An evaluation of cyber-bookshops: The WebQual method. *International Journal of Electronic Commerce, 6*, 11–30.

Cao, M., Zhang, Q. Y, & Seydel, J. (2005). B2C e-commerce web site quality: An empirical examination. *Industrial Management & Data Systems, 105*, 645–661.

Froehle, C. A., & Roth, A. V. (2004). New measurement scales for evaluating perceptions of the technology-mediated customer service experience. *Journal of Operations Management, 22*, 1–21.

Mathwick, C., Malhotra, N., & Rigdon, E. (2001). Experiential value: Conceptualization, measurement, and application in the catalog and Internet shopping environment. *Journal of Retailing, 77*, 39–56.

Parasuraman, A., Zeithaml, V. A., & Malhotra, A. (2005). E-S-QUAL: A multiple-item scale for assessing electronic service quality. *Journal of Service Research, 7*, 213–233.

Pitt, L., Berthon, P., and Watson, R. (1999). Cyberservice: Taming service marketing problems with the World Wide Web. *Business Horizons, 42*(1), 11–18.

Schubert, P. (2002). Extended Web Assessment Method (EWAM): Evaluation of electronic commerce applications from the customer's viewpoint. *International Journal of Electronic Commerce, 7*, 51–80.

REFERENCES

Bennett, A. W., Edens, P. S., & Bell, S. T. (2003). Effectiveness of training in organizations: A meta-analysis of design and evaluation features. *Journal of Applied Psychology, 88,* 234–245.

Buckingham, M., & Coffman, C. (1999). *First break all the rules.* New York: Simon & Schuster.

Cummings, D. E. (2009). The evolution of current status of process safety management metrics. *Process Safety Progress, 28,* 147–155.

Davenport, T. H., & Stoddard, D. B. (1994). Reeingineering: Business change of mythic proportions? *MIS Quarterly, 18,* 121–127.

Fitz-enz, J. (2000). *ROI of human capital.* New York: Amacom.

Glad, E., & Becker, H. (1996). *Activity-based costing and management.* Chichester, NY: Wiley.

Gunasekaran, A., & Kobu, B. (2007). Performance measures and metrics in logistics and supply chain management: A review of recent literature (1999–2004) for research and applications. *International Journal of Production Research, 45,* 2819–2840.

Hicks, D. T. (1999). *Activity-based costing: Making it work for small and mid-sized companies.* New York: Wiley.

Lewis, R. J. (1993). *Activity-based costing for marketing and manufacturing.* Westport, CT: Quorum.

Meyer, C. (1994, May-June). How the right measures help teams excel. *Harvard Business Review, 72*(3), 95–103.

Page, T. J., & Iwata, B. A. (1986). Interobserver agreement. In A. Poling & R. W. Fuqua (Eds.), *Research methods in applied behavior analysis* (pp. 99–126). New York: Plenum.

Ritchie, L. D. (1991). *Information: Communication concepts 2.* Newbury Park, CA: Sage.

Rubin, Z. (1970). Measurement of romantic love. *Journal of Personality and Social Psychology, 16,* 265–273.

18 COLLECTION OF INDICATORS AND METRICS

CHAPTER OVERVIEW

This chapter presents a laundry list of various metrics and indicators that managers can use as a reference to create metrics that fit their special needs. These lists were the product of years of masters of business administration projects in which students specialized in various areas added to metric lists in previous sources. For a simplified list of metrics, Kaplan and Norton's *Balanced Scorecard* (Kaplan & Norton, 1996) is still a classic. Brown's *Keeping Score* (Brown, 1996) is another excellent source for key metrics. J. Fitz-enz's *ROI of Human Capital* (Fitz-enz, 2000) is the definitive work on metrics for human resources.

When relevant, some indicators are classified in two areas. For example, quality metrics are relative under both customer and process headings. Many human resource metrics are key financial metrics. The following general topics are included:

- Financial
- Employee: Human Resources
- Employee: Learning
- Ethics
- Operations and Processes: Quality
- Operations and Processes: Productivity
- Operations and Processes: Other
- Customers and Marketing
- Community: Contributions and Citizenship
- Community: Environmental Processes
- Community and Employee: Safety
- Strategic Variables: Synergy
- Strategic Variables: Innovation

This chapter also includes a special section on "Performance Appraisal Elements."

Financial

Activity-based costing (ABC)
Accounts receivable
Altman's Z
Asset per worker $: Assets/# of workers
Asset under management
Asset turnover ratio (ATR): Net Revenue/Average total assets
Asset utilization
    Building
    Employee
    Land
Book-to-market (BM) ratio: Book value per share/Market value per share
Benefits
    Cost per employee
    Percent of payroll
    Percent of revenue
Brand equity (see also "Customers and Marketing")
Budget variance
Business risk (BR): σ of operating income/mean operating income
Capital ratio (CapR):
    (Risk-adjusted Equity + Adjusted Subordinate Debt)/Risk-Adjusted Asset
Cash coverage ratio (EBIT [Earnings Before Interest and Taxes]+ depreciation/interest)
Cash flow
Cash flow to long-term debt (CF/LTD): CFO/(BV of long-term debt + PV of operating leases)
Cash flow volatility (the firm's cash flow coefficient of variation divided by the market's cash flow coefficient of variation)
Cash ratio (CaR): (Cash + marketable securities)/Current liabilities
Cost of quality (labor and materials for rework)
Credit rating changes from major agencies
Current ratio (CR): Current asset/Current liability
Debt payments as percent of net income
Debt-to-equity ratio (DER): Total long-term debt/Total equity
Debt ratio (DR): (current liabilities + total long-term debt)/(total debt + total equity)
Delinquent loans to total loans
Earnings per share (earnings available to stockholders/shares outstanding)

EBIT margin (percent): EBIT/Sales Revenue

Earnings per share (EPS) $: Earnings/number of shares

Equity multiplier ratio: Total assets/Total equity

Equity ratio (percent): Shareholder's equity/Asset

Equity turnover ratio (ETR): Net revenue/Average equity (book value)

Earned value added (EVA): Operating Profit − Taxes − Cost of Capital

Expenses: Planned/Actual

Financial activity measures

Financial leverage (total assets/shareholders' equity)

Fixed asset turnover (sales/net fixed assets)

Fixed charge coverage ratio (EBIT + lease payments/interest + lease payments)

Fixed ratio (percent): Fixed asset/Equity

Functional department (e.g., engineering) as a percent of sales

Global marketing and competition

Gross margin: Net selling price − purchase price

Gross profit margin (gross profit/sales)

Gross revenue

Growth rate: $g = RR \times ROI = (1 − \text{Dividend payout ratio}) \times ROI$

Human capital (see also "Employee: Human Resources")

    Revenue divided by full-time employees (FTEs)

    Costs (pay, benefits, absence, turnover, contingents, training)

Inspection costs

Insurance costs

Inventory costs (total)

Interest coverage ratio (ICR): EBIT/Net interest expense

Inventory conversion period (365/inventory turnover)

Inventory turnover (percent): COGS/Ending inventory

Invested capital (IC) turnover (Sales/IC)

Jensen's alpha

Labor costs per unit

Liquidity

Litigation costs

Loan turnover ratio (LTR): Net revenue/Average total loans after deducting reserves

Long-term debt to total capital (LTD/TC): Long-term debt/Total capital = Long-term debt/(Long-term debt + Equity)

Management earnings

Market capitalization (a.k.a. firm value) (share price multiplied by outstanding shares)

Market position

Market share

Market-to-book ratio (stock price/book value of stock per share)

Market value added (MVA): (All capital invested since start of business)/ (MV of all equity + Debt)

Mergers and acquisitions

Net charge-offs to average loans

Net income

    Net income before one-time charge-offs

    Net income before taxes, depreciation, amortization, and interest payments

Net profit margin (net profit/sales)

Net worth to total assets

New markets entered

Net operating profit after tax NOPAT margin (NOPAT/sales)

Operating income before/after depreciation divided by sales

Operating margins

Operating return on assets (ROA) (NOPAT/sales)

Outstanding orders

Pay/Benefits (see also. "Employee Human Resources")

Price to Earnings Ratio (P/E ratio)

Planning (financial) to support processes

Price leadership

Profitability (overall and by market or customer segment)

Profit margin

Profit per employee

Projected sales

Proposals (dollar value of proposals weighted by probability of proposals accepted into sales)

Quick ratio (percent): (Current assets − Inventories)/Current liabilities

Receiving costs

Relative size and growth in industry or markets served

Research and development (R&D) investment/profit

Retirement costs

Return on assets (ROA) (percent): Net income/Total assets

Return on equity (ROE):   Net income
                        Shareholder's equity

Return on investment (ROI): Cumulative Contribution or Gain from investment-Cost of investment divided by Total Assets Costs of Investment

Revenue

    Revenue broken by sources: acquisitions, grants, endowments, divestitures, new partnerships and alliances, and new employee relationships

    Revenue broken by domestic and international

    Revenue growth broken down by new products or services

    Revenue growth broken down by markets

    Revenue per employee

    Revenue-to-expense ratio (RER)

Sales variability (SV): σ of sales/mean sales

Sales (see also "Customers and Marketing")

   By low versus high margin products

   Gross sales

   Gross sales average per customer

   Sales per customer

   Sales per employee

   Sales per square feet

   Sales variability

Sending back defective products (costs)

Shareholder's equity per share (dollars): Shareholder's equity/Number of shares

Size of bid-ask spread

Stock returns before and after news events

Stress-related illness (dollars spent)

Subsidiary rate of return versus Parent rate of return

Times interest earned ratio = EBIT/interest

Tobin's Q (ratio of the market value to the cost of replacing the firm's assets)

Total assets turnover (sales/total assets)

Total expense per worker: Total expense/Number of workers

Total units sold (see also "Customers and Marketing")

Trading turnover (TT): Number of shares traded during the period/Total shares outstanding

Training cost as a percent of payroll

Value added per employee

Warranty costs

Workman's compensation

Employee: Human Resources

Absenteeism

Absenteeism costs = 0.5 × Revenue per hour per employee × Absenteeism percent

Accession rate (replacement hires and new positions as a percentage of the workforce)

Accident costs (see also "Community" and "Employee: Safety")

Aging workforce

Alignment: Employee and corporate goals

Benefit change paperwork (turnaround time)

Benefits cost per employee (see also "Financial")

   Benefit costs versus competitors

   Benefit costs versus industry

Black belt status (percent of employees/managers who achieve)

Commitment (would you like to work here X years from now?)

Communication/Information breakdown surveys
Compliance with fair-employment practices (federal and state)
Counseling services
Costs (pay, benefits, absence, turnover, contingents, training)
Cross-functional teamwork
Cultural values (respecting chain of command, making the budget, team orientation, risk minimization, etc.)
    Strong versus weak (widely held/weakly held)
Day care
Employee assistance program (costs, usage)
Equal Employment Opportunity (EEO) complaints (rate of)
Employee grievances
Employee growth
Empowerment (percent who feel they can act on the customer's behalf)
Employee referral bonuses
Employee suggestions (received/processed)
Ergonomic indicators
Exit interviews (percent reasons for leaving broken by categories)
Family programs launched
Flexible hours
Flexible location
FTEs (full-time employees versus part-time employees, total number)
Grievances
Health of employees
Hiring
    Costs
    Percent of college hires
    Cycle time (external and internal time to fill, time to start)
    Percent of female and minority hires
    Percent of employee referral
    Percent internally hired
Hours worked per week
Insurance costs (see also "Financial")
Internal promotion rates
Job coverage: Number of employees on hand
                   Number of employees needed
Job rotation or sharing
Job satisfaction (Gallup measure, global measure, Job Description Index not recommended)
Knowledge of organizational direction
Leave (for volunteer work or family)
Link between compensation and performance
Litigation costs (HR related)
Manager satisfaction with hires

Merit increases benchmarked versus industry average
Metrics: Percent automated
Metrics: Percent data gathering methods in place
Number of female and minority hires
Number of HR transactions processed
Organization citizenship behaviors (OCB) indicators
Offer-to-acceptance ratio
Orientation time
Occupational Safety and Health Administration (OSHA) audits
Outsourcing costs
Overtime (average, as percent of total labor hours)
Pay/Benefits: FTE/Contingent (see also "Financial")
Performance appraisals (percent completed)
Performance appraisals (average score change over time)
Professional/Nonprofessional ratios
Promotions (percent female and minority)
Recognition (programs to promote)
Recreational or cultural activities
Recruiter costs
Recruiting (number of applicants by recruiting source)
Recruiting (turnover by source)
Retention (employee)
Revenue per employee (see also "Financial")
Retirement benefits (see also "Financial")
Revenue/FTEs
Sales per employee (see also "Financial")
Stress-related illness
Succession planning (percent of positions for which this is planned)
Supervisory ratios
Salary (benchmark against competitor levels)
Salary (differential between high and low performers)
Salary (speed of change)
Security indicators
Sick days per year
Stress-related illness (dollars or days lost)
Strikes and other job actions
Telecommuting
Time to fill jobs
Transfer requests per supervisor
Transfer requests rate (in/out)
Turnover costs (estimate as 6 months pay for nonexempt, 1 year pay for exempt, includes termination, replacement, vacancy, learning curve)
Turnover rate
    Average tenure

Number of employees over 6 months tenure
Minorities over 6 months tenure
Overall as percent of total population
Turnover by job category
Voluntary versus involuntary as a percentage of head count (Fitz-enz, 2000, refers to this as "Separation Rate")
Women over 6 months tenure
Utilization (match of skill level to job level)
Vacancies (average number of days jobs unfilled)
Well-being indicators
Workmen compensation claims (see also "Financial")

Employee: Learning

Awards conferred (certificates, technical ratings)
Bilingual (percent)
Career development
Coverage
Job coverage measure of competence: number of employees qualified
number of employees needed for specific jobs
Competency ratings
Costs per training (and by hour)
Cross-training (percent trained to do another job)
Diversity training
Education level (percent with bachelors, masters, doctoral, and technical degrees)
Employee input to training needs
Employee input to training delivery preferences
Ethics training
Employee training (linked to performance measurement, performance improvement, and technological change)
High potential employee programs
Improvement efforts (and indicators that they take place)
Internships
Invited scholars
Job rotation (see also "Employee: Human Resources")
Knowledge of job roles
Knowledge transfer (systematic effort to gain knowledge from departing employees)
Management and leadership development
Mentoring versus training
Non-work-related education
Objectives linked to training (balanced for short- and long-term organizational objectives)
Orientation training
Perceived information sharing

Percentage meeting competencies
Percentage with special skills (e.g., special certifications, language skills, etc.)
Safety training
Skills attained
Succession planning (percent of jobs with backup)
Tenure
Training costs
    Per employee
    Percent of payroll (see also "Financial")
Transfer new skills to long-term organizational use

Ethics

Adverse impacts on society from products, services, operations
Audit and ethical reviews
    Numbers of hours spent conducting
    Results
Board members (percent who are independent)
Breaches (number of instances)
Health (and conditions) for employees
Number of calls to ethics hotline
Investigations (percent of breaches investigated)
Preparation for disaster
Processes to monitor ethical behavior (partners, customers, and other stakeholders)
Regulatory compliance (processes, measures, and goals for achieving or surpassing)
Relationships between stockholder and nonstockholder constituencies
Safety of employees
Survey results on employee perceptions of ethics
Theft (employee, dollars per year)
Training (number of ethics training hours)

Operations and Processes: Quality

Customer shortfall (wait times, dissatisfaction, etc.)
Defects by cause (e.g., paint, parts, etc.)
Defect prevention
Endorsements by customer (see also "Customers and Marketing")
Endorsements by trade reporters
Errors (broken down by type)
Field service requests
First pass yields
Labor cost per unit
Number of units divided by raw material costs

Requirements met by processes
Returns
Rework: First pass yield
Sample size of checked items is large enough (if not 100%)
Scrap
Service errors
Six Sigma results
Statistical process control (percent of processes under)
Survey (postproject)
Treatment of defects
Warranty costs (see also "Financial")
Waste
Yields (ratio of good items produced to good items entering the process)

Operations and Processes: Productivity

Automation (percent of processes automated)
Back order percentage (back ordered products/total ordered products)
Bottlenecks (length of time of the slowest step in the process)
Costs
    Activity based
    Materials
    Per batch
    Per service or product
    Per support call
    Per unit
    Per volume
    Percent of net sales
    Activity-based costing systems
Cycle time
Cycle time for product introduction
Deliveries versus headcount
Downtime
Labor rate (average hourly)
Lead times
Manufacturing cycle effectiveness (MCE): Processing time/Throughput time
On-time delivery
Productivity
Profit per employee (dollars)
Rework
Sales per employee (dollars)
Set-up times
Time to market
Time variance from proposed project schedules

Turnaround defined with consideration of the following elements (see also MCE)

- Order is received from the customer
- Materials for work are ordered
- Work is scheduled
- Raw materials are ordered
- Raw materials are received
- Production on the order is initiated
- Order or batch is in finished goods inventory
- Inspection
- Storage
- Order is shipped
- Delivery to customer

Waste, scrap produced

Operations and Processes: Other

Administrative costs as a percent of sales
Agility (can adapt to changing requirements, demands, and decisions)
Audit, inspection, and testing costs
Collection period (accounts receivable/credit sales per day)
Continuity in case of emergency (percent of plans in place)
Damaged equipment (broken down by error or cause of damage)
Delivery speed
Documentation
    Completion (percentage of processes documented)
    Errors
Engineering change requests
    Number submitted
    Percent completed
E-technology (usage)
Environmental impact
Financial planning to support processes (see also "Financial")
Forced outage rate (forced outage hours/period hours)
Freight carrier accuracy tracking (percent)
Freight carrier damage tracking (percent)
Future sales (processes for developing)
Green manufacturing (see also "Community: Environmental Processes")
Help desk tickets (number per year)
Improvement processes in place
Innovation rates
Input from customers, suppliers, partners, and collaborators
Inventory over budget
Inventory turnover = Cost of good sold/Inventory

Long-term performance indicators
Number of retail channels
Plant availability (hours available/period hours)
Plant utilization rate (output/design capacity)
Paperwork errors
Payment processing
Price weighted availability rate (period revenue/period revenue + outage losses)
Parts shortages
Price weighted forced outage rate (outage losses/period revenues + outage losses)
Processes aligned with current business needs and directions
Process control (percent of processes under statistical process control)
Process learning with other organizational units
Projected units to be completed
Production flexibility
Reduced variability
Reformulating products (time/costs)
Service usage by site
Shipments (correct address, paperwork)
Shipping per unit (shipping costs/units shipped)
Tooling costs
Utilization (e.g., revenue per hotel rooms, load factor on airplanes)
Value added per employee
Warehouse utilization
Work instructions completed (percentage)

Customers and Marketing

Accuracy
Advertising/Sales
Amount of transaction (average)
Brand awareness
Brand equity (see also "Financial") (Web sites such as Young & Rubicam's Brand Asset Valuator (http://www.valuebasedmanagement.net/methods_brand_asset_valuator.html) can provide a calculation. The Young and Rubicam formula considers brand equity to be a function of differentiation, relevance, esteem, and knowledge.
Brand image
Brand loyalty
Brochure requests
Cancellations (dollars, number, percentage)
Changing customer requirements or needs that can influence future purchase decisions
Checkout ease

Competitor customers (analysis thereof)
Complaints/Returns
  Average number of complaints per customer
  Total number
  Mean time to respond
  Mean time to complex request
  Ratio of returns to do with dissatisfaction, not defect
  Satisfaction with complaint handling
Complaints translated into improvement
Confidentiality and security of transactions
Contacts, number of customer visits, sales calls, etc.
  Contact via e-mail
  Contact via phone
  Contact via face-to-face visit
Contracts, number of contracts per customer visit
Cost per customer
Cost to serve customer
Cross-sales (percent)
Customer account histories
Customer base growth
Customer/Employee ratio
Customer endorsements
Customer equity
Customer expectations (including product and service features)
Customer lifetime value (CLV)
Customer loyalty
Customer referral value
Customer requirements met
Customer retention/Repeat business
Customer satisfaction (compare to American Customer Satisfaction Index [ASCI], http://www.theacsi.org/)
Delivery speed
Differentiation factors: Price, reliability, value, delivery, timeliness, easy of use, technical support, and sales relationship
Ease of use (products or service)
Field service requests
Financial loss for customer
Flexibility
Focus group results
Follow-through
Free trials (and purchase rate)
Help availability
Incomplete online transactions (percent)
Innovation, novelty, and creativity

Length of contracts (average)
Likelihood of continued patronage by customer (survey)
Listening (percent who believe problems are listened to)
Lost sales: Survey of reasons why customers gave project to another company
Marketing expense
Market share: Total or segmented
Net promoter score
New versus existing customers (percentage of total sales, or total dollars)
New customers versus prospective inquiries
Number of new customers versus solicitation expense
Number of customers
Market segments: Percentage of customers by market segments or other groupings
    Core versus strong and continuing versus future versus possible breakout markets
Open measures: What could we offer? How can we improve? Strengths? Weaknesses?
Parking
Perceived value relative to competitors
Potential customers and market segments
Price (relative to others)
Price per call (e.g., customer complaint, support, etc.)
Price per unit
Problem resolution
    First-time resolution to problems (percent first time or number of repeats)
    Percent of customers who believe employees can solve their problems
Process improvements
Product quality
Public relations coverage (positive, negative, and neutral media references)
Rank of product and service attributes that are the most important
Referrals
Relative importance of product and service features to purchase or relationship decisions
Retention
    Average length of customer relationship
    Repeat versus lost customers
    Retention of "A" customers
    Revenue lost due to lack of retention
Requests or transactions not fulfilled
Response time to customer-initiated contact
Returns by customers
    Return total dollars
    Return and percent of total products

Sales (see also "Customers and Marketing")
    By low versus high margin products
    By new products or services
    Gross sales
    Gross sales average per customer
    Sales from proprietary products
    Sales per customer
    Sales per employee
    Sales per sales representative
    Sales per square feet
    Sales variability
Satisfaction relative to satisfaction with your competitors
Secret shopper ratings
Service quality
Shelf space
Supplier of choice (percent of customers who choose you)
Technical support (needs met)
Time
    Customer calls
    Processing time per customer
    Response time
Total count of service-months committed
Total count of unit-months leased
Total units sold
Transaction completion rates
Up sales (percent)
Value
    Overall (service/product was worth the price)
    Price satisfaction
    Relative perceived value (us versus competitors)
Visits by customers (and conversion rates to sales)
    Store
    Web site
Waiting time in queues
Waived fees to maintain customer satisfaction
Wallet share
Warranty claims
Web site
    Mouse clicks (number to complete a purchase)
    Satisfaction measure
    Screen load time (average)
Weighted value of prospective orders (weighted by probability of closure)
Win/loss analysis

Community: Contributions and Citizenship

Attendees to town meetings
Blood donations
Boards (number of employees serving or number of boards)
Career fairs/outreach
Charitable contributions to nonprofit (dollars)
Charity dollars raised
Classes offered to the community
Clothing drives
Community program involvement (number broken down by program)
Community satisfaction index (completed by main stakeholders)
Complaints
Events: Corporate sponsorships
Food donations
Hardware donations
Hiring (percent recruited locally)
Internships sponsored
Jobs created by project
Matching programs (employee contributions matched by corporate dollars)
Percent of community accessing services
Percent of company profit given back to the community
Presentations to the public
Software donations
Suggestions
    Made
    Implemented
Toy drives
Traffic problems caused by company
Trees planted
Used equipment donated (computers, furniture, etc.)
Volunteer time
    Nonprofits
    Schools

Community: Environmental Processes

Audits/checklists
Complaints from community
Emissions (percent of reduction)
Environmental Protection Agency (EPA) warnings (number)
EPA violations (number)
Processes
    By-product use
    Green manufacturing

Hazardous waste disposal
Recycling
Reduced omission levels
Waste stream reductions
Regulatory violations
Waste (percent of reductions)

Community and Employee: Safety

See Chapter 17 for a list of leading and lagging metrics.
Accidents (number of)
Accidents (costs)
Accident safety ratings
Accident severity ratings
Checklists completed
Complaints
Employee Assistance Programs (EAP)
Ergonomic indicators (see also "Employee: Human Resources")
EPA violations
EPA warnings
False alarm rate
Fatalities
Lost time accidents (total)
OSHA audits per year
Response time to injuries
Safety training
Security breaches
Training
    Percent trained
    Average hours training
Workman's compensation claims (see also "Financial" and "Employee: Human Resources")
Workplace preparedness for disasters or emergencies

Strategy Variables: Synergy

Common technologies across business units
Percentage of time in meetings (reflecting only one person goes to a meeting rather than extras)
Shared services (purchasing, distribution, etc.)

Strategy Variables: Innovation

Adoption rate of new products
Awards: Product design awards (bronze, silver, gold)

Communication technology
    Efficiency from shifts (phone versus e-mail versus future technologies)
    Satisfaction with shifts (Web site review, satisfaction with communications)
Cost savings due to new technology
Customer perceptions of innovativeness
Customer endorsements (see also "Customers and Marketing")
Break-even time (from beginning of product development to getting profit to pay for it)
Functions (number available with new release)
Ideas generated/Turned into pitches
Industry awards for new products
Innovation (identification of customer needs) to operations/delivery to post-sales service
Missed innovations (dismissed ideas)
New designers (number hired per year)
New products produced
    By product line
    Our company versus competitors
Patents
    Number filed by your company per year
    Number issued to your company per year
    Number competitor patents
Percentage of innovations that were initiated at your own company
Prototypes (number per quarter)
R&D/Profit ratio
R&D/Sales
R&D spent (basic and applied research)
Research projects
    Number of joint projects
    Number of grants
    Number of white papers
Sales
    Percent sales from new products
    Percent sales from proprietary products
Suggestions (number per month, received and/or implemented)
Time (amount/percent) to employees to spend innovating

PERFORMANCE APPRAISAL ELEMENTS

This section is based on a content analysis of 55 performance appraisals that were readily obtained on the Web in 2006. The goal is to give an idea of all possible contents that might be included. The following are major appraisal sections:

- Introduction
- Employee Data
- Job Descriptions/Responsibilities
- Company Value Statements
- Rating Section and Competencies
- Performance Planning/Personal Development for the Coming Year
- Comments
- Signatures
- Thank You

Introduction

Possible Contents

The purpose of this performance appraisal process is to:

- Provide a written record for the staff member and his or her supervisor on the nature of the former's job performance.
- Pinpoint areas of greatest/least achievement
- Improve performance
- Aid in promotion, retention, and salary decisions
- Develop mutual goals
- Improve employer/employee communication

Performance Planning: Review the current job description and send significant updates to the human resources department. Using your previous review, your job description, and new job demands, develop your plans for the upcoming year.

Performance Appraisal/Review/Summary: Discuss the job, rate each item, sign the appraisal, and send to human resources.

For additional information on how to complete this form, go to http://
_____.

Distribution Instructions:
This form is to be completed by _____ .
When finished, it should be delivered to _____ through
_____ (medium).
The supervisor and employee are encouraged to be frank and open.

Employee Data

Possible Contents

Name: _____

Employee ID: _____ Social Security Number: _____

Location/Department:_____ Supervisor/Evaluator: _____

Job Title: _____ Function: _____ Class Code: _____

Occupation Code: _____ Business Unit: _____

Period of evaluation: From _____ to _____

Employee status: Exempt_____ Nonexempt_____

   Managerial _____ Nonmanagerial _____

Does this position supervise others? Yes/No

   If yes, how many? Total directly supervised: _____

      Total indirectly supervised: _____

Time with the company: _____ Length of time in this position: _____

Appraisal meeting date: _____

Evaluation type: 3-month Probation __ Trial Period __ Annual __ Other ___

Bargaining unit: _____

Job Description/Responsibilities

Possible Contents

Essential duties and tasks associated with this position (insert specific job description).

Company Value Statements

Possible Contents

The mission of this company is to provide_____ products to _____ customers.

   This company seeks to be _____ with the _____ level of excellence.

Rating Section and Competencies

Both leader and worker competencies are in alphabetical order and shown in Table 18.1. A typical scale of 1 to 5 could be used, but it is recommended that the numbers are coupled with a verbal description that reflects what the numbers mean. It is also recommended that a column for "Notes" or "Not applicable" be included.

A line can also be written in for specific competencies and goals. It is also highly recommended that two different versions be written, one for managers and one for employees.

Table 18.1 List of Competencies

Ability to follow directions	Effectiveness/Results orientation	Personnel relations (judgment in hiring, promotion, termination, and evaluation)
Ability to Improve/Learn	Effort/Goes the extra mile	Planning/Forecasting
Accuracy	Ethics	Policy and procedure knowledge/Follows
Analytical and Data Analysis	External relations	Pressure—Steadiness under pressure
Attention to Detail	Feedback—uses constructive feedback to improve	Problem solving/Judgment
Attendance/Punctuality	Flexibility and adaptability	Project coordination
Attitude Displayed	Goal setting	Quality of work
Budget/Fiscal Awareness (utilizes resources)	Health and safety	Quantity of work (productivity)
Communication: Written	Helps others	Reliability
Communication: Keeping Others Informed	Helps—Seeks assistance when needed	Research/Investigation skills
Communication: Listening Skills	Improvements—Suggests ways to improve; continuous improvement	Respectfulness
Communication: Communicates Expectations to Employees	Influencing	Responsibility
Communication: Direction and Department Vision	Initiative	Responsiveness (how quickly does this employee get back to people)
Communication: Presentation Skills	Integrity (honest, fair, honors commitments)	Safety
Conflict Management	Interpersonal (get along with staff members)	Teamwork
Company Values Upheld	Interpersonal (develop relationships with customers)	Technical knowledge
Cooperation	Information technology/Equipment skills	Time management (deadlines met, prioritizes, effectively multitasks, efficient)

(Continued)

Table 18.1 List of Competencies (Continued)

Courtesy	Knowledge, skills, abilities/Knowledge of job	Willingness/Volunteers for special assignments
Creativity	Leadership	Work independently
Customer Service (internal/external)	Metrics—Defines and monitors metrics for key business activities	Work practices/Professionalism (lump together attendance, punctuality, safety, clothing, organization of work area)
Delegation/ Empowerment	Organization	
Dependability	Participation with employees in decision making	
Develops Self (skill training, reads up on latest professional developments)	Personal appearance	
Develops Staff		

Source: © Ruth A. Huwe.

Performance Planning/Personal Development for the Coming Year

Possible Contents

Training Goals: _____
Job/Assignment/Project Goals: _____
Community Service: _____
    What can you do to achieve these goals? _____
    What can your supervisor do to achieve these goals? _____
    What opportunities/training can the company provide that will help you achieve these goals? _____
Career path: _____
State the following in relation to each goal that you set:
    Competency: _____
    Goal: _____
    Timeframe: _____

State the following in relation to each goal that you set:
    Goal: _____
    Specific action: _____
    Timeframe: _____

Comments

Possible Contents

Employee Comments:

Comments about this appraisal: _____.
Comments about your supervisor: _____.
Comments that have not been addressed in this appraisal: _____.

Major accomplishments in the previous year: _____.
Evaluator comments: _____.

Signatures

Possible Contents

A signature does not necessarily mean agreement with the appraisal.
A signature signifies that I have been advised of my performance ratings and
have discussed the contents of this appraisal with my supervisor.
____ I would like to discuss this evaluation with an appropriate administrator.
____ I decline to sign.
____ I will submit a rebuttal
Employee Signature: _____ Date: _____
Supervisor Signature(s): _____ Date: _____
Sr. Manager Signature: _____ Date: _____
Our next review will be on the following date: _____
____ I would like to discuss this evaluation with an appropriate administrator.
____ I decline to sign.
____ I will submit a rebuttal

Thank You

Possible Contents

The next step in this process is _____.
Thank you.

REFERENCES

Brown, M. G. (1996). *Keeping score.* New York: Productivity Inc.
Fitz-enz, J. (2000). *The ROI of Human Capital.* New York: Amacom.
Kaplan, R. S., & Norton, D. P. (1996). *The balanced scorecard: Translating strat-
egy into action.* Boston, MA: Harvard Business School Press.

Index

ability and capability: performance attributes, 67; and personality, 68, 69

absenteeism, 110, 123, 242; cost of, 297, 315; employee attributes, 51; project management metrics and, 301; and withdrawal, 244

accomplishment measures, sales department, 113

accounting department, 35, 108, 109

accounting practices, 11

accounts receivable, 312, 321

accuracy, 57, 109, 111, 165, 182, 196, 203, 287, 322, 331

actionable, choice of measure, 25, 115, 258; first-level team scorecard, 86; as measurement issue criteria, 171, 180

activity-based accounting, 54, 294

activity-based costing (ABC), 312, 320

adjectival anchors, 64, 71; combined with numbers, 74, 139

adjusted subordinate debt, 312

administrative department, 109

advertising, 111, 119, 322

affective commitment, 244

aggregate metrics, 301. *See also* roll-up metrics

airline performance, 306

ambidexterity, 52

analysis of variance (ANOVA), 193, 197, 200

anecdotal reports, 183

application, 179

asset metrics, organization scorecard, 119

asset per worker, 312

asset utilization, 54, 312

assimilation effect, 150

associations, types of, 186, 203–205

attitudinal outcomes, 242

attributes, 63, 156, 181; in basic metric model, measuring, 22, 24, 27; of employees, 51; key metric scorecard elements, 18, 19; in performance appraisals, 76; of scale, 137; summary of, 52–53; of team, measuring, 48–49; and variables, 20

audience analysis and presentation, 217

autonomy, 249, 254

backup, 38, 319

balanced metric system, 6, 84

balanced scorecard, 4, 10–11, 84–87, 96, 286; of first-level team, 90; organization scorecard, 118, 125–127

Balanced Scorecard Model (BSC), 40, 49, 120–122, 179–180; comparison of, 126

Baldrige criteria, organization scorecard, 11, 35, 41, 42, 120, 128, 129;

comparison of, 126; performance
under, 118, 122–123, 124
Baldrige National Quality Award, 11–12
bank service, 306
basic metric model, 17, 21, 82, 89;
consequences of applying, 28; key
concepts of, 18; in manufacturing
industry, 87–88; technique of, 21–27;
work performance of, 17–21, 84
basic team scorecard, 44–45
behavioral event interviews, 70
behavioral goals, 10
behaviorally anchored ratings scales
(BARS), 64, 71, 72, 139
behavioral metrics, 18, 21, 24, 274; in
departmental scorecard, 275; as drivers
of performance, 33n2; first-level team
scorecards and, 89, 90, 93; and goals,
257; organization scorecard, 119, 121,
126; and outcome metrics, 18, 26–27,
286; potential regulations, 27
behavioral outcomes, 51, 242, 261
behavior change and training, 305
behavior management, motives for
measures, 95
behavior measures, sales department, 113
behavior modification, 242, 251
behavior observation scales (BOS), 64, 71,
73, 139
benchmark, first-level team scorecards, 83
bid management cycle time, 304
billing hours, 296
biserial correlation, 197
book-to-market (BM) ratio, 312
boundary, defining systems, 35
brainstorming sessions, 90, 212, 259
brand equity, 312
brand value metrics, organization
scorecard, 119
budget, 294
budget variance, 312
business administration projects, 311
business administration students, 293
business metrics: and defect questions,
203; and survey questions, 202–203
business metrics, application to, 192;
central tendency, 192; dispersion,
192–194; kurtosis, 194; skewness, 194

business metrics, relevance for:
actionable, 180; construct validity,
174; content validity, 173–174;
convergent validity, 175; divergent
validity, 175; ecological validity, 177;
face validity, 176; feasibility, 178; logic,
179–180; parsimony, 180–181;
predictive validity, 176; reliability, 177
business process metrics, organization
scorecard, 118
business risk (BR), 312

canonical correlation, 198
capacity utilization, 304
capital ratio (CapR), 312
"capture-tag-recapture" methods, 202
cascade metrics, 38, 107, 301. See also
roll-up metrics
cash flow, 276; to long-term debt (CF/
LTD), 312; organizational scorecard,
279; volatility, 312
cash ratio (CaR), 312
causal associations, 41
causality, 203–204
cause and effect diagram, 303
census, 20, 186
central tendency, 192
change initiatives, 210, 213
check sheet, 303
Chi square, 198, 199
classified count metrics, 55
closed and open systems, distinguishing,
34–35
closed-ended question, 182
coaching, 64, 223, 225
coding process, 36
cognitive evaluation theory (CET), 27,
242, 249
cognitive feedback, 226
collaboration scorecard, 271
collaborative goals, 81, 294–295
collective unconscious, 245
combination scorecard, departments,
114
command and control, 245
comments, performance appraisals, 66
communication facilitation, motives for
measures, 95

community, metrics and indicators of, 326–327; contributions and citizenship, 326; and employee, 311, 327; environmental processes, 326–327
company value statements, 64, 65
compensation distribution, motives for measures, 95
competency, 68; and individual performance attributes, taxonomies of, 69–71
competency scale, 64, 71, 75, 77, 78
complete metric report, 210
conceptual definition, 138, 141
conceptualization, 71, 185; of customer surveys, 156–157; of metrics as feedback, 224–230; of organizational scorecards, 117–120; of performance appraisal, 66–67; of scale construction, 136–138; of scorecards, 17–21; of statistics primer, 186–191
concurrent validity, 176
confidence interval, 178
confidentiality, 285, 286
conformance to requirements, 156
construct, 137, 139, 174
construct validity, 174–175, 285, 286
consulting, 294
consumer satisfaction, 158
contemporary metric systems: basic ideas behind, 33–34; performance improvement under, 39; and STS approach, 43, 44, 45
content analysis, reliability of, 145
content selection and presentation, 217
content validity, 173–174, 285
contingency lines, first-level team: and indexes, techniques in, 93; for performance dimensions, 100; steps for completion of, 98; technical support score translated to, 99, 101; translation into, 82, 97
contingency question, 139
continuance commitment, 244
contract employees, cost of, 296
contract negotiation, 299
contrast effect, 150
control chart, 303

convergent validity, 175
corporate America, metrics in, 106
corporate culture, variables influencing, 52, 86, 214, 225, 289
corporate measures, 276; and departmental metrics, 106; translated to departmental scoreboard, 114
corporate scorecard, 269; drawing attributes from, 81, 90; and initiatives, linking categories of, 277
correlation, 197, 203
cost computation, 296
cost-cutting, strategic variables, 52
counterproductive behavior, 243
count metrics, 271; and project size, 93
creating metrics, 21; visual checklist and, 31
creative department, 299
critical capabilities, 298, 299
critical customer factors, 299
critical tasks, 298, 299
criticism, methods for inviting, 90
Cronbach's alpha, 148, 149, 177, 288
cross-buying metrics, organization scorecard, 119
cross-functional process steps, 298
cross-reference sales, 286
customer acquisition, 276
customer and quality metrics, 311
customer attitude, 59, 156, 157, 158, 159
customer dissatisfaction, 306
customer lifetime value (CLV), 57, 119, 125–126
customer metrics, organization scorecard, 118
customer retention, 276
customers: category and team performance, 48, 49; and marketing, metrics and indicators of, 311, 312, 322–325; measuring effectiveness of outcome, 50; type of, 156, 158
customer satisfaction, 57, 156, 158, 295; internal and external customers, 298; and quality, 96; ratings of, 276, 277, 283, 286; survey of, 89, 97
customer service departments, 109
customer service orientation scale, 71
customer service performance, 293

customer service scale, 156; concepts related to, 157; construction process, 161–167
customer service surveys, 57
customer survey, 277
customer value metrics, organization scorecard, 119
customer versus overhead, scorecard balancing of, 125
customization, strategic variables, 52

dashboard approaches, 97
Dashboard Incorporated, 267–268; basic metric model for, 272–274; example organizational scorecard for, 276; first-level scorecard for, 269, 271; general customer service survey for, 278; metrics-to-action, 280; Service Bureau Employee, personal scorecard for, 286
data gathering, 143, 216, 268, 289, 317
datum, 186
debt ratio (DR), 312
debt-to-equity ratio (DER), 312
defective products, cost of sending back, 315
defining terms: in creating departmental scorecards, 114–115; in customer surveys, 163; in first-level scorecard construction, 85; in performance appraisal measurement, 76; in scale construction, 141–142
delinquent loans, 312
deliverable performance, dimensions of, 54
delivery reliability, 304
demographics: employee metrics and, 51; in scale construction, 150–151
department, definition of, 103–104
departmental managers, 290
departmental metric models, 106
departmental scorecards, 81; attributes for, 105; customer satisfaction and, 107; functional and process metrics, 114; measuring variables under, 106; process metrics, 104, 113–114; scrutiny of, 116; steps for creation of, 105
dependent variable, 197; motivation and, 242

descriptive statistic, 33n1, 187
designing metrics: efficiency indicators in, 54; input indicators in, 53
deviation, 186
diagnostic versus strategic measures, scorecard balancing of, 127
dichotomous independent variable, 197
differentiation, 37, 38, 39
dimension, 138–139, 142; key metric scorecard elements, 18, 19, 23, 27
directive function feedback, 226
direct metrics, 286; first-level team, 90
director scorecard, 301
discontinuous strategic transformations, 38, 39
disengagement, 209–210
dissatisfiers, 252
distal goal, 10, 257
distribution channels, organization scorecard, 119
distributive justice, 260
divergent validity, 175
doing it right the first time, 156
dotted-line relationships, 294
double loops, 183–184; learning, 42–43, 45; questions, 213
dynamic homeostasis, 37, 39

EBIT (Earnings Before Interest and Taxes) margin, 313
ecological validity, 176–177
e-commerce: as strategic variable, 52; Web site quality, 308
economic value added (EVA), 118, 123, 126, 276, 280, 313; organization, 126
effective ingratiation, 141
efficiency, 85; concept of, 175; engineering team and, 94–96; in manufacturing industry, 84–85, 87–88; metric scoreboard, 47, 48, 49; as productivity measurement, 53
Eight Great competencies, 64; contemporary performance appraisals and, 71
e-mails, 178, 220, 294, 323, 328
emergency signs, 97, 99
emotional feedback, 226
employee, 315–319; human resources, 315–318; learning, 318–319;

monitoring of, 84; variables classifying, 51; virtual work teams under, 12

employee behavior, 67, 150, 234, 247, 258

employee commitment, manufacturing industry, 84–85

employee cross-training: engineering team and, 96; manufacturing industry, 84–85, 87–88; as renewal variable, 85

employee data, 64, 65

employee engagement scorecards, 209; conceptualization of, 218; gathering data for, 216; links associated with, 215; methods for, 211; reports, 210, 215–216; scientific practice of reporting, 218–219

employee involvement, 44

employee involvement scorecard, 209, 210; limitation in data gathering, 219

employee motivation, 290; behavior modification as, 10; motives for measures, 95

employee participation, 209

employee renewal, 51; first-level team scorecard and, 85; metric scoreboard, 47

employee satisfaction, 90, 107, 276, 295

employee survey, 295

empowerment, 13, 182, 209, 210, 211, 316, 332

engagement, 209; arguments for, 211; of employees, 44; metrics analysis and, 216; and performance, 91; processes, 104

engineering department, 109–110

enterprise resource planning (ERP) system, 85, 216, 289

environmental protection and safety processes, 311

equifinality, 37, 39, 211

equity, 313

equity turnover ratio (ETR), 313

error, 187; and justice, theories of, 242, 259–260; reporting probability of, 287; Type One Error, 186, 187; Type Two Error, 186, 188

ES (effect size) indexes and values, 199

esteem needs, 247

ethics, 179; metrics and indicators of, 319

EVA (economic value added), 118, 123, 126, 276, 280, 313; organization, 126

evaluation, 226; costs, 296

exempt employees, 306

expectancy theory, 242

expenses, 313

explication, 138, 142

external customers, 56, 158, 298

external hard quality metrics, 56

external versus internal process, scorecard balancing of, 125

extinction, 250

extrinsic motivation, 242, 248–249

face validity, 176, 177, 180, 286

facility department, 110, 296. *See also* safety department

facility savings and profit, 296

factor analysis: in customer service scale construction, 165; in performance appraisals, 78; in scale construction, 147–148

feasibility: choice of measure, 25; departmental metrics, 115; of first-level team scorecard, 86; as measurement issue criteria, 171, 178; of measurement unit, 26

federal government, 307

feedback, 250, 254; in business contexts, 223; conceptualization of, 224–225; consistency in, 232, 235; and contemporary performance management systems, 225–226; content of, 230, 233–234; delivery of, 235–236; demographic differences across senders of, 231; effectiveness of, 229, 235–236; of first-level team, 98; format of, 236–237; gap concept in, 227; and goal setting, 10; key sources of, 231; logic and emotion, effects of, 228; metrics' power as, 229; milestones in research on, 226–229; novelty in, 234; of organization scorecards, 121; relevance in, 234

feedback effects, 226; nature of, 229–230; on turnover, 236

feedback research, 24

fill-in model, 44–45

fill-in-the-blank approach, 21

finance departments, 108
Financial Accounting Standards Board (FASB), 11
financial activity measures, 313
financial benefits, 296
financial category, metrics and indicators of, 312–315; revenue, 314
financial incentives, 250
financial metrics, organization scorecard, 118
financial performance, 84
first-level scorecards, 104; creation of, 82–93; roll-up metrics of, 107–108
first-level team scorecard, 81–101, 269, 270, 271, 277; attributes of, 85; basic metric model for, 272–274; crib sheets for, 90; defining terms in, 85; deliverables in, 86–89, 96; dimensions of, 89; engineering team and, 94–96; execution methods, 82; meta-process behind, 82–83; and organizational scorecard, 281–282; reflecting corporate strategy in, 90; report form, translation into, 91, 92; scrutiny of, 85–86, 90–91; single index, reduction into, 82, 97; statistical issues concerning, 90–91
Fleishman Job Analysis Survey (FJAS), 69
flexibility, 303
flextime, 12, 13
flowchart, 303
focal goal, 257–258
forced distribution, 64, 71, 73, 139
forecasting, accuracy in, 304
forecasts creation, motives for measures, 95
frequency, 73, 186, 189, 192, 225
functional job analysis (FJA), 64, 69
functional metrics, 104, 108, 269
functional organizations, indicators for, 108–109
functional performance, departmental metrics, 106
future implications, employee engagement scorecards, 219
future-oriented marketing metrics, 57

gain-sharing level, 294
Gallup organization, 181; measure of, 316; work of, 295

general systems theory (GST), 33, 35, 39–43
generic competencies, 68, 69
generic customer service survey, 278
generic organization scorecard, 123
generic quality attributes, 57
Gibson models, 49
global item, 75, 159–160
globalization, 12, 13, 39; strategic variables, 52
global marketing and competition, 313
goal myopia, 119
goals, 10, 21, 89, 290, 332; category and team performance, 48; as pilot survey item, 50
goal setting, first-level team scorecards and, 83, 89
goal-setting examples, contingency table with, 204
goal-setting theory, 4, 96, 117–120, 226, 242, 257–258; and feedback, 227–228; organizational behavior and, 228
"green" methods, strategic variables, 52
gross profit margin, 313
group as level of analysis, 44
growth, 268, 275, 276, 280; for software products, 278
growth rate, 313

hard and soft measures, difference between, 48, 59
hard versus easy goals, 117–120
higher-level organizational scorecards, 210; and individual-level activities, 211
high-level scorecard, 130
high-performance teams, 95, 293
histogram, 303
homeostasis principle, 37, 39
hospitals, 307
hotelling, 12, 13
human capital, 296–297; ROI of, 311
human resources, metrics and indicators for, 315–318
human resources department, 290; indicators for, 108, 110
human resources information system, 216

implementation challenges, 81
importation of energy, 36

incentive function feedback, 226
incentive system development, motives
    for measures, 95
incremental renewal, 38, 39
independent variable, 197; motivation
    and, 243, 247
index, 20, 93
indicator: and dimensions, 19; and
    measure, 18; and metrics, collection
    of, 311–328
indicator of scale, 137; categories of,
    144–145; identifying of, 144; in scale
    construction, 142–143
indirect metrics, 286; first-level team, 90
INDSAT, 159
inductive reasoning, 69
Industrial Revolution and scorecards,
    10–11
inferential statistics, 31n1, 186
information about ethics, 150, 151
informational justice, 260
information input, 36
information support department,
    110–111
information technology consulting, 307
informative feedback, 234
infrequency, 73
ingratiation items, in factor analysis, 149
initiative performance, departmental
    metrics, 106, 114
initiatives, metrics for, 213
initiative scorecards, 211, 212, 214;
    standard indicators for, 215; vision
    bullets and, 214, 215
innovation, 90, 296, 312, 327–328
innovation initiative, 215
inspection costs, 313
instructions, in scale construction,
    150, 151
insurance costs, 313
intangible assets, organization scorecard,
    118
intangible interventions, 296–297
intangible output, 157
intangibles, ROI of interventions
    computed, 296–298
integrated products, revenue by, 279
integration, 276; and coordination, 37,
    38, 39

intellectual advances, 4, 12, 96
interactional justice, 260
intercoder reliability, 145, 177–178
interest coverage ratio (ICR), 313
intermediate variables, 104; departmental
    metrics, 106
internal customers, 158
internal survey, 294
International Electrotechnical
    Commission (IEC), 107
International Organization for Standards
    (ISO), 106
Internet shopping, 309
interpersonal justice, 260
interpersonal understanding scale, 71
interval measurement, 186, 195, 196
intervention costs, 296
intrinsic motivation, 242, 248–249
intuitive approach, first-level team, 89
inventory costs, 304, 313
inventory turnover, 313, 321
ISO 14000, 117
ISO 9000, 117, 213

Job Characteristics Inventory (JCI), 254
job characteristics model and work
    design, 253–254; outcome effects of,
    254
job content models and theories, 242
job demands, 210
job demands-resources (JD-R) framework,
    210
job descriptions and responsibilities, 64, 65
job description taxonomies, 63, 69
Job Diagnostic Survey (JDS), 254
job knowledge, 44
job performance, 243
job resources, 210, 211
job satisfaction, variables driving, 51
job-specific competencies, 68–69

key performance indicators (KPI), 124
knowledge: and cognitive ability, 68;
    performance attributes, 67
knowledge management, information
    theory and, 305
knowledge of performance (KP), 228
knowledge sharing, 305
kurtosis, 150, 191, 194, 287; types of, 195

labor costs, 313
labor efficiency, 304
lagging metrics, 302–303
lagging versus leading outcomes,
    scorecard balancing of, 125–126
layman usage, 218
lead by example, idea of, 256
leading metrics, 303
lead time, 304
lean manufacturing, 54, 96, 254
lean production, 52; process approaches
    to productivity metrics, 54
learning: metrics and indicators of,
    318–319; organization scorecards, 121
level of analysis, 19, 20, 55, 107–108, 114,
    225; in basic metric model, 22;
    departmental scorecards, 105; in
    first-level scorecard construction, 84;
    and performance appraisals, 226; in
    roll-up measure, 179; in scale
    construction, 146–147; scorecard for,
    268–269
level of measurement, 19, 20, 31
library service, 307
Likert scale, 139, 196
liquidity, 313
litigation costs, 313, 316
loan turnover ratio (LTR), 313
logic: choice of measure, 25; departmental
    metrics, 115; first-level team
    scorecard, 86; as measurement issue
    criteria, 171, 179
logistics departments, 109
logit regression, 197
log-linear analysis, 198
long-term debt: cash flow to, 312; to total
    capital, 313
long-term metrics, 90, 286
lost productivity cost, 306
lower-level individual scorecards, 210
lower-order scorecards, 130

management, asset under, 312
management and metrics, 12–13, 75
management earnings, 313
management information system (MIS),
    55, 216
management journals on measuring
    performance, 85

managerial performance, 71
MANOVA, 197
Manual for Ability Requirements Scales
    (MARS), 69
manufacturing cycle effectiveness (MCE),
    320
manufacturing departments, 108, 111
manufacturing industry, 307; first-level
    team scorecards in, 82; reason for
    designing, 83; scope for, 83–84
market conditions, 234
marketing departments, 109, 111
marketing metrics and financial
    outcomes, 119
market position, 313
market-to-book ratio, 313
market value added (MVA), 314
Maslow's hierarchy of needs, 242, 247
material costs, 296
materials savings and profit, 296
mean, 186, 192, 195
measure, 63; of behavior modification,
    251; deciding focus of, 33; equity
    theory, 261; of expectancy theory, 253;
    of goal-setting theory, 259; intangible
    factors under, 11; of job characteristics
    model, 254; and metric, differentiating
    of, 4–5; of motivation-hygiene theory,
    252; of needs theory, 248; of person-
    environment fit, 255; of reinforcement
    theory, 251; reliability, 24; validity, 25
measurement, levels of, 185, 196–197
measurement issues, 285–287
measurement unit, 5–7, 18, 26; first-level
    team scorecards and, 89; practicality
    in business context, 63
median, 192, 195
mediator variable, 204–205; effects of,
    205
media usage and reports, 289
meeting costs, 296
meeting invitations, 294
mental starvation, 245
mergers and acquisitions, 314
meta-analysis, 10
metric creation process, 104
metric manager, 290
metrics: in business context, reasons for,
    95; creation of, 311; future sociological

trends of, 12–13; historical overview of, 96–13; and human motivation, 95; and measure, comparison of, 4–5; measurement unit and, 5–7; as motivation theory or practice, 13; task performance, 12, 84

metric scorecard, remembering essential elements of, 18

metrics to action tool, 91, 93, 211, 212, 295; double-loop questions in, 213; for organization scorecard, 279–280; team agenda for, 212; for using scorecard, 277

metric system, 209; and action, 277; actions, link between, 210; boundary's impact on, 35; decisions on, 271; implementation of, 277; offsite disease and, 209; process steps, comparison of, 270; in real life scenario, 267, 290; responsibility for creation of, 290

milestones met, 30, 54, 55, 74, 95–96, 97, 99, 109, 110, 111, 174, 183, 236, 237, 300, 306

missing data, 285

mission and vision, articulation of, 211, 214

mission identification, first-level team and, 86

mission statement, organizational metrics, 86, 128

mobile populations, sampling of, 202

mode, 192, 195

moderator variable, 204

moments of distribution, 185, 186, 191–195

motivation: "carrot and stick" flair, 245–246; cognitive theories of, 255; definitional ingredients of, 242; and human needs, 247; and job satisfaction, 243; key concepts of, 241–243; metrics and, 241, 242; organizational behavior and, 256; overview of, 244–246; performance improvement, 250; theories and models on, 246–247

motivation-hygiene theory, 242, 251–252

motivation techniques, 295

motivation theories, 51

motive: in customer service scale construction, 162; for departmental scorecards creation, 105; in first-level scorecard construction, 83; key metric scorecard elements, 18; for performance appraisal measurement, 75–76; in scale construction, 140–141

multichannel shopping metrics, organization scorecard, 119

multiple discriminant analysis, 198

multiple goals, 41, 119–120, 257

multiple regression, 197

needs-based theories, motivation, 242

needs theory, 247, 248

negative association, 42

negative entropy, 36, 38

negative feedback, 36, 38, 224, 226–228, 230–231, 236, 237

negative reinforcement, 250

nerd index, for software engineers, 18–19

net income, 314

new products, organization scorecard, 119

nominal definition, 138, 141

nominal measurement, 186, 195, 196

nonexempt employees, 306

nonfinancial indicators, 11

nonlinear associations, 82; organizational effectiveness and metric scores, 101

nonmanagerial competencies, 71

normality, criterion for, 192; central tendency, 192; dispersion, 193; kurtosis, 194

normality of items: in customer service scale construction, 165; in scale construction, 150

normative commitment, 244

null hypothesis, 186

object, 63; key metric scorecard elements, 18, 19

objective versus subjective measures, scorecard balancing of, 127

obsolescence cost, 304

Occupational Safety and Health Administration (OSHA) audits, 317, 327

off-site impact, 303

off-site meetings, creating goals at, 209
one-shot goals, 81
one-shot initiative, 74
O*NET, 64, 69–70
online services, 306
on-site impact, 303
open-ended item, 139
open-ended quality measures, 58
open-ended question, 56, 58, 139, 144, 178, 182, 288
open systems, 33, 34–39
operating margins and income, 314
operational definition, 85, 138, 218, 285
operationalization, 85, 138, 142
operations and processes, metrics and indicators of: productivity under, 320–321; quality of, 319–320
optimal scale, productivity measure, 54
oral comprehension, 69
ordinal measurement, 186, 195, 196
organizational attribute, 42–43
organizational behavior, 10, 224, 228, 236, 246; variables driving, 51
organizational changes, 39, 43
organizational effectiveness, 82
organizational goals, conflicts in, 104
organization alignment and execution, motives for measures, 95
organizational initiatives, 269; and first-level team scorecard, 281
organizational mind-set, 38
organizational performance: BSC model, 120–122; combined model, 125; creation of, 127–130; indicators of, 108; and metrics, 10, 11, 84–87, 106, 117; outcomes of, 11; stakeholders model, 123–125; strengths and weaknesses under, 127
organizational scorecard, 123; attributes, 269, 270, 274, 276; business planning under, 121; combined model of, 277; communicating, 130; conceptualization of, 117, 127–130; executives under, 81; research and development under, 126; scrutiny of, 118; variables of, 104
organizational systems, 41
organization citizenship behaviors (OCBs), 243

organization commitment, 51
organization development department, 108, 290
outcome effects: of cognitive evaluation theory (CET), 249–250; of equity theory and procedural justice, 261–262; of expectancy theory, 253; of goal-setting theory, 259; of job characteristics model, 254; of motivation-hygiene theory, 252; of needs theory, 248; of person-environment fit, 255; of reinforcement theory, 250
outcome metric, 18, 22, 274; in departmental scorecard, 275; first-level team scorecards and, 89, 90, 93; and goals, 257
outcomes, rewards for, 234
outcome variables, 44
outliers, 192, 256, 273
output, 36, 303; productivity metrics, indicators of, 53
overhead costs, 296, 304

parameter, 20, 186
Pareto chart, 303
parsimoniousness: choice of measure, 25; first-level team scorecard, 86
parsimony: departmental metrics, 115; first-level team, 93; as measurement issue criteria, 171, 180–181
participant thanks, 150, 151, 166
participative decision making, 44
past versus future outcomes, scorecard balancing of, 125–126
peer feedback, 230
pen-and-paper survey, 184
perceived equity, 260
perceived product quality, 156, 158
perceived service quality, 156, 158; in customer service scale construction, 162
perceived value, 304, 309
performance: conceptualization of, 66; and project management, 300
performance appraisal elements: comments, 333; company value statements, 330; employee data, 329–330; introduction, 329; job

description and responsibilities, 330; metrics and indicators of, 328–329; performance planning/personal development, 332; rating and competencies, 330, 331–332; signatures, 333; thank you, 333
performance appraisal form, 290
performance appraisals, 63, 225, 226; additional contents in, 77; components of, 64–67; concepts of, 66; establishing scope, 76; reasons for, 75; worker attributes on, 65, 67
performance attributes, 285
performance dimensions, organization scorecard, 118, 129
performance feedback, 210
performance gap, 227
performance improvement, 27, 29, 33; engaging employees in, 91; feedback interventions and, 10; motives for measures, 12, 95; and positive goals, 41
performance management, 258
performance management feedback, 225–226
performance management system, 64, 224, 226
performance measures, organization scorecard, 119
performance planning, 65, 66
period of time, choosing measurement, 26
personal relationships, support to, 295
person-environment fit, 242, 254–255
person-job (PJ) fit, 254, 255
person-organization (PO) fit, 254
person-supervisor (PS) fit, 254–255
phenomenon, 136–137, 157
physiological needs, 247
pilot test: in customer service scale construction, 166; in scale construction, 152
"Plan, Do, Check, Act" cycle, 106
planning costs, 296
population, 186, 187; mental leap from samples to, 188–191
portal service quality, 307
positive association, 42
positive feedback, 224, 226, 230–231, 236, 237
positive reinforcement, 250

postsales service, 56
power analysis, 185, 198, 200–202; equations of, 186
precision, 182, 196, 203, 287
preconscious, 24
predictive validity, 175–176, 286
prescription, in feedback, 229, 230, 235, 258
present, and future metrics, 286
price leadership, 314
price promotions, 119
price weighted forced outage rate, 322
principles of metrics, application of, 17
Pritchard models, goal achievement under, 49
private feedback, 235
problem solving, 85, 106
procedural justice, 260
process and quality metrics, 311
process cycle time, 304
processes, 42; improving quality of, 95
process measurement, 54, 55
process metrics, 269; departmental metrics, 106; steps for, 298–300
procurement, lead time for, 304
product, 157; improving quality of, 95; and service variety, 304
product development time, 304
product feature metrics, 56
production, 299
production costs, 294
production flexibility, 304
productivity, 28, 295, 311; dimensions of, 48, 53; effectiveness of, 48, 49; and first-level team, 90; and incentives, 230; measurement of, 44; with quality in work performance, 28; and quality metrics, 58, 286; techniques in measuring, 53, 54
productivity category and team performance, 48; measuring effectiveness of outcome, 50
product quality, 157
product reformulation, 294
product return metrics, organization scorecard, 119
profit, 276; organizational scorecard, 279
profitability, 295
profit margin, 314

project collaboration: format for, 295; participants in, 294
project management metrics, 300–301; cost under, 300; time or scheduling, 300–301
proofreading: in customer service scale construction, 166; in scale construction, 151–152
prototypical product, 157
prototypical service, 157
proximal goal, 257
public display, 287
public feedback, 235
punishment, 226, 230, 250, 255, 256
purchase behavior, 156, 158
purchase intention, 156, 158
purchasing department, 111–112
purpose of measurement, 26

qualitative feedback, 236
quality, 85, 156–157; metric scoreboard, 47
quality category and team performance, 48, 49; measuring effectiveness of outcome, 50
quality control, charts of, 303
quality improvement, 40
quality measurement, 47, 49, 52, 277; approaches to, 48; standard qualitative questions, 58; techniques in, 55–58
quantitative feedback, 233, 236
quantity, 85; engineering team and, 94–96; manufacturing industry, 84–85, 87–88
quantity of work, metric scoreboard, 47, 52
quick ratio (percent), 314

random sample, 202
ratings, 233
rating scales, 71, 156; types of rating scales, 160–161
rating section, 65; and competencies, 330–332
ratio measurement, 186, 195, 196
reaction time, 69, 259
recognition of employees, motives for measures, 95
recruiting costs, 306

reengineering efforts, 298
referrals, organization scorecard, 119
regulations, compliance to, 304
reinforcement theory, 242
relative percentile, 71, 74–75, 139
reliability, 24, 286; departmental metrics, 115; as measurement issue criteria, 171, 177–178
reliability analysis: in customer service scale construction, 165; in performance appraisals, 78; in scale construction, 148–149
reliable measures, first-level team scorecard, 86
renewal, 45; and strategic contribution, departmental metrics, 107, 114
renewal concept, 52; scorecard and systems theory, 49; tracking, 51; variables reflecting, 48
report dissemination, media choice, 219–220
report formats, first-level team scorecards and, 82
reports: communication of, 289; and corporate scorecard, linking categories of, 277, 281–282; dissemination of, 217; by first-level team, presentation of, 91; gathering data for, 289; presenting of, 85; result of, 218
representativeness, 202
research and development (R&D), 112, 314
research hypothesis, 186
resources and capabilities, 38
resource utilization, 303
response rate bias, 178
results communication, techniques for, 210
retail, 119, 226, 309
retention and acquisition metrics, organization scorecard, 119
retrofitting hypothesis, 152–153
return on assets (ROA), 11, 123, 314
return on capital employed (ROCE), organization, 126
return on equity (ROE), 314
return on investment (ROI), 276, 304; organizational metrics, 126; organizational scorecard, 279

revenue mix, 276; organizational scorecard, 279
revenue-to-expense ratio (RER), 314
risk-adjusted asset cash coverage ratio, 312
risk-adjusted equity, 312
roles and teams, 44
roll-up first-level metrics, 269
roll-up measure, 179
roll-up metrics, 38, 104, 106, 107, 287, 301
RVFLAPS: departments, 115; mnemonic, 24, 31n3

sacrifice, 156, 158
safety, in manufacturing industry, 84–85, 87–88, 90
safety department, 112
safety metrics, 302
safety needs, 247
salary, 306; discussions, 261
sales, 299, 315; revenue by, 296; turnaround time for paperwork in, 299
sales growth, 276; organizational scorecard, 279
sampling methods, 106, 185; wildlife studies and, 202
SAS (statistical software), 198
satisfiers, 252
scale, 20, 157; construction concept, 137; construction of, 139–153; definition of, 135; items of, 145–147
scaling methods, 63, 64
scatter diagram, 303
scheduling, accuracy of, 304
scientific definition process, 138–139
scientific goals, hallmarks of, 117
scientific management, 245
scientific method, 289
scope, 183; in customer service scale construction, 162; defining, 35; in first-level scorecard construction, 83–84; in performance appraisals, 76; in scale construction, 141
scorecard, 31, 183; attributes and dimensions of, 269; fixing flaws in, 285; gathering data for, 285; implementation of, 277; issues of,

288–289; logic in, 286; and performance appraisals, 285; presentation of results and issues of, 288–289; for service bureau, 286; translation of, 211; using of, 116
scorecard models and attributes, 104
scorecard variables, measurement of, 47–59
scrutiny, 115, 116
self-actualization needs, 247
self-determination theory, 242
self-efficacy, 242, 256, 259
self-feedback, 230
self-regulation, 255
self-transcendence needs, 247
selling price, 304
service bureau employee, 286
service quality, 157, 162
service value, 156, 158
SERVPERF, 156, 159
SERVQUAL, 156, 159, 182, 293, 306; attributes of service quality, 160; measure, 277
shared incentives, 294
shareholders, 95
shareholder's equity, 315
shareholder value, action metrics of, 119
short-term metrics, 90, 286
signatures, performance appraisals, 66
simple feedback scheme, 40
simple regression, 197
simple task, 299–300
simplicity, departmental metrics, 107
Six Sigma, 96, 285
skill, performance attributes, 67
skill variety, 253
SMART, 258–259
social cognitive theory, 242, 255, 256
social learning theory, 242, 255; and managers, 256
social needs, 247
social recognition, 250
social systems, 43
social unit and scorecard, choice of, 268
socioecology, 44
socio-technical systems (STS), 33, 43, 211
soft-skill intervention, 296
spatial differentiation, goal-setting theory, 119

special projects, 294
specifications, conformance to, 304
specific versus ambiguous goals, 117
split-half reliability, 178
SPSS (statistical software), 198
squares, sum of, 186
stakeholder model, 4, 11, 96; comparison
    of, 126; organization scorecard, 118
standard, meaning of, 107
standard deviation, 186, 190–191
standards movement, 117–120
standard strategic variables, 52
standard supervisor manuals, 229
statistic, 20, 185, 186; concepts from, 187;
    packages in, 198; types of, 197
statistical inferences, 185, 186, 188–191
statistical process control, 303
statistical soundness: choice of measure,
    25; departmental metrics, 115;
    first-level team scorecard, 86; as
    measurement issue criteria, 171, 181
statistics issues, 287–288
steady state homeostasis, 37, 39
stock out cost, 304
strategic business unit, organization
    scorecard, 117
strategic contribution, 45; first-level team
    scorecard and, 85; identifying
    variables reflecting, 48; organization's
    vision and, 52
strategic initiatives, organization
    scorecards, 125
strategic renewal, 38
strategic variables, 312, 327–328;
    innovation, 327–328; metric
    scoreboard, 47; synergy, 327
strategy, organizational metrics, 127,
    129, 130
strategy and metrics, first-level team, 91
strategy and scorecard, organization
    scorecard, 118
strategy map, 120, 121
subdimension, 138–139
subjective and objective metrics, 286;
    first-level team, 90
subsystem, defining, 34, 35, 42, 45
sufficient cause, 205
supervisory feedback, 230

supply chain management, performance
    indicators for, 303–304
supply chain performance, 309
supply chain response time, 304
suprasystem, defining, 34, 35, 40
survey, 20, 157
survey items, 139
synergy, 312, 327
SYSTAT (statistical software), 198
system elements, understanding
    associations between, 34
systems as cycles of events, 36, 45
systems theory, 33; and concept of
    renewal, 48; and feedback, 227

tangible and intangible referents, 286;
    first-level team, 90
tangible assets, organization scorecard,
    118
task identity, 253
task performance, 243
task significance, 254
team attributes, 90; renewal category,
    49–52; strategy performance, 52
team by activity matrix, 213, 305
team metric collections, 104
team outcome effectiveness, measuring,
    50, 59
team performance: attributes of, 107;
    dimensions of, 48; measuring
    effectiveness of outcome, 50
team productivity, dimension of, 48
team scorecards: report, 283–284; and
    strategic contribution, 48
team strategic contribution, and first-level
    team scorecard, 85
technical resolution, 286
technical services department, scorecard
    for, 106
technical support team, first-level team
    scorecards and, 89, 101
technical systems, 43
technological base, 38
technology-mediated customer service,
    309
telecommuting, 12, 317
temporal differentiation, goal-setting
    theory, 119

temporary employees, cost of, 297
term definition, in customer service, 162
test marketing, 294
test-retest reliability, 178
throughput processes, 35, 36, 37, 40
timeliness, 48, 49; choosing measurement, 26; measuring effectiveness of outcome, 50
times interest earned ratio, 315
timing issue, feedback, 232
total quality control, 96
total quality management (TQM), 4, 211; paradigms for programs, 106; understanding metrics, 10
tourism, 309
traffic department, 299
training: costs of, 296, 304, 315; results of, 305
training department, 112
training metrics, 304–305; attendance, 304; reaction under, 305
transportation cost, 304
travel agency services, 309
travel budget, 296
Trotter matrix, 280
trunk strength, 69
T-test, 197
turnover costs, 306
Type One Error, 186, 187
Type Two Error, 186, 188

underutilization, 84
union and management, negotiation between, 267
unit of analysis, 19, 20, 22, 31, 183; in customer service scale construction, 162; in performance appraisals, 76; in scale construction, 141
unit of observation, 5–6, 19
unit size, posing problem, 182–183
up-buying metrics, organization scorecard, 119

validity: departmental metrics, 115; first-level team scorecard, 86; as measurement issue criteria, 171, 172–173
validity check: in customer service scale construction, 165; in performance appraisals, 78; in scale construction, 147, 149–150
validity coefficient, 288
value chain monitoring, motives for measures, 95
value quality metrics, 56
variable, 19, 20, 137, 181; definition of, 218; measurement, first-level team, 84
variance, 186
vice president scorecard, 301; with managers, 302
virtual work teams, 12
vision scorecard, 214
vision statement, 269; organizational metrics, 127, 128, 130
visual demonstrations, 218
volunteer work, 90

wage and employment trends category, 70
warranty cost, 304
Web site metrics, 306
work applications, 21
work characteristics models, 242
workman's compensation, 315, 327
work performance: basic metric model, 17; deliverable in, 28; efficiency category, 48–49, 52, 53; engineering example for, 30; learning as dimension of, 49; scorecards on, 51; technique of, 27–31
work units, collaborations between, 294
work utilization, concept of, 175

zero defects, 156

About the Author

RUTH A. HUWE is a full-time lecturer at the Foster School of Business at the University of Washington. She received her PhD from the University of Washington in 1995 and is the sole proprietor of Huwe Management Consulting. Dr. Huwe has created survey scales and scorecards for dozens of teams, including the former Puget Power Company and the Boeing Company. She specializes in metrics for first-level teams and stresses the use of scorecards in overall programs of motivation. She teaches courses in metrics, motivation, organizational behavior, leadership, and business communication.